COLUMBIA COLLEGE CHICAGO

3 2711 00152 6940

D1762138

DATE DUE

JUL 1 3 2011		
APR 2 9 2013		
		JUL 2 3 2009

WITHDRAWN

ICONS OF CRIME FIGHTING

Recent Titles in
Greenwood Icons

Icons of Horror and the Supernatural: An Encyclopedia of
Our Worst Nightmares
Edited by S.T. Joshi

Icons of Business: An Encyclopedia of Mavericks, Movers, and Shakers
Kateri Drexler

Icons of Hip Hop: An Encyclopedia of the Movement, Music, and Culture
Edited by Mickey Hess

Icons of Evolution: An Encyclopedia of People, Evidence, and Controversies
Edited by Brian Regal

Icons of Rock: An Encyclopedia of the Legends Who Changed Music Forever
Scott Schinder and Andy Schwartz

Icons of R&B and Soul: An Encyclopedia of the Artists Who Revolutionized
Rhythm
Bob Gulla

African American Icons of Sport: Triumph, Courage, and Excellence
Matthew C. Whitaker

Icons of the American West: From Cowgirls to Silicon Valley
Edited by Gordon Morris Bakken

Icons of Latino America: Latino Contributions to American Culture
Roger Bruns

ICONS OF CRIME FIGHTING

Relentless Pursuers Of Justice

VOLUME 1

Edited by Jeffrey B. Bumgarner

Greenwood Icons

GREENWOOD PRESS
Westport, Connecticut • London

Library of Congress Cataloging-in-Publication Data

Icons of crime fighting : relentless pursuers of justice / edited by Jeffrey Bumgarner.
    p. cm.
   Includes bibliographical references and index.
   ISBN-13: 978-0-313-34129-8 ((set) : alk. paper)
   ISBN-13: 978-0-313-34130-4 ((vol. 1) : alk. paper)
   ISBN-13: 978-0-313-34131-1 ((vol. 2) : alk. paper)
   1. Law enforcement—United States—History. 2. Crime prevention—United States—History. 3. Criminal investigation—United States—History. 4. Criminal justice, Administration of—United States—History. 5. Personality and history. I. Bumgarner, Jeffrey B.
   HV8138.I36 2008
   363.2092′273—dc22   2008018447

British Library Cataloguing in Publication Data is available.

Copyright © 2008 by Jeffrey B. Bumgarner

All rights reserved. No portion of this book may be reproduced, by any process or technique, without the express written consent of the publisher.

Library of Congress Catalog Card Number: 2008018447
ISBN-13: 978-0-313-34129-8 (set)
          978-0-313-34130-4 (vol. 1)
          978-0-313-34131-1 (vol. 2)

First published in 2008

Greenwood Press, 88 Post Road West, Westport, CT 06881
An imprint of Greenwood Publishing Group, Inc.
www.greenwood.com

Printed in the United States of America

The paper used in this book complies with the Permanent Paper Standard issued by the National Information Standards Organization (Z39.48–1984).

10 9 8 7 6 5 4 3 2 1

Icons of Crime Fighting is dedicated to all the individuals who have made it their life's work to fight crime and injustice in the United States and elsewhere. While this publication recounts the service of many individuals who are well known for this fight and are deserving of accolades, there are countless more men and women who work visibly in their own communities or behind the scenes in all realms of the criminal justice system—as police officers, federal agents, prosecutors, victims' advocates, social workers, etc. They too are deserving of tribute. This book set is for them.

Contents

List of Photos	ix
Series Foreword	xi
Preface	xiii

Volume 1

Gun Fighters: U.S. Marshals of the Old West, *Tusty Zohra and Jeffrey T. Walker*	1
Allan Pinkerton, *Scott H. Belshaw and Amanda L. Belshaw*	27
The Texas Rangers, *Ronald Burns*	57
August Vollmer, *Willard M. Oliver*	83
J. Edgar Hoover and the FBI, *Kilby Raptopoulos and Jeffrey T. Walker*	117
Thomas Dewey, *Clarrisa Breen*	143
Robert Kennedy: The Enforcer Within, *J. Scott Granberg-Rademacker*	167
Jim Garrison, *Elvira M. White*	197
Buford Pusser, *Jacob Rodriguez*	235
Eddie Egan and Sonny Grosso, *Ellen Leichtman*	257
Bob Woodward and Carl Bernstein: Presidential Crime Fighters and Shapers of American Public Opinion, *Christopher Larimer*	291

Volume 2

Francisco Vincent Serpico, *Morris A. Taylor*	319
Joseph Pistone, AKA "Donnie Brasco," *John Dombrink*	343
Vincent T. Bugliosi: Justice Purist—The Prosecutor with a Heart, *Edward J. Schauer*	371
For Adam: The John Walsh Story, *Elizabeth Quinn DeValve*	421
FBI Profilers, *Richard N. Kocsis*	437
Sheriff Joe Arpaio, *Kelli Stevens*	463
Mark Fuhrman, *Scott H. Belshaw*	493
Rudolph "Rudy" Giuliani, *Camille Gibson*	521
Curtis Sliwa: Vigilantism, Victims' Rights, and the Guardian Angels, *Brion Sever, with Al Gorman and Greg Coram*	553
Dr. Henry Lee: Leading Practitioner in Forensic Criminal Investigations, *Janet E. McClellan*	577
Dr. Bill Bass, *Cécile Van de Voorde*	605
Selected Bibliography	623
About the Editor and the Contributors	645
Index	651

Photos

Sculptured bust portrait of James Butler "Wild Bill" Hickock, atop tombstone (page 1), Deadwood, SD. © 2008 Chaiba.

Dodge City Peace Commission, 1882 (page 2). From left to right, members are shown as follows. Back row: W. H. Harris, Luke Short and Bat Masterson. Front row: Charles Bassett, Wyatt Earp, F. McClain and Neil Brown. Courtesy AP Images.

Allan Pinkerton of Antietam (page 27), MD, 1884. Courtesy of the Library of Congress.

Hon. James Francis Miller of Texas (page 57), ca. 1875. Courtesy of the Library of Congress.

Captain Samuel Hamilton Walker (page 58), ca. 1846. Courtesy of the Library of Congress.

August Vollmer (page 83), 1929. © Corbis/Bettmann.

J. Edgar Hoover (page 117), 1969. Courtesy of the Library of Congress.

Special prosecutor Thomas E. Dewey (page 143), holds up his right hand as he is sworn in by Supreme Court Justice Philip J. McCook in New York City, 1935. Courtesy AP Images.

Robert Kennedy (page 167), appearing before the Platform Committee, 1964. Courtesy of the Library of Congress.

Jim Garrison (page 197), who stands 6-foot-6, towers over assistants James Alcock, right, and Andrew "Moo Moo" Sciambra as they huddle prior to the trial of Clay Shaw, Jan. 16, 1969. Courtesy AP Images.

Sheriff Buford Pusser of Tennessee (page 235), shortly before he was killed in a suspicious car crash, 1998. © Getty Images.

From the 1971 film "The French Connection", directed by William Friedkin. Shown from left: Sonny Grosso as Det. Phil Klein, Eddie Egan as Lt. Walter Simonson (page 257). Courtesy of Photofest.

Washington Post writers Carl Bernstein, left, and Robert Woodward (page 291), who pressed the Watergate investigation, are photographed in Washington, D.C., May 7, 1973. Courtesy AP Images.

New York City detective Frank Serpico (page 319), with beard, sits in front of his attorney, Ramsey Clark, at the Knapp Commission's investigation of alleged police corruption at a hearing in New York, 1971. Courtesy AP Images/Jim Wells.

Joe Pistone (page 343), the American F.B.I agent upon whom the film 'Donnie Brasco' was based, 1997. © Fotos International/Getty Images.

Deputy District Attorneys Aaron Stovitz (left) and Vincent Bugliosi (page 371), display an aerial photograph of the home of Leno and Rosemary LaBianca. Courtesy of Photofest.

The death of the prime suspect in the kidnapping and murder of 6-year-old Adam Walsh (page 421), shown in this 1981 file photo, doesn't close the still-unsolved case. Police believed Ottis Elwood Toole killed Adam, who disappeared from outside a Hollywood, Florida shopping mall in 1981. Courtesy AP Images.

John Douglas working in his Virginia office (page 437), 2002. Larry Stone Photography.

Maricopa County Sheriff Joe Arpaio (page 463), speaks during a news conference in Avondale, AZ. The conference was held May 10, 2006, to kick off the beginning of the sheriffs' departments efforts to find illegal immigrants. Courtesy AP Images/Roy Dabner.

Former police Detective Mark Fuhrman (page 493), shown testifying at the O. J. Simpson trial, March 10, 1995. Courtesy AP Images/John McCoy.

U.S. Attorney Rudolph Giuliani (page 521), talks to media in New York City, Dec. 13, 1984. Courtesy AP Images/Debbie Hodgson.

Radio talk show personality and Guardian Angels founder Curtis Sliwa, center (page 553), enters Manhattan federal court in New York surrounded by other Guardian Angel members, Feb. 27, 2006. Courtesy AP Images/Louis Lanzano.

Forensic scientist Dr. Henry C. Lee (page 577), shows the court a cotton swab similar to the one he used to collect evidence from the crime scene at music producer Phil Spector's home, during Spector's murder trial for the murder of actress Lana Clarkson, 2007. Courtesy AP Images/Paul Buck, Pool.

Dr. Bill Bass (page 605), carefully cleans a skull before examining it in his laboratory at the at the University of Tennessee in Knoxville. Courtesy of the University of Tennessee.

Series Foreword

Worshipped and cursed. Loved and loathed. Obsessed about the world over. What does it take to become an icon? Regardless of subject, culture, or era, the requisite qualifications are the same: (1) challenge the status quo, (2) influence millions, and (3) impact history.

Using these criteria, Greenwood Press introduces a new reference format and approach to popular culture. Spanning a wide range of subjects, volumes in the Greenwood Icons series provide students and general readers a port of entry into the most fascinating and influential topics of the day. Every two-volume title offers an in-depth look at approximately 24 iconic figures, each of which captures the essence of a broad subject. These icons typically embody a group of values, elicit strong reactions, reflect the essence of a particular time and place, and link different traditions and periods. Among those featured are artists and activists, superheroes and spies, inventors and athletes—the legends and mythmakers of entire generations. Yet icons can also come from unexpected places: as the heroine who transcends the pages of a novel or as the revolutionary idea that shatters our previously held beliefs. Whether people, places, or things, such icons serve as a bridge between the past and the present, the canonical and the contemporary. By focusing on icons central to popular culture, this series encourages students to appreciate cultural diversity and critically analyze issues of enduring significance.

Most importantly, these books are as entertaining as they are provocative. Is Disneyland a more influential icon of the American West than Las Vegas? How do ghosts and ghouls reflect our collective psyche? Is Barry Bonds an inspiring or deplorable icon of baseball? Designed to foster debate, the series serves as a unique resource that is ideal for paper writing or report purposes. Insightful, in-depth entries provide far more information than conventional reference articles but are less intimidating and more accessible than a book-length biography. The most revered and reviled icons of American and world history are brought to life with related sidebars, timelines, fact boxes, and quotations. Authoritative entries are accompanied by bibliographies, making these titles an ideal starting point for further research. Spanning a wide range of popular topics, including business, literature, civil rights, politics, music, and more, books in the Greenwood Icons series provide fresh insights for the student and popular reader into the power and influence of icons, a topic of as vital interest today as in any previous era.

Preface

Americans have always been fascinated by the social problem of crime and society's response to it. This fascination is easily diagnosed by the number of murder mysteries that have been published over the ages, the fictional and nonfictional police television shows peppered throughout the network and cable channels, and the innumerable cinematic productions that focus on police officers, detectives, and federal agents marching through adversity to make the case and thwart the violent criminal villain.

Indeed, much of what Americans and others around the world know about crime fighting has been learned through these mediums. This often results in an incomplete, and in many cases, inaccurate, understanding of crime fighting and crime fighters. Criminal investigators and prosecutors are in wide agreement, for example, that securing a conviction in certain types of criminal cases has been hampered by popular television. The so-called "CSI effect" has resulted in many juries harboring an expectation that there will be significant scientific evidence in every serious case to link an alleged offender to the crime, just as on television. The fact is that most crimes continue to be solved through old-fashioned police work, eyewitness accounts, solid suspect interviews, and other circumstantial evidence. Most cases do not involve definitive forensic evidence, and certainly most cases are not resolved in the span of a sixty-minute television show (where none of the cops take notes, suspects' rights are marginalized, search warrants materialize out of thin air, and the offenders always seem willing to talk to the police in custody without an attorney).

In *Icons of Crime Fighting*, and in keeping with America's fascination with criminal justice and criminal investigation, readers are introduced to different individuals and organizations that have made significant contributions to general or particular realms of fighting crime. However, an emphasis is placed on historical accuracy and an accounting of how criminals are actually countered and thwarted. Most of the twenty-two chapters in this two-volume set relate to individuals who are noteworthy for their crime-fighting efforts and accomplishments. A few of the chapters relate to organizations that are regarded for their respective contributions to fighting crime. All of the individuals and organizations are "iconic" in the sense that people are aware of them, certainly in criminal justice circles, but also in popular culture. Their notoriety in popular culture, however, does not diminish their serious and significant professional contributions to the areas in which they operate or operated.

The two-volume set starts off with a historical chapter: "Gunfighters: U.S. Marshals of the Old West." This chapter explores the history of America's oldest federal law enforcement agency and profiles famed federal lawmen from the nineteenth century, including Wyatt Earp, Bat Masterson, and Pat Garrett. Chapter 2 continues with a nineteenth-century American historical theme by profiling Allan Pinkerton, America's most famous nonfictional private eye. Indeed, it was Pinkerton and his National Detective Agency that coined the term "private eye" to begin with. Rounding off the discussion of law enforcement in the American West and Southwest during the 1800s is Chapter 3, which focuses on the famed Texas Rangers. Texas lawmen from this organization such as W. J. McDonald (for whom the expression "one riot, one ranger" was coined) and Frank Hamer (who tracked down Bonnie and Clyde) are introduced.

Chapters 4, 5, and 6 bring readers forward into the early twentieth century. Chapter 4 profiles the life and career of August Vollmer, the most significant of police reformers. Vollmer was an early twentieth-century police chief who is credited with many innovations and approaches to crime fighting and police professionalization that are still in place today. Chapter 5 is concerned with the famous FBI director, the late J. Edgar Hoover. There is no law enforcement leader, past or present, who possesses a legacy that can rival Hoover's. This chapter also necessarily delves into the history of the Federal Bureau of Investigation, which by itself readers will find to be inherently interesting. Chapter 6 explores the career of one of New York City's most famous prosecutors, Thomas Dewey. His crime-fighting career was at its zenith during the 1930s—an accomplished career that would propel him eventually to become governor of New York and the Republican presidential candidate in 1948. Although he has been immortalized in the famous photo of President Truman holding up a *Chicago Daily Tribune* newspaper with the erroneous headline "Dewey Beats Truman" in 1948, his efforts at fighting organized crime and mobsters such as Dutch Schultz and Lucky Luciano were among his most significant accomplishments.

Beginning with Chapter 7, *Icons of Crime Fighting* shifts to more recent history, particularly the last half of the twentieth century through the present day. Chapter 7 is devoted to Robert Kennedy. Although well known as President John F. Kennedy's brother and attorney general, his service as an attorney for the U.S. Senate in the 1950s really marks the beginning of his crime-fighting career. In that capacity, he investigated the influence of organized crime in the labor unions as well as the infiltration of communists in American public service. Of course, his life tragically ended when he was assassinated as a presidential candidate in 1968. Speaking of the Kennedys, Chapter 8 examines the career and crusade of famed prosecutor Jim Garrison. He was a very well-known district attorney in New Orleans during the 1960s and 1970s, but Garrison became iconic when he prosecuted Louisiana businessman Clay Shaw as a conspirator in the John F. Kennedy assassination. Shaw was found "not guilty" by a jury after less than an hour of deliberation. Nonetheless, the case raised enough doubt about President Kennedy's death to warrant an Oliver Stone film (*JFK*) on the matter, with Kevin Costner playing the lead role—that of Jim Garrison.

Garrison isn't the only iconic individual profiled in this book about whom movies were made. Chapter 9 examines the life of Buford Pusser, the three-term sheriff of McNairy County, Tennessee, in the 1960s. His fight against the criminal element in his county inspired the movie *Walking Tall*. Pusser survived an assassination attempt in 1967, but his wife was killed in the attack. The resolve Pusser possessed to continue the fight for justice in the wake of this tragedy is truly an inspiration. Chapter 10 profiles two crime fighters: Eddie Egan and Sonnie Grosso. These two New York City police detectives were partners in the 1960s and conducted one of the most famous drug-trafficking investigations in American history. The international drug-trafficking scheme they investigated is famously known as the French Connection because of the fact that the drugs came into the United States through France. Egan and Grosso were the inspiration for the characters Jimmy "Popeye" Doyle and Sonny Russo, played by Gene Hackman and Roy Scheider, respectively, in the 1971 movie *The French Connection*.

The movies keep on rolling in Chapter 11. Here, readers will learn about the story of Bob Woodward and Carl Bernstein. The movie *All the President's Men* highlights the significance of their fight for justice in the political realm. These two *Washington Post* reporters investigated the 1972 burglary of the Democratic National Committee's office at the Watergate Hotel in Washington, D.C. Their efforts (and others') ultimately resulted in the convictions on conspiracy and perjury charges of several high-ranking government officials connected to President Richard Nixon. President Nixon eventually resigned over the scandal.

Chapter 12, which begins Volume 2, also deals with an individual associated with a fight against government corruption—Frank Serpico. Serpico was instrumental in fighting corruption in the New York City Police Department (NYPD) during the 1960s. He exposed widespread criminal activity among NYPD officers, including routine acceptance of gratuities and kickbacks, as well as acts of bribery and extortion. Al Pacino starred in the title role of the 1973 movie *Serpico*.

Interestingly, Al Pacino also starred in a movie about the icon profiled in Chapter 13, the 1997 film *Donnie Brasco*. Joe Pistone, aka "Donnie Brasco," was an FBI agent who went deep undercover to infiltrate the New

York Mafia. His six-year undercover effort resulted in more than one hundred convictions of members of organized crime. Pacino does not star as Pistone in the movie, but rather as a mobster befriended and investigated by Pistone. Johnny Depp plays Pistone in the movie.

Chapter 14 is the most exhaustive chapter in the book and profiles the life of famed prosecutor Vincent Bugliosi. Chapter author Ed Schauer interviewed Bugliosi extensively in preparing the chapter and brings a unique perspective on this influential and contemporary crime fighter. Bugliosi is mostly known for his successful prosecution of Charles Manson and Manson's associates. Later, he wrote *Helter Skelter,* a book chronicling Manson's crimes. Chapter 15 explores another contemporary crime fighter in the public eye: John Walsh. Walsh is best known for hosting Fox television's long-running show *America's Most Wanted*. He is a tireless victims' advocate. Sadly, personal tragedy propelled him into his life's work. In 1981, Walsh's own 6-year-old son was abducted and murdered by a child predator. He has crusaded against child predators and for victims' rights ever since.

In Chapter 16, readers have the opportunity to learn about a group of individuals that has captured the imagination of America and Hollywood for many years: the profilers of the FBI. The chapter explores the history of profiling as a criminal investigative technique and delves into the FBI's early effort to develop profiling as a viable tool. Famous FBI profilers such as Greg McCrary, John Douglas, Robert Ressler, and Roy Hazlewood are introduced. These individuals, along with the FBI's Behavior Analysis Unit, inspired several popular movies and books, such as Thomas Harris' *Silence of the Lambs*.

Chapter 17 deals with another contemporary icon, the current and long-serving sheriff of Maricopa County, Arizona, Joe Arpaio. Some have labeled him "America's Toughest Sheriff." He is famous for housing county prisoners in tents and subjecting them to unconventional forms of punishment. The chapter goes further to explore the efficacy of these alternate forms of punishment. The author of this chapter also had an opportunity to interview Arpaio personally and secure his unique perspective on his service as sheriff.

Although Joe Arpaio is controversial in many quarters, Chapter 18 deals with probably the most controversial individual profiled in *Icons of Crime Fighting*: Mark Fuhrman. Detective Fuhrman first received national attention as one of the investigating officers of the O. J. Simpson case. His denial of using the "n" word, which later proved to be false, impeached the credibility of the entire investigating team. However, his stature as an investigator has been resurrected after privately investigating the 1975 murder of Martha Moxley. His investigation resulted in renewed official interest in the case and the conviction in 2002 of Michael Skakel, who is a relative of the Kennedy family. He has similarly investigated and written about several other high-profile crimes.

Chapter 19 explores the career of Rudy Giuliani. Most recently, he was a presidential candidate in the Republican Party who dropped out of the race after the 2008 Florida primary. However, his career before that included many high notes and accomplishments as a crime fighter. Giuliani was the mayor of New York City from 1994 to 2001. He was affectionately dubbed "America's mayor" after his handling of the tragedy on 9/11. He presided over a sharp decline in violent crime in the city and was very supportive of aggressive police tactics. He also served as a U.S. attorney and is well known for his fight against organized crime in that capacity.

Another New York City icon is the subject of Chapter 20, Curtis Sliwa and the Guardian Angels. Sliwa is the founder of the Guardian Angels, a worldwide crime prevention organization that relies on citizen patrols. The chapter explores Sliwa's efforts in crime prevention as well as the issue of vigilantism and citizen crime prevention efforts generally.

Icons of Crime Fighting ends with its final two chapters devoted to iconic forensic scientists. Chapter 21 profiles Dr. Henry Lee, who is perhaps the world's most famous forensic scientist. He has consulted on hundreds of murder and sexual assault investigations, including many high-profile cases. He is affiliated with the University of New Haven, Connecticut, which is home to one of the most renowned forensic science degree programs in the world. Chapter 22 examines the career of Dr. Bill Bass. Dr. Bass, a professor at the University of Tennessee, is renowned for founding the "Body Farm," which is an outdoor forensic laboratory where donated dead bodies are permitted to decay. As a forensic anthropologist, Dr. Bass has consulted on numerous homicide investigations involving decomposed human remains. Both Dr. Lee and Dr. Bass are counted among the most famous and highly regarded criminal investigative scientists in the world.

It is hoped that readers of *Icons of Crime Fighting: Relentless Pursuers of Justice* will find the profiles of individuals and agencies contained therein to be interesting and informative. Certainly the chapters can serve as a springboard for further research into their respective and associated crime-fighting topics. In fact, each chapter ends with a Further Reading list, and there is an extensive Selected Bibliography at the end of Volume 2 to aid further exploration and study. Ultimately, my desire and the desire of the various chapter authors is that readers will be edified and inspired by the stories of dedication and professionalism relating to the many crime-fighting icons, past and present, who serve or have served to protect society from those who would perpetrate evil.

Jeffrey B. Bumgarner, Ph.D.
Minnesota State University, Mankato

© 2008 Chaiba

Gun Fighters: U.S. Marshals of the Old West

Tusty Zohra and Jeffrey T. Walker

Courtesy AP Images

The legends of the Wild West have become a part of American history and folklore. Stories of lawmen and cowboys facing death in the town square have been passed on from generation to generation. The images behind western folklore have often been exaggerated by movies and books, stretching the truth to provide an interesting climax in western stories. Such stories typically portray lawmen as heroic symbols, devoted to keeping the peace and upholding the law. They are responsible for apprehending criminals and restoring justice.

The oldest known lawmen in American history and folklore are the U.S. Marshals. They were depicted as the image of bravery and heroic virtue. They stood by their post in front of the marshal's office or town saloon, watching for trouble and keeping the peace. Equipped with their pistols and the occasional shotgun, they were ready to apprehend any criminal who violated the law.

Movies and books often portrayed these lawmen as possessing supernatural characteristics of strength, poise, and speed in drawing their pistols. Classic scenarios illustrated dusty streets, full of horses and carriages; men, women, and children walking the streets in fear; and cowboys pillaging the town for personal gain. Typically, for the purpose of exemplifying the existence of evil, the story would begin with villains breaking the law, usually at the town saloon. There is usually a bartender, always a bystander, polishing glasses in a room full of town residents who were fearful for their lives. Then in walks the hero, the marshal, who will apprehend the criminals. The story will typically end with a gunfight at the climax of the story.

These stories possess a romanticized, yet fictional interpretation of gunfighters in the Wild West. Marshals such as Wyatt Earp, James Butler Hickok (Wild Bill), Edward and Bat Masterson, and many others are heroic symbols of lawmen in the Wild West. They were portrayed as drifters who came into town, apprehended the outlaws, and moved on in search of new adventures. They were, typically, hired for their swiftness and skills and not for their ability to police the towns.

Where these myths ended and the true stories began is an ambiguous line. Although the gunfighting days are over, the stories still remain. In all reality, the lawmen from the past are not so different from the lawmen of today. Their objectives and responsibilities are to uphold the law and provide peace in the communities. The men of the Wild West are gone, but their spirits and stories are still very much alive today.

THE WILD WEST

The stories of the Wild West represent engaging parables of the struggles of the beginning of western civilization. Although many of the tales are deceiving accounts of history, the origins and establishment of the western region is truly enticing. During the 1850s to the early 1900s, people moved west looking for new adventures, the lure of land, and the dream of gold and silver. Settling the West often meant coming into direct contact with Indian tribes. The West consisted of miles of open land, where the buffalo grazed and the Indians resided. There were no boundaries and few regional limits. It was full of mystery, adventure, and dangerous possibilities. The conflict between the settlers and the Indians began with claiming territories, westward extension of the railroads, and competition for wildlife.

In 1803, the Louisiana Purchase doubled the area of land owned by the United States. The first attempts to explore the new territory came in 1804 when Lewis and Clark launched an expedition. The exploration progressed westward to the Pacific Ocean and affirmed that the West could be settled. Not long after, settlers began to move into the unclaimed territories, especially in California when the gold rush became prevalent around the end of the 1840s. Farmers, businessmen, and others packed their belongings and headed to western states such Oregon, Kansas, and California.

Even after conflicts with the Indians were over and most of the Indian population was confined to reservations, peace was not guaranteed. Anarchy and disarray characterized many towns because of minimal law enforcement, no direct control from the East, and lack of communication. Any crimes committed would often go unreported because the nearest law enforcement agency could be located hundreds of miles away. Many times, the settlers could not get word to the lawmen because of the lack of communication or lack of time to make a difference.

Communication between the settlers and the law finally became more useful when the telegraph system was implemented around the 1860s. This invention was followed by the telephone in the late 1870s. At this time in history, law and order became a demand in western towns, resulting in the rise of the six-shooter lawman. The rise of the lawmen was mainly due to the high criminal activity of what history calls the "outlaws." Bank, train, mine, and ranch robberies increased in alarming numbers and residents of the towns demanded justice. They needed men who could fight, shoot, and apprehend the criminals. Residents felt fear when walking down the streets, especially at night when the saloons and brothels were filled with rowdy cowboys and outlaws. Many of these criminals were attracted to the West during the California gold rush because they were driven by the thought of hidden fortunes. Many were disappointed and resorted to other means for money.

Before the U.S. Marshals became the men of law, residents had to defend themselves when crimes were committed. Residents of the town conducted citizen courts and executed sentences on those who were found guilty. Outlaws who violated the law were caught and hung, often without a proper trial. This method became problematic when too much blood was being spilled. Although outlaws were being caught, other members of their gangs sought revenge on the town; therefore, many town residents would live in fear because of the repercussions of their actions. Soon the residents realized that they needed some sort of police organization to deal with the criminals. They wanted a police structure that would prevent criminals from participating in criminal activities or apprehend those who had.

This precipitated the rise of the marshals. At this time, both outlaws and lawmen were equipped with six-shot, revolver pistols made popular during the Civil War. This symbol of the Wild West demanded expert shooters, because the six-shooter was known for its lack of dependability and capabilities. Lawmen who were proficient with six-shooter pistols were sought out.

Here begin the tales of gunfights in town squares and heroic figures who rescued the residents of their towns. Although many stories regarding lawmen are true in nature, they often include an engaging account that may have been distorted through years of retelling stories and producing fictional movies.

Six-shooter lawmen were initially created at the local or state level. Cities would hire a city marshal (often to cover the whole county). Sometimes this was done privately by landowners; other times it was an effort of the state. For example, Kansas set up a police system where the towns were run by city marshals. Each town would have one city marshal and several deputies. Usually the deputies would work during cattle season and were terminated when the season ended. One of the most famous attempts at local-level law enforcement in the West began with the development of the Texas Rangers in 1870. Federal agents such as the U.S. Marshals were also moving into the West as the need for assistance became pronounced.

"The duties of the town's police force varied in detail from place to place, but followed an overall pattern. The police had power to enter any saloon, billiard hall, or other place of amusement and arrest drunks or others who refused to 'be restored to order and quiet'" (Drago 1975). With the number of people carrying guns, especially pistols, and with the number of people willing to use them in the aftermath of the Civil War, keeping the peace often meant engaging in a gunfight.

THE BEGINNING

The U.S. Marshal system is the oldest federal agency in the United States. Its purpose was to handle civil, criminal, and judicial matters. The Marshals were established by the Judiciary Act of 1789, which implemented the new judiciary system. The act created district and circuit courts and established positions for judges and clerks, along with the U.S. Marshals. The Judiciary Act set up thirteen U.S. Marshal offices across the nation. In Section 27 of the Judiciary Act of 1789, Congress asserted that the following were the responsibilities of the marshals:

> That a marshal shall be appointed in and for each district for the term of four years, but shall be removable from office at pleasure, whose duty it shall be to attend the district and circuit courts when sitting therein, and also the Supreme Court in the District in which that court shall sit. And to execute throughout the district, all lawful precepts directed to him, and issued under the authority of the United States, and he shall have power to command all necessary assistance in the execution of his duty, and to appoint as there shall be occasion, one or more deputies, who shall be removable from office by the judge of the district court, or the circuit court sitting within the district, at the pleasure of either; and before he enters on the duties of his office, he shall become bound for the faithful performance of the same.... (Judiciary Act of 1789, 1 Stat. 73)

Congress developed the U.S. Marshals for several reasons. First, as discussed above, they were to assist in court proceedings for both lower and higher courts, by transporting prisoners, executing processes, and implementing legal documents such as judicial writs. They were also responsible for upholding peace and law among residents in their communities.

Judiciary Act of 1789

Creation of the Office of U.S. Marshal

Section 27. And be it further enacted, That a marshal shall be appointed in and for each district for the term of four years, but shall be removable from office at pleasure, whose duty it shall be to attend the district and circuit courts when sitting therein, and also the Supreme Court in the District in which that court shall sit. And to execute throughout the district, all lawful precepts directed to him, and issued under the authority of the United States, and he shall have power to command all necessary assistance in the execution of his duty, and to appoint as there shall be occasion, one or more deputies, who shall be removable from office by the judge of the district court, or the circuit court sitting within the district, at the pleasure of either; and before he enters on the duties of his office, he shall become bound for the faithful performance of the same, by himself and by his deputies before the judge of the district court to the United States, jointly and severally, with two good and sufficient sureties, inhabitants and freeholders of such district, to be approved by the district judge, in the sum of twenty thousand dollars, and shall take before said judge, as shall also his deputies, before they enter on the duties of their appointment, the following oath of office: "I, A.B., do solemnly swear or affirm, that I will faithfully execute all lawful precepts directed to the marshal of the district of _____ under the authority of the United States, and true returns make, and in all things well and truly, and without malice or partiality, perform the duties of the office of marshal (or marshal's deputy, as the case may be) of the district of _____, during my continuance in said office, and take only my lawful fees. So help me God."

Section 28. And be it further enacted, That in all causes wherein the marshal or his deputy shall be a party, the writs and precepts therein shall be directed to such disinterested person as the court, or any justice or judge thereof may appoint, and the person so appointed, is hereby authorized to execute and return the same. And in case of the death of any marshal, his deputy or deputies shall continue in office, unless otherwise specially removed; and shall execute the same in the name of the deceased, until another marshal shall be appointed and sworn: And the defaults or misfeasances in office of such deputy or deputies in the mean time, as well as before, shall be adjudged a breach of the condition of the bond given, as before directed, by the marshal who appointed them; and the executor or administrator of the deceased marshal shall have like remedy for the defaults and misfeasances in office of such deputy or deputies during such interval,

> as they would be entitled to if the marshal had continued in life and in the exercise of his said office, until his successor was appointed, and sworn or affirmed: And every marshal or his deputy when removed from office, or when the term for which the marshal is appointed shall expire, shall have power notwithstanding to execute all such precepts as may be in their hands respectively at the time of such removal or expiration of office; and the marshal shall be held answerable for the delivery to his successor of all prisoners which may be in his custody at the time of his removal, or when the term for which he is appointed shall expire, and for that purpose may retain such prisoners in his custody until his successor shall be appointed and qualified as the law directs.

The U.S. Marshals played several notable roles in American history. For example, in 1850 when Congress passed the Fugitive Slave Act, marshals were assigned to capture and return all fugitive slaves to their owners. During this time, all free slave states were mandated to return any slave who was not yet free, as deemed by the state that they resided in. This brought a lot of anguish to the marshals from citizens who did not believe in having slaves. Another role was the responsibility of guarding the home front of the United States against enemies. On April 6, 1917, the U.S. Congress declared war against Germany, entering what is now known as World War I. During this time period, the marshals guarded the United States against enemies, spies, and attackers. They were responsible for protecting the American citizens against hostile attacks.

The range of responsibilities of the U.S. Marshals is broad, and they differ depending on the situation in which they are needed, although overall, they were implemented to execute court proceedings and federal responsibilities. After the Judiciary Act of 1789 was passed, President George Washington appointed thirteen U.S. Marshals to office. By 1791, President Washington had appointed sixteen U.S. Marshals, one for each of the original sixteen districts. The first sixteen Marshals were Allan McLane (Delaware), Henry Dearborn (Maine), Isaac Huger (South Carolina), Nathanial Ramsay (Maryland), Jonathan Jackson (Massachusetts), Clement Biddle (Pennsylvania), William Smith (New York), Lewis Morris (Vermont), Robert Forsyth (Georgia), Thomas Lowry (New Jersey), Samuel McDowell (Kentucky), Edward Carrington (Virginia), John Skinner (North Carolina), John Parker (New Hampshire), Phillip Bradley (Connecticut), and William Peck (Rhode Island).

About seven of the sixteen original marshals lived and remained agents their entire lives in the district to which they were assigned. Others remained as marshals for an average of six years and moved on to higher governmental positions. The sixteen marshals were appointed to office because of their loyalty, dedication, and leadership shown for the government. After they were assigned to their district, they executed their duties, although their responsibilities sometimes differed.

For example, when the Secret Service was established in 1865, the marshals were assigned to assist them in counterfeiting investigations. Before the twentieth century, currency in the United States was not standardized; therefore, counterfeiters were not uncommon. The marshals were designated to help control this problem. Also during this period, the marshals were assigned to the Old West to capture fugitive outlaws such as Billy the Kid, the Dalton Gang, and several other criminals.

The population of the Wild West was growing in massive numbers as citizens realized that the western regions could be settled. As the population grew, the need and demand for law and order became fierce. The government started appointing U.S. Marshals to western regions to assist in creating and maintaining some sort of police structure. Hence, we have the rise of the marshals in the Wild West.

Although the U.S. Marshals played an important role in taming the Wild West, many iconic figures who established the name of being a U.S. Marshal had different policing duties. For example, western heroes such as Wyatt Earp, Ben Thompson, and Pat Garrett were never really U.S. Marshals, although they are portrayed as such. Because of fictional movies and books, much of the truth has been greatly exaggerated. For the purpose of this chapter, iconic figures who were U.S. Marshals and city marshals in western history are discussed.

ABILENE: A MARSHAL CITY

Abilene, Kansas, was a small, cattle-roaming town that was often violent and prone to crime. The first city marshal was appointed in Abilene on May 2, 1870. The marshal was Thomas J. (Bear River Tom) Smith. Bear River Tom received his nickname for his shooting abilities, illustrated during some riots on the Union Pacific Railroad. The riots were a result of infuriated railroad workers who were tired of being robbed by local outlaws. The retaliation was known as the Bear River Riot, and through the assistance of various gunmen, the railroad workers defended themselves against the attacks.

Soon after the riots, Smith arrived in Ellsworth, Kansas, and noticed an announcement of an opening for city marshal in Abilene, Kansas. Smith was intrigued by the position, because he had spent several years in the New York Police Department. Soon after arriving in Abilene, Smith was appointed city marshal, receiving $125 a month and an additional $2 for each apprehension.

At first, Smith's policing methods seemed unusual to many residents and officials. He prevented crime and apprehended criminals without using his pistols. He believed in policing with logic and reason, instead of by instilling fear with firearms. This concept surprised many residents of the town because firearms had been the means of controlling criminals. He also strictly enforced the no-gun law in town. Smith quickly gained respect when the no-gun method was equally as effective as that of his predecessors, who policed with weapons. In contrast to many lawmen in the West, Smith also policed his city on horseback instead of walking the streets. This technique allowed him to have a broader view of the town.

Bear River Tom's unique policing techniques, poise, and mysteriousness gained much respect in Abilene. Although he seldom used his pistols, residents and criminals were fully aware of his shooting abilities and knew that his pistols were always hanging in the sides of his leather belt. The city was so impressed with Marshal Smith that they even raised his salary to $225 per month.

Sometime in the latter part of 1870, Abilene began to experience a decline in prosperity, which led city officials to dismiss several deputy marshals until the town could afford them. Smith assumed he was going to be fired as well and attempted to turn in his resignation, although the officials would not accept it. Historians now claim that his resignation may have been the best thing for him, because Smith's death was soon to follow.

Marshal Smith's death came when he and Deputy James H. McDonald went to arrest Andrew McConnell. McConnell was charged with the murder of a local resident. McConnell had been on a hunting trip and upon his return, realized his neighbor's cows were in his pasture. He was further enraged after realizing the cows were the property of a particular neighbor, John Shea, whom he despised. When McConnell went to Shea's farm, they got into an argument, at which time Shea was killed. Later in court, McConnell claimed Shea drew his firearm first, although the gun malfunctioned and did not fire. According to McConnell, Shea attempted to shoot him three times before McConnell shot back in self-defense. When an examination of Shea's gun revealed it was working properly, the court issued a warrant for McConnell's arrest and told Sheriff Cramer to make the arrest.

Cramer had recently been elected Sheriff of Abilene and was a somewhat cowardly man. Sheriff Cramer and Deputy McDonald requested Marshal Smith to assist with the arrest, although on the day of arrest, Cramer found reasons not to go with them. Smith and McDonald found McConnell and a friend, Moses Miles, in a dugout near Chapman Creek. When Smith and McDonald attempted to make the arrest, McConnell and Smith got into a fight and McConnell shot Smith in the stomach. While wounded, Smith still continued to fight until Miles came from behind and nearly decapitated Smith with an axe. McDonald ran to town when the struggle began, claiming he left to get help. Both McConnell and Miles were arrested and sentenced to the state penitentiary. McConnell was sentenced to twelve years in prison, and Miles was sentenced to sixteen years. The city townsmen were outraged at the court's decision, asserting that the sentences were too lenient. The city mourned the death of their beloved marshal and thereafter compared his successors to the level of Smith's capabilities as a lawman.

Years after the death of Marshal Smith, the city constructed a statue in his honor. With Smith gone, the city faced the need for a new marshal who would be fierce enough to control the brutal and aggressive city of Abilene.

ENTER WILD BILL

Just over a year after the death of Bear River Tom, James Butler (Wild Bill) Hickok was appointed the new marshal of Abilene in April of 1871. Wild Bill Hickok has been one of the most popular U.S. Marshals known throughout history. Even at the time, he received some notoriety as a scout, spy, bodyguard, and stage driver, among other things. He was also known for his quick draw with his pistols and excellent shooting ability. He first began to gain notoriety in the shootout at the Rock Creek (Nebraska) station of the Overland Express, in which he had killed—murdered, his critics have it—Dave McCanles, the former station owner, and two others. During this time, he was a town constable. For most of the well-known part of his career, Wild Bill was typically either a city marshal or sheriff. He became a U.S. Marshal in the latter part of his career, and not many tales are told about that period in his life.

The tales of Wild Bill Hickok began in Fort Riley, Kansas, where he was appointed deputy city marshal around 1866. During this time, he became associated with other frontier icons such as Wyatt Earp (Deputy Marshal of Wichita, Kansas), Bat Masterson (Sheriff of Ford County, Kansas), and Doc Holliday. After his time in Fort Riley, Wild Bill moved on to other ventures including being a part of Buffalo Bill's Wild West Show. Around 1869, Wild Bill ended up at Hays City, Kansas, where he was appointed the sheriff of Ellis County and city marshal.

Hays City became the stomping ground for cattle runs and railroad trails. Thousands of cattle runs made their way through Hays City to places like Nebraska, Wyoming, and Dakota. With the population boom, the officials of Hays City realized the need for someone to maintain law and order. Shortly thereafter, the city council decided to hire James Butler Hickok, known as "Wild Bill," or the "Prince of Pistoleers," as the sheriff and city marshal.

As the sheriff of Hays City, Wild Bill patrolled the streets with a shotgun and two pistols. He went from gambling saloons to brothels, maintaining a fierce presence. Having the reputation of being one of the best gunmen in the West, Wild Bill was constantly challenged by outlaws or troublemakers who wanted to prove their skills. They usually wanted to fight the best gunfighter in the West. Wild Bill typically avoided such confrontations, although he did not retreat from a challenge.

Although Hickok kept the peace in Hays City, his time there was controversial. One instance brought Wild Bill into direct confrontation with the U.S. Army stationed nearby. Wild Bill was a friend of an Army officer named Captain Tom Custer, although many of the members of the Army did not care for Wild Bill. On one occasion, Captain Custer was racing up and down the streets of Hays City shooting his pistols. Hickok arrested Custer and took him back to the military fort. Captain Custer was outraged by Wild Bill's actions and sought retribution for the embarrassment that he had endured. A few days later, Custer and some other soldiers went to a saloon where Wild Bill was located and attempted to settle the matter. Wild Bill shot several of the soldiers before some of his friends stopped him by reminding him of the repercussions of the actions. After the event, Wild Bill either quit or was fired from Hays City and moved to Ellsworth, Kansas, until the situation had subsided.

When the upheaval from Hays City settled down, Hickok sought out the position of city marshal in Abilene, Kansas. Hickok began his duties at a salary of $150 a month and 25 percent of all fines executed by the courts. The city council also gave him three deputy marshals, James Gainsford, Tom Carson, and James McDonald (Tom Smith's previous deputy). Hickok's policing methods raised concern when residents realized that he policed the town quite differently than Marshal Smith. Wild Bill had no problems utilizing his gun power. He maintained peace and order with his pistols.

Wild Bill was also strict on the no-gun laws, although he was not quite as friendly about administering the law. He used his weapons and sharp tongue to police the town, which made him a target for attacks from those who found his manner undesirable. Wild Bill was also a careful and cautious man. He distrusted most of his deputies and many of the residents of Abilene. He rarely supervised the town at night, always watched carefully when walking by dark alleys, and (contrary to popular depictions) usually had his back to the wall at saloons and gambling pubs. Although many felt that Tom Smith's techniques were better, Abilene residents soon came to respect Wild Bill as an authoritative figure. However, outlaws who felt like they had something to prove constantly challenged Wild Bill.

On one occasion, Hickok and a man known as Phil Coe came to a face-off. Coe was part of a gambling problem occurring in Abilene around October 1871, and story has it that Coe was also messing around with Jessie Hazel, a woman Hickok had claimed as his own. When Wild Bill heard this rumor, he went and found them drinking wine in a secluded room. He was outraged, and the men got into a fight, during which Coe got the better of Hickok. After the brawl, Coe bragged to the town about how he got the best of Wild Bill, which did not please the marshal at all, although Wild Bill took no action at the time.

One night, Coe and several of his friends were drunk and indirectly challenged Wild Bill to a gunfight. Surrounded by fifty Texan friends, Coe was ready to fight the marshal of Abilene, Kansas. During the fight, Coe was shot in the stomach twice, and Hickok was grazed when two bullets hit his coat. During the showdown, Hickok's friend, Mike Williams, ran in to save Hickok but was killed. History states that Hickok was responsible for accidentally shooting his friend, assuming the person running up behind him was an enemy. In a rage because of his friend's death, Hickok then went into every bar, brothel, and gambling burrow in town and cleared out all the gamblers, prostitutes, and drunks.

The report of this gunfight was very exaggerated and was misinterpreted by the newspapers. Many newspapers applauded Hickok for his efforts in keeping the peace and maintaining order, while other reporters criticized Hickok for his violent actions. Various demeaning accounts of the story portrayed Hickok as the "Wild Bill," "terror of the West," and "notorious gambler and desperado." Other accounts of the story indicated that Hickok killed Coe by shooting him in the back. Although many versions of the story were relayed, most residents of Abilene still respected Hickok. They sought him out as an authoritative figure, friend, and considerate individual.

James Butler Hickok's days at Abilene, Kansas, were ultimately short-lived. He was the marshal for about eight months. His problems were not due to the gunfights but were because of the differences he had with the city council. Around late 1871, because of a reduction of the cattle business, the city council ordered Hickok to fire a number of deputies. Hickok refused to do so, which caused conflict between Wild Bill and the officials.

James Butler Hickok was relieved of his marshal duties around December of 1871. The rationale behind this decision was unclear; the city council only claimed that they no longer needed his services. Some believe many residents of Abilene still compared him to Marshal Smith and remained disappointed about his policing techniques. The council later hired James A. Gauthie at a substantially lower salary. Hickok was later appointed U.S. Marshal of Ellsworth, Kansas. Although Wild Bill was a U.S. Marshal, most of the stories about him are of when he was a sheriff or city marshal.

Numerous tales have it that Wild Bill was responsible for many deaths, although the number of deaths was never quite clear. Legend has it that many Indian chiefs and tribe members died at the hands of Wild Bill, although this account remains unclear, as well. "On the other hand, court records reveal that he was responsible for the death of eleven white men and absolved of responsibility in each instance by reason of self-defense or accident" (O'Conner 1959).

Wild Bill spent many years policing towns in the West. He was a lawman by trade and a gambler by habit. In 1876, he was killed during a poker game in Deadwood, Dakota. Ironically, on that day, for the first time since Hays City, Wild Bill sat without his back to the wall. He was a very cautious man and always sat where he was able to view everything occurring around him. It seems to be unclear if there were no seats by the wall or if his friends were playing a joke on him, but reluctantly, Wild Bill sat in the game room with his back to the door. All of sudden, a man named Jack McCall shot Wild Bill in the back of the head, killing him instantly. McCall was only twenty-five years old at the time and wanted to be the best gunfighter in the West. McCall claimed he was seeking revenge for the killing of his brother. It was later found out that McCall had no brothers at all. Legend has it that when Wild Bill was shot, he was holding a pair of aces and a pair of eights, which is now called the Dead Man's Hand.

After the shooting, McCall was caught by the residents of the town. At the first trial, he was found not guilty and was permitted to go free; however, McCall's boasting about the killing of Wild Bill resulted in his demise. He was charged for the second time, found guilty, and sentenced to death for the murder of Hickok.

History indicates that Wild Bill was a both lawman and a gambler. It was not uncommon for lawmen to be gamblers, as well. Some men were businessmen, lawmen, gamblers, family men, and even outlaws. One of the most notorious lawmen-outlaws was Ben Thompson.

A GUNMAN OR LAWMAN: BEN THOMPSON

The story of Ben Thompson is not as well known as other marshals, but is indicative of the multiple roles/personalities of lawmen of this time. Thompson was never a U.S. Marshal, although he played a unique role as a city marshal. He was a gunman, a soldier, a gambler, an outlaw, a businessman, and a marshal. He was known as a fierce gunman, a loyal friend, and a drunk. He never had much money, although he was loved by his friends for his loyalty and reliability. He was a soldier for the U.S. Army during the Civil War. Shortly after the war, he was sentenced to prison on murder charges for killing an acquaintance. After being released from prison, he became a gambler and businessman.

Around 1870, he traveled to Abilene, Kansas, completely broke. After a lucky gambling streak, he and his friend Phil Coe bought the Bull's Head Saloon. During this time in Abilene, Wild Bill Hickok was the marshal of the town. Thompson's business partner, Phil Coe, was the same person who had issues with Wild Bill. The Bull's Head Saloon proved to be a profitable venture. After a while, Thompson left the saloon in the hands of Coe while he went to Kansas City to meet with his wife. After the death of Coe, Thompson sold the saloon and went to Ellsworth, Kansas.

Ben Thompson could never seem to stay out of trouble, especially when his brother, Billy, was involved. In August 1873, Thompson was at a saloon gambling when one of the gamblers, John Sterling, claimed that if he won the hand, he would split the winnings with Thompson. After the gambler won, he left the saloon without splitting the winnings. Thompson later found Sterling and demanded his half of the winnings. Sterling refused, slapped Thompson in the face, and left the saloon. This ultimately led to a gunfight involving Thompson, Sterling, and others, during which the local sheriff was shot. Thompson was forced to leave town because he was wanted by the law.

After leaving Ellsworth, Thompson went to Austin, Texas. In Austin, he ran for city marshal but was defeated. Ben blamed this defeat on a man known as Mark Wilson, who was a local businessman. When Thompson confronted Wilson, Wilson started firing his shotgun. Thompson retaliated by shooting Wilson several times and killing him. Many believe that the death of Wilson was premeditated, although Thompson was acquitted on the basis of self-defense.

Around 1883, Thompson ran for city marshal for the second time and was elected marshal of Austin, Texas. After he became marshal, Austin reported a dramatic decline in the crime. During this time, he ran into another enemy, Jack Harris, who attempted to kill him, but Thompson shot back and killed Harris. Thompson was indicted for the murder but was acquitted on the grounds that both men had threatened each other at various times in their lives. After this incident, Thompson was asked for his resignation. Thompson was killed on March 13, 1884, after a gunfight broke out between he and some old enemies. Thompson was hit eight times.

Ben Thompson's story was different in the sense that he was a lawman and an outlaw. He was also known for his many acquaintances. One of Thompson's close friends was Bat Masterson, the sheriff of Ford County, Kansas. The Masterson brothers were also lawmen who were a central part of western history.

A TALE OF DODGE CITY: THE MASTERSONS

Stories of Dodge City have captivated western movie lovers all over the nation. Heroic western icons such as the Masterson brothers, Wyatt Earp, and Doc Holliday made Dodge City a central part of western lore. In 1872, Billy Brooks became the first unofficial city marshal for Dodge City, because it was not yet incorporated. History indicates that Billy "Bully" Brooks was an unruly, cowardly man, who was ultimately driven out of town. Many assumed it was because of murder charges for the death of Matt Sullivan, a saloonkeeper. Other reports indicated that he was killed in 1877 by Virgil Earp, Wyatt Earp's older brother.

In 1876, Lawrence E. Deger became the first official city marshal of Dodge City. In 1877, he was later replaced by Edward J. Masterson, who was the younger brother of Bat Masterson, sheriff of Ford County, Kansas. Ed Masterson was killed when Masterson and Assistant Marshal Nat Haywood were patrolling the streets of Dodge City one night. They heard a commotion coming from the Lady Gay Theatre, a local entertainment center. When they arrived at the theater, they realized that Jack Wagner had been frantically waving his gun around the theater. Marshal Masterson approached Wagner and took away his weapons. Masterson then handed the weapons to Wagner's employer, who was also in the crowd.

After the crowd had settled down, the two lawmen turned around to leave. Wagner had reclaimed his weapons and followed them to the sidewalk. Ed Masterson began to take away his weapons again, and Wagner and Masterson started to brawl. Haywood attempted to intervene but Wagner threatened to shoot him if he did. Wagner shot Masterson in the stomach and the gunshot set his clothes on fire. Ed Masterson, in return, shot Wagner through the body, killing him on the spot. Another account of the story claims that Bat Masterson, Edward Masterson's older brother, heard of the trouble and came to the rescue, although it was too late to save his brother. Upon arriving at the scene, Bat Masterson shot both criminals to death, Wagner and another individual who came to rescue him.

After the death of Edward Masterson, city officials of Dodge City appointed Charley Bassett as the new city marshal. By this time, Wyatt Earp had returned to Dodge City from his travels and should have been a prime candidate for the marshal position, although he was appointed assistant city marshal instead. A couple years earlier, Wyatt Earp was the assistant city marshal of Dodge City, but left in 1877 to travel through Texas on gambling ventures. During this time in his life, he met his soon-to-be close friend, Doc Holliday, a gambling dentist from Georgia. Upon his return to Dodge City, he was reappointed assistant city marshal. As discussed below, the time Wyatt Earp spent in Dodge City was suspicious because when he arrived in Dodge City, he was penniless, but when he left he had enough money to buy the Oriental Saloon in Tombstone, Arizona.

Historians credit Earp's increase in money to the legend of Dora Hand. Hand was a prosperous, attractive saloon singer who was murdered accidentally by a culprit who thought she was someone else. The murder suspect was a man known as Spike Kenedy, who was seen running away from the murder scene. As the investigation began, Sheriff Bat Masterson, Marshal Bassett, Assistant Marshal Wyatt Earp, and Deputy Sheriff Tilghman set off to find Kenedy. After Kenedy was arrested, his father, who was wealthy, came to his son's assistance. At the indictment hearing, no press or public was allowed to watch the proceedings, and the charges were dropped because of lack of evidence. Legend has it that Bat Masterson may have also been involved in the suspicious circumstances of the Kenedy case. He had the reputation of being a gambler and was known to be paid minimal wages, although shortly after the Kenedy incident, Masterson bought a saloon/dance hall without explaining where he had acquired the funds.

The legend of Bat Masterson is more prominent than the tales of his brothers. He was born the second of seven children in Quebec, Canada, although his family moved to the United States around the mid-1850s. Masterson was born Bartholomew Masterson (shortened to "Bat") but changed his name to William Barclay Masterson years later. Throughout history, Bat Masterson has been recognized as one of the most iconic of western figures.

Along with his brothers, Jim and Edward, Bat was a lawman by trade. He began his career as a scout for the U.S. Army, and toward the end of his life, he became a sportswriter. His close friends included Wyatt Earp, Ben Thompson, Wild Bill Hickok, and Alfred Henry Lewis.

Legends have it that his first fight was in Sweetwater, Texas, probably over a woman. During the gunfight, Bat was shot in the pelvis, which crippled him and caused him to use a cane for the rest of his life. Around 1877, Bat ended up in Dodge City with his brothers Jim and Edward. Jim was a saloon owner, while Ed was a deputy sheriff for Dodge City. Around the first week of November 1877, Bat was elected sheriff of Ford County, and he filled that role for about two years. Most of the stories told about Bat Masterson were during his years as the sheriff of Ford County.

After Bat was elected sheriff of Ford County, he was eager to show his ability to do the job. He got his opportunity soon enough when a group of outlaws attempted to rob the trains of Santa Fe, close to Kingsley. At first, two groups were dispatched to apprehend the criminals. The first group was led by Edwards County Sheriff Fuller. The second group was led by ex-Sheriff Bob McCanse. After a somewhat exhaustive search, both groups came back empty handed. The agents of the Adams Express Company requested the assistance of Bat Masterson to apprehend the criminals.

Bat was eager to take on this task and formed a party to assist his search. As they rode to a nearby ranch, Masterson saw several outlaws riding toward the ranch. When the outlaws arrived, Josh Webb, one of the inhabitants at the ranch, went to greet them at the door. Bat Masterson quickly reacted, sensing that this was an opportune time to capture the outlaws. One account of the story follows:

> Bat suddenly kicked wide the partly open door and leaped out with leveled rifle. "Throw up your hands!" he snapped as Riley and Morrow scurried to his flanks with drawn guns. The startled West quickly complied with Bat's orders, but Rudabaugh was a tougher customer. His hand flew from his saddle horn to his gun butt. He froze with the weapon half out of the scabbard as Josh Webb's six-gun hammer clicked behind him. Then the man whom Wyatt Earp once called "the most notorious outlaw in the range country" slowly

raised his hands, and Bat told Riley to disarm the pair. From the gun belt of each outlaw, Big Kinch extracted a Colt and a .45-caliber government carbine. He stepped back, thinking his task complete, but the sharp-eyed Bat detected a suspicious-looking bulge under Rudabaugh's greatcoat. He pulled open the coat and reached for the revolver the bandit had hidden in his waistband. Rudabaugh made one last desperate attempt to escape capture. He grabbed for the gun as Bat extricated it from his clothing, but Bat wrenched it away from him. (DeArment 1979)

Masterson's quick-wittedness and diligent reactions apprehended the wanted outlaws. The residents of Dodge City and Ford County acclaimed him a hero for capturing the train robbers.

Although there are many tales of Bat Masterson, his time as sheriff of Ford County was short-lived. He was not reelected in 1879, serving only two years as sheriff. He later became a U.S. Marshal for Trinidad, Colorado, but lasted only a few months as marshal. He then traveled from city to city gambling and conducting business ventures. Later in life, he left the West and moved to New York City, where he was appointed deputy U.S. Marshal of the lower part of New York City in 1908. His life as U.S. Marshal didn't generate as many stories as when he was a sheriff of Ford County. Toward the end of his life, he became a prominent sportswriter for a New York newspaper. William Barclay (Bat) Masterson died in 1921, at the age of sixty-seven. He died sitting at his desk, while writing his sports column for the *Telegraph*.

WYATT EARP: REALITY OF THE MAN

Wyatt Earp was one of the most legendary lawmen of western history. The legend of Wyatt Earp has been interpreted by many scholars and journalists and by the media. Because of the movies and media attention, the image of Wyatt Earp has almost become fictional. Wyatt Earp was a lawman, gambler, businessman, and gunfighter. His legendary reputation characterized him as a tall, courageous frontiersman who wore a long black coat and an ironed white shirt. He was portrayed as a man who was fearless no matter what the situation. As are many iconic figures, Wyatt Earp was portrayed as a U.S. Marshal, although he was never actually a federal agent. His occupation as a lawman was typically limited to deputy city marshal. However, Wyatt's brother, Virgil, was a U.S. Marshal during his lifetime.

Wyatt Berry Stapp Earp, the third of six children of Nicholas and Virginia Earp, was born in 1848 in Illinois. The Earp family moved around quite a bit, a trend that continued with the next generation. Earp had very little formal education but picked up the survival tricks of the streets. In 1870, Earp obtained his first lawman position as the town constable in Lamar, Missouri. He left Lamar in 1871 after the sudden death of his first wife from an unknown illness. Earp traveled the next few years through several states, including Kansas, Texas, and New Mexico.

Through his travels, he earned his travel expenses by being a gambler and a law enforcement officer. He was a deputy city marshal for Wichita, Kansas, and then ended up in Dodge City, Kansas, where he was briefly an assistant deputy marshal. While Earp was in Dodge City, he met a prostitute named Cecilia Ann Mattie Blaylock. Wyatt and Mattie lived together for years and eventually had a common-law marriage. Wyatt and Mattie continued to travel through various states and even ended up in Dodge City again, where he was appointed deputy city marshal for the second time. As mentioned above, he was deputy marshal when Bat Masterson was sheriff of Ford County. After his time in Dodge City, he and Mattie went to Tombstone, Arizona, in 1879.

Wyatt Earp became legendary because of one particular fight that took place at the O.K. Corral. The Earp family and the half-bloods, a local outlaw gang, became rivals when the Earps tried to restore law and order in the city of Tombstone. The members of the gang were well-known outlaws such as Ike Clanton, Tom McLaury, Billy Clanton, and Billy Claiborne. They were known for their savage behavior and red sashes, which indicated their membership in the gang.

Shortly after arriving at Tombstone, Wyatt Earp became a shotgun messenger and then a deputy sheriff for Pima County, Arizona, for about three months. Wyatt Earp had wanted to become the sheriff of Tombstone, but lost that position to a politician named John H. Behan. Wyatt soon after resigned as the deputy sheriff because he felt that he should have been the sheriff of Tombstone.

Virgil Earp was appointed Deputy U.S. Marshal for the Arizona Territory before he arrived in Tombstone. After his arrival, he became the city marshal, as well, and appointed his brothers Warren and Morgan as his deputies. As mentioned before, during this time Wyatt was no longer a deputy sheriff and spent most of his time at a local saloon called the Oriental Saloon, which he purchased with other investors.

The showdown between the Earp family and the half-bloods began when a Kinnear and Company carriage was robbed. During the attack, the driver of the carriage was murdered. To apprehend the criminals, two groups were formed to find the murderers. Sheriff John Behan and his deputies led the first group, and the second group consisted of the Earp brothers, Frank Leslie, and Bat Masterson. Both groups were competing against each other, which made the search difficult.

The group led by Sheriff Behan found Luther King and made him name the other participants in the robbery, who were Bill Leonard, Harry Head, and Jim Crane. King was arrested but managed to escape and leave town. When the Earp brothers heard about King's escape, they decided that they needed to find the culprits first. Stories indicated that soon thereafter, Doc

Gun Fighters

Holliday was also implicated in the robbery and murder. Doc Holliday was eventually acquitted. The Earps were enraged at the accusations against Doc Holliday, which only caused more conflict between Wyatt Earp and Sheriff Behan. The struggle between the lawmen split the city of Tombstone between those who favored the Earps and those who favored the sheriff. Meanwhile, Sheriff Behan established a support group by involving himself with outlaws and gang members.

The rivalry between the half-bloods and the Earp family began when Wyatt Earp tried to bribe Ike Clanton to divulge information on the whereabouts of the criminals. Earp offered Clanton all the monetary rewards for the capture of the murderers in return for information on his friends. A few days later, the outlaws were killed and rumors began that Ike Clanton had ratted out his friends to Wyatt Earp. In one incident, Clanton started screaming in the middle of town that he did no such thing and that the stories were all lies. After several conflicts between the outlaws and the Earps, Virgil Earp, now U.S. Marshal and city marshal, appointed Wyatt Earp and Doc Holliday as deputy marshals. There were several stories that indicated that some of the members of the half-bloods, including Ike Clanton, were threatening to kill the Earps, who expected a showdown almost every day.

On October 25, 1881, the Earp brothers and Doc Holliday decided to take action. Earlier that morning, Ike had some heated words with Virgil Earp after playing cards in a saloon. Later that afternoon, Virgil and Morgan Earp stopped Ike in the middle of the street, where Ike threatened the Earp brothers again. Virgil and Morgan arrested Ike and took him to the courthouse, where the Judge charged him 25 cents for possession of a weapon.

On the same day, the Earp brothers heard that several members of the half-blood gang were near the O.K. Corral. The brothers started on their way down to the O.K. Corral, first Wyatt and Morgan, who were joined by Holliday and Virgil. Sheriff Behan heard of the upcoming showdown and urged Virgil Earp to remove the weapons the outlaws were carrying with them. Tired of all the threats against his family, Virgil Earp refused that idea and asserted that if they wanted to fight, he would let them fight. Sheriff Behan, at this time, went to disarm the outlaws and urged everyone to follow him to his office, although both parties resisted. The Earps claimed they intended to disarm the cowboys, although the situation turned out differently. One account of the showdown went like this:

> Later Behan was to testify that when the Earps reached the McLaurys, one of them—he thought it was Wyatt—said, "You sons of bitches, you have been looking for a fight, and now you can have it." Wyatt testified that as his group came up to the Clantons, Billy Clanton and the two McLaurys had their hands by their sides and Frank McLaury's and Bill Clanton's six-shooters were in plain sight. Virgil ordered them to throw up their hands, saying that he had come to disarm them. Immediately, Billy Clanton and Frank McLaury

dropped their hands to their pistols. Virgil called out, "Hold, I don't mean that; I have come to disarm you." Billy Clanton cried out, "Don't shoot me, I don't want to fight." Tom McLaury quickly threw open his coat to show that he was not armed saying either, "I have nothing," or "I am not armed" (according to Behan, who later reported the conversations under oath). Behan claimed that Holliday fired the first shot from a nickel-plated pistol. Almost instantaneously two more shots were fired. No accounts of the fight seem to agree, but it is apparent that Wyatt Earp and Billy Clanton got off the first shots. (Rosa 1969)

The Earps claimed they were trying to disarm the troublemakers and therefore were defending their lives. All that is certain is that several participants of the gunfight were injured. Billy Clanton, Tom McLaury, and Frank McLaury were all killed in the fight. Virgil Earp was shot in the leg, Morgan was shot in the spine, and Doc Holliday had a bullet tear in the skin on his back. Wyatt Earp went untouched, as did Ike Clanton and Billy Claiborne.

One account claims that Wyatt Earp and Doc Holliday were arrested because of the deaths at the O.K. Corral. The warrants were issued by Sheriff Behan and Ike Clanton. The bail bond was set at $20,000, which was raised by friends of the Earp family. The trial date was never set because the judge threw out the case on the grounds that Tom McLaury had access to a gun; therefore, they were not shooting at unarmed men.

Around the end of November, Virgil Earp was shot in the arm and side, which crippled him for life. About four months after Virgil Earp's incident, Morgan Earp was killed while playing pool at a saloon. Another version of the story claims that, instead of being arrested for the deaths at the O.K. Corral, Wyatt Earp and Doc Holliday were arrested because they killed Frank Stillwell, one of the murderers of Morgan Earp.

The Earp family soon realized it was too dangerous for them to be in Tombstone and moved out of the city. Stories have it that Virgil Earp and his family accompanied Morgan's body to Colton, California, the hometown of their parents. Wyatt Earp went his separate way, accompanied by Doc Holliday. Legend has it that Wyatt Earp traveled westward to avenge the death of his brother, during the time frame that Frank Stillwell was killed. Wyatt and Doc were charged with Stillwell's murder but were acquitted. After this, Wyatt and Doc left Arizona, never to return again because of the possible dangers it possessed.

During his time in Tombstone, Arizona, Wyatt left Mattie for the town sheriff's girlfriend, Josephine Marcus, also known as Josie. Josie was a young actress from San Francisco, who lived with Wyatt for the rest of his life. They were married in San Francisco, California. The couple then moved from town to town, seeking business opportunities and participating in gambling ventures.

The gunfight at the O.K. Corral became popular after the release of the western film, *Tombstone*. The recap of history illustrated in this movie was truly exaggerated at points, yet was quite interesting to the general populace. Toward the end of Wyatt's life, several versions of his life story were published in local newspapers, which enraged him. The articles portrayed the Earp brothers as troublemakers, who initiated the fight between the members of the half-bloods at the O.K. Corral. To set the stories straight, Wyatt Earp tried to recapture the past in words, twice. A biography of Wyatt Earp's life, *Wyatt Earp: Frontier Marshal* by Stuart Nathaniel Lake, formed the basis of many movies about the Earp family. Facts of Lake's book have been widely criticized as fictional, although it remains the primary account of Wyatt Earp's life. Scholars argue that Wyatt Earp and Lake exchanged letters and had meetings with each other, although Earp died two years before the book was actually published.

Scholars have indicated that Wyatt Earp was much cared for and loved by many of his friends and was viewed as one of the true western frontiersmen. "When asked by Teddy Roosevelt why he had not written about Earp's colorful life, Bat Masterson is said to have answered, 'Mr. President, the real story of the Old West can never be told unless Wyatt Earp will tell what he knows...'" (Cohen 2003). Wyatt Earp died in 1929 in Los Angeles, at 83 years of age. Virgil died in Nevada in 1906.

Around 1885, the West started becoming more modernized as its population increased. The days of the cow towns and the cowboys were at an end. Law enforcement agencies became more organized and structured. "In 1885, the Kansas cattle boom was ended by passage of a state law banning the trail-cattle industry. Soon the boom days were only memories—of two-gun marshals who shot it out with the lawless on the dusty streets or in the smoky saloons of the cow towns. The days of the men who ruled with revolvers." (Cohen 2003).

THE U.S. MARSHALS TODAY

Currently, there are ninety-four U.S. Marshal offices throughout the country, one for each congressional district in the United States. The president of the United States appoints the U.S. Marshals, and deputy marshals are recruited through a hiring process. They are responsible for fugitive investigations, court security, the witness protection program, transporting prisoners, and assets relinquishment, as well as other duties.

Fugitive responsibilities for the U.S. Marshals include investigating and apprehending criminals. They investigate escapees and those who fail to pay bond and/or fail to appear in court, arrest parole and probation violators, and assist the other federal agencies in various investigations. They are responsible for arrest warrants until the warrants are either executed or dismissed. "The U.S. Marshals work with other federal, state and local law enforcement agencies on multi-agency task forces. These task forces focus law enforcement resources and attention to the most serious cases. Task forces allow law enforcement officers to work together, increasing the opportunities to locate and capture dangerous violent fugitives."(Cooley 1959).

Judiciary responsibilities involve protecting court administrators, including judges, witnesses, and jurors. Currently U.S. Marshals protect more than two thousand judges, witnesses, and jurors and more than four hundred federal courthouses. Marshals are responsible for court security during and after proceedings and also for transporting prisoners to court proceedings and from court back to confinement. "When a person is arrested, they must go before a magistrate (judge) to be charged (told why they were arrested)… While in Marshals Service custody (hold) each prisoner is safely moved to and from court, securely housed and, provided meals and medical care. The Marshals Service may be required to escort prisoners many times during several legal proceedings." (Cooley 1959). This includes the preliminary hearing, all trial examinations, sentencing, and transportation to specific locations.

U.S. Marshals are also in charge of the witness protection program. "The Marshals Service protects witnesses who testify against dangerous defendants such as drug traffickers, organized crime members, terrorists, and other criminals. For a witness' testimony, the government offers protection, a new name and a safe location" (U.S. Marshal Homepage). This includes 24-hour surveillance, counseling, physical examinations, documents providing new names and locations, and finding the witnesses new jobs.

The marshals conduct asset repossessions, as well. They work with the Drug Enforcement Agency (DEA), the Federal Bureau of Investigation (FBI), Immigration and Customs Enforcement (ICE), and the Internal Revenue Service (IRS) when properties need to be seized by federal agencies. This responsibility also requires the marshals to manage properties or assets such as houses until the court decides either to sell the asset or dispose of it.

The responsibilities of U.S. Marshals have grown over the years, although the core duties still remain the same. They are mainly responsible for court proceedings and handling prisoners. The duties of the western icons of crime fighting were similar to the responsibilities of the U.S. Marshals today, although because of the media, the perception of much of what the western marshals did is skewed. Much of their occupation did involve apprehending criminals and enforcing the law, but the romanticized, fictional versions portrayed in movies and books fails to include the tedious details involved in the marshals' occupation.

Becoming a Deputy U.S. Marshal (http://www.usmarshals.gov)

Major Duties

Under the close supervision of senior U.S. Marshals law enforcement personnel, Deputy U.S. Marshals will perform the following vital law enforcement responsibilities:

- fugitive apprehension
- court security
- transporting and processing prisoners
- conducting body searches of prisoners and persons under arrest
- producing prisoners in court and maintaining custody of prisoners throughout court proceedings
- protecting sequestered juries
- providing protection for court facilities and personnel
- executing civil and criminal processes, and
- enforcing court orders and Attorney General orders involving civil disturbances, acts of terrorism, etc.

Qualification Requirements

You must be a U.S. citizen, be between the ages of 21 and 36, be in excellent physical condition, have a bachelor's degree or three years of qualifying experience, or an equivalent combination of education and experience, possess a valid drivers license with a good driving record, complete agency FCIP requirements and structured interview, and undergo a rigorous $17\frac{1}{2}$ week basic training program at the U.S. Marshals Service Training Academy in Glynco, GA.

General Experience Requirements (GS-5): You must have had a minimum of three years of responsible volunteer or paid experience, or you must substitute a four year degree from an accredited college or university. The following types of experience are illustrative of acceptable experience.

- Law enforcement
- Work involving the correctional treatment and supervision of criminal offenders in correctional institutions
- Classroom teaching or instruction
- Sales (other than taking and filling orders as in over-the-counter sales)
- Interviewing experience in a public or private service agency which involved making determinations on individual requests for services, benefits, etc., and explaining, interpreting, and applying rules, regulations, and procedures

(continued)

- Work involving contacts with the public for the purpose of gathering information, such as credit rating investigator, claims adjuster, journalist, etc.
- Volunteer teaching or counseling
- Other experience that has demonstrated the ability to take charge and make decisions, such as civilian/military supervisory, managerial or leadership responsibility

Specialized Experience (GS-7 only): In addition to the GS-5 experience requirement above, you must have one year of responsible law enforcement experience that required the exercise of tact, courtesy, and the ability to deal effectively with associates, subordinates, the general public, and prisoners. This experience must demonstrate your abilities as a competent law enforcement officer, to include the ability to make arrests and use firearms proficiently. (Superior academic achievement may also qualify you for the GS-7 level.)

Substitution of Education for Specialized Experience (Superior Academic Achievement) GS-7 only: A bachelor's degree and one of the following Superior Academic Achievement provisions:

1. A grade point average (GPA) of 3.0 or higher for all completed undergraduate courses, or for those courses completed during the last 2 years of undergraduate study.
2. Rank in the upper one third of your college or university undergraduate class.
3. Membership in a national scholastic honor society (other than freshman honor societies) recognized by the Association of College Honor Societies.
4. Successful completion of graduate education in law, or in a field related to law enforcement (e.g., criminal justice), or completion of one full year of graduate study (minimum of 18 semester or 27 graduate quarter hours).

Combination of Education and Experience: If you do not qualify based on education or experience alone we will combine your education and experience in an attempt to satisfy the minimum general experience requirements, at the GS-5 level, for Deputy U.S. Marshal positions.

Medical Qualifications: Deputy U.S. Marshals must be physically able to safely and efficiently perform the full range of duties of the position. Any medical or physical condition which affects this ability is disqualifying.

Some conditions which may be disqualifying are: diabetes mellitus, convulsive disorders, hernias, orthopedic conditions that affect mobility, stability, flexibility and strength, hypertension, heart disease, color vision deficits and eye surgery.

(continued)

> Specific medical requirements are: 20/20 binocular vision is required and may be corrected with lenses to meet this standard. Uncorrected vision must test 20/200 or better in each eye. Any surgery to correct vision may be disqualifying dependent on the outcome of the surgery. Near vision, corrected or uncorrected, must be sufficient to distinguish basic colors and depth perception must be clinically normal.
>
> Hearing must test at 30 decibels (dB) or better in each ear at 500, 1000, and 2000 hertz (Hz) and 40 dB or better at 3000 Hz.
>
> Fitness in total standards in the categories of flexibility, push-ups, sit-ups, and 1.5 mile run must be met by all candidates before the hiring process is completed. (Call a District Recruitment Officer for more information)

CONCLUSION

Western movies and books have portrayed the U.S. Marshals as possessing supernatural powers, excelling in their abilities to fight and shoot. These men typically possessed extraordinary courage. They rode their horses with poise; they shot their guns from many yards away and never missed a shot; they saved the town from evil outlaws; and when they were done for the day, they rode off into the sunset.

In reality, U.S. Marshals were designated to assist court proceedings, court security, and citizen protection. Many of the actual responsibilities of the U.S. Marshals have been overlooked and misinterpreted by fictional stories. Also, city-elected law enforcement officers have been confused with true western U.S. Marshals. Icons such as Wyatt Warp and Ben Thompson are known for being marshals, although the fact that they were city-elected officers has been lost in the stories.

Interestingly enough, contrary to popular belief, the Wild West was not so long ago. For example, many of the marshals were in their prime when the use of the telephone was first established. Many of the marshals even drove around in automobiles before they died. The first powered car was built in 1872. The first car run by gasoline engine was built in 1893, and after that, various car companies started building different versions of the automobile. When we think about the Wild West, we imagine it to be so long ago, but many of the heroes of the Old West died after the automobile became popular.

Western legends and tales provide an interesting version of the beginning of western civilization. The U.S. Marshals are important figures in history. The origin of the West was established through the help of these men. They controlled and maintained law and order in towns and cities that were run by criminal outlaws. Icons such as James Butler (Wild Bill) Hickok, Wyatt

Earp, Bat Masterson, and Thomas J. (Bear River Tom) Smith will be forever remembered for their services and the roles that they played in history.

FURTHER READING

Cohen, Hubert I. 2003. Wyatt Earp at the O.K. Corral: Six versions. *Journal of American Culture* 26 (2): 204–23.
Cooley, Rita W. 1959. The Office of United States Marshal. *Western Political Quarterly* 12 (1): 123–40.
DeArment, Robert K. 1979. *Bat Masterson: The Man and the Legend.* Norman: University of Oklahoma Press.
Drago, Harry S. 1975. *The Legend Makers: Tales of the Old-time Peace Officers and Desperadoes of the Frontier.* New York: Cornwall Press.
Judiciary Act of 1789, 1 Stat. 73.
O'Conner, Richard. *Wild Bill Hickok.* New York: Doubleday, 1959.
Peterson, Roger S. 1994. Wyatt Earp. *American History* 29 (3): 54–62.
Rosa, Joseph G. 1969. *The Gunfighter: Man or Myth?* Norman: University of Oklahoma Press.
United States Marshal Homepage. http://www.usmarshals.gov.

Courtesy of the Library of Congress

Allan Pinkerton

Scott H. Belshaw and Amanda L. Belshaw

Allan Pinkerton (1819–1884) is regarded as the father of modern private investigation, an interesting title to hold considering he happened upon that career entirely by accident. With his hands-on approach to business, he pioneered several innovations in the field, the derivatives of which are still practiced today. Several government agencies today have their roots in a Pinkerton-run enterprise. It was the Pinkerton National Detective Agency that comprised the first Secret Service for the United States, serving as undercover antiespionage agents for the Union during the Civil War. Pinkerton also employed the first female investigators in America, a notable feat because women were not permitted to become police officers until just before the dawn of the twentieth century. It was Allan Pinkerton's agency that created the first central files on criminals, keeping notes of their crimes, their habits, their hangouts, and their photographs. These files became the predecessor to the criminal databases for the U.S. Federal Bureau of Investigation and other law enforcement agencies. Allan Pinkerton was well known across the country in his time for his strong work ethic and for the cases his agency successfully resolved, but many people today are not aware of Pinkerton's contributions to the law enforcement community that still exist today.

THE EARLY YEARS

Allan Pinkerton was born in Glasgow, Scotland, on August 25, 1819. Pinkerton proved to be an adventurous child, full of energy, who often ignored his schoolwork in favor of hunting and fishing in the Scottish countryside. His parents, William and Isabell, often had difficulty encouraging their inquisitive child to pay attention to his studies. Life for the Pinkerton family was tough in the working-class Gorbals area of Glasgow. William Pinkerton was a police sergeant who was removed from active duty after an on-the-job injury. When Allan was still young, his father was killed by a mob during a political riot, leaving Allan to assist his mother, a weaver, with caring for the family. Pinkerton quit school and went to work to earn living wages—first as a patternmaker, then as a cooper, or barrel maker. As a young adult, he joined a young revolutionary group called the Chartists, who wanted the working class to have a larger voice in the country's system of government.

On March 13, 1842, twenty-two-year-old Allan married a young woman from Edinburgh, Joan Carfrae. Shortly after their ceremony ended, a friend arrived and hastily informed Allan that the authorities would arrive almost immediately to arrest Allan for his involvement with the Chartists. The following morning, the newlywed Pinkertons set sail for North America for a new beginning. Starting over would prove to be challenging for the young couple, for their troubles started before they ever set foot in North America. A terrible storm, catching the couple's ship in a whirlpool, happened as the boat was nearing Halifax. The ship took on water and then rammed against a reef near the shore. Almost everything in the storage compartments was lost, including everything the Pinkertons owned, save what they were wearing on their bodies. The exhausted and injured survivors made their way to land, only to meet a group of Indians who demanded that they hand over any shiny trinkets they had. Joan Pinkerton was forced to give up her new silver wedding ring, which held great importance for her; Allan nearly refused to allow her to give it away, but an officer from their ship convinced Pinkerton that it was better to give the Indians his wife's ring rather than his own life.

The Pinkertons had intended to move to Quebec, but after hearing stories about a fast-growing city in the northern United States, Pinkerton opted instead to settle in Chicago. He believed he could find a good deal of work there as a cooper. The couple disembarked their next ship near Detroit and bought supplies: food, a wagon and horses, and tools. Making their way slowly across the unknown landscape, the Pinkertons slept in the barns of kind farmers and hunted and foraged for food when they ran out. Upon arriving in Chicago, Pinkerton met fellow Scotsmen who told him of a brewery that needed barrel makers. Pinkerton was hired quickly and began earning his living in America. The family lived reasonably and had stability, but the adventurous Pinkerton eventually grew restless. He wanted to own his own business and began exploring how to best make that happen. He learned of a town forty miles from Chicago, named Dundee, which also had a large population of Scots, but no barrel-makers. The Pinkertons packed up their home and moved to Dundee, and Pinkerton soon earned a reputation as an excellent craftsman and fair businessman. Pinkerton's One and Original Cooperage of Dundee grew very quickly, and soon he employed several craftsmen who worked six days a week in his shop. Pinkerton was flexible with his customers, often taking payments in produce and farm goods from area farmers and never insisting on being paid during slow farming seasons. His patience with his clients furthered his positive reputation.

In 1846, the first Pinkerton to be born in America, William, arrived, followed later by twins Robert and Joan. Four other daughters followed over the next five to six years, but none of them survived childhood, and very little is known about them. Save for the deaths of their youngest children, the Pinkerton family appeared to be living the early version of the American Dream, complete with a prosperous business and three healthy, happy children. Pinkerton continued to improve the business by devising cheaper ways to make his product without sacrificing its quality. In fact, Pinkerton took a very hands-on approach with his business; even though he was the owner and supervisor, he was not above performing hard labor himself if it got the job done. It was this work ethic that unwittingly led the future "private eye" to the career for which he became renowned.

Careers in Private Investigation

Significant Points

Work hours are often irregular, and the work can be dangerous.

- About 30 percent are self-employed.
- Applicants typically have related experience in areas such as law enforcement, insurance, the military, or government investigative or intelligence jobs.
- Keen competition is expected for most jobs despite faster-than-average employment growth.

Nature of the Work

Private detectives and investigators assist individuals, businesses, and attorneys by finding and analyzing information. They connect small clues to solve mysteries or to uncover facts about legal, financial, or personal matters. Private detectives and investigators offer many services, including executive, corporate, and celebrity protection; pre-employment verification; and individual background profiles. Some investigate computer crimes, such as identity theft, harassing e-mails, and illegal downloading of copyrighted material. They also provide assistance in criminal and civil liability cases, insurance claims and fraud, child custody and protection cases, missing persons cases, and premarital screening. They are sometimes hired to investigate individuals to prove or disprove infidelity.

Private detectives and investigators have many methods to choose from when determining the facts in a case. Much of their work is done using a computer, recovering deleted e-mails and documents, for example. They may also perform computer database searches or work with someone who does. Computers allow investigators to obtain quickly huge amounts of information such as a subject's prior arrests, convictions, and civil legal judgments; telephone numbers; motor vehicle registrations; association and club memberships; and even photographs.

Detectives and investigators also perform various other types of surveillance or searches. To verify facts, such as an individual's income or place of employment, they may make phone calls or visit a subject's workplace. In other cases, especially those involving missing persons and background checks, investigators interview people to gather as much information as possible about an individual. Sometimes investigators go undercover, pretending to be someone else to get information or to observe a subject inconspicuously.

Most detectives and investigators are trained to perform physical surveillance, which may be high- or low-tech. They may observe a site, such as the home of a subject, from an inconspicuous location or a vehicle. Using photographic and video cameras, binoculars, and cell phones, detectives often use surveillance to gather information on an individual; this can be quite time-consuming.

The duties of private detectives and investigators depend on the needs of their clients. In cases that involve fraudulent workers' compensation claims, for example, investigators may carry out long-term covert observation of a person suspected of fraud. If an investigator observes him or her performing an activity that contradicts injuries stated in a worker's compensation claim, the investigator would take video or still photographs to document the activity and report it to the client.

Detectives and investigators must be mindful of the law when conducting investigations. They keep up with federal, state, and local legislation, such as privacy laws and other legal issues affecting their work. The legality of certain methods may be unclear, and investigators and detectives must make judgment calls when deciding how to pursue a case. They must also know how to collect evidence properly so that they do not compromise its admissibility in court.

Private detectives and investigators often specialize. Those who focus on intellectual property theft, for example, investigate and document acts of piracy, help clients stop illegal activity, and provide intelligence for prosecution and civil action. Other investigators specialize in developing financial profiles and asset searches. Their reports reflect information gathered through interviews, investigation and surveillance, and research, including review of public documents.

Computer forensic investigators specialize in recovering, analyzing, and presenting data from computers for use in investigations or as evidence. They determine the details of intrusions into computer systems, recover data from encrypted or erased files, and recover e-mails and deleted passwords.

Legal investigators assist in preparing criminal defenses, locating witnesses, serving legal documents, interviewing police and prospective witnesses, and gathering and reviewing evidence. Legal investigators also may collect information on the parties to the litigation, take photographs, testify in court, and assemble evidence and reports for trials. They often work for law firms or lawyers.

Corporate investigators conduct internal and external investigations for corporations. In internal investigations, they may investigate drug use in the workplace, ensure that expense accounts are not abused, or determine whether employees are stealing merchandise or information. External investigations attempt to thwart criminal schemes from outside the corporation, such as fraudulent billing by a supplier.

Financial investigators may be hired to develop confidential financial profiles of individuals or companies that are prospective parties to large financial transactions. These investigators often are certified public accountants (CPAs) who work closely with investment bankers and other accountants. They

(continued)

might also search for assets to recover damages awarded by a court in fraud or theft cases.

Detectives who work for retail stores or hotels are responsible for controlling losses and protecting assets. *Store detectives*, also known as *loss prevention agents*, safeguard the assets of retail stores by apprehending anyone attempting to steal merchandise or destroy store property. They prevent theft by shoplifters, vendor representatives, delivery personnel, and even store employees. Store detectives also conduct periodic inspections of stock areas, dressing rooms, and restrooms, and sometimes assist in opening and closing the store. They may prepare loss prevention and security reports for management and testify in court against people they apprehend. *Hotel detectives* protect guests of the establishment from theft of their belongings and preserve order in hotel restaurants and bars. They also may keep undesirable individuals, such as known thieves, off the premises.

Work Environment

Many detectives and investigators spend time away from their offices conducting interviews or doing surveillance, but some work in their office most of the day conducting computer searches and making phone calls. When the investigator is working on a case, the environment might range from plush boardrooms to seedy bars. Store and hotel detectives work in the businesses that they protect.

Investigators generally work alone, but they sometimes work with others during surveillance or when following a subject in order to avoid detection by the subject. Some of the work involves confrontation, so the job can be stressful and dangerous. Some situations call for the investigator to be armed, such as certain bodyguard assignments for corporate or celebrity clients. In most cases, however, a weapon is not necessary because the purpose of the work is gathering information and not law enforcement or criminal apprehension. Owners of investigative agencies have the added stress of having to deal with demanding and sometimes distraught clients.

Private detectives and investigators often work irregular hours because of the need to conduct surveillance and contact people who are not available during normal working hours. Early morning, evening, weekend, and holiday work is common.

Training, Other Qualifications, and Advancement

Most private detectives and investigators have some college education and previous experience in investigative work. In most states, they are required to be licensed.

There are no formal education requirements for most private detective and investigator jobs, although many have college degrees. Courses in criminal justice and police science are helpful to aspiring private detectives and investigators. Although related experience is usually required, some people enter the occupation directly after graduation from college, generally with an associate or bachelor's degree in criminal justice or police science. The 2006 educational attainment for private detectives and investigators, in percent, was as follows: high school graduate or equivalent, 18 percent; some college, no degree, 26 percent; associate's degree, 8 percent; bachelor's degree, 34 percent; master's degree, 13 percent; professional degree or Ph.D., 3 percent.

Most corporate investigators must have a bachelor's degree, preferably in a business-related field. Some corporate investigators have a master's degree in business administration or a law degree; others are CPAs.

For computer forensics work, a computer science or accounting degree is more helpful than a criminal justice degree. An accounting degree provides good background knowledge for investigating fraud through computer forensics. Either of these two degrees provides a good starting point, after which investigative techniques can be learned on the job. Alternatively, many colleges and universities now offer certificate programs, requiring from fifteen to twenty-one credits, in computer forensics. These programs are most beneficial to law enforcement officers, paralegals, or others who are already involved in investigative work. A few colleges and universities now offer bachelor's or master's degrees in computer forensics, and others are planning to begin offering such degrees.

Most of the work of private detectives and investigators is learned on the job. New investigators will usually start by learning how to use databases to gather information. The training they receive depends on the type of firm. At an insurance company, a new investigator will learn to recognize insurance fraud. At a firm that specializes in domestic cases, a new worker might observe a senior investigator performing surveillance. Learning by doing, in which new investigators are put on cases and gain skills as they go, is a common approach. Corporate investigators hired by large companies, however, may receive formal training in business practices, management structure, and various finance-related topics.

Because they work with changing technologies, computer forensic investigators never stop training. They learn the latest methods of fraud detection and new software programs and operating systems by attending conferences and courses offered by software vendors and professional associations.

Licensure

The majority of states and the District of Columbia require private detectives and investigators to be licensed. Licensing requirements vary, however. Seven states—Alabama, Alaska, Colorado, Idaho, Mississippi, Missouri, and South

(continued)

Dakota—have no statewide licensing requirements, some states have few requirements, and many others have stringent regulations. For example, the Bureau of Security and Investigative Services of the California Department of Consumer Affairs requires private investigators to be eighteen years of age or older; have a combination of education in police science, criminal law, or justice and experience equaling three years (6,000 hours); pass a criminal history background check by the California Department of Justice and the FBI (in most states, convicted felons cannot be issued a license); and receive a qualifying score on a two-hour written examination covering laws and regulations. Detectives and investigators in all states who carry handguns must meet additional requirements for a firearms permit.

There are no licenses specifically for computer forensic investigators, but some states require them to be licensed private investigators. Even where licensure is not required, a private investigator license is useful to some because it allows them to perform follow-up or complementary tasks.

Other Qualifications

Private detectives and investigators typically have previous experience in other occupations. Some have worked in other occupations, for insurance or collections companies, in the private security industry, or as paralegals. Many investigators enter the field after serving in law enforcement, the military, government auditing and investigative positions, or federal intelligence jobs. Former law enforcement officers, military investigators, and government agents, who are frequently able to retire after twenty-five years of service, often become private detectives or investigators in a second career.

Others enter from jobs in finance, accounting, commercial credit, investigative reporting, insurance, and law. These individuals often can apply their prior work experience in a related investigative specialty.

Most computer forensic investigators learn their trade while working for a law enforcement agency, either as a sworn officer or a civilian computer forensic analyst. They are trained at their agency's computer forensics training program. Many people enter law enforcement specifically to get this training and establish a reputation before moving to the private sector.

For private detective and investigator jobs, most employers look for individuals with ingenuity, persistence, and assertiveness. A candidate must not be afraid of confrontation, should communicate well, and should be able to think on his or her feet. Good interviewing and interrogation skills also are important and usually are acquired in earlier careers in law enforcement or other fields. Because the courts often are the judge of a properly conducted investigation, the investigator must be able to present the facts in a manner that a jury will believe. The screening process for potential employees typically includes a background check for a criminal history.

Certification and Advancement

Some investigators receive certification from a professional organization to demonstrate competency in a field. For example, the National Association of Legal Investigators confers the Certified Legal Investigator designation on licensed investigators who devote a majority of their practice to negligence or criminal defense investigations. To receive the designation, applicants must satisfy experience, educational, and continuing-training requirements and must pass written and oral exams.

ASIS, a trade organization for the security industry, offers the Professional Certified Investigator certification. To qualify, applicants must have a high school diploma or equivalent; have five years of investigations experience, including two years managing investigations; and must pass an exam.

Most private-detective agencies are small, with little room for advancement. Usually, there are no defined ranks or steps, so advancement takes the form of increases in salary and assignment status. Many detectives and investigators start their own firms after gaining a few years of experience. Corporate and legal investigators may rise to supervisor or manager of the security or investigations department.

Employment

Private detectives and investigators held about 52,000 jobs in 2006. About 30 percent were self-employed, including many for whom investigative work was a second job. Around 34 percent of detective and investigator jobs were in investigation and security services, including private detective agencies, while another 9 percent were in department or other general merchandise stores. The rest worked mostly in state and local government, legal services firms, employment services companies, insurance agencies, and credit mediation establishments, including banks and other depository institutions.

Job Outlook

Keen competition is expected for most jobs despite faster-than-average employment growth.

Employment Change

Employment of private detectives and investigators is expected to grow 18 percent over the 2006–2016 decade, faster than the average for all occupations. Increased demand for private detectives and investigators will result from heightened security concerns, increased litigation, and the need to protect confidential information and property of all kinds. The proliferation of criminal activity on the Internet, such as identity theft, spamming, e-mail harassment, and illegal downloading of copyrighted materials, will also increase the demand for

> private investigators. Employee background checks, conducted by private investigators, will become standard for an increasing number of jobs. Growing financial activity worldwide will increase the demand for investigators to control internal and external financial losses, to monitor competitors, and to prevent industrial spying.
>
> ### Earnings
>
> Median annual earnings of salaried private detectives and investigators were $33,750 in May 2006. The middle 50 percent earned between $24,180 and $47,740. The lowest 10 percent earned less than $19,720, and the highest 10 percent earned more than $64,380. Earnings of private detectives and investigators vary greatly by employer, specialty, and geographic area.
>
> *Source:* Excerpted from Labor Statistics, U.S. Department of Labor. *Occupational Outlook Handbook, 2008-09 Edition*, Private Detectives and Investigators, on the Internet at http://www.bls.gov/oco/ocos157.htm.

A SURPRISING TURN OF EVENTS AND A NEW CAREER

Pinkerton, in an ongoing effort to be thrifty, often cut his own wood in the wild to make barrel staves rather than spending the money to buy poles. One day, Pinkerton went to a small island in the middle of the nearby Fox River to cut wood. While there, he noticed a thin trail had been worn through the tall grasses. It had long been thought by locals that the island was uninhabited, so Pinkerton became curious. Following the trail, he found what appeared to be a well-used, and probably just recently used, campsite. Pinkerton went back to town and reported his discovery to the sheriff, thinking the campsite was used for suspicious activities. The sheriff, impressed with Pinkerton's keen observation skills, deputized Pinkerton and asked for his assistance. The sheriff speculated that the campsite might be involved with an elusive counterfeiting ring that had been in the Dundee area for some time. Several local residents were suspected of being involved in the ring, but no money had been found in their homes or on their persons, so the trails had gone cold. Sheriff Yates believed Pinkerton might have found a link to the counterfeiters and reasoned that the island would have made an excellent place to hide the false money. Pinkerton and the sheriff, armed with rifles, watched the island campsite and arrested several participants in the ring one night when they returned to the hideout.

The Dundee town council was pleased with Pinkerton's work and asked him to help discover and arrest the ringleader. Pinkerton agreed and began monitoring the home of a local landowner named Crane. An older, well-dressed man would ride to Crane's home frequently, meet with some of the local suspects, and then leave again. Pinkerton met the gentleman, a Vermont man named John Craig, at a local watering hole and struck up conversation. Pinkerton pretended to be interested in taking over the local operations from Crane, whom Pinkerton said was starting to falter in the business because many of his cohorts had recently been arrested by the police. Pinkerton used $125, a large amount of money at that time, to buy false bills from Craig. Thinking that the police would like to know where Craig's central operation was housed, Pinkerton arranged to meet Craig at the latter's home base, using the excuse that the police might be watching him at the Dundee tavern. The sheriff made arrangements with the Chicago police, and they were waiting when Pinkerton met with Craig at the Sauganash Hotel in Chicago for lunch some days later. When the deal was being made, police rushed out and arrested Craig. Many patrons in the bar appeared to be watching the scene with great interest, and Pinkerton and the police believed some cohorts of Craig's were present and saw the bust. The counterfeit money disappeared from the Chicago area soon after Craig's arrest.

The Cook County sheriff heard about Pinkerton's work on the counterfeiting case and offered him a job as an investigator. Pinkerton and his family once again packed their things and moved, this time back to Chicago, where Pinkerton began work as a police officer, following in his father's footsteps at a later age in his own life. Pinkerton discovered that Chicago had changed dramatically in his absence: the city had exploded in population and several areas had been improved. He also learned that with the advancement of progress came the dregs of society—pickpockets, robbers and burglars, rapists, and murderers. At the time, before 1850, Chicago claimed to house a population of approximately 30,000, but only twelve police officers were employed to enforce the laws. In addition, there were several neighborhoods that the officers would not approach or patrol, for they were seen as too dangerous and unsafe, further causing a breakdown in societal norms.

Pinkerton wholeheartedly dove into his job as a police officer and earned a reputation for his toughness. He would not accept bribes and would not tolerate cheekiness, sass, or disrespect from suspects. He was so successful as an officer that he was asked to become Chicago's first detective. Pinkerton was also tremendously successful in this role because of his bravery and his ability to trick suspects into confessing to their crimes before they realized they had done so.

A PRIVATE VENTURE LEADING TO NEW ADVENTURES

After some time, Pinkerton grew tired of his rather meager policeman's pay, which was not helpful to his growing family. Pinkerton found himself in the predicament of deciding whether to return to barrel making or perhaps, to remain an investigator, but in the private sector, not employed by the police. There were, after all, very few private investigators in the United States at that time, and there were none in the Chicago area. Pinkerton went to some of his clients and determined that they would continue to use his services and pay well for them, if he broke free of government work and opened his own business. In particular, Pinkerton created a working relationship with the Rock Island and Illinois Central Railroad, which eventually became his first large client. He had investigated, and successfully solved, several shipping thefts for the company. Pinkerton would frequently be seen about town, dining with the railroad's president, George B. McClellan, and the company attorney, Abraham Lincoln.

Confident with the belief that he could successfully support his family as a private investigator, Pinkerton resigned from police work and opened an office in Chicago's market district, partnering with Chicago attorney Edward Rucker. The North-Western Police Agency, later called the Pinkerton Agency, was born. Pinkerton advertised his services and ethics in newspapers around the United States. He was committed to honesty and integrity in business and promised openly to accept no bribes or make agreements with criminals. Pinkerton would not accept divorce cases or other matters that might create embarrassing scandals for his clients, and he would not keep reward money offered on any cases. He also did not raise his fees without authorization from his clients, and Pinkerton kept those clients informed of the work's status as the cases progressed. Pinkerton promoted his company by freely discussing his agents' successes with the press as the company solved murders and apprehended crooks. Anyone who hired Pinkerton was impressed with not only his company's reputation but also with the results it promised—and provided. Pinkerton enforced a strict code of conduct and decorum among his workers. He insisted that his agents not smoke or drink alcohol and that they not gamble or use foul language. Pinkerton worked with telegraph operators, gun experts, and others in technological fields to make sure that his employees were current with the latest advances and inventions.

Pinkerton created a catchy, distinctive logo for his company, the Pinkerton National Detective Agency. The logo featured an open eye with the words, "We Never Sleep" underneath it and the name of the company surrounding it. The graphic could soon be spied in newspapers and magazines and on billboards and wanted posters. This logo apparently led to the birth of the term "private eye," which is still used today as a moniker for a private investigator. The country, in fact, began referring to Pinkerton as "The Eye."

Another innovative move made by Pinkerton was his hiring of the first female investigator, Kate Warne. When she appeared in his office looking for work, Pinkerton assumed that she was hoping for a clerical position. Not so, she informed him, and the surprised Pinkerton found himself interviewing Warne for an investigator's position he had advertised in a Chicago newspaper. Pinkerton was initially reluctant to hire Warne, but she argued her case with such fervor and eloquence that he decided to take a chance. Women, Warne stated, were able to put themselves into certain situations more easily than men could, becoming confidantes of wives, girlfriends, and mistresses and learning information through collateral sources; men, Warne pointed out, would often brag in the presence of females and give away more information than they believed the women paid attention to. Some time later, after her successes on many investigations, Pinkerton made Warne his supervisor of female agents. Warne was recently widowed when she joined the agency, and she had no children, so she was able to wholly emulate the roles that she played, from Southern society matron to cleaning woman to street fortune teller. The fact that Pinkerton hired women was highly unusual, because women were not even allowed to join police forces until 1891 and the first female police investigators did not arrive upon the crime-fighting scene until 1903.

The case that made Pinkerton and his agents famous involved the Adams Express, a railroad and stagecoach mail and cargo carrier. The line repeatedly experienced missing money from strongboxes on its route between Columbus, Georgia, and Montgomery, Alabama. Pinkerton placed some of his best agents on the case, including the effective Kate Warne. On the basis of the available information and clues, Pinkerton knew the missing money had to be the work of an operative inside the agency. Assuming undercover identities, Pinkerton's agents were able to determine that the sending agent in Columbus was actually sealing up the strongboxes without putting the money in them, hoping that the messenger would be blamed for the thefts. The sending agent and his wife, who knew about her husband's actions, were arrested, and Pinkerton personally returned the remainder of the $50,000 reward to Adams Express. The grateful carrier helped spread word around the country of the tremendous success.

Pinkerton and his agents quickly earned a reputation for diligence and thoroughness. The agency took on the most difficult cases and solved them when law enforcement could not. Pinkerton himself became well known among members of the underworld. They knew Pinkerton the man was incorruptible, as was Pinkerton the agency. They also knew that both the man and the agency would continue pursuing them, looking in every nook and cranny, until the scoundrels were found and justice was done.

Some years later, in 1866, the Pinkerton Agency would again come to the rescue of Adams Express by capturing the thieves who stole $700,000 from the carrier on a New York, New Haven, & Hartford train; the agency also recovered all but approximately $12,000 of the missing money.

WARTIME "PROFIT"EERING

In 1860, tensions ran high in the United States, which was not yet even one hundred years old. Slavery was a divisive issue, and the presidential election of 1860 would be the final deciding factor on whether the United States remained one nation or went to war against itself. Pinkerton and his agency had become hugely famous after the first Adams Express job, having been discussed in newsprint around the country. Their popularity nearly overshadowed developments in another area entirely. In the political arena, an antislavery lawyer, Abraham Lincoln, was expected to be nominated for president of the United States, and the proslavery South was expected to secede from the Union if Lincoln were elected. Pinkerton himself was antislavery and used his barrel making shop near Chicago as a stop on the Underground Railroad, providing shelter to runaway slaves in transit to Canada and freedom. Pinkerton's old friend Abraham Lincoln, also an abolitionist, was elected the 16th president of the United States. The political and emotional climates in the United States were strained to their breaking points.

In January 1861, Pinkerton was hired by the president of the Philadelphia, Wilmington, and Baltimore Railroad to protect the trains and the line, which was a major mail route on the eastern seaboard, from Confederate insurgents. Pinkerton placed agents all along the route, but his agents were unable to find a plot to destroy the rail line. Rather, Pinkerton investigators began to learn bits and pieces of information that, when added together, suggested that there might be a plot to assassinate newly elected President Lincoln on the way to the inauguration ceremony. Most of the information came through Pinkerton's agent Timothy Webster, who had worked his way deep undercover into a Baltimore-based group of secessionists named the Knights of the Golden Circle. Webster learned that men had been assigned to shoot the new president in Baltimore as his train chugged through the town at a particular hour. At the time, the newspapers printed the entire schedule of Lincoln's trip from Illinois to Washington; the group was able to accurately estimate Lincoln's arrival and departure times in Baltimore on February 23.

Pinkerton acted immediately, as Lincoln had already left Illinois when the information was learned. Pinkerton knew one of Lincoln's staff members—his new press secretary, Norman Judd—and believed that Judd would assist him in speaking personally to the president. Pinkerton contacted Judd as the president's train stopped in Philadelphia. His hunch proved to be right, because Judd scheduled a meeting between Pinkerton and Lincoln. Lincoln turned out to be surprised to see his old friend from some years past, and Pinkerton felt bad at giving Lincoln the news. Lincoln was obligated to keep appointments in Philadelphia and Harrisburg the following day, so his evening and nighttime schedule would have to be changed to avoid the assassination attempt. Pinkerton had made arrangements to have Lincoln leave Harrisburg that night on a private train to Baltimore, and the tracks would be kept clear so that the train could safely travel at top speed. The president would arrive in Baltimore hours before he was expected to and would board an express train that had already been hired by Pinkerton, which would take Lincoln to Washington before the sun rose. Governor Curtin of Pennsylvania, with whom Lincoln was scheduled to attend dinner while he was in Harrisburg, would tell his guests that Lincoln had become ill and had to rest in his quarters in the gubernatorial home. Pinkerton, however, would take Lincoln out through the carriage entrance and into a waiting transport. The plan would be divulged to only those parties who needed to know in order to maintain the appearance that Lincoln would be traveling as scheduled. Telegraph lines would be cut so that anyone who learned of the changes to the president's schedule could not wire ahead to their co-conspirators. The conspiracy, unfortunately, even included the Baltimore chief of police, who had scheduled very little police protection during Lincoln's stop in the city.

The following night, Lincoln was placed quickly into a carriage with darkened windows, which also carried Pinkerton and another agent, both armed. Another agent placed Lincoln on the waiting train and then sliced the telegraph wires. Kate Warne and other Pinkerton agents were already on the train, heavily armed. Pinkerton joined the crew on the train and retreated to the back of the train to make sure the charter was not being followed. A light signal system had been implemented along the train's route so that Pinkerton's agents could signal each other that things were proceeding as planned. The signals worked, and Lincoln's train arrived in Baltimore at 3:30 A.M. In Baltimore, another group of Pinkerton agents formed a protective circle around the president and led him to the connecting train. Hearts stopped briefly when the second train was late, but it arrived not far behind schedule, and the plan was back in action. The train was inspected, the president took his seat, and for the final 50 miles to Washington, the same safety precautions with the light signal system were taken. Lincoln's train arrived in Union Station at approximately 6:10 A.M., with General Winfield Scott and the secretary of state waiting to meet the president. Lincoln made it safely to Washington for his inauguration, which happened a few weeks later, but the slave states in the South made good on their promise to secede from the Union if Lincoln became president. The Confederate States of America fired guns upon Fort Sumter, located in Carolina harbor, on April 13, 1861. This proved to be the first act of what would become known as the Civil War.

Political conditions in the United States deteriorated rapidly once the antislavery Abraham Lincoln took office. President-Elect Lincoln had not yet been inaugurated, and he already had an impending civil war to address. Lincoln was determined to maintain the wholeness of the Union and would send the army marching into the South if it was needed to squash the rebellion of the slave states. Lincoln approached some old friends to help him set up his new network: George McClellan, whom he placed in command of the Army of the Potomac, and Allan Pinkerton, whom Lincoln asked to organize a "secret service" undercover police force for Washington, because there were many Southern sympathizers in the city. Pinkerton was ready to accept the assignment as the head of the secret service, but General Winfield Scott, commander-in-chief of the Union army, wanted someone else to do the job. Instead, McClellan made Pinkerton his personal spy to ferret out any potential espionage by Confederate operatives.

Pinkerton placed agents around the South, including Kate Warne and Timothy Webster. Warne posed as a southern matron in Tennessee and Virginia, making her way around the social circuit, while Webster remained in Maryland, a confidante of the Knights of the Golden Circle, the same group that had plotted to assassinate the president on the way to his inauguration. Pinkerton himself accepted some particularly special assignments, some of which resulted in nearly getting him discovered. Utilizing the name "Major E. J. Allen," Pinkerton operated in Tennessee, Georgia, and Mississippi, pursuing spies who helped the Confederate cause.

In 1861, General Scott retired, and Lincoln made McClellan the commander-in-chief of the army. McClellan maintained regular counsel with Pinkerton, and the general gave Pinkerton credit for some of the Union army's victories because Pinkerton and his operatives passed on accurate information about troop movements and the like. Pinkerton assigned some of his agents to McClellan so they could spy on the Southern army on-site, but he remained behind in Washington to take on a new apprentice.

The newest recruit of the Pinkerton agency was sixteen-year-old William Pinkerton. William proved to have keen observation skills and could easily blend in with his surroundings. William was in charge of several agents who worked in the Confederate states. The younger Pinkerton was wounded in the knee at Antietam by an exploding shell, but after he healed, he went right back on the job with his father. Pinkerton paid a good deal of attention to his son, teaching him everything he knew about the industry, down to his high standards for ethics and for the work. Pinkerton particularly trusted Kate Warne with some of the agency's more difficult assignments. Warne lived in the South, as a southern belle, under a false name and family background and flirted with many a Southern man to learn information about the secessionist movement. One of the southern sympathizers Warne met was a Shakespearean play actor named John Wilkes Booth, who would later earn fame not on stage but in another area of the theater. Each bit of information was transmitted back to Pinkerton in Washington city.

Another Pinkerton operative who assisted with special projects was a newcomer, Elizabeth Baker, from Richmond, Virginia. Baker was a Union loyalist and would assist with any case that furthered, directly or indirectly, the Union cause. Baker helped discover the existence of a new invention, the submarine, being built at an iron works in Richmond. The submarine was said to travel underwater so that it could blow up Union ships that were blockading the James River. Baker was able to secure a visit to the iron works and actually see the submarine being built; she made a sketch of the ship and its external breathing system, which could be detected easily by an observant sailor on the surface who knew what to look for. Baker presented her sketches to the Secretary of the Navy, and the South was never able to disrupt the blockade at the James River. The ever-growing Pinkerton agency reportedly employed more active agents than the standing army of the United States of America, causing the agency to be outlawed in the state of Ohio. There were fears from locals that the Pinkerton agency would be hired out by the presidency as a private army to quell any resistance.

Despite the growing number of Confederate spies being arrested by Pinkerton agents, Allan Pinkerton knew that there was an extremely well-hidden source of the information the spies leaked to the South. Pinkerton was determined to find the source of the leak, which he believed was from a high-ranking person within the Lincoln administration because of the type of information that was being provided to the South. With persistence, the Pinkerton agents found the source of the information being leaked to the Confederacy—Rose O'Neal Greenhow, the widow of a newspaper editor whose paper supported slavery. Greenhow had managed to befriend many influential members of the upper-class circles in Washington city through her familial connection to Dolly Madison, widow of the late President James Madison. Greenhow passed Union army plans and other information to the South using the cipher code of the Confederate Signal Corps. Greenhow's information helped the Confederate Army plan several successful defenses or counterattacks against the Union army. It was Greenhow who warned Confederate General Pierre Beauregard about an approaching Union advance upon Manassas, Virginia. After an extensive ongoing investigation, Greenhow was arrested on August 23, 1861, and placed under house arrest. In her possession was a great deal of information that included troop movements, supply routes, maps, and names of other spies she used, mostly female. Many of the female spies were arrested and placed in the Greenhow home, which became referred to jokingly as "Fort Greenhow." Greenhow was not put to death by hanging because she was a woman and had a child; instead, she and her fellow agents were held until they could be escorted to Richmond, Virginia, where they could no longer pass information that would harm the North's cause.

While not putting Greenhow and her fellow female conspirators to death was appropriate for the times, the act of generosity lead to the undoing of Pinkerton Special Agent Timothy Webster. Webster had remained in Baltimore, acting as a double agent by passing information to and from the Knights of the Golden Circle, who were loyal to the Confederate cause. Webster had garnered such favor with the Knights of the Golden Circle that the Confederate secretary of war, Judah Benjamin, hired Webster as a special agent of the underground spy network. Webster would often haul mail between Richmond and Baltimore, usually traveling via Washington. Webster would open letters from the South, find pertinent information, then carefully reseal the letters, and deliver them to their rightful recipients. Using this method, Webster could notify Pinkerton, who in turn advised General McClellan, of any planning done on behalf of the South on both sides of the Mason-Dixon line. Webster carried out his duties as a double agent until he began suffering from inflammatory rheumatism. The work became too much for him to handle alone, so he requested two additional operatives to assist him. Pinkerton sent Pryce Lewis and John Scully, both of whom had worked in the Chicago Pinkerton office, to Richmond to assist Webster. The three spies carried out their work successfully and quietly until an unfortunate incident happened. The Union War Department unwittingly released Rose O'Neal Greenhow from house arrest too early, while Webster and his assistants were still active in the rebel community. Pinkerton became aware of the snafu and dispatched an agent to Richmond to warn Webster, Lewis, and Scully, but by the time the agent arrived in Richmond, it was too late. Greenhow and her sister spies had seen Scully and Lewis, both of whom had been instrumental in Greenhow's arrest, in their hotel and identified them to the Confederate government. The Confederate legislature captured Scully and Lewis and tried them via court martial. Webster, who remained out of sight because of his ailments, was safe for the moment, but Scully and Lewis were convicted as traitors to the Confederacy and ordered hanged. On the night before the executions, Scully sent for a priest to make his confession as a Catholic. The South sent a false priest to do the job, and although Lewis did not confess, Scully did—and by doing so, he implicated Timothy Webster as the Baltimore chief of the Secret Service for the U.S. government. Webster was later arrested and found guilty in a court-martial and then ordered by Confederate President Jefferson Davis to be hanged. Webster, though still sick, bravely met his death when he was hanged on April 30, 1862. Pinkerton buried his loyal detective in his own family's cemetery plot in Chicago.

Shortly thereafter, Pinkerton's role as an operative for the North came to an end. A Union colonel, Lafayette Baker, convinced the Secretary of War to appoint his own operatives as the official antispy unit for the presidency. Furthermore, President Lincoln had become dissatisfied with his friend George McClellan's performance as commander-in-chief of the Union army and had him replaced. Pinkerton left Washington, where he had worked for two and a half years as the chief antiespionage officer in the Union, to perform other jobs for the government. One such job was the location of dishonest suppliers who were cheating clients by overcharging for supplies and deliveries.

Years later, Pinkerton would lament that he did not supervise Washington city's security on April 14, 1865. That night, during a stage production at Ford's Theater, actor John Wilkes Booth fatally shot President Lincoln in the head, an act that Pinkerton believed would never have occurred if his agents had been in place.

POSTWAR VENTURES: A CHANGE IN DIRECTION

During Pinkerton's tenure in Washington, his business had grown dramatically. His trusted employees George Bangs and Francis Warner not only managed the Chicago office, but they also opened offices in New York City and Philadelphia. After the end of the Civil War, Pinkerton returned to his home office in Chicago with his son William. His second son, Robert, joined his father and brother in the family business. The sons researched traits of fugitive criminals and the criminal mind in general. William proved to be an excellent and driven detective, while Robert excelled in administrative duties, even creating a filing system that later became the basis for filing systems for other law enforcement agencies in this country. By the 1870s, the Pinkerton agency owned the most extensive collection of criminal mug shots in existence. The collection was maintained regularly by field agents who cut news stories and notations from the media and sent them to the home office with notes. The country dubbed the Pinkerton agency's investigators the "Pinks," and they were everywhere.

Pinkerton had turned the pursuit and capture of professionals into a successful private enterprise. Pinkerton seemed to possess an innate ability to sniff out guilty criminals before the police were able to do so. He used his experience and determined that criminals have their own personal traits and techniques that give them away. When lecturing in front of an audience in 1880, Pinkerton stated: "On reading a telegraphic newspaper report of a large or small robbery, with the aid of my vast records and great personal experience and familiarity with these matters, I can at once tell the character of the work, and then, knowing the names, history, habits, and quite frequently, the rendezvous of men doing that type of work, am able to determine, with almost unerring certainty, not only the very parties who committed the robberies, but also what disposition they are likely to make of their plunder, and at what points they may be hiding." In this way, Pinkerton became a sort of early criminal profiler. Pinkerton and his sons William and Robert consulted with banks, shipping companies, mail services, and other money-handling businesses to provide them with advice or preventive measures to protect their assets. Pinkerton also kept lines of communication open with those companies—and with police agencies—to exchange mug shots and felon identification cards, circulating information with which to better apprehend criminals around the country. Pinkerton and his agents compiled a glossary of terms used by bank and train robbers and their associates. Put together in the 1880s, the glossary gives the reader a glimpse into the seediness of the criminal element of the time. A sample of these terms, taken from the Pinkerton Web site follows:

Bull	A law enforcement officer
Chip	A money drawer in a bank
Ditched	Arrested
Jimmying a bull	Shooting a law enforcement officer
Rattler	Freight train
Sapper	An officer who freely uses his club
White Liner	An alcoholic

One tragedy that befell the Pinkerton agency early in the postwar years was the loss of crack agent Kate Warne. Warne became ill with pneumonia very suddenly at the end of 1867 and died on January 1, 1868. Pinkerton was greatly saddened by the loss of one of his best agents and had Warne buried in his own family's plot, near Timothy Webster.

GO WEST, YOUNG CRIMINAL, GO WEST!

With the end of the Civil War came American expansion into the West. As pioneers and settlers moved toward California, so did the criminals. Pinkerton followed the trend and opened offices in trail towns between Kansas and California, as far north as the Canadian border and as far south as Texas. Whenever a bank, stagecoach, or train was robbed, Pinkerton agents were always close by to solve the crime. Pinkerton, now aging physically, allowed William to manage field officers more often. William assembled posses to hunt down some of the Wild West's most famous bad men: Jesse James, Cole Younger, and Butch Cassidy and the Sundance Kid. These men, and more, were brought to justice one by one by Pinkerton agents. The Pinkerton agency developed a constantly moving, constantly updated network of agents who exchanged information and closed in on the outlaws as they traveled through the West. The Pinkertons would use their knowledge about the criminals' habits to taunt them and cause them stress, forcing them to panic and do something foolish, which would ultimately lead to their captures.

One of the first desperado busts by the Pinkerton agency was that of the Reno brothers, a gang of six brothers who robbed trains. In 1867, they robbed an Adams Express car, and the Pinkertons were set upon their trail. The Reno brothers were doggedly pursued by the Pinkertons at every crevasse in the badlands, until the Renos were so desperate that they tried several times to kill William Pinkerton in an effort to throw his men off their trail, even momentarily. William survived all the deadly encounters to see that all the Reno brothers were either dead and buried or imprisoned by the end of 1868.

The frontier outlaws who probably found the Pinkerton agents most irritating were Frank and Jesse James, former Civil War activists who became law-dodging gunmen. In southern Missouri, the homeland of the James boys, they were considered heroes long into the 1870s. Much of the population there still fumed that the Union had won the war and portrayed Jesse as a kind of modern-day Robin Hood who railed against wealthy Yankee bankers and railroads. The Pinkertons, including Allan himself, who joined on some of the searches, were the evil agents of the conglomerates and were given no assistance whatsoever when they came through the Smoky Mountains, where they frequently lost the James brothers. It was their pursuit of the James brothers that led to a frenzy of rare negative press for the "Pinks."

The Pinkerton detectives had reputations for fairness that even the most insidious outlaws tended to respect. In 1875, that reputation was seriously damaged when two members of the James family were attacked by a posse led by Pinkertons. Pinkerton agents surrounded a small cabin near Kearney, Missouri, believing Jesse was hiding inside. The posse called out demands for Jesse to surrender peacefully, but nobody reportedly answered the cries. Supposedly, someone threw an explosive device through a window that had been found open. Jesse's mother, Zerelda James, was so injured that a hand had to be amputated, and a mentally challenged stepbrother was killed. Allen Pinkerton, from his Chicago office, expressed his sincere regrets, but flatly denied that any of his agents had thrown a bomb. He admitted that his men were present at the scene, but they had only waited in the surrounding underbrush for James to come out with his hands up. It was obvious that an explosion had happened, but nobody publicly accepted the blame for its cause. The Pinkertons' reputation wore this blemish for some time afterward. Some historians believe one of the hired deputies threw the bomb; others claim that the warning shot from a detective's gun had possibly broken and ignited a kerosene lamp inside the cabin.

Later, when the James brothers branched out into Minnesota for a bank robbery, the populace was much less sympathetic to them. The Pinkertons warned the town of Northfield, Minnesota, of the impending arrival of the James gang, which included three of the Younger brothers, also on the run from the law. The citizenry prepared itself and met the James posse with firepower. The bandits escaped from the gun battle injured and vulnerable and thus began their downfall. One of Jesse's men, desperate for money, killed him in April of 1882. Frank served time in prison and retired peacefully to his farm back in Missouri.

Another group of outlaws in the Wild West who found its freedom at the mercy of the Pinkertons was known as "The Wild Bunch," who terrorized banks and money-carrying trains between Texas and Wyoming. Their two most well-known members were Butch Cassidy and the Sundance Kid. Operating from 1895 to 1902, the Wild Bunch had at least twenty members in its heyday. After a robbery, the Wild Bunch would retreat to Wyoming and hide in canyons and caves; then, when public outcry ceased, the group would return to west Texas to plan subsequent heists. On June 2, 1899, the Wild Bunch stole $30,000 in unsigned banknotes from the Union Pacific Railroad's *Overland Flyer*. The Pinkerton agents were asked to assist local law enforcement with the apprehension of the gang. One diligent Pinkerton agent located a group photo of some of the Wild Bunch at a photography studio in Fort Worth, Texas. This photo was made into wanted posters and circulated in towns all over the West, making it much more difficult for the gang to hide out without being recognized. The Wild Bunch pulled off two more large heists after the posters were circulated: one in 1900 at a Nevada bank and one more train robbery, this time in Montana, a year later. While the Pinkertons had slowly but surely captured or killed many of the Wild Bunch, a one-hundred-man posse and a special train were commandeered to chase the gang after the Montana train robbery. The Wild Bunch retreated to Fort Worth, where they disbanded before they were all killed or captured. Butch Cassidy and the Sundance Kid, with his wife Etta Place, left the country and moved to Bolivia, where they could not be extradited because they had no detectable criminal records in that country.

Despite the violence in the West in the late 1800s, the Pinkertons were able to survive as an agency by diligently pursuing lawbreakers and practicing their honest, strict work ethic. A reformed safecracker, George White, said of the Pinkertons in his 1895 memoir: "...I had to acknowledge that they were honest and it was dangerous for a crook when a Pinkerton was on his trail" (Geringer, 2007).

PINKERTONS AS STRIKEBREAKERS

In 1871, the Pinkertons found themselves contractors for government work again. In that year, Congress gave $50,000 to the newly founded Department of Justice to create a subcommittee that would investigate and prosecute federal lawbreakers, including bank robbers and forgers. Although the amount of money given was not enough to create an internal investigations unit, it was enough to contract the investigative services to the Pinkerton agency.

Also in the 1870s, the Pinkerton agency began investigating labor unions for various industries. In an odd twist of fate, the same Allan Pinkerton who had once advocated for workers' rights in Glasgow had become known as one of the driving forces behind squashing the growing labor union movement in the United States. One notable union investigation was conducted under the authority of the Philadelphia and Reading Railroad, based in Pennsylvania. One of Pinkerton's agents, James McParlan, used an alias to penetrate and infiltrate a labor organization named the Molly Maguires. The Mollies were a secret organization of Irish Catholics who banded together as militant strikers in response to a 20 percent wage reduction at their coal mines. Beatings and murders, some committed by the Mollies, were rampant throughout the mining region. Over time, membership in the Mollies grew to 30,000, or more than 80 percent of the area's anthracite coal miners. For years, McParlan's investigation labored, until December 10, 1875. On that date, three men and two women were attacked in their home by masked vigilantes. McParlan had secretly identified the three men as Mollies, and somehow this information found its way to unauthorized parties. One of the Molly men was shot inside the home, and the other two were wounded but escaped death. One of the women—a wife of one of the Mollies—was also killed. McParlan became outraged that his undercover information had been used to kill a woman and nearly resigned from his undercover assignment. He remained in the position after heavy coaxing from the Pinkertons. Union leaders were imprisoned, and after six months, the strike failed. The starving strikers reluctantly, but out of necessity for their families, accepted the 20 percent pay cut. In 1876, ten union leaders were convicted of committing or inciting vigilante violence on behalf of the Molly Maguires. The men were hanged in June of 1877 at two different prisons in Pennsylvania. Ten more accused Molly leaders were convicted and executed at four separate prisons over the next two years.

THE LATER YEARS: AN AGENCY REFOCUSED

Pinkerton wrote seventeen books in the decade of 1874–1884, including *The Expressman and the Detective* (1874) and a memoir titled *Thirty Years a Detective* (1884). Just a few weeks shy of his 65th birthday, Allan Pinkerton had a freak accident with tragic results. He slipped while walking down a Chicago street and badly bit his tongue when his chin hit the pavement. Pinkerton failed to properly care for the injury and developed gangrene. Pinkerton died on July 1, 1884. He was buried in Graceland Cemetery in Chicago, near two of his favorite agents who preceded him in death. Pinkerton had allowed Timothy Webster and Kate Warne to be buried in his family's plot as tribute to their years of faithful service to his agency. Today, Pinkerton, a member of the Military Intelligence Hall of Fame, lies in the same spot, near his wife, Warne, and Webster.

Pinkerton's sons, William and Robert, were in charge of the agency after their father died. Pinkerton had left behind a strict code of ethics that was faithfully followed by his boys. William and Robert Pinkerton worked fluidly, almost as one mind. They kept their father's best interests at the forefront, but they expanded the agency to look beyond American borders for outlaws. The more "modern-era" criminal had discovered that the one way to escape the Pinkertons was to travel overseas. New steamships could sail from New York to England within one week, vastly increasing the amount of time it would take for the Pinkertons to capture any sea-bound fugitives. Because of foreign policies, the Pinkertons were usually unable to directly arrest any criminals in Europe, but the agents would work with national authorities, such as Scotland Yard and the Paris Surete, to locate fugitives for extradition back to the United States. One of these fugitives who fled to Europe, Adam Worth, led the Pinkertons on a multinational chase, only to be apprehended by another person. In a strange turn of events, the Pinkerton's ethics and compassion led to a partnership between pursuers and the pursued.

Worth gained William Pinkerton's attention when in 1869 he robbed the Boylston Bank in Boston, Massachusetts, to the tune of one million dollars. Worth fled to Liverpool, then Paris, then London, living the high life and portraying himself as a director of many illegal money-taking businesses. In 1876, he led a group to steal a famous painting, *Duchess of Devonshire* by Thomas Gainsborough, from an art gallery in London. Worth then remained on the run from the Pinkertons for several years, moving between several major cities in Europe to avoid apprehension. Somehow, despite his illegal business, Worth earned William Pinkerton's admiration to a degree, for Worth despised guns and never physically harmed anyone during his illegal activities. William always believed that, had Worth not ventured down a criminal path, he might have been a successful leader in the business world. Pinkerton followed Worth across Europe, often visiting his foreign associates and updating the Pinkerton data files on Worth's travels. Worth, who knew Pinkerton by sight, would often dine at particular restaurants or frequent various watering holes, only to be joined at his leisure activities by Pinkerton. Pinkerton and Worth chatted regularly about different subjects, but the subtle message Pinkerton sent to Worth was the fact that he was being watched. After their last meeting at the Criterion Restaurant in London, Worth told Pinkerton that he had always respected the Pinks. The men shook hands upon parting and Worth reportedly said, "May the best man win" (Geringer, 2007).

Years later, in 1891, Worth was arrested for mail theft in Belgium. The Belgian police wired international law enforcement and detective agencies for any information on Worth in the hope that they could force a longer sentence on him. While Scotland Yard and Surete responded to the wire, William Pinkerton ignored it, telling his brother Robert, "The old man's going to suffer enough. Let's leave him be" (Geringer, 2007). Worth spent almost ten years in prison and then returned to America to visit William Pinkerton. While in prison, Worth had learned of the kindness William had done him and wanted to repay the favor. The offer could not have come at a better time.

During the labor movement of the late 1800s, the Pinkerton National Detective Agency had once again received bad press after assisting the Carnegie Steel Company with a strike of the Amalgamated Association of Iron and

Steel Workers at its steel plant in Homestead, Pennsylvania, in 1892. The union had won a sliding-scale contract in 1889 after striking; the contract based the employees' wages on the fluctuating prices of Bessemer steel billets. The contract expired on June 30, 1892, while company owner Andrew Carnegie, who had often shown compassion for union members, was in Scotland. Carnegie left mill manager Henry Clay Frick, a vocal antiunionist, in charge of operations. Before the deadline had arrived, Frick ordered a wood-and-barbed-wire fence constructed around the perimeter of the mill property. While negotiations between the company and the union continued through June, Frick ordered the mill to begin shutting down operations on June 28, and the union was locked out of the mill on the morning of June 30. On July 6, a company of three hundred Pinkerton detectives arrived from New York and Chicago, having been called by mill manager Henry Clay Frick to protect the plant and its replacement workers, known as "scabs." A bitter fight erupted upon the arrival of the Pinks when union workers and their families tore through the new fences around the mill. Gunfire was exchanged for more than twelve hours that day, which resulted in the deaths of approximately nine strikers and three Pinkerton men. The strike-breaking Pinkerton agents had been fired on by a group of armed picketers. The Pennsylvania National Guard was brought in on July 12 to weaken and disrupt the union fighters. Although both Pinkerton men and union members were killed, the media capitalized on the event and portrayed the plight of the working class as it was oppressed by crooked conglomerates who used paid mercenaries to get their way. The Pinkertons were labeled as turncoats who were disloyal to the cause of the common man, and after years of international praise, their reputation suffered desperately, though they continued to be used as guards for coal, iron, and lumber strikes in four states and for the railroad strikes that swept the country. After the Homestead fiasco, in fact, Pinkerton agents were immortalized in popular culture in song lyrics.

Lyrics: "Father Was Killed By the Pinkerton Men"
V1. 'Twas in a Pennsylvania town not very long ago,
Men struck against reduction of their pay.
Their millionaire employer with philanthropic show
Had closed the works till starved they would obey.
They fought for home and right to live where they had toiled so long
But ere the sun had set some were laid low.
There're hearts now sadly grieving by that sad and bitter wrong.
God help them for it was a cruel blow.

CHORUS:
God help them tonight in their hour of affliction
Praying for him whom they'll ne'er see again.
Hear the orphans tell their sad story
"Father was killed by the Pinkerton men."

V2. Ye prating politicians, who boast protection creed,
Go to Homestead and stop the orphans' cry.
Protection for the rich man ye pander to his greed,
His workmen they are cattle and may die.
The freedom of the city in Scotland far away
'Tis presented to the millionaire suave,
But here in Free America with protection in full sway,
His workmen get the freedom of the grave.
(CHORUS)

Adam Worth, seeing the Homestead debacle as an opportunity that would mutually benefit him and the Pinkertons, offered a solution. He wanted to return the stolen *Duchess of Devonshire* to the art gallery in London—but only if William Pinkerton brokered the deal. Worth acknowledged that Pinkerton had known all along that he had stolen the painting, but, rather than apprehending Worth outright, he allowed other law enforcement entities to do so, which dramatically decreased his time in prison. Worth wanted to repay William's kindness and professionalism by allowing him to be the "face man" on the return of a long-lost famous painting. The newspapers gobbled up the story and praised the wonderful job and ethics of the Pinkerton agency, and the company's reputation for diligence and fairness was once again restored.

THE AGENCY OF OLD MORPHS INTO A NEW ENTITY

After the deaths of Robert in 1907 and William in 1923, the Pinkerton agency remained a family-run business. Robert's son, Allan, ran the agency after his tenure as a World War I soldier until he died in 1930. The final Pinkerton descendant to run the business was Robert II, the great-grandson of its founder. After he died in the 1960s, the Pinkerton National Detective Agency became a corporation. At that time, the agency was divided into six regions around the United States: Cleveland, Ohio; Kansas City, Missouri; Atlanta, Georgia; Dallas, Texas; Saddle Brook, New Jersey; and San Francisco, California. There were also Canadian and international headquarters in Montreal, Canada, and London, England.

In modern times, as more specialized law enforcement agencies have been established, the Pinkerton agency found that it was needed less often as a fugitive hunter and strikebreaker, but its security services were in higher demand. The Pinkerton agency ceased its labor spying after revelations made by the La Follette Civil Liberties Committee hearings in 1937, which publicized that businesses using espionage to prevent unions from forming and to harass union members was unfair. The creation of the Federal Bureau of Investigation and the police modernization movement contributed to the decrease in detective work for the agency. By the middle of the 1950s, the Pinkerton agency spent most of its time investigating frauds, particularly insurance frauds, and providing constant security for corporations. In the 1960s, the word "Detective" was dropped from the agency's official name and letterhead, due in part to its change in focus. The original company founded by Allan Pinkerton was sold in 1983 after having been managed by Pinkerton descendants for more than 118 years. In 1999, the company merged with Securitas AB, based in Stockholm, Sweden, making Pinkerton a senior partner in the world's largest security company, holding offices in more than thirty countries. All this came from a crime-fighting company begun by a Scottish barrel maker who believed in ethics and humanity.

An independent grant-making organization was founded by Robert Pinkerton, great-grandson of Allan Pinkerton, in 1966, just one year before he died. The Pinkerton Foundation, based in New York City, was established with the broad goals of reducing crime and preventing juvenile delinquency. At this time, the foundation assists with establishing and supporting youth-based programs in at-risk and impoverished communities. When Pinkerton's, Inc., was sold in 1983, the foundation did not retain any affiliation with the company.

In 2000, the Pinkerton Agency celebrated 150 continuous years of service. To commemorate the anniversary, the agency donated numerous materials to the Smithsonian Institution in Washington, D.C. Among these materials are rare files, photographs, and other documents on such individuals as Jesse James and Butch Cassidy. Included in the collection are the wanted posters of the Wild Bunch and documentation and case notes pertaining to the Pinkerton agents' pursuit of those outlaws. The donated files, some dating back to 1850, also detail firsthand the formation and history of the Pinkerton National Detective Agency.

Also in 2000, an organization calling itself the Old Pinks Association, was formed, dedicated to former employees and agents of the Pinkerton's National Detective Agency. The group has assembled a collection of documents, photographs, paintings, and other memoirs related to their former agency. The group even has an employees' reunion every two years in a different American city, which is attended by former investigators and their families. The group is not affiliated with the current Pinkerton's, Inc.

EXAMPLES OF THE PINKERTONS IN MODERN POPULAR CULTURE

Samuel Dashiell Hammett, known by his middle name, served as a Pinkerton agent from 1915 to 1921. Calling on his experience as a private eye, he wrote detective novels and short stories and is credited with the invention of the American hard-boiled detective novel. Some of the most famous characters he has penned include Sam Spade of *The Maltese Falcon*, Nick and Nora Charles of *The Thin Man*, and the Continental Op from *Red Harvest* and *The Dain Curse*.

Popular singer-songwriter Sir Elton John includes a reference to the Pinkertons in his song, *Ballad of a Well-Known Gun*.

The Pinkerton Agency, and some agents by name, is often referred to in the Home Box Office television series *Deadwood*. The series takes place in Deadwood, South Dakota, in the 1880s, shortly after the incident known as

Custer's Last Stand. Deadwood is an uncivilized town rife with crime and corruption, and Pinkerton agents frequently arrive in or near town to locate outlaws.

In the 1994 movie *Bad Girls*, starring Madeline Stowe, Mary Stuart Masterson, Andie MacDowell, and Drew Barrymore, four Wild West prostitutes on the run from the law are pursued by hired Pinkerton detectives Graves and O'Brady.

Actor Timothy Dalton portrays Allan Pinkerton in the movie *American Outlaws* (2001). Pinkerton is shown pursuing American outlaw Jesse James, played in the movie by actor Colin Farrell.

Author Sir Arthur Conan Doyle included a Pinkerton agent in his fourth, and last, Sherlock Holmes novel, *The Valley of Fear*. In the book, a Pinkerton detective is featured among a renegade gang of Freemasons in the western United States.

Allan Pinkerton and the Pinkerton National Detective Agency were influential in the evolution of modern law enforcement. Without the Pinkertons, our modern Secret Service and Federal Bureau of Investigation might not operate as we know them today. Maintaining a central headquarters but dividing the agency into regions around the country vastly improved the ability of the agency to apprehend mobile criminals. Pinkerton taking the chance to hire Kate Warne as the first female private investigator helped pave the way for women to become law enforcement officers and eventually investigators and detectives. Wanted posters in the Wild West took on a whole new life when Pinkerton agents included an actual photo of the wanted individuals along with the descriptions of their appearances and their possible whereabouts. Pinkerton even contributed colorful terms, such as "Pinks" and "private eye," to the modern American vernacular. In summation, Allan Pinkerton's effects on the investigations and law enforcement communities have stood the test of time and can still be witnessed today—if one does a little investigation.

Note

The authors thank an old gumshoe, Edmund Pankau, for his kindness and for teaching us the tools of the trade. Rest in peace, my friend. We also thank private investigator Ralph Thomas for his assistance with this project, and we do not want to leave out our children Clayton and Dillon, who are the true meaning of what love really is.

FURTHER READING

Allan Pinkerton. http://www.thrillingdetective.com/eyes/pinkerton.html.
Allan Pinkerton and His Detective Agency. http://www.pbs.org/wgbh/amex/james/peopleevents/p_pinkerton.html.

Allan Pinkerton and His Secret Role in the Underground Railroad. http://www.suite101.com/article.cfm/the_underground_railroad/114256.

Axelrod, Allen. 1992. *The War between the Spies*. New York: The Atlantic Monthly Press.

Deadwood. Home Box Office Online. http://www.hbo.com.

Detective Allan Pinkerton Was Born in Glasgow, Scotland, August 25, 1819. Library of Congress. http://www.americaslibrary.gov/cgi-bin/page.cgi/jb/nation/pinkerto_1.

Father Was Killed By the Pinkerton Men. The Musical Saga of Homestead. http://historymatters.gmu.edu/d/5322.

Geringer, Joseph. 2007. Allan Pinkerton and His Detective Agency: 'We Never Sleep.' http://www.crimelibrary.com/gangsters_outlaws/cops_others/pinkerton/1.html.

Lavine, Sigmund A. 1963. *Allan Pinkerton—America's First Private Eye*. New York: Dodd, Mead.

Macintyre, Ben. 1997. *The Napoleon of Crime*. New York: Delta Books.

Mackay, James. 1997. *Allan Pinkerton: The First Private Eye*. Indianapolis: Wiley.

Morn, Frank. 1982. *The Eye That Never Sleeps: A History of the Pinkerton National Detective Agency*. Bloomington, IN: Indiana University Press.

Nash, Jay R. 1994. *Western Lawmen and Outlaws*. New York: DaCapo Press.

Pinkerton, Allan. http://www.factmonster.com/ce6/people/A0839106.html.

Pinkerton Corporate Web site. http://www.ci-pinkerton.com/index.html.

The Pinkerton Foundation official Web site: http://www.thepinkertonfoundation.org.

Pinkerton Government Services Web site. http://www.pinkertons.com.

Plot Summary for *Deadwood*. Internet Movie Database. http://www.imdb.com.

The Old Pinks' Association official Web site. http://www.oldpinks.com.

Courtesy of the Library of Congress

The Texas Rangers

Ronald Burns

Courtesy of the Library of Congress

The history of the Texas Rangers is rife with accounts of tradition, valor, and controversy. As one of the oldest state law enforcement agencies in North America, the Rangers faced several unique challenges and responded admirably to most of them. The story of the Texas Rangers has been the subject of many books, movies, and television shows, and their legend is shaped largely by their ability to respond, often successfully, to the call of duty. Their success, however, has been tempered in part by criticism of some

Ranger practices. Nevertheless, the Rangers have been compared to other famous law enforcement agencies such as the Federal Bureau of Investigation, Scotland Yard, Interpol, and the Royal Canadian Mounted Police. The Rangers' success is highly attributable to the tenacity with which they perform their duties, the legend of the Rangers, and their ability to adjust to fluctuating societal conditions.

Law enforcement agencies are often assessed on their ability to adapt to changing situations. Criminal behavior changes with the times, thus generating the need for law enforcement to keep pace. Recently, we've seen law enforcement agencies change their practices to address the need for homeland security. Historically, the Rangers engaged in their own version of homeland security when dealing with various threats from different groups, spread out over the frontier. Early on, the Rangers figured prominently in many battles related to the independence of Texas, while later in their history they confronted a wide array of social issues that commanded law enforcement intervention. The group's significant contributions to social control remains one of the most interesting stories in American folklore.

Many authors suggest the Texas Rangers are the oldest state law enforcement agency in North America. Others refute the complete accuracy of this suggestion, noting that Texas was not yet a state when the Rangers were created in 1823, nor was it a U.S. territory. Instead, Texas was still part of Mexico. The debate regarding the Rangers' status as possibly the first state law enforcement agency symbolizes the historical and current ethos of the group: prestigious, yet subject to controversy.

The storied history of the Texas Rangers can be discussed according to four distinct eras. The first era (1823–1866) pertains to Ranger involvement in fighting Indians and protecting the frontier border. The second era (1874–1900) involves Rangers as Western lawmen. The third (1900–1935) and fourth eras (1935–present) relate to changes and political patronage with regard to the Rangers, and the Rangers as part of the Texas Department of Public Safety (DPS), respectively.

ORIGINS (1823–1866)

The storied history of the Texas Rangers begins when the sparsely populated province of Texas was under the control of Spain. In 1821, Mexico would gain independence from Spain, and the area currently recognized as Texas fell under the control of the Mexican government. The impact of Mexican independence, including the newly established Mexican government in Mexico City, would have little effect on Texans.

Indian attacks continuously made it difficult for any settlers to begin life in the province of Texas, and the Mexican government realized the need to populate the area if the Indians advances were to be quelled. Moses Austin proposed colonizing the area with American settlers who would become Spanish citizens. In 1821 Austin received approval to distribute 20,000 acres among three hundred American families. Austin's death coincided with the end of Spanish rule, but his son, Stephen F. Austin, continued his father's work. Soon, Texas would become inhabited and residents would begin facing many challenges as they established the area.

Initially, the settlers were content with their situation. The American settlers were pleased to receive free land with no taxes, have a liberal constitution, and have the right to retain slaves even though slavery had been abolished by the Mexican government. The settlers, however, had no intention of acculturating into Mexican society. They viewed themselves as an independent group, ready to protect their lives and property by fighting marauding Indians.

About 90 percent of the American settlers were Southerners who brought with them a ranger tradition. The term ranger was used in Scotland in the 1600s to describe armed men who ranged the countryside to protect against enemy groups. The practice made its way to the American colonies as early as 1739, and became the basis for one of the world's most storied crime-fighting groups, the Texas Rangers.

Although the Rangers didn't officially appear in a piece of state legislation until 1874, the group's roots are traced back to 1823 when Tonkawa and Karankawa Indians raided the coast of the Mexican province of Tejas. Historian Robert Utley notes that modern day Rangers prefer to believe the Rangers originated in 1823, although contemporary records suggest the Rangers originated in 1835 when they served as soldiers. Stephen F. Austin, the impresario of Tejas, and his lieutenant Moses Morrison, assembled a group of men to protect the coast and the developing colony. The Anglo families that constituted Austin's colonists in the areas settled away from established Spanish-Mexican towns and Comanche trails, yet this did not protect them from invasion and the need to establish protection. The Mexican government agreed to assist the colonists; however, appropriate military support was too distant. With permission from the Mexican government, Austin established a ten-person force in 1823 and allegedly paid the men with his own money. The group of rangers expanded to twenty as Austin led an expedition against a group of Tonkawas who had stolen horses.

These Rangers, as they were called, would eventually assume the jurisdiction of Texas and adopt the name Texas Rangers. The early Rangers were organized along the legal lines of a militia, as opposed to a military, given their lack of uniforms and their freedom from military laws and regulations. They were also distinct from what would today be considered municipal or county-level law enforcement, particularly in light of their region-wide jurisdiction.

This early group of peacekeepers consisted of armed and mounted individuals from all backgrounds. The early forces were also multicultural, as

Hispanics, Anglos, and American Indians served as Rangers as early as the 1820s. The terms of their Ranger volunteer enlistment ranged from three to six months. They were called upon as needed, and returned to their occupations as blacksmiths, masons, farmers, and other occupations when their services weren't required.

More than thirty thousand Anglo colonists were in Texas by 1830 and the Mexican government began efforts to limit Anglo settlement. Over the next five years, relations between the American settlers and the Mexican government deteriorated, eventually leading to Mexican troops sent to garrison San Antonio. The colonists, now intent on independence, began establishing volunteer troops.

Mexican authorities provided little assistance in preventing Indian attacks against settlers. Austin called a conference of the six districts in the settlement with the goal of providing a system of defense. The leaders agreed to keep a permanent force of twenty to thirty Rangers. By 1835 the Rangers had a force of fifty-six men organized among three companies. These early Rangers were required to provide their own weapons and horses, although the government would provide both for a charge if a recruit so requested. Rangers were also required to be prepared for action at a moment's notice. The early Texas Rangers often fought battles in which they were outnumbered. Accordingly, they often carried several weapons and were skilled in using each.

With the impending movement toward Texas independence in 1835, a council of Texas representatives established a "Corps of Rangers" to protect the frontier from Indian advances. Corps members enlisted for one year and were paid $1.25 per day. It was during this period that the Ranger legend and lore largely began, as the Rangers participated in some of Texas's most famous battles with Indians.

The Texas Rangers played a limited role during the Texas Revolution, serving primarily as scouts and couriers for those seeking protection from the Mexican army. The Rangers further served by retrieving cattle and destroying produce or equipment abandoned by those seeking shelter. Their limited role would continue as the region became the Republic of Texas (1836–1845) under its first president Sam Houston, who sought favorable ties with the Indians. Mirabeau Lamar succeeded Houston as President of the Texas Republic in 1838. He sought to enhance Ranger forces out of concern for Indian advances. Texas was alone as a nation and in turn formed a navy, an army, and an organized militia. Charged with protecting the frontier, the Rangers were instrumental in the battles against the Indians.

Indian raids continued through the late 1830s, and both the Indians and settlers recognized that there was more to the conflict between the groups than stolen horses or disputes over hunting grounds. Accounts of Comanche atrocities were prominent, and to many Texans the Indians represented a savage threat that threatened the spread of civilization. In return, Texans responded at times with similar or even more brutal attacks. The conflicts between the groups "became a brutal race war, a clash of vastly incongruous world views." (Hardin 1991, 7).

By the end of Lamar's tenure in office the Republic had successfully defeated many of the more powerful Indian tribes. Sam Houston was reelected to the presidency in 1841 and soon realized the significance of the Rangers in protecting the frontier. The Rangers were effective and inexpensive. In response, 150 Rangers were notably helpful in repelling Mexican and Indian invasions over the next three years under the direction of Captain John Coffee Hays. In the 1844 Battle of Walker Creek just outside of San Antonio, Captain Hays and fourteen men equipped with Colt revolvers defeated seventy Comanches, killing twenty-three and wounding another thirty. The revolvers, procured by Hays from the Texas Navy, contributed largely to the fifteen-minute battle that resulted in Hays' troops suffering only two lance wounds. Hays instilled Ranger traditions and recruited skillful individuals who could help protect the frontier.

It was during the Battle of Walker Creek that three elements converged to further establish the Ranger tradition. First, the event showcased the battle-worthiness of the Rangers and their expertise in fighting while on horseback. The swiftness and effectiveness with which the Rangers won the battle is testament to their fighting abilities. Second, Captain Hays further established the Ranger tradition of having superiors lead by example as opposed to command. Hays' involvement in fighting alongside his troops would help him become the preeminent Ranger captain following Texas' annexation into the United States and the standard by which subsequent Ranger captains would be evaluated. Third, the introduction of the revolving pistol by the Rangers further solidified the tradition of hard-fighting law enforcement agents.

In the early 1840s, Ranger Samuel H. Walker visited with firearm maker Samuel Colt. Colt was interested in getting Walker's endorsement for Colt's revolving pistol, which was opposed by the Ordnance Department. Walker commented on the usefulness of the Paterson Colt, particularly as used by the Rangers to subdue the large number of Comanche fighters during the Battle of Walker Creek. While meeting with Colt, Walker purchased weapons for the Rangers and offered suggestions to Colt regarding improvements to the handgun. Particularly, Walker was interested in a lethal weapon that could be used while one was mounted on a horse. Colt embraced the idea and created a .44-caliber, six-shot revolver with a nine-inch barrel. The Walker Colt, as the gun was named, significantly impacted Ranger law enforcement practices and, arguably, historical and modern day law enforcement practices. The new revolver would better equip the Rangers to fight the many battles in which they were outnumbered. The Rangers' adoption and use of the revolver would help establish and contribute to the legend of the Rangers.

The annexation of Texas into the United States and the Mexican-American War, which began in 1846, provided the Rangers another opportunity to showcase their abilities. As federalized volunteers, the Rangers had garnered the admiration of many in society and were loosely accountable to the regulations of commissioned regiments. In doing so, they were also able to maintain many of their traditions, including short terms of service, the absence of uniforms and flags, and scorn for military proprieties and the chain of command. They also maintained enough freedom to inflict atrocities on Mexican civilians and exact revenge for Mexican actions at the Alamo.

The ability of the Rangers to navigate the frontier and their guerilla-style warfare contributed to the American offensive during the Mexican-American War. Ranger assistance was notably showcased in the battles in Palo Alto and Resaca de la Palma, and they provided effective guidance for the American army to Monterrey, where U.S. forces invaded the city. After being furloughed following a brief armistice, the Rangers returned to battle and secured and provided information that significantly helped win the battle in Buena Vista. Their role in the war would soon change from one involving guidance and intelligence to involvement in combat actions in March 1847.

Involvement in the Mexican-American War enabled the Rangers to prove themselves worthy fighters. Under the direction of Jack Hays and Samuel Walker, the Rangers assisted the U.S. forces and created an impressive reputation that remains. Their fierce fighting tactics led some, including General Zachary Taylor, who would become the twelfth president of the United States, and General Winfield Scott to comment that the Rangers perhaps acted too violently toward military and civilian Mexicans. Taylor and Scott, who commanded Rangers during the fighting in several battles, commented that the Rangers were "unsurpassed both as fighters and troublemakers." (Croke 2002). Ranger behavior was applauded and bemoaned during this period, and General Taylor would eventually request that no more Rangers be provided for assistance. Their brutalities, which in some ways tarnished and in other ways enhanced the reputation of the Rangers, exemplified the racism existent in nineteenth century Anglo-Texas. It was during this period that some Mexicans referred to the Rangers as *los Diablos Tejanos*, the "Texas Devils."

The Treaty of Guadalupe Hidalgo signed in 1848 ended the Mexican-American War and the Rangers retreated to Texas. The United States and Mexico agreed that the Rio Grande River would serve as the national border. The war was costly to the Rangers, who lost several soldiers including Samuel Walker, who perished leading a group called the U.S. Mounted Rifles. Ranger involvement in the war against Mexico would be the only time the Rangers would operate as a military unit.

After the Mexican-American War, the Rangers became less involved in social control practices and most of the force was disbanded. Captain Hays relocated to California, and his wartime adjutant John Salmon "Rip" Ford took his place as Captain. The U.S. army now assumed the responsibility of protecting the Texas frontier, and Ranger assistance was not requested. Most Rangers returned to their "non-Ranger" lives, while some, including Jack Hays, headed to California as part of the gold rush.

Despite the lull in activity, the Rangers were not disbanded and were sometimes called on to settle skirmishes between Indians and settlers who wanted to locate in what was previously Indian land. The United States had set up reservations for the Indians, although not all Indians were content with the establishment. The Army forces now assuming primary law enforcement in Texas would prove ineffective in deterring Indian advances. Now a U.S. senator, Sam Houston requested federal funding for the Rangers to confront the Indian threat, but received nothing in return.

This seemingly dormant period in Ranger history would not last, however. Apache raids on southwestern Texas in 1855 inspired Governor Elisha M. Pease to assemble three companies of Texas Rangers under the direction of James H. Callahan. Many Texans volunteered for the expedition, which would involve chasing Indians who had recognized the effectiveness of evading law enforcement by crossing the Mexican border. Callahan refused to recognize international boundaries, or international laws for that matter, and led his troops across the Rio Grande in pursuit of fleeing Indians. Mexican authorities objected to the intrusions, as did Washington officials. Nevertheless, the Rangers would not be deterred and Governor Pease, who supported the Rangers, became the target of criticism from several directions. The Ranger practice of unlawfully crossing the border eventually ceased in response to the pressure, though the renegade practices of Callahan and troops would perpetuate the Ranger legend. The Rangers continued to cross the border, albeit during hot pursuits deemed "expedient," a term that encompasses much subjectivity.

The election of Hardin Richard Runnels as governor in 1857 and the appointment of "Rip" Ford as senior captain in 1858 further reinvigorated the Rangers. Runnels allocated $70,000 to support the Rangers, who saw their forces increase to roughly one hundred members who were tasked with controlling the invasive acts of the Comanche and other tribes whose raids against settlers generated concern. During the 1858 Battle of Antelope Hills in what is now Oklahoma, Ford proved his worthiness as a leader. Rip Ford was only thirty-four years old when he began his career as captain, and his troops destroyed the sizeable village of Chief Iron Jacket while killing seventy-six Indians. Only two Rangers were killed and three wounded. Eighteen Indian women and children were taken as prisoners for future trade for white captives. The tactics used by Ford and his troops during this battle were soon emulated by U.S. army forces in subsequent attacks on Rush Springs and Crooked Creek.

Ford, whose nickname "Rip" stood for "rest in peace," was a tenacious fighter who led the Rangers against Juan Cortina, who had seized the border city of Brownsville. Cortina's troops, some 400 strong, were defeated in the bloody battle that consumed 151 of Cortina's men and roughly 90 Texas citizens including a few Rangers. After this expedition, the Rangers ceased to significantly impact social control for the next fourteen years. The beginning of the Civil War led many Rangers and other law enforcement officials to support the Confederacy. The federal forts that had been established were abandoned with Texas' secession from the Union, leaving Texas with little law enforcement and the reemergence of Indian advances. Further, rebel deserters from various parts of the South made their way into Texas, which at the time was ill prepared to confront the unruly behavior.

Despite taking place mostly outside of Texas, the Civil War impacted the Texas Rangers. Many suitable candidates for the Texas Rangers left the state. In response, Texas relied on those left behind, including young boys, older men, and men who were deemed unfit to fight in the war, to protect its frontiers. Immediately following the war, law enforcement in Texas was "disorganized and haphazard" (Horton and Turner 1999, 97).

The Ranger legend continued during the Civil War. For instance, the well-known Terry's Rangers and several other units from the Texas cavalry adopted the Ranger title; however, they were not true Texas Rangers. The adoption of the term "Ranger," nevertheless, depicts the significance of the group.

The period of Reconstruction (1865–1873) is referred to as "the darkest period in the history of the organization" (Texas Department of Public Safety: Texas Rangers). Federal troops commanded by General Philip Sheridan occupied the state, and under the direction of the Governor E. J. Davis, the Rangers were charged with enforcing unpopular laws. It is argued that, for all practical purposes, the Rangers disbanded for almost a decade after the war. The State Police of Texas, created by Governor Davis and consisting of many carpetbaggers, were charged with enforcing martial law, which compounded the problem. The State Police eventually disbanded as a result of their inefficiency and citizen distrust of any authority, either civil or military, after the Civil War. The Rangers, who were busy fighting Indians, were left to enforce the laws in Texas.

The current stereotype of the Texas Rangers as lawmen neglects the citizen soldier practices of the early Rangers. Early Rangers largely engaged in soldier-like practices when defending against Indian advances. These early Rangers pursued justice as vigorously as the current and more recent Rangers; however, the concept of justice has changed and procedural law and police professionalism have impacted Ranger practices. The concept of justice recognized and enforced by early Rangers involved limited concern for individual rights, particularly as applied to Mexican and Indian foes. Nevertheless, justice, as applied by the early Rangers was understood and accepted by the Anglo-Texans, who dominated the Republic of Texas and later, the state of Texas.

THE LEGEND CONTINUES (1874–1900)

Crime and social disorder were problematic in Texas after the Civil War. A poor economy and displaced veterans contributed to the problems, as did the presence of a Reconstruction government that maintained a different ethos from many Texans. Unlike the period prior to the War, however, Indians no longer posed the primary threat. The enhanced military presence provided by the Johnson and Grant administrations in their attempts to address the "Indian problem" largely contributed. Law-breaking Anglos and Mexican bandits provided notable challenges for Texas. Unfortunately, there was no full-time organized law enforcement agency to provide adequate protection.

Democrats regained political power in 1873, officially ending Reconstruction in Texas. Following a period of federal intervention, the new state government attempted to restore some of what Texas was all about, including the Texas Rangers. The legislation attempted to recast the Texas Rangers as a permanent military outfit to perform the tasks of citizen soldiers, but more effectively. The Rangers maintained many of the defining features of earlier Ranger groups, only they were no longer citizen soldiers. The Rangers would fight Indians as the need arose, but for the most part, the Rangers became more recognizable as state law enforcement agents than protectors against Indian advances.

Particularly, the legislation authorized funding for two Ranger forces to provide formal social control. The Frontier Battalion, the first of the two Ranger forces, was led by Major John B. Jones and consisted of six companies comprised of seventy-five men in each. Their primary responsibility was to protect the border with Mexico along the Rio Grande and prevent crime. The second force, known as the Special Force, was led by Captain Leander H. McNelly and was responsible for controlling general lawlessness across the state. The Special Force engaged in a wide array of activities, including tracking down robbers and horse thieves. The significance of this legislation is notable in many ways, not the least of which involves its being the first time the Rangers were provided legislatively directed responsibilities and statewide jurisdiction.

It was around this time that a half-century of war with Indians in Texas would come to an end. The Frontier Battalion under John B. Jones defeated a group of Comanche Indians during the 1874 Red River War. With the exception of a few skirmishes with Apaches along the New Mexico border in 1880, the Red River War signified the end of major battles fought by Texans against the advancing Indians.

The $75,000 allocated to the Frontier Battalion was expected to cover two years, when legislators would once again meet and appropriations could be made. Unfortunately, the funding was consumed too quickly, and after about five months the number of troops in the six companies of the

Frontier Battalion was reduced from seventy-five men to forty. The need for fighting Indians had decreased, and the Rangers shifted their attention to traditional law enforcement activities.

Major John B. Jones designed the Frontier Battalion and presided over the Rangers' transformation into an agency set on state law enforcement. Jones was able to effectively address the administrative, logistical, financial, and political challenges associated with the transition of the Rangers from protectors of the frontier to law enforcement agents. He was also able to maintain command of his troops, and, holding to tradition, led through example by riding the frontier several times each year. Jones was able to transform the Rangers into a state law enforcement agency while maintaining many Ranger traditions. For instance, the Rangers still provided their own horses and arms, wore no uniforms, and enjoyed great camaraderie with their colleagues and officers.

For all intents and purposes, the Rangers were a military organization subject to discipline, order, accountability, and other characteristics associated with a military outfit. They nevertheless maintained their informal relationships within the companies. They faced a continuous struggle in that they retained much of their tradition and took pride in their social control expertise, yet were consumed by the changes, particularly as they pertained to law enforcement, associated with a developing state and country.

Leander McNelly would play a significant role in furthering the Ranger reputation as protectors of Texas. McNelly, whose standards for Rangers was rigorous and whose fighting tactics were brutal, led a militia group requested by the governor to quell the violent Sutton-Taylor feud. The company largely resembled the Frontier Battalion, and the public and those in the militia regarded themselves as Rangers: McNelly's Rangers. McNelly and his men failed to quell the Sutton-Taylor feud, but the group soon took on the task of confronting Mexican cattle thieves on the Rio Grande. It is suggested the group used tactics not legally permissible by government-sanctioned groups. Unconventional law enforcement tactics such as violently improper interrogations were not beyond McNelly's approach (Utley 2002a). McNelly, who was tough on his Rangers, yet even tougher on outlaws, engaged in questionable practices such as "shoot first and ask questions later," and the historical Spanish practice of *la ley de fuga*, which holds that prisoners were to be summarily shot in the event of a rescue attempt.

McNelly's legend, and that of the Texas Rangers, would thrive in 1875 as he and thirty Rangers attempted to find stolen cattle. McNelly and company crossed the Rio Grande and mistakenly entered a village thought to be the refuge for the cattle thieves and shot a dozen or so men in the streets. A large Mexican contingent drove the Rangers back to the Rio Grande where fighting took place over two days. The Rangers continued the fight despite the advice of U.S. army officers to cease fire, and the presence of four hundred Mexican troops gathering to stand up for their sovereignty. The

Mexican leader of the troops agreed to turn over the cattle and the thieves upon ceasefire, and the Rangers returned home.

Although only one-third of the cattle were returned, none of the bandits were turned over, and his Rangers' actions nearly provoked an international incident, McNelly's reputation as a leader soared as a brave man who fought for justice. The public viewed the Rangers entering Mexico and killing men of uncertain guilt for the sake of a few cows as justifiable. The Rangers were standing up for and representing justice. McNelly died from tuberculosis in 1877, and his company was incorporated into the Frontier Battalion.

The practices of the Frontier Battalion generated controversy, particularly with regard to their use of firearms while investigating crimes and maintaining order. As peace officers, the Rangers could legally make arrests with or without arrest warrants and were encouraged to use all reasonable means to do so. At this time, justifiable homicide was permitted by Texas peace officers to prevent arson, burglary, castration, maiming, murder, rape, and other offenses. Further, Texas was among the states that changed the common-law tradition of requiring one to retreat prior to engaging in self-defense, which encouraged further violence by both Texans and their law enforcement officers.

The Rangers engaged in two distinct types of social control during this period. When interacting with outside agents such as Indians or bootlegging Mexicans, the Rangers acted in a soldier-like manner. In contrast, they performed like detectives and policemen when confronting the unruly within their society, such as outlaws and train robbers. The law enforcement aspect of the Rangers largely involved dealing with bloody feuds, lynch mobs, cattle thieves, killers, and the like. Ranger crime-fighting energies were, in part, directed by the creation of a "crime book" compiled by Adjutant General William Steele. The book contained a list of known outlaws, which guided the Ranger lawmen.

The organization and scope of the two Ranger units created in 1874, the Frontier Battalion and the Special Force, had outlived their purpose with the settlement of the West and the demise of the Western outlaw at the turn of the century. The need for frontier justice was fading, and along with it went the Frontier Battalion in 1891. Nevertheless, the vast lands of southwestern Texas provided fertile ground for cover to many outlaws, and local law enforcement was ill equipped to respond. In response, the Rangers would continue to contribute. In 1894 and 1895 the Rangers rode 173,381 miles, arrested 676 suspects, recovered and returned 2,856 head of stolen livestock, and assisted local law enforcement on 162 occasions. These numbers attest to the ongoing need for Ranger intervention regardless of substantial societal changes.

The Rangers, toward the latter part of this era, were no longer citizen soldiers who assembled in times of need and returned home when their services were no longer required. Now they were recruited and served as long as financial support for the Rangers existed. Nevertheless, changing from a militia-type group of frontiersmen to a formal law enforcement agency provided particular challenges for the Rangers. For example, the Rangers needed to keep pace with the rise of the professionalism in policing that was taking place at the time. Emphasis on careerism, scientific techniques of crime detection, and the increased use of technology, resulting from the industrialization of America, perpetuated changes in Ranger practices. The move toward crime prevention, as opposed to crime enforcement, was something new to the Rangers, while new technologies such as telephones, repeating firearms, trains, and cars also challenged the Rangers. These developments provided new crime-fighting threats while simultaneously offering new crime-fighting tools. The Rangers were forced, in large part, to adapt to a new society and move beyond their historical social control practices. Accordingly, the Rangers were able to continue protecting the frontier while transforming into a professional state law enforcement organization dealing with more conventional forms of crime and disorder.

The eighteenth century Rangers were described as hard but fair men during a period when hardness was required and fairness a bonus. In his insightful work *Lone Star Justice: The First Century of the Texas Rangers*, Robert Utley closely examines the events and practices that shaped the Texas Rangers. He notes the distinctively different functions of the Rangers during 1823–1910. From 1823 until 1874 the Rangers were citizen soldiers called on to confront unruly Indians or Mexicans. After 1874, the Rangers became "Old West lawmen" under the institution known as the Frontier Battalion.

Much of the legend and lore associated with the Texas Rangers originated in this period, for instance, as the Rangers tracked down and arrested (or killed) notorious outlaws. Included among the outlaws were John Wesley Hardin, a preacher's son who allegedly killed thirty-one men, train robber Sam Bass, and gunfighter King Fisher. Things would change with the arrival of the twentieth century, as the lawmen Rangers faced a new set of challenges with which they had to contend.

CHANGE AND POLITICAL PATRONAGE (1900–1935)

The twentieth century brought about notable change for the Texas Rangers. Particularly, law enforcement practices evolved from a frontier style, through which the Rangers had established much of their reputation, to a more mundane domestic approach. Second, gubernatorial intervention and political patronage hampered the Ranger reputation. Modernization and urbanization were impacting the group, for instance, as the introduction and widespread use of automobiles and trains rendered the horseback Ranger almost obsolete.

Nevertheless, the Rangers would continue to provide social control in Texas. In July 1901 the Texas Legislature passed legislation charging the Rangers with protecting the frontier against marauding or thieving parties and suppressing lawlessness and crime throughout the state. Four companies of no more than twenty Rangers would now be officially recognized as a state law enforcement agency. The Rangers were authorized and funded by the Texas adjutant general, who was appointed by the governor and charged with overseeing the Texas National Guard. In other words, the Rangers became highly susceptible to gubernatorial influence. Despite greater accountability and enhanced bureaucratic concerns, the Rangers were able to maintain particular traditions including control over who became a Ranger and the refusal to wear a uniform and badge. In fact, there has never been an official Texas Ranger uniform. Part of the ongoing Ranger tradition is their style of dress, which they continue to proudly wear today: western wear with a white or tan hat, cowboy boots, western cut shirt, tie, pants, and boots.

The early part of the twentieth century found the Rangers expanding their duties to include a wide range of peacekeeping duties with which they were somewhat unfamiliar. This role was unpopular with many Texans, who had come to expect something different from the Rangers. Things would soon change as the Rangers responded to trouble along the Texas-Mexico border between 1910 and 1920. Ranger responses to the situation brought negative attention to the group. Specifically, the Rangers were called on to deal with Mexican revolutionaries, outlaw groups, war-time spies, draft dodgers, liquor smugglers, and other social problems, and the Rangers resorted to the some of the controversial practices of McNelly's Rangers. At a 1919 legislative hearing initiated by State Representative J. T. Canales, who made eighteen charges against the Rangers, they were accused of unscrupulous behavior including pistol-whippings, cold-blooded murders, and intimidations. The investigation led to the dismissal of questionable Rangers and the reorganization of the group. The hearing helped to restore public confidence in the force; however, it did not end the political influence in Ranger affairs.

Between 1919 and 1935 the Rangers showcased their ability to adapt to meet the needs of a changing society. Particularly, the Rangers confronted many significant social issues and problems, including labor strikes, violations pertaining to Prohibition, Mexican border raids, and Ku Klux Klan activities. In 1918, National Prohibition, as provided by the Eighteenth Amendment, generated a new set of challenges for the Rangers, because bootleggers would cross the border from Mexico with the intent of selling liquor. Shootouts between Rangers and smugglers were not uncommon, although some Rangers viewed Prohibition as ludicrous and often chose not to enforce the associated laws. The Rangers also had to contend with providing protection during the oil boom, particularly during the 1920s and 1930s. The oil boom areas during this period seemed to attract unruly citizens looking to illegally cash in on the fortunes in the area.

Compounding the need for the Rangers to change was the transition of Texas away from a frontier era into a more domestic period. Although some Texans didn't appreciate the Rangers' new focus on peacekeeping or some of their heavy-handed tactics, the Ranger crime-fighting reputation would persist and Texans would remain proud of their state law enforcement agency. Captain Frank H. Hamer is among the most famous Rangers, for instance, in light of his role in shifting the Rangers from horse to car and his ability to subdue the infamous outlaws Bonnie and Clyde.

The Great Depression brought about a number of bank robberies and murders, leading the Texas Bankers Association to offer a standing $5,000 reward for killing bank robbers. Some outlaws staged bank robberies and killed their accomplices to receive the reward. Facing a somewhat new type of crime, the Rangers reacted by enlisting the services of the media. Captain Hamer got the press involved, which ultimately led to the banking association changing its reward policy.

Hamer was not done, however. Subduing the infamous Texas natives Clyde Barrow and Bonnie Parker greatly enhanced the Ranger reputation as crime fighters and kept alive the spirit of the force, which had dwindled. Captain Hamer was given responsibility for apprehending the fugitive couple, and after 102 days he and fellow officers ambushed and killed the couple on a rural country road in May 1934. This incident served to reinvigorate the Rangers, who had seen their role as true crime fighters dwindle and their reputation suffer. Political intervention and patronage would contribute to the hard times faced by the Rangers.

Placing the Rangers under the auspices of the Texas adjutant general meant that the Rangers were largely accountable to the Texas governor. Several governors would take an active role in filling the ranks of the Rangers during this period; however, the most controversial of the group was Miriam A. Ferguson, who served from 1933 to 1935. Ferguson summarily fired all Texas Rangers who supported her opponent, incumbent Governor Ross Sterling, in the gubernatorial election. About forty Rangers who weren't fired resigned in disgust. Governor Ferguson then replenished the diminished Ranger ranks with "Special Ranger" commissions to political allies. Ferguson appointed roughly 2,300 Special Rangers, and commission as a Ranger became easier to obtain. With that move, however, came the hiring of less-than-worthy Rangers. Those selected by Ferguson would be termed, in a derogatory manner, "Ferguson's Rangers." Some of Ferguson's appointees were ex-convicts, and many were convicted of various crimes while Rangers. The Rangers would see their reputation become tarnished, earning them the title: "the most scandal-ridden law enforcement agency in American history" (Horton and Turner 1999). The Rangers would become "a source of patronage, corruption, and ridicule" and the effects on state law enforcement in Texas were "catastrophic" (Proctor 1991, 11). Needless to say, criminals took advantage of the absence of an effective Ranger group and negative attention was again directed toward the Rangers.

In 1934 the Texas Senate reacted to the problematic state of law enforcement in Texas and formed a committee to investigate. The committee's report was critical of law enforcement in Texas. The Rangers were forced to revisit their place in law enforcement and made several changes in the period that followed. Perhaps most significant among the changes was the 1935 incorporation of the Rangers into the newly created Texas Department of Public Safety (DPS), which originated following the senate committee's recommendation.

MODERN DAY RANGERS (1935–PRESENT)

Texas Governor James V. Allred is credited with restoring the Texas Ranger reputation and maintaining the Rangers as a legitimate law enforcement organization. Upon taking office in 1935, Allred canceled all of the Special Ranger commissions created by former Governor Ferguson and persuaded the Texas Legislature to move the Rangers from the Texas adjutant general's office to the newly created Texas DPS.

Until the 1940s Ranger law enforcement practices largely resembled the frontier ethos of the State of Texas. The Rangers became increasingly professional following their incorporation into the Texas DPS, because they now had access to a top-notch crime laboratory, improved communications, and political stability. Although smaller in numbers, the quality of the Texas DPS Rangers was better than in years past. The Rangers would also be protected from their recent role as a political pawn. These changes largely assisted the Rangers in making the transition from a seemingly lawless group ranging over the frontier to a state-of-the-art law enforcement agency. However, the early DPS Rangers were still personally ill equipped by today's law enforcement standards. They were provided a Colt .45 and a Winchester .30 caliber rifle by the state; however, they were required to provided their own car, horse, and saddle.

Although part of a new agency, Ranger duties were essentially the same: enforce the state's laws, particularly with regard to felonies, gambling and narcotics; locate fugitives; and suppress riots. The Rangers were also charged with maintaining order during labor disputes and working with other law enforcement agencies across Texas, and more generally, the United States.

Rangers provided internal security in Texas during World War II, with duties ranging from showing educational training films regarding air raid alarms to tracking down escaped German prisoners of war. By 1945 there were forty-five Rangers, and two years later the number increased to fifty-one. The Rangers were once again adapting to a changing society and locating and establishing their place within modern state law enforcement.

The Ranger legend was perpetuated during the 1950s when Ranger Captain R. A. Crowder single-handedly calmed rioting inmates at the Rusk

State Hospital for the Criminally Insane in 1955. During the rioting the inmates had taken several hostages. Crowder entered the maximum-security unit, conversed with the leader of the mob, and quelled the riot. The Rangers were also instrumental in providing a much-needed law enforcement presence while schools were being racially integrated, assisting with violent labor disputes, shutting down illegal gambling functions, and providing many other law enforcement services.

The cultural revolution of the late 1960s again drew negative attention to the Rangers as many Americans questioned much of what the Rangers stood for—authority. The Rangers became a target of protest, and sometimes adopted earlier, questionable tactics in quelling riots, which would perpetuate public criticism (and praise). Some questioned their effectiveness working within the boundaries of modern-day procedural law, while others still held to the belief that the Rangers "get things done" at all costs.

Recent decades have brought about ongoing professionalism with the Rangers. They continue to investigate felonious crimes, suppress riots, and apprehend fugitives, and their efforts are enhanced through notable government support. Ranger appropriations have increased in recent times, and the Rangers receive great assistance from computerized information systems. Rangers are more experienced and better organized than in years past. The training and education of recent Rangers is also much better. The overall increased professionalism is much needed in today's society where issues concerning procedural justice are seemingly more common than ever.

The history of the Texas Rangers suggests they are indeed icons in crime fighting. The following section sheds further light on the group, through examination of the day-to-day duties of the current Rangers, issues pertaining to their organization and personnel, and finally, the story behind the Texas Ranger badge.

Duties

The Texas Rangers currently derive their statutory authority from the *Texas Government Code*, and the Rangers are responsible for many law enforcement functions as provided in the *Texas Penal Code*. Among their primary functions are the following:

- criminal and special investigations,
- apprehending wanted felons,
- suppressing major disturbances,
- protecting life and property,
- rendering assistance to law enforcement officials,
- gathering and disseminating criminal intelligence,
- serving as officers of the court at the request of a judge,
- providing protection for designated elected officials, and

- participating in educational training and providing training to other law enforcement agencies.

(Texas Department of Public Safety: Texas Rangers)

The Rangers have become increasingly active in law enforcement since their 1935 incorporation into the Texas DPS. Their significant involvement in the crime scene investigation of the Branch Davidian compound and their investigations of mass murderers, drug lords, and serial rapists demonstrate the Rangers' continued importance to state-level law enforcement.

The Rangers took part in an estimated 255 cases during their first year in the new agency, followed by involvement in 16,701 cases two decades later in 1955. In 2005 the Rangers conducted 5,488 investigations resulting in 1,496 felony arrests and 137 misdemeanor arrests. They executed 475 search warrants and obtained 3,437 statements, including 563 confessions to various crimes. Rangers recovered stolen property valued at $1,832,101 and seized contraband valued at $1,518,392. Their activities contributed to 1,828 convictions for various crimes, resulting in 23 death sentences, 52 life sentences, and a total of 10,168 years in prison time being served. They issued 546 subpoenas and 823 warrants. Further, in 2005 the Rangers provided nine hypnosis sessions in criminal investigations. The ability to have such a large impact with a relatively small staff speaks volumes about the Rangers' capacity to fight crime.

In 2000 the Texas Legislature authorized the Unsolved Crimes Investigation Team (UCIT), which is led by a Ranger captain and lieutenant and staffed by eight Ranger sergeants. The UCIT is tasked with providing Texas law enforcement agencies a process for investigating unsolved murders or what seem to be serial or linked criminal transactions.

During the same year, the Rangers acquired a forensic artist who is based at the Ranger headquarters in Austin. The artist assists law enforcement agencies throughout the state by providing various forms of investigative-related artwork. Composite drawings, age progression updates of missing individuals or fugitives, courtroom displays, postmortem drawings, computer facial imaging, and skull reconstruction are among the types of artwork provided by the forensic artist. The services help identify victims of violent crimes and apprehend criminal offenders. Providing such services demonstrates the Rangers' capacity to adapt to changing times while maintaining a distinct specialization in law enforcement.

ORGANIZATION AND PERSONNEL

The historically fluctuating mission and organization of the Texas Rangers contributed to consistent organizational and personnel changes. Perhaps the simplest manner of describing the historical organizational design of the Rangers is to focus on the highest level of accountability. Early in the history of the Texas Rangers, captains, lieutenants, or sergeants in charge of companies spread throughout Texas reported to the Austin-based headquarters officers. The Adjutant General oversaw the Rangers once Texas became a state. However, this arrangement only lasted until 1935, when the Rangers became accountable to the Texas DPS.

The Ranger Headquarters remains in Austin while six companies and the headquarters for the UCIT are spread throughout Texas.

Texas Ranger Division Locales

Headquarters: Austin
Company A: Houston
Company B: Garland
Company C: Lubbock
Company D: San Antonio
Company E: Midland
Company F: Waco
Unsolved Crimes Investigation Team: San Antonio

As noted, the number of Rangers has fluctuated over the years. Recent numbers suggest that the Ranger force has been small since the demise of the Ferguson Rangers, with fewer than one hundred Rangers being the norm. There were only thirty-four Rangers when the force was reorganized in 1935. As of April 2007 the Texas Rangers Division consisted of 140 members, including 118 commissioned officers, three crime analysts, a forensic artist, a fiscal analyst, and seventeen civilian support personnel.

As noted, early Rangers were primarily volunteer citizens. Formal selection and recruitment practices were established as the Rangers became increasingly institutionalized. Rangers were typically recruited from county sheriff or municipal police departments between 1935 and the early 1980s. That approach changed when Texas DPS Director James Adams mandated that Texas Rangers be recruited and selected from the ranks of the DPS. Little recruiting has ever been necessary, as it was not unusual for the Rangers to receive more than two hundred applications for a small number of openings.

To become a Ranger one must first meet the requirements for entry employment with the Texas DPS. Candidates must also meet special requirements to be eligible to be a Ranger. Accordingly, each applicant must

- be a U.S. citizen,
- be in excellent physical condition,
- have an outstanding record of at least eight years of investigative experience with a bona fide law enforcement agency,
- be currently employed with the Texas DPS as a commissioned officer with the rank of at least Trooper II,

- pass a thorough background investigation,
- possess a valid Texas driver's license,
- be at least twenty years of age, and
- have a minimum of ninety semester hours from an accredited college or three years or more of military or law enforcement experience.
(Texas Department of Public Safety: Texas Rangers)

These requirements are much more stringent than those in place in 1919, when state legislation led to the reorganization of the Rangers. The 1919 Rangers had no specific requirements for enlistment; physical condition, previous law enforcement experience, and formal education and training were not examined.

The average age of the Rangers in 1987 was forty-five and remained there as of 2005. The level of education of the Rangers, however, increased during that period. In 1987 the Rangers' average level of education was 42 hours of college. As of 2005 that number increased to 117, with 56 Rangers possessing a college degree compared to 28 in 1987.

It wasn't until the Rangers became part of the Texas DPS that they received formal in-service training. Current Rangers are required to attend at minimum forty hours of in-service training every two years, although most Rangers attend far more than the minimum number of required hours.

While the early Rangers were demographically diverse, the modern Rangers have been criticized for a lack of diversity. The changing demographics of society and increased societal concern for multiculturalism provided new challenges for the Rangers. Although they have constantly sought to maintain their core attitude amidst many changes, questionable hiring practices recently attracted negative attention to the Rangers.

Females were appointed Special Rangers in the 1930s and 1940s; however, they were generally administrative assistants or handled security for the governor or projects involving sensitive information. The most recent and first full-time female Rangers were appointed in 1993, or 170 years after the Rangers first assembled. Racial and ethnic minorities have also been underrepresented as Rangers. The 1969 hiring of a Hispanic recruit was the first in more than fifty years and in 1988 Sergeant Lee Roy Young, Jr., became the first African American Texas Ranger in the twentieth century. Ranger hiring practices had been criticized, as some questioned whether the Rangers adhered to the "good ol' boy" approach of hiring and promotion. Some questioned the absence of Hispanic Rangers in 1967 following farm worker strikes, which brought the question of diversity to light.

In 1986 the Ranger oral interview board denied a position to Texas DPS trooper Michael Scott who scored well on all tests and seemingly did well in the interview although he received a low score. Scott applied again, scored well again, and was once again denied a position. Scott noticed that the Rangers had no African Americans on the force, leading him to speculate that race played a factor in his inability to be hired. Along with other African American troopers who wondered the same thing, Scott approached that NAACP which in turn filed a complaint with the Equal Employment Opportunity Commission (EEOC) on behalf of the officers in 1988. Texas DPS officials agreed to negotiate and two African American Rangers were hired that year. Neither Michael Scott nor any of his colleagues who filed the complaint with the NAACP were among those hired.

The complaint filed with the EEOC caught the attention of the DPS who, in turn, reacted. Historically, the Ranger candidate-interviewing practices involved several Rangers, all of whom were white. After the complaint, the practice changed to involve more diversity in the interview process. This change was not enough, however, as the Texas state government was becoming increasingly diversified and more politicians were paying attention to DPS and Ranger hiring practices. Particularly, in 1993 several minorities on the Texas House Appropriations Committee made strong recommendations that greater diversity was needed among the ranks. Then-governor Ann Richards supported the claims and suggested the need to include women on the force.

Despite the earlier, fringe involvement of females in Ranger practices, no woman had ever served as a full-time Ranger. The idea of a female Ranger did not sit well with many current and former Rangers, who voiced their concerns. Nevertheless, the pressure was too much. On August 1, 1993, the Texas DPS announced the hiring of nine new Rangers: two women, two white males, three Hispanic males, one black male, and one Asian American male. The goal was to diversify the force and make it reflective of the state as a whole.

Michael Scott was not among those hired. The applicant pool of minorities and women was small, and some suggest the Rangers failed to hire the most qualified of the pool. Based on the inexperience of several of those who became Rangers, it is suggested that the only thing the new hires had in common was a low likelihood of generating controversy.

THE BADGE

The Texas Rangers are often associated with law, justice, and a badge on their chest. The early Rangers of the nineteenth and twentieth centuries, however, didn't proudly display a badge. It wasn't until later in the twentieth century that the five-pointed star became part of the Ranger attire. The badge has come to symbolize much of what the Rangers stand for.

The original group of Rangers didn't wear or have a badge primarily because they weren't official lawmen. The star now proudly worn by many Texas law enforcement officials was created in 1835 by Texas's first secretary of state Charles B. Stewart. However, it wasn't worn by law enforcement officials until 1870 during Reconstruction. It was during 1870 when Governor E. J. Davis created the state police to control unruly former Confederates that the badge was first worn by law enforcement.

It was not until the Rangers were through devoting much of their efforts toward troubles at the border and Indian attacks and began considering themselves peacekeepers around 1875 that they began carrying badges. Still, only a few Rangers carried a badge and those who did generally placed the badges out of sight until they needed to display it as a sign of authority. The purpose for this was twofold: wearing a badge provided a target for outlaws, and it was better that nobody knew they were a Ranger until the need for an arrest arose.

The original badges were carved out of Mexican silver coins and early Ranger badges were not made to specific standards. Some Rangers molded the coins into a shield with a star, while others placed the star within a circle. Still, others simply carved a star from a tin can or used jewelry, leather, or wood. Regardless of the material used for the badge, the five-pointed star was present in the design.

In 1900 the state issued the Rangers a five-pointed star inscribed "Texas State Ranger." Only a few were made, and some Rangers continued the tradition of carving their own badge when the government supply of badges ran out. The most common design used by the Rangers was the wagon wheel. Ranger badges changed in 1917 when a star-shaped badge with a circle on the inside was issued. Still, some Rangers preferred to create their own, contributing to the historical inconsistency of Ranger badges.

The badge once again changed in design when the Rangers became part of the Texas DPS in 1930 and a diamond-shaped badge featuring the star and the wheel was issued. Most Rangers carried the badge until 1967 when the DPS redesigned the badge, choosing the earlier circle-star used in the 1800s for the design. Despite the changes, Mexican coins are still used to create Ranger badges, one of the many traditions maintained by the Rangers.

IN THE END

In his 1935 work documenting the history of the Texas Rangers, William Prescott Webb predicted the group would soon disappear. Webb's prediction failed to materialize, as the Rangers have adapted to the many challenges they've encountered. They've done so while maintaining, despite some disruptions, a reputation as an exceptional crime-fighting group. In fact, several states have attempted to create law enforcement groups along the lines of the Texas Rangers. The Arizona Rangers and the New Mexico Mounted Police, established in the early twentieth century, are among the more successful attempts. It is said that "imitation is the sincerest form of flattery." To be sure, the Rangers have received a lion's share of flattery.

The history of the Texas Rangers is aptly described by several authors, including Harold Weiss (1994), who suggests, "The reality of the Texas Rangers in the late nineteenth and early twentieth centuries lay between the images of the good guys in white hats and '*los Diablos Tejanos*' in black hats." Robert Utley describes the two contrasting views of the Rangers that have taken shape. The first view depicts the Rangers as "fearless men of sterling character and unswerving dedication to the mission" (Utley 2002b, xii). They appear as a highly efficient and effective group that provide shining examples for generations to come. As citizen soldiers they outfought their opponents. As lawmen, they always brought the criminal to justice. The other view of the Rangers, as described by Utley, depicts the group as "ruthless, brutal, and more lawless than the criminals they pursued" (xii). As citizen soldiers they indiscriminately killed innocents and enemies of all sorts. As lawmen, they used unscrupulous tactics without concern for individual rights.

One must consider Ranger practices within the time period when they exist. To judge their earlier, legend-generating practices by today's standards would render many Rangers criminals. However, nineteenth-century Ranger practices occurred at a time when violence was more common than it is today, and procedural law was a figment of one's imagination. Many of the individuals the Rangers killed were trying to kill them or do harm to others. There was little, if any, crime-fighting technology and very little concern for police professionalism, at least by today's standards. The criminals were sometimes ruthless, and law enforcement, as it existed, needed to keep pace.

Consideration of Ranger practices with regard to the time does not justify the sometimes barbaric and illegal Ranger practices of law enforcement. Instead, it helps temper the negative attention sometimes drawn to the group. Many early local law enforcement officials avoided procedural concerns, and little procedural law controlled law enforcement practices.

The ability of the Rangers to survive as a group despite questionable practices and occasionally being the target of public and government discontent speaks loudly of their success. To be sure, the group would have been permanently disbanded if they were systematically barbaric in their practices. Instead, it can be safely argued that the Rangers, like some modern law enforcement groups, went to extreme measures in taking the law into their own hands. Yet, along the way the Rangers established a legend unlike any other law enforcement group. The Rangers had the benefit of establishing their reputation at a time of little media scrutiny or concern for police professionalism, and even less concern for procedural law.

Regardless of sporadic negative public opinion, political controversy, questionable personnel practices, and a sometimes skewed view of justice, the Rangers remain well respected among law enforcement agencies and the general public. The Rangers have been the topic of volumes of academic writings and the subject of many popular culture features. The legend and lore of the Rangers have been acknowledged and perpetuated in various forms of popular culture, ranging from comic books to Hollywood motion pictures. Movie stars such as John Wayne, Robert Duval, and Clint Eastwood have all portrayed Texas Rangers. Mike Cox's "Texas Rangers Filmology" identifies 161 television and big screen movies about the Rangers that were made between 1910 and 1995. Such a large number of movies is, at the very least, testament to Hollywood's fascination with the group.

> **Media Portrayals of the Texas Rangers**
>
> There have been hundreds of motion picture and television productions focused on fictional and nonfictional, dramatic accounts of the Texas Rangers. The Texas Rangers have been popular fodder for Hollywood for decades. This is evident as far back as 1936, with the release of the Oscar-nominated motion picture *The Texas Rangers* starring Fred MacMurray from Universal Pictures.
>
> More recently, of course, the Texas Rangers have been depicted fictionally through the long-running television series *Walker, Texas Ranger* starring Chuck Norris. This series, which chronicles the fictional life and casework of Dallas-based Texas Ranger Cordell Walker (Chuck Norris) premiered on April 23, 1993, on NBC. The show ran nine seasons, with the last episode airing on May 19, 2001. The show continues to entertain in reruns on the USA Network.

Television series such as *The Lone Ranger* and *Walker, Texas Ranger* and famous novels such as *Lonesome Dove* also recognize the Rangers, and poet Walt Whitman's 1892 poem *Song of Myself* pays tribute to the Rangers. A major-league baseball team bears the name, and the Texas Ranger Hall of Fame located on the Brazos River in Waco, Texas, opened in 1968, provides evidence of the significance of the Texas Rangers to law enforcement. The Hall is a repository for historical artifacts associated with the Rangers and helps keep alive the legend and lore of the Rangers.

The Rangers began as a small, informal group that used exceptional personal skills and a host of freedoms to their advantage on the range. Their historical successes, albeit controversial at times, helped the force establish a reputation among the elite law enforcement agencies in the world. Times change, however, and the Rangers had to make adjustments. For instance, early Rangers countered Indian arrows with bullets from a revolver. Indians fought on horseback, so in response the Rangers rode a superior horse, the large, American horse that was fed grain or corn instead of grass. The adjustments have been in tune most of the time, yet there have been blemishes. However, a strong argument can be made that no law enforcement agency has aptly changed with the times without missteps. The high-profile nature of the Rangers often places them in the spotlight, which can both help and hinder the group.

The legend of the Texas Rangers feeds on and contributes to the public's perception of Texas as a "law and order," "do-it-yourself justice" territory. The historical rebellious nature of Texas and the pride maintained by its citizens are unlike most, if not all, other states. To have a state law enforcement agency with a reputation for "getting the job done," sometimes at all costs, seems apt for the state. Unfortunately, times change and law enforcement practices must respond. A strength of the Rangers is their ability to succeed in challenging situations. There are seemingly few obstacles they cannot overcome.

The popular culture and research literature provide for interesting study in depictions of the Rangers. As with any historical account there is a notable amount of subjectivity in the storytelling. Historians and other researchers use official records, Ranger biographies and autobiographies, news accounts, and other artifacts to tell the story of the Rangers. However, each of these sources is filtered in the sense that an individual at some earlier point in time documented what happened. Such filtering involves subjectivity that distorts storytelling in one way or another. For instance, official records, as well as biographies and autobiographies, contain few accounts of self-incrimination. With regard to the biographical and autobiographical accounts of Rangers and their practices, all, for a large part, are framed in the heroic mold. The role of the historian is to determine what information most accurately depicts the story being told. This task is often easier said than done and undoubtedly involves subjectivity.

Given the emotion attached to the Texas Rangers, with some recognizing the group as icons in enforcing social control and others recognizing them as brutal, lawless demagogues, the subjectivity becomes more pronounced. It is not uncommon to encounter skewed accounts of the Rangers in the popular culture, commercial, and academic literatures. Some accounts of the Rangers neglect the ruthlessness associated with Ranger practices, choosing instead to focus on the bravery and valor. Other accounts challenge the historical Ranger reputation through highlighting the injustices inherent in early Ranger attempts to ensure justice. Yet other accounts, for instance, television shows such as *The Lone Ranger*, glamorize the violence used by the Rangers as part of their social control efforts. Unfortunately, the real truth regarding Ranger practices may never be known. This dilemma is associated with many historical accounts of people, places, and things.

So, what's next for the Rangers? Despite their placement under the Texas DPS, their legend continues and the group maintains many traditions. The Rangers will continue to contribute to the Texas' most serious crime cases, because their ability to move with more freedom than most law enforcement agencies, their access to the sophisticated DPS crime lab, and their ability to avoid departmental red tape makes them extremely useful. The Rangers will continue to find ways to significantly contribute to law enforcement and retain their status as an icon in crime fighting.

FURTHER READING

Cox, Mike. 1999. *Texas Ranger Tales II*, 265–79. Plano, TX: Republic of Texas Press.
Croke, Bill. 2002. Lone Rangers: When Texas was really Texas. *The Weekly Standard* 7 (43): 31–33.
Draper, Robert. 1994. The twilight of the Texas Rangers. *Texas Monthly* 22 (2): 76–83, 107–8, 110, 112–13, 118.
Eckhart, Jerry. 1993. Texas Ranger's badge. *True West* 40 (9): 46–49.
Gathman, Roger. 2007. They didn't ride off into the sunset. *Austin American-Statesman* March 25: J05.
The Handbook of Texas Online. Available at: http://www.tsha.utexas.edu/handbook/online/articles/TT/met4.html (accessed May 2, 2007).
Hardin, Stephen L. 1991. *The Texas Rangers*. New York: Osprey.
Horton, David M., and Ryan Kellus Turner. 1999. *Lone Star Justice*. Austin, TX: Eakin Press.
Oliver, Willard M., and James F. Hilgenberg, Jr. 2006. *A History of Crime and Justice in America*. Boston, MA: Allyn & Bacon.
Proctor, Ben. 1991. *Just One Riot: Texas Rangers in the 20th Century*. Austin, TX: Eakin Press.
Roth, Mitchel P. 2005. *Crime and Punishment: A History of the Criminal Justice System*. Belmont, CA: Wadsworth.
Texas Department of Public Safety: Texas Rangers. Available at http://www.txdps.state.tx.us/director_staff/texas_rangers/index.htm. (Accessed April 14, 2007).
Texas Ranger Hall of Fame: Visitor Information. http://www.texasranger.org/visitor/visitor.htm/. (Accessed April 14, 2007).
Utley, Robert M. 2002a. Tales of the Texas Rangers. *American Heritage* 53 (3): 40–44, 46–47.
Utley, Robert. 2002b. *Lone Star Justice: The First Century of the Texas Rangers*. New York: Oxford University Press.
Webb, Walter Prescott. 1935. *The Texas Rangers: A Century of Frontier Defense*. Boston: Houghton Mifflin.
Weiss, Harold J., Jr. 1994. "The Texas Rangers revisited: Old themes and new viewpoints." *Southwestern Historical Quarterly* 97 (4): 620–40.
Wilkins, Frederick. 1998. The Texas Rangers: Birth and legend. *Wild West* 11 (2): 42–48.

August Vollmer

Willard M. Oliver

> The citizen expects police officers to have the wisdom of Solomon, the courage of David, the strength of Samson, the patience of Job, the leadership of Moses, the kindness of the Good Samaritan, the strategical training of Alexander, the faith of Daniel, the diplomacy of Lincoln, the tolerance of the Carpenter of Nazareth, and, finally, an intimate knowledge of every branch of the natural, biological, and social sciences. If he had all these, he *might* be a good policeman.
>
> —August Vollmer

If ever there was an individual who deserves to be called an "icon of crime fighting," it is assuredly August Vollmer. Hailed by many as the "Father of American Policing," Vollmer established a reputation for fighting crime, not through brute force, as was common at the turn of the twentieth century, but rather as an educator, an educator of the police officer. While only having a vocational education himself, Vollmer became a self-educated man through his voracious appetite for reading. Combined with his early experiences as a town marshal (1905–1909), which later evolved into an appointment as police chief in the city of Berkeley, California (1909–1932), Vollmer began to innovate on how best to fight crime. The adoption of an emergency signal system, the department-wide adoption of bicycle patrols, a fully motorized police department, the installation of radios in patrol vehicles, a police training academy, the lie detector, and the establishment of a crime lab are but a few of the innovations with which he is credited.

It was, however, his dedication to educating the police officer and turning policing into a profession for which he is most renowned. It was specifically the establishment of a criminology (police science) program at the University of California at Berkeley, to ensure that his police officers were educated and received a college degree, that would lead him down the path of being remembered as an educator. Vollmer would receive the first professorship in Police Administration at the University of Chicago and then later, a similar position at the University of California at Berkeley, where he continued to call for the professionalization of the police through education. Eventually, Vollmer would create what would become the American Society of Criminology (ASC), and its spin-off, the Academy of Criminal Justice Sciences (ACJS), two associations dedicated to scientific research and education related to the issue of crime fighting.

Born in humble conditions in New Orleans, Louisiana, with little evidence that he would go on to a career in policing, August Vollmer is credited with moving policing out of the political and corrupt era of the nineteenth century and into the modern era of police professionalization. Through his dedication to police reform and education, August Vollmer had a significant impact on policing and should be remembered as one of the greatest icons of crime fighting in America.

THE EARLY YEARS

He was born in New Orleans, Louisiana, to John and Philippine Vollmer, both of German descent, who had been brought to America by their parents.

John and Philippine met and married in the city of New Orleans. John Vollmer ran a local grocery store that turned out to be reasonably profitable for the family. John and Philippine had three children: Josie, August, and Edward. Josie had been adopted five years before Philippine gave birth to August, who was born on March 7, 1876. Two years later, in 1878, she gave birth to another son, Edward.

In May 1884, at the age of eight, August was beaten and bloodied by a local ruffian. His father, finding out that August had run from a fight, chastised his wife for encouraging this type of behavior. John Vollmer would not have one of his children run from an honest fight. So, John Vollmer sent his son to Pierre La Blanc at a local gymnasium to teach him how to box and defend himself. John taught his son never to run from a fight. It would be the last lesson his father would teach him about life, as three months later, he died of a heart attack.

In the following months, August was challenged by another one of the local boys. Remembering all his father had taught him and drawing on his new-found skills in boxing, he handily defeated his opponent. Yet, the victory was somewhat lost on August, for life had changed greatly with the unexpected death of his father. His mother had to take over the duties of running her husband's grocery store, thus allowing her to spend very little time at home. Prior to John's death, she had always been at home for the three children, and August had found her presence comforting. Now that she was forced to work full-time, he lost the stability of what had been a secure home. There were, however, some benefits to not having a watchful mother's eye, for he could go anywhere he chose during the day. He and his friends took many hikes to Lake Pontchartrain where he would fish and swim the days away. He was also able to roam the streets of New Orleans and explore the various alleys, storefronts, and neighborhoods that had continued to spring up around the city.

Working full-time in the grocery store had, however, taken a toll on his mother's health and, after running the store for nearly two years, she was forced to sell it. With the proceeds from the sale and realizing she still needed to care for her three children, Philippine decided that her best option was to return to Germany to be close to her family. They packed up what they could and embarked on the long journey across the Atlantic Ocean to live in a small town in Germany. Vollmer was ten years old.

Although at first August and his siblings did not like their new life in Germany, they did find that they had more freedom to roam about and there were many new and interesting things to explore. They were enrolled in a local school and they began learning to speak German. Just as Vollmer started to adapt to life in Germany and was becoming proficient in the language, his mother decided they needed to return to the States. Life in Europe is vastly different than in the States, for America has always held much more in the way of conveniences. So, after two years in Germany, they once again crossed the Atlantic Ocean on board a ship headed for what had once been their home.

The Vollmers returned to New Orleans and quickly settled back into life in the city. August was sent to the New Orleans Academy, a vocational school, where he worked hard in his studies. Under the encouragement and tutelage of the principal, John Wilson, August set his sights on becoming a stenographer and was enrolled in classes on bookkeeping, typing, and shorthand. August enjoyed being back in New Orleans, and despite his studies, he continued to find time to roam the city streets and venture back to Lake Ponchartrain.

New Orleans assuredly offered more opportunities for those who lived there and it continued to grow, but it also faced many problems with corruption, local gangs, and crime. Philippine decided it was not the proper place to continue raising her children. After a visit to California, she decided to move the family to San Francisco, a city that afforded many new opportunities and where she had a number of friends. Vollmer wasn't sure he wanted to leave New Orleans, but he did recognize that he stood a better chance of getting a job as a stenographer in such a large and established city. So, after he finished his course work at the New Orleans Academy, the family packed up, and took the train west to San Francisco. The year was 1888.

The family rode on one of the cars that consisted of benches, not exactly the best of accommodations for the long trip, but with Philippine's dwindling cash reserves, it was the best they could afford. Josie was not happy about the move, as she had developed a group of friends, not to mention a boyfriend she did not want to leave. Yet, that was, in part, one of the reasons for the move. Philippine was not happy with the crowd that Josie was running with, and she also feared the same for August. Perhaps highlighting the realities of life in New Orleans at the time was the fact that a woman riding in the same car as the Vollmer's was the widow of New Orleans' police chief David Hennessy, who had been assassinated by the Mafia. This murder, by the "Black Hand," a Sicilian gang that was fast growing into the Mafia, which would dominate America's attention in the 1920s and 1930s, was the incident that forced American law enforcement to finally acknowledge the existence of the Mafia. Although nineteen Sicilians were arrested and placed on trial, including one as young as nine, all of them were acquitted of the murder charges. Incensed by the failure of the local justice system to convict, a vigilante group formed, broke into the jail, and killed ten of the accused.

In a sense, the widow of David Hennessy was fleeing to San Francisco to start a new life, and so was Philippine. Vollmer, at thirteen years of age, was well aware of this. He was sad for his mother, who had lost her husband, and he was sad for Mrs. Hennessy, who also had lost hers. He was also disappointed in the New Orleans' Police Department for failing to protect the city. As O. W. Wilson, writing shortly before Vollmer's death, queried, "it is interesting to conjecture the extent to which knowledge of the Hennessy tragedy may have influenced the future law-enforcement activities of August, who was then twelve" (1953, 92). If it had, it must have been on a subconscious level, for August never gave thought to becoming a police officer, even less a police chief.

The Vollmers rented an apartment on O'Farrell Street in San Francisco, and true to form, on day one, August began exploring the new city. August told his mother the next day that he was going to find a job as a stenographer to help the family make ends meet. Try as he might, no one was willing to hire a thirteen-year-old self-professed stenographer, despite his training at the New Orleans Academy. He finally had to settle for a job as assistant shipping clerk and messenger at W. and J. Sloane and Company, Household Furnishings. He quickly fell into a routine with working during the day delivering packages around San Francisco, working out at a gym after work, taking hikes, going to the beach, and becoming active in the local church.

In 1890, when he was fourteen, his mother decided she was going to have a home built for the family in a small college town across the bay—Berkeley, California. The process of having the house built took almost a year, and during this time, Josie, who had never liked the idea of moving to San Francisco, and assuredly did not want to move to a small town like Berkeley, ran away from home. The family never heard from her again.

In 1891, the family moved into the house in North Berkeley, located on Bonita Street. Mrs. Vollmer was able to secure a job as a practicing nurse, thus allowing her to supplement the family's funds. Around the same time, August was hired as a stenographer by E. H. Driggs. Driggs had refused August a job two years previously but had stayed in contact with August when he delivered packages to his office. August worked for Mr. Driggs for almost a year, but it meant a daily commute from Berkeley into San Francisco. Mrs. Vollmer encouraged August to find a local job in Berkeley, but Vollmer was comfortable with the life he was leading. He worked during the day, hiked the hills around Berkeley, swam in the San Francisco Bay, sailed in his old boat, *The Ruby*, and even bought a guitar and learned how to strum the popular songs of the day.

August also began taking an interest in girls around this time. He met a young lady named Pat Fell at one of the church socials in San Francisco, whom he continued to date even after moving to Berkeley. He also met a young lady named Lydia Sturdevant in Berkeley. Although he liked Pat enormously, having listened to his mother and quit the job in San Francisco, he was now in and out of jobs in Berkeley. Although he wanted to get more serious in his relationship with Pat Fell, she would not condone his transience in the job market; they quarreled and subsequently parted.

In 1895, at the age of nineteen, August did manage to land a steady job by becoming a partner with a friend, Ted Patterson, in the opening of a coal and feed store in Berkeley. Despite their age, Vollmer's steady personality won over many of the locals who at first did not take the boys seriously. Many of the locals began to deal with Vollmer and Patterson and over several years, the two made the coal and feed store into a relatively prosperous venture.

During this period of his life, August also helped to organize a volunteer fire department for the area in which he lived, North Berkeley. Two years later, Vollmer received the town's Fireman Medal for his role in forming and maintaining the volunteer fire department. It is clear that August was quickly settling into life in Berkeley and he was fast becoming a well-respected member of the little college community. His life, however, would quickly change when America declared war on Spain in April of 1898.

Within minutes of hearing that America was at war with Spain he told his mother he was leaving in the morning for San Francisco. He was going to sell his half of the business to Ted Patterson and enlist in the Army as a volunteer. His country had issued the call for volunteers, and out of a profound sense of duty he knew he had to answer that call. True to his word, he sold his interest in the coal and feed store and left for San Francisco the next morning. Arriving at the Presidio he enlisted and was assigned to the Third Artillery, Company G. After being issued his khaki uniform, campaign hat, and bed roll and receiving six weeks of military training and drill, he was deemed ready for war. He was allowed to return home for a one-day leave, where he discovered his mother had tried to enlist herself, in the Army Nurse Corps, but she had been turned down because of her age. However, his brother Edward had also enlisted in the Army, and, after being accepted, served for a year in the military band.

In June of 1898, at the age of twenty-two, August boarded a ship destined for Manila in the Philippines. The trip across the Pacific was tedious, but August was familiar with long voyages, having previously crossed the Atlantic twice. He passed the time reading aloud from his Bible to his new buddy, Jim Ball. The troopship arrived in Manila Bay in June of 1898, and they witnessed the remains of the flagship of the Spanish admiral, the *Reina Christina*, as they entered. Seeing the destruction that had been wrought by Admiral Dewey's fleet, August began to think that the war was probably over and there would be no fighting left for him and the army. However, despite the fact that Dewey had utterly destroyed the Spanish fleet, the Spanish still held Manila, and the army continued to form for its assault on the city. Vollmer began to grow impatient and wondered why the attack did not commence.

The reality of the matter was the Spanish wanted to surrender, but they were afraid the local Filipinos would rush in and destroy them, showing no quarter. Hence they were much more willing to surrender to the Americans as they knew they would receive safe passage from them. However, Spanish machismo and military dictates would not allow the Spanish to surrender openly, hence a fight had to ensue before they could actually surrender. Thus, an informal agreement was reached that dictated that the Americans would attack, the Spanish would surrender, and the Filipinos would be kept out of the city. August joined in the fight, which lasted longer than intended because of some miscommunication, but still resulted in the taking of Fort Malate. The Spanish surrendered; Manila was captured.

August thought that was the end of his fighting days, but little did he know that would quickly change and his more serious engagements were still to come. In the meantime, however, Vollmer's unit began conducting police duty in and around Manila, something he came to relish, despite its lacking the glory of battle. This lasted for nearly six months. During that time, Aguinaldo began generating a strong following of Filipino insurgents who were attacking soldiers along the roads and rivers and at the ports. As the amount of damage and destruction increased, the military was forced to order the capture of Aguinaldo and his men. It was February of 1899.

Captain Randolph, Vollmer's company commander, was given charge of the *Laguna de Bay*, a steam-engine riverboat that was converted into a gunship by nailing sheets of steel to the wooden sides of the old boat and installing three-inch gun turrets on the upper deck. The mission of the *Laguna de Bay* was to secure the rivers and keep them open to travel as they were the main arterial highways of the island. The problem was that Aguinaldo was employing snipers along the river-way, who would shoot at the passing boats and then melt into the dense foliage. Vollmer's boat had to patrol the rivers and engage the Filipinos, which proved difficult for there were skirmishes and engagements nearly every day. The other difficult part of the operation was that the rivers were often very narrow and the boat did not have adequate turning room. Soldiers on board, like Vollmer, had to enter the water and turn the boat in place, exposing themselves to gunfire. It was a dangerous job and one in which many men were killed. August somehow survived; his only injury was to his hearing from the repeated firing of the three-inch guns on the upper deck.

One aspect of fighting any insurgency is trying to win over the locals who are not sympathetic to the insurgents' cause, but are not necessarily assisting in the fight against them. Vollmer had heard Captain Randolph talk of the Macabebes, an indigenous tribe that was against the insurgency, but were located far upriver. Vollmer volunteered to lead an expedition to make contact with the Macabebes to see how the army could help them to fight the insurgents. At first the commander refused, but after much persuading, August was allowed to try to make contact. A friend, Alfred Vanza, agreed to go with him. They hid in a boat manned by friendly locals underneath a cargo load of nipa grass. At one point they were stopped by some of the insurgents, and the nipa grass was prodded with bayonets. Luckily, Vollmer and Vanza were not detected and their guides did not give them away. Eventually, they made contact with the Macabebes, learning that they were in need of both weapons and ammunition. Vollmer and Vanza stayed with the Macabebes for two days, assessing their situation and promising them the guns they needed.

Vollmer and Vanza returned safely, having found that the weapons and ammunition were available, but that the greater problem of supply was the ability to deliver them to the Macabebes. Again Vollmer volunteered to take charge of the mission to get the weapons and ammunition to the Macabebes. He decided to take the local train as far as it would go and then transfer the weapons to small canoes, which were far more maneuverable in the Philippine rivers. Armed with better weapons, the Macabebes were able quickly to drive the insurgents from the main waterways and, combined with other actions led by General MacArthur (the father of the famed World War II general), the insurgents were defeated and Aguinaldo surrendered. The insurgency was over. In the end, Vollmer had been involved in the taking of Manila and twenty-four major battles and engagements during the Philippine insurgency. On August 17, 1899, Vollmer boarded a ship, ready to cross the Pacific Ocean once again, this time heading for home.

August returned home to a celebratory parade through the streets of San Francisco, followed the next day by the less-than-glamorous process of being mustered out of the army. Vollmer was once again a civilian with no job, but an adequate amount of money saved from both the sale of his interest in the feed store and his year in the military. He arrived home, again to a hero's welcome, where he found his brother had beat him home by two weeks. In fact, he had been home long enough to land a job with the local telephone company. Although Mrs. Vollmer encouraged August to take some time off, August was restless from the long voyage across the ocean and was ready to move on with his life. He quickly landed a job with a local grocery store, delivering groceries via a horse-drawn wagon. It was not what he wanted, but it managed to keep him busy and he was making money again.

Several months later he saw in the local paper that the examination for mail carrier was to be held in Berkeley, a job that interested him more than the delivery of groceries. He tested, passed, and became one of the mail carriers for the little town of Berkeley. He enjoyed the job immensely for it kept him out-of-doors, walking the streets of Berkeley, and he came to be friends with all the people on his delivery route. It also gave him the time to pursue his interests, and the pay was very acceptable for his lifestyle. Although he had toyed with going back into business for himself, he never actively pursued self-employment.

The routine of being a mail deliverer was punctuated one day in 1904, when a railroad flat car broke away from its mooring and raced down the hill toward a local commuter train. Although the train operators were not aware of their loss, several passersby attempted to throw bricks underneath the wheels to stop it. Although the bricks momentarily slowed the train car, it continued to race downhill. Vollmer, seeing all that had occurred, dropped his bag and took off in a run, leaping onto the runaway car. He managed to get to the hand break and pulled back hard. The car slowed and came to a halt. He managed to not only avert what would have no doubt ended in enormous property damage, he most likely saved the lives of dozens of people by his heroic actions. The newspaper reported that "Vollmer is very modest about his performance and refuses to admit that he did anything unusual, despite the fact that his friends are congratulating him on his bravery." (Carte and Carte 1975, 21). Although his reputation was already well established, the railcar incident demonstrated his "grit and courage," so that one day in January 1905, after Vollmer had served as a mail carrier for four years, Mr. Friend Richardson, the editor of the *Berkeley Daily Gazette,* asked August to stop by his office; he had something he wanted to talk about.

A CAREER IN POLICING

Richardson greeted Vollmer, engaged in some small talk, and then got to the point of his request for August's visit. Richardson asked Gus, as he was generally known, to run for town marshal. The current marshal, Charles Kearns, had allowed gambling and opium dens to operate openly in Berkeley, and he failed to enforce the liquor laws. Kerns' defense was that his small force of only three marshals was too small to enforce the laws. The reality, however, was the corrupt nature of policing during that period, and Kern was as corrupt as they came. While the citizenry grew tired of the lack of enforcement, many of the Berkeley political elites grew tired of the corruption, and they saw Vollmer as the right man for the job.

Vollmer had never given policing any consideration, although he had enjoyed his time serving as military police in the Philippines. It was the military experience that Richardson recognized as giving Vollmer credence for the job, coupled with his intimacy with so many citizens of Berkeley from being a mail carrier; he reasoned that Vollmer's chances of winning the election were good. Richardson told Vollmer that he was needed to clean up the dope dens and gambling joints and to staunch the flow of criminals coming into Berkeley from the surrounding cities. Vollmer was hesitant and told Richardson that he needed to think it over. He spoke with family and friends about the idea, and although his family was united in opposition, all of his friends agreed he was the right man for the job. Vollmer acquiesced and Richardson announced his candidacy the next day in an editorial explaining that

> Gus Vollmer is a man of mental acumen and sagacity and his service in the army has particularly fitted him for the job of hunting down and

apprehending criminals. He is a man of great physical powers. He has the physical strength to cope with any criminal and besides he has the necessary grit and courage. (Parker 1961, 41–42)

Another Berkeley newspaper, the *Advocate,* endorsed Vollmer for marshal by explaining, "this man is a Berkeley product and *known of Berkeley men,*" and that "he is ambitious to make a record for himself and the record will be good" (Carte and Carte 1975, 17). The fact that Thomas Richard, the mayor of Berkeley; Jim Kenney, the fire chief; Professor Jacques Loeb, a world-renowned biologist from the University of California; George C. Schmidt, the local postmaster (whom Vollmer had worked for as a letter carrier); and Mr. Friend Richardson, the editor of the *Berkeley Daily Gazette,* along with the Republican Party, were all behind his candidacy, Vollmer handily defeated the long-time incumbent, Marshal Kearns, by a three-to-one vote. On August 15, 1905, at the age of twenty-nine, August Vollmer was installed as the marshal of Berkeley, California.

It should be noted that policing at the time Vollmer began public service as the marshal of Berkeley was not a well-respected career. In fact, it was not even perceived as a career, much less a profession. Policing in America up to that point was rife with political corruption and brutality. As Raymond B. Fosdick, one of the leading police reformers at the turn of the century had argued, the police were "perhaps the most pronounced failure in all our unhappy municipal history" and that "it cannot be denied that politics lies at the root of much of it" (Walker 1977, 3). The political machines controlled much of what policing did, which tended to revolve around the procurement of money through graft. And, in many situations, whether warranted or not, the police resorted to brutal violence over suspects, criminals, and innocent people. As Vollmer himself would later point out, "the only requirement necessary for appointment as policeman was political pull and brute strength…No preliminary training was necessary, and the officers were considered sufficiently equipped to perform their duties if they were armed with a revolver, club and hand-cuffs, and wore a regulation uniform." It was, as Vollmer so succinctly concluded, an "era of incivility, ignorance, brutality and graft."

Vollmer, however, was an innovative individual and according to Douthit, at the time in 1905, "Berkeley proved to be a good place for an innovative police leader to begin his work" (Douthit 1975, 104). And innovate he did. Drawing on his previous military experience, Vollmer quickly identified the problems of the marshal's office, began developing a plan for improvement, and set about working to put that plan into action. His first move was to petition the city council in person to expand the force from three to twelve deputy marshals to develop a night patrol to supplement the existing day patrol. In addition, he asked for the funds to put uniforms on all his deputies; up to that point the Berkeley marshal's deputies simply wore plain clothes and a copper badge. This would be the first of many battles with the city council, for as Vollmer would later write, one of his former officers who, having become a police chief himself, was having difficulties with his own city council:

> What you are suffering right now was endured by me when I first entered police service. It was a constant battle and there was never an occasion in the first few years when I had any more than a bare majority of the Council. It was fight every day and fight every night. (Douthit 1975, 107)

In order to use his force to clean up the town's crime problem, Vollmer began his policing career by ordering a raid on an opium-gambling den. Although he and his men managed to break up the illegal activities despite advance warning obtained by the gambler, those arrested were let go by the court because of insufficient evidence. Vollmer and his men had failed to adequately identify each of the men for they were all Chinese. Although discouraged, Vollmer redoubled his efforts to avoid those kinds of oversights in the future by educating his marshals on how to not only secure an arrest, but to secure the evidence as well. At about this time there were several attempts to bribe Vollmer to steer clear of certain opium dens and gambling parlors, graft that his predecessor had accepted readily. This was simply an effrontery to August and he took it personally. He specifically targeted these dens, ensuring he had the necessary evidence to convict.

Vollmer's early success with implementing his ideas encouraged him to think more about how best to implement the duties and responsibilities of policing. He adopted the use of bicycles to make his force more mobile and, after several timed checks verified it, faster in its response to calls for service. Thus, Vollmer became the first police chief in the nation to implement such a practice. This action put him not only in the local spotlight, often with much derision, but it brought him national attention as well. Also, after hearing about an emergency signal system being used in Los Angles by a private detective, Vollmer visited the city and brought back the concept to Berkeley. After much harassment on his part, the city council floated a $25,000 bond to pay for the emergency light signal system, which was implemented and proved quite successful. Once again, Vollmer had implemented a first for a public police agency and found himself in the national spotlight, this time receiving much praise, even from the locals.

Another innovation developed by Vollmer was through an early study of criminal behavior. As he and his men arrested criminals, he interviewed them to learn not only why they committed crimes, but what kind of crimes they committed and how. Through this careful study he was able to begin classifying the different types of crimes and associating them with certain types of criminals. Vollmer then began writing letters to other police chiefs in the surrounding area to learn about the types of crimes and criminals they were experiencing. In one particular incident, Vollmer found that several ministers' homes were being burglarized in a very similar manner to crimes occurring in Berkeley. One contact with another police department provided Vollmer with a picture and identification of the individual committing these crimes. A short time later the individual was arrested in Berkeley by one of Vollmer's deputies.

As a result of these early experiments, Vollmer adopted the modus operandi file system originally developed by the English constable L. W. Atcherly. Drawing on what he had learned, as well as the knowledge of one of his deputies, Clarence D. Lee, who had been a business clerk before becoming a police officer, Vollmer was able to modify the older Atcherly system of classification and update it into a better and more modern system. Vollmer once again became the first police administrator in America to advance this innovation.

On the morning of April 18, 1906, having served in his position of town marshal a little less than one year, Vollmer was startled awake by his bed moving from side to side and his entire house shaking. Berkeley had just experienced the same earthquake shocks that devastated the city of San Francisco. He ran to wake his mother and told her to leave the house. He then reached his brother Edward's room upstairs where he woke both him and his wife and snatched up his niece, Laura, taking her outside to safety. Once the tremors had stopped, Vollmer ran back inside to get dressed, for he knew there would be plenty of work for his marshals and he needed to get to police headquarters. Once there, he and Jack Le Strange, his executive officer, began riding around Berkeley on their bicycles trying to assess the amount of damage. Eventually their journeys took them to the hill overlooking San Francisco where they witnessed the heavy black smoking rising from the city. San Francisco was on fire. Vollmer knew that the ferryboats and trains would be carrying people fleeing the city and that they would have a refugee problem of epic proportions. The marshals had to act and act fast.

The response organized by the city of Berkeley was as efficient as it could be under the circumstances. They opened up many of the city buildings, the local ice skating rink, and the university itself to shelter incoming refugees. Vollmer put out a call for veterans of the Spanish-American War in the local newspaper, for them to come to his aid to police the refugees. His marshals and these newly deputized veterans would prevent looting, police the refugee camps, and investigate any allegation of criminal behavior. Vollmer's organized response, as part of the larger city response to the earthquake, was efficient and highly effective for dealing with the influx of more than fifty thousand refugees. All of this after only having been in the job of marshal for a little less than a year won him the admiration and respect of all.

The refugees who remained in Berkeley, an estimated 25,000, would translate the small town of 20,000, into a rather large town of 45,000 citizens, creating far more work for Vollmer's growing force. Additional deputies were added to the force, bringing the total number to twenty-six regular deputies and one special officer on the payroll. Their uniforms also finally arrived by early 1907.

Vollmer, during this same time period, sought not only to advance his own police department, but to advance policing in general. In 1906, police chiefs across California organized the California Police Chiefs Association, a forum for police chiefs to share information and innovations. After having only served as the chief police administrator for Berkeley for two years, Vollmer was elected the president of the new association.

In early 1907, another event would spark Vollmer to innovate further, generating a number of ideas that would create a lasting legacy for Vollmer. A dead body found in Berkeley was reported to have been a suicide, but Vollmer thought it might be a homicide. He drew upon his own knowledge and that of his friend at the University of California at Berkeley, Jacques Loeb, a professor of biology, to obtain evidence that it was in fact a homicide. The individual was thought to have committed suicide by taking the poison potassium cyanide. However, Professor Loeb explained that the poison relaxes the body, so there would have been no way in which the dead body could have remained clutching the bottle of pills. The grand jury, however, decided there wasn't enough proof to rule the death a homicide, stating that without a photograph it could not be proved the dead body had been clutching the pill bottle, thus rejecting what Vollmer thought to be incontrovertible evidence. Rather than wallow in self-pity, Vollmer set himself to learning more about the natural sciences and how they could be better applied to the "science" of policing. Vollmer began educating himself, not only in the natural sciences, but also in the areas of criminal psychology, criminology, and criminal investigation, by reading works by such people as Gross, Pinkerton, Garofalo, Ferri, and Lombroso.

By this point it was clear that Vollmer had taken to his position with such relish that he was fast becoming an instrumental leader of the community. In 1907 he became an active member of the Berkeley Charity Organization and the president of the Berkeley SPCA. When his two-year term as marshal was about to expire, he eagerly ran for a second term and won with a wider margin than in his first election. This affirmation of his abilities, mixed with his new-found education, moved him further into his innovation period.

Realizing he shouldn't be the only one on his force with this special knowledge, Vollmer proposed creating a police training school. Vollmer started a police school with the assistance of Walter Peterson, an officer from the Oakland Police Department. Vollmer then drew on his contacts with many of the professors from the university, in order to solicit their support and to teach such topics as "police methods and procedures, fingerprinting, first aid, criminal law, anthropometry, photography, public health, and sanitation, as well as occasional lectures on related subjects in criminology, psychiatry, and anthropology" (Douthit 1975). While the town of Berkeley once again found humor in Vollmer's ideas, his deputies took well to the implementation of his suggestion. As Frank Morn, a leading historian of criminal justice, has pointed out, Vollmer's establishment of the police school "was one year before Philadelphia's School of Instruction was set up, in effect, making Vollmer the father of the police academy movement" (Morn 1995).

As Vollmer's ideas began to prove their worth, the city council of Berkeley voted unanimously to change the position of marshal to that of police chief. Rather than being elected every two years, the office of the chief of police would be an appointed position, serving under the will and pleasure of the mayor and city council indefinitely. The city council, of course, voted to make August Vollmer their first police chief, granting him this appointment on August 13, 1909.

While Vollmer's professional life continued to prosper, his relationship with Lydia Sturdevant, now a respected soprano with the Milan (Italy) Opera Company, did as well. In the summer of 1911 they were married and the newlywed couple honeymooned in Los Angeles. While there, he came to the assistance of two police officers who, while affecting an arrest, had come under a mob attack.

Back at work, Vollmer began lobbying the city council to build a new police headquarters, because his current office was located in the basement of city hall. In addition, he adopted the use of motorcycles to further enhance the mobility of his officers. However, after several years of contending with injuries from motorcycle accidents and having half of his force in the hospital in 1914, he switched his entire force to police cars, becoming the first police department in the nation to be a fully mobile patrol force. Once again, however, he faced much derision for his actions, only to be vindicated later when the entire nation's police agencies moved to motor vehicle patrols.

In the summer of 1916, he added a full-time criminologist, Dr. Albert Schneider, a professor at the University of California Medical School, to be in charge of the department's brand new criminal investigation laboratory. This was another first for Vollmer, the first police crime lab in the United States, making him also the father of American criminalistics. It proved beneficial and Schneider quickly demonstrated his worth when a bomb left by the Mafia was recovered and Schneider's analysis of the bomb led to the arrest of two suspects. This example of the hard sciences being applied to policing would lead Vollmer to create, through a joint effort with the University of California, the first crime lab in the United States.

Around the same time, Vollmer decided to move toward not just trying to educate his officers, but to hire college-educated men for his police department. He placed an advertisement in the local paper that read, "College men wanted for police force. Interesting experience. Learn a new profession. Serve on the Berkeley police force while you go to college. Contact August Vollmer, Chief of Police" (Parker 1961, 100). Employing the intelligence tests used by the U.S. military for World War I, Vollmer screened the college applicants, using some of the earliest screening applications in policing in America. Once again the newspapers derided Vollmer's actions and once again Vollmer was vindicated over time; one of his hires included O. W. Wilson, who not only became the police chief of the Wichita Police Department, but the first dean of the school of criminology at the University of California at Berkeley. In addition, as Wilson explained, "among the 'college cops' were men destined to become the heads of a number of law enforcement agencies, several college and university professors, the Chairman of the California Adult Authority, a psychiatrist, a notable physician, and a Major General in the Army" (Wilson 1953, 99). As Vollmer himself would later explain, what "distinguishes the Berkeley police department from others is the fact that rigid entrance requirements were set up many years ago and have been strictly adhered to since that time" (Douthit 1975, 107).

In addition to hiring college students to be police officers, Vollmer also worked with the University of California at Berkeley to create a three-year course of study for his new hires in police sciences. The curriculum that he had devised nearly a decade earlier and that saw some developments and changes over time was crafted into a very demanding program. In the first year, students would take such classes as physics, chemistry, biology, physiology, anatomy, anthropology, toxicology, and criminology. In the second year, the students would take courses in criminal psychology, psychiatry, police organization and administration, police methods and procedures, and both theoretical and applied criminology. Finally, in the third year they would take such classes as microbiology and parasitology, police microanalysis, public health, first aid, and criminal law. The police and criminology courses were offered exclusively every year from 1916 to 1932 (except for 1927) to Berkeley officers during the summer sessions, but the other courses could be taken throughout the academic year.

In order to advance his thoughts related to a police school, Vollmer, along with Schneider, coauthored an article for the *Journal of Criminal Law and Criminology,* related to the Berkeley Police School in 1916. In that same issue, a Chicago newspaper editorial was reprinted that encouraged policing to develop into a profession and cited the Berkeley police school model as the most efficient means for achieving this. The editorial quoted Vollmer, who compared police training with that of the well-established models for educating doctors and lawyers by explaining that "inefficiency and all the ills that follow in its wake may be expected until this professional status is recognized by the public and prepared for by the press" (Carte and Carte 1975, 28). Vollmer's ideas of policing as a profession were starting to gain traction in America, and not just among a few innovative police chiefs. It was beginning to enter the mainstream and was becoming, albeit slowly, conventional wisdom on how best to create a better police force.

In addition to writing for the *Journal of Criminal Law and Criminology*, Vollmer's friend Professor Kidd was a member of the American Institute of Criminal Law and Criminology, which published the journal out of Northwestern University. He recruited Vollmer to join the association. Vollmer joined without hesitation and threw himself immediately into a leadership role. He was elected the president of the California chapter in 1917 and was elected the national vice president the very next year. At the same time that he was elected president of the California chapter, he was also appointed as an associate editor of the journal, thus establishing a long-term dedication to the journal, for Vollmer would author and coauthor a number of articles for the journal over the next several decades.

Vollmer had always had an interest in children throughout his career. He helped to organize the junior police in the years just before World War I and after the war, the School Boy Patrol. During this time frame, hundreds of boys would join, receiving instruction on military drill, and they became actively involved in community service projects. However, it was toward the study of juvenile delinquents that Vollmer would dedicate much of his time. He fully believed that the criminal behavior one exhibited as an adult had its source in childhood and that the only proper means of deterring future criminality was to deal with juveniles when they were young. As early as 1906 or 1907, Vollmer served notice to his deputies that juveniles were not to be placed behind bars. In 1915, Vollmer ordered the department to begin separating crime statistics into two categories: adult and juvenile. In 1919, he helped organize the first Community Coordinating Council for the Prevention of Delinquency, a series of councils that would be adopted by other jurisdictions throughout the United States.

One of the initiatives of this council was known as the Hawthorne School Study, a study of juveniles in the first six grades in Berkeley. What the study attempted to understand was the relationship between the personal abnormalities of juveniles and their criminal behavior with that of their social and familial conditions. The study found that some juveniles exhibited the same abnormalities, both personal and social, that many adult criminals exhibited. These children, the study argued, as did Vollmer, should be labeled "predelinquents," and they should be afforded attention from the social agencies to avoid the onset of criminal behavior.

Vollmer was largely reflecting the leading movements of the day. These movements were aimed at "saving the child" from poor social conditions and entering a life of criminality and became the popular reforms by those known as the "child savers." Even Vollmer's speeches, such as the one on "predelinquency" that he delivered at the annual meeting of the International Association of Chiefs of Police (IACP) in 1921, reflected this progressive movement when he stated that "when parents are unable, by reason of economic or other conditions, to furnish the proper home training and their offspring acquires delinquent tendencies, or when temptations tear the moral fabric, or where bad habits of defective or neglected children are transmitted to others, the community and the child would profit were it possible to place these potential offenders in parental schools until they are taught how to adjust themselves in a normal environment" (Douthit 1975, 114).

The problems with this popular movement, however, were many. The child savers in reality neglected the rights of children and grossly overestimated their abilities to actually improve the child's situation, thus becoming, in many cases, part of the problem. In addition, it was very much a government intrusion on the private lives of not only the child, but the family unit as a whole. In fact, the interventions were plainly a violation of the Fourth Amendment of the Constitution, namely the protections against illegal seizures. Moreover, Vollmer never fully explained what the interventions by the social-science-trained police officers or others would consist of, sticking rather to very vague language suggesting they work closely with the schools and other agencies. Finally, it has been noted that even when relegated to the role of making referrals, Vollmer was not clear as to whether or not the referrals would be mandatory, hence depriving children of their rights without due process, or merely a suggestion, which could simply be ignored.

Vollmer's dedication to developing the police sciences and his work ethic caused him to spend little time at home with his wife Lydia. At the same time, Lydia continued singing with the Milan Opera as well as giving voice lessons to others. Their lives were vastly different and both were wrapped up in their own respective careers. The marriage of nearly a decade began to falter, for they had simply drifted apart. In 1920, although it was unusual for the time, they quietly filed for a divorce and they both went their separate ways.

Remaining wrapped up in his work, Vollmer continued to find ways to innovate. In the early 1920s, one of Vollmer's lasting innovations was his initiative to develop a means of screening his police applicants based on the physical responses the body exhibits when lying. Vollmer called on one of his college cops and future psychiatrist, John Larson, to develop a machine that would do just that. In coordination with Robert Gesell of the Physiology Department at the university, they were able to develop a rudimentary "lie-detector" machine. Vollmer became its first subject, with Larson administering the test. The test was successful as Larson was able to catch Vollmer lying on two occasions. Additional tests supported this anecdotal test; thus the lie detector became not only a means of screening police applicants, but for determining if suspected criminals had committed a crime. Although the polygraph was never fully accepted by the judicial system, it has remained an integral part of the police hiring process, because well over 90 percent of police agencies screen their applicants with the machine.

In 1921, Vollmer's next idea was the creation of a radio communication system that could be placed in the police cars so that headquarters could communicate with officers while on patrol. Vollmer once again put his college-educated police officers to work and they adapted a crystal radio set for use in the Model-T Ford patrol cars. Now Vollmer could communicate with his officers in the field, thus providing him the ability to respond faster to crimes and calls for service. Once again, the Berkeley Police Department was the innovator for something that would rapidly become a staple of American policing.

That same year, Vollmer, on a visit to San Francisco, happened to run into his former girlfriend, Pat Fell. They went out to dinner. Pat had heard much about August in the San Francisco newspapers. Although they picked up where they had left off in their relationship, Vollmer feared that his work ethic would get in the way of a relationship. Despite this hesitation, he invited Pat to his home for dinner the following week, and they continued to date in this manner until their marriage in the summer of 1924.

Vollmer's reputation and that of the Berkeley Police Department continued to rise. One of the premier police authorities of the day, Raymond B. Fosdick, praised the Berkeley police force in his book *American Police Systems*, which was published in 1920. Fosdick explained that between 1908 and 1915, the city of Berkeley saw a 73 percent increase in population, but criminal complaints only rose 14 percent during the same time period. Even more impressive was the fact that stolen property had actually decreased by 28 percent during the time frame. Although Vollmer consistently tried to add more officers to his police force, he was only able to add five additional officers during this time period. Fosdick credited Vollmer's movement of the police department to full motorized patrol for keeping the crime problem in check.

Because of the number of innovations on the part of Vollmer and his willingness to speak out on behalf of the Berkeley Police Department, the department—through Vollmer—had become an active member of both the California Association of Chiefs of Police and the International Association of Chiefs of Police (IACP). Having served as the president of the California association in 1908, he began attending meetings of the IACP in the mid-1910s, giving a number of speeches on police work. These early speeches were quite often filled not only with his convictions of educating police officers and adapting the hard sciences and technology to policing, but also with rhetoric that the police should be seen as professional social workers.

At the 1919 convention, Vollmer gave a speech titled "The Policeman as a Social Worker." It was assuredly just as controversial then as it would be if given today. Vollmer argued, however, that police officers must engrain themselves in the community, recognize the needs of individuals in the neighborhoods they police, especially the needs of juveniles, and work toward providing and coordinating the necessary social resources to improve the individual and the quality of life in each neighborhood. These ideas are highly reflective of the concepts in policing that became popular in the 1980s and 1990s in American policing, referred to under the rubric "community policing." His advocacy for these and other ideas and, more importantly, his outspokenness on policing overall, would earn him election to the presidency of the IACP in 1921.

At the annual convention in June 1922, presiding as president and giving the annual president's speech, Vollmer advocated for the creation of a centralized national bureau of criminal records and statistics. His argument was that as technology improved and criminals became more mobile, agencies must have a way of communicating with each other to know if a certain individual entering their community had a criminal past or was wanted for a crime in another jurisdiction. In addition, simply having reliable statistics on crime in various towns and cities would give the police agency the information necessary to determine how best to deploy the police to fight crime more effectively. His advocacy would never wane and in time the IACP would adopt a system that eventually gave way to the Federal Bureau of Investigation's criminal records and fingerprint system.

As Vollmer was recognized by this time as a leading authority in policing, several representatives from the Los Angeles Police Department, an agency facing numerous allegations of corruption and brutality, came to recruit him for police chief. August declined the offer, but the Mayor of Los Angeles was both persistent and desperate. Eventually a deal was worked out where Vollmer would be "on loan" to the police department for one year, while his administrative staff in Berkeley would continue to operate the police department. Thus, on August 4, 1923, August Vollmer became the police chief of one of the largest police departments in the United States.

Vollmer's first day on the job was taken up with a reception held in his honor. This was not how Vollmer wanted to start on the job; almost immediately he was inundated with the politics of the job, something that was far less prevalent in Berkeley. In fact, Vollmer quickly learned that the political influence had control of most of the department and the city administration. In much the same manner as in his past, Vollmer immediately set about trying to identify the problems of the police department by beginning a study of the issues through both a formal review and with private contacts with the criminal underworld. As in Berkeley, he also organized a vice squad and wanted this squad to fly under the radar of political influence by being untouchable. He gave the responsibility of the unit to a no-nonsense officer, Clyde Plummer.

Vollmer also tried to apply the same methods of hiring qualified candidates and educating them for the job in Los Angeles. He implemented the Army alpha-rating intelligence test not only to new candidates, but to the entire force of three thousand officers. He then used the information for purposes of reassigning certain officers to certain duties. He also began moving the police department toward the adoption of a police academy. The new police school would soon develop ties with the University of

Southern California, and the university's extension division would soon offer courses in police administration.

It did not take long before these changes and his crackdowns on vice operations began giving Vollmer undue political grief. Those who were affected by the attempts at shutting down the vice by loss of graft quickly crafted a way to get rid of Vollmer. They implemented a civil service examination that was structured so the highest score by those who took the test would become the police chief. The political hacks figured Vollmer, with nothing more than a grade school education, wouldn't be able to pass. Vollmer took the test, writing for eight hours, and handily scored the highest score of the seventy-five individuals who took the test. Vollmer would remain the chief of police of Los Angeles.

In the meantime, Vollmer effected a review of the Los Angeles City Jail, of which he was ultimately in charge, and found the conditions to be deplorable. He pushed for the building of a new jail by appealing to both the mayor and the city council. His appeal was for the building of a modern jail, one that would "consist of one-story buildings with modern plumbing and kitchen facilities and with space for growing flowers and vegetables" (Douthit 1975, 117). He also made the proposal that to cut costs, the prisoners should be the ones to build the new jail as they would stand to benefit the most. The mayor and city council, however, thought the proposal was too soft on the criminals and immediately rejected the idea. However, a grand jury that investigated the conditions of the city jail found the same deplorable conditions Vollmer had witnessed. They ordered the city to build a new jail in the manner that Vollmer had called for and to use prison labor. Vollmer's prison was an early concept of the prison farm, a prison style that would become popular during the 1920s and 1930s in America.

Vollmer made it to the end of his temporary tenure as the Police Chief of Los Angeles. In the summer of 1924, his report on the Los Angeles Police Department was issued, and in it he made a number of recommendations for its improvement. The report was met with mixed reviews and controversy, and the rousing cry became "the first of September will be the end of August." Vollmer's tenure had come to an end and he returned to his comfortable position as police chief in Berkeley. The report was filed away and ignored for twenty-five years. In 1949, the report was pulled from the shelf and a number of the recommendations were acted on. While simply too far ahead of their time, their adoption in the 1950s coincided with the movement toward a professionalized police system under Chief William H. Parker. Once again, Vollmer's ideas were vindicated. This time, the vindication was more personal and one he relished.

Vollmer, having stepped down from his one-year appointment as president of the IACP and knowing that his departure from Los Angeles was imminent, found the timing to be right, and he proposed to Pat Fell, who accepted. They were married on July 23, 1924, and moved into a new house in the Berkeley hills. Unlike his previous marriage, this one would stand the test of time, as Pat's interests were in her husband and she became his confidante in his work as a police executive. This proved helpful for his reputation as a leading police expert, and his willingness to assist the Los Angeles Police Department gave other agencies the idea of calling on Vollmer for assistance.

Many would call on Vollmer for assistance in a variety of ways. One of those calls was from Alameda County, the county in which Berkeley was located. The district attorney's office made it a policy to send their assistant deputy district attorneys to work in solid and respectable departments to gain experience in noncorrupt jurisdictions. In 1923, one of the new assistants sent to work in Berkeley was Earl Warren. Vollmer and Warren would work on a number of projects together, and they developed a working friendship. In 1925, when Warren was elected the district attorney himself, he continued to work with Vollmer on a number of projects. For instance, when raids were ordered against bootlegging, prostitution, or gambling operations, Warren would call upon Vollmer and his police force because he knew they were not corrupt themselves and, hence, would properly effect the arrests. In addition, whenever evidence needed to be collected and preserved to ensure it wasn't tampered with, Warren would call on Vollmer's police department. Thus, Warren was heavily influenced by Vollmer in his understanding of professional police work. When he became the California attorney general, he again called on Vollmer to help establish an education program for all California law enforcement officers. One can only speculate as to the influence that Vollmer had on the future governor of California and Chief Justice of the U.S. Supreme Court, but there is little doubt that he heavily influenced that young assistant district attorney.

Another individual who would call on Vollmer during this same time was J. Edgar Hoover, the acting director of the Federal Bureau of Investigation. He visited the Berkeley Police Department to review Vollmer's records system, as well as to learn first-hand about Vollmer's other innovations. Although Hoover was clever enough to learn from others and determine how best to apply the innovations of others to his bureau, he was politically astute enough to avoid giving anyone else credit. Therefore, it is not known how much influence Vollmer had on Hoover, but they did maintain a professional correspondence over the ensuing years.

In the summer of 1926, Vollmer received another request to conduct a police survey, this time from the Havana Police Department in Cuba. He requested temporary leave from the Berkeley City Council and, once it was granted, he and Pat traveled to Havana. He spent time investigating the status of the agency and authored a report with a number of recommendations for the department's improvement. Upon his return, he found a similar request for assistance awaiting him from the Detroit Police Department. He conducted the study of Detroit's department and again returned to find more requests. One of the requests was from as far away as Nanking, China. This time he sent one of his trusted captains to conduct the police survey.

The next police survey request to which he responded came from the Kansas City Police Department in Missouri, where he recommended that, because of political corruption, the police department should be placed under the authority of a state commission. No sooner was this survey completed than Vollmer received another request from the city of Chicago. It was this survey that opened up a number of new doors for Vollmer. The first door was to serve as the police chief of Chicago, which he declined. His experience in Los Angeles had taught him the true value of remaining Berkeley's police chief.

The second door opened when Vollmer received a call from Robert Hutchins, president of the University of Chicago, who offered Vollmer an appointment as Professor of Police Administration in the Department of Political Science. Once again, Vollmer requested a leave of absence from Berkeley, and again it was granted. In 1929, Vollmer served as the first professor of police administration in America, a post he would hold for two academic years. During this time frame, Vollmer would also assist in the organization of a regional peace officer's association, the creation of the Illinois State Identification Bureau, and with the assistance of his graduate student Spencer Parratt, the completion of a survey of all the police departments within a fifty-mile radius of Chicago.

The final door opened was to serve on President Herbert Hoover's National Law Observance and Enforcement Commission, which was directed by George Wickersham and was commonly referred to as the "Wickersham Commission." Vollmer served as the primary consultant and lead author for volume 14, the report on *The Police*. The majority of the work on this monograph was completed while he served as a professor in Chicago. One benefit to his having moved to the University of Chicago was the fact that he was given two graduate students from the Department of Political Science, David Monroe and Earle Garrett, who helped Vollmer prepare his report.

Recognizing the valuable asset they had in their own backyard and having worked with Vollmer over the previous two decades, the University of California in his hometown of Berkeley offered him a similar position. He began his tenure in the spring of 1932. Recognizing the difficulties of managing both careers, feeling satisfied with his run as a police executive and excited about the prospects of continuing a new career as a professor of Police Administration, Vollmer resigned his position as chief of police of Berkeley, a post he had held for twenty-six years.

Rather than immediately moving into his teaching duties, he and Pat traveled the world for one year, visiting Honolulu, Tokyo, Manila, Singapore, Amsterdam, Glasgow, and London. Along the way, he mixed business with pleasure as he visited all of the major city police departments along the way.

His reputation, which had become international, preceded him wherever he went.

It was also around this time that Vollmer's career would earn him several prestigious awards. The first came in 1929 when he received the Harmon Foundation Medal, which recognized him for the most notable contribution to the social sciences in the previous year. The second, awarded in 1931, was the Benjamin Ide Wheeler "Distinguished Citizen of Berkeley" award. Finally, the third award was from the Academy of Science, which awarded him the "Public Welfare Medal," in recognition of his application of scientific principles to police administration.

Timeline of Police Innovations Credited to August Vollmer

In 1906, the department installed a basic records system (One of the first in the United States)

- In 1906, installed the first Modus Operandi (MO) System.
- In 1907, first use of scientific investigation (Kelinschmidt case—analysis of blood, fibers and soil).
- In 1907, the department's police school was established. It included instruction from professors on such subjects as the law and evidence procedures. This was the first school of its kind in the world and had a far-reaching effect on law enforcement.
- In 1911, organized the first Police Motorcycle Patrol.
- In 1913, changed to automobiles for patrolling.
- In 1916, Chief Vollmer established the first School of Criminology at University of California, at Berkeley. Chief Vollmer became a strong advocate of college-educated police officers.
- In 1918, began using intelligence tests in recruiting police officers.
- In 1920, the first lie detector instrument was developed at University of California and used by our department.
- In 1921, began using a psychiatric screening in recruitment.
- In 1923, the first Junior Traffic Police Program was established.
- In 1924, established one of the first single fingerprint systems.
- In 1925, established our first Crime Prevention Division and hired the first police woman.

Source: City of Berkeley, CA, http://www.ci.berkeley.ca.us/police/history/history.html.

A CAREER IN ACADEMIA

What had made Vollmer's second career as a professor possible was the receipt of a Rockefeller Foundation grant for a project regarding the administration of criminal justice, which was obtained by the Bureau of Public Administration and the Department of Political Science. The project was able to lure away Herman Adler from the University of Chicago, and it obtained the appointment of Hugh Fuller, an expert on criminal statistics. Vollmer was to teach courses in police administration and conduct research in his area to support a new group major in criminology that was launched in the fall of 1933. The group "major" idea was established as a topical area of concentration that was housed in an existing academic discipline. The study of police sciences, in this case the topical area, or group major, was housed in the Department of Political Science.

Vollmer had returned to Berkeley from his work-styled vacation around the world and took up his duties at the University of California at Berkeley as Professor of Police Administration. Just prior to his assumption of his professorial duties, the report he had worked on for the Wickersham Commission was finally published. Although Vollmer's report presented a police movement that was beginning to adopt professional standards like other bona fide professions, the other Wickersham Commission report on the police that explored police corruption, titled *Lawlessness in Law Enforcement*, was much more damning of the police in general. Vollmer's portion of the overall report on *The Police* was very much a compilation of all he had learned from his police department surveys and was highly reflective of Vollmer's philosophy of policing. He made numerous recommendations for the betterment and professionalization of the police, including the removal of the police from politics, an independent police chief, higher recruitment and training standards, the adoption of modern communication and record systems, improved working conditions for the police, and the use of an active crime prevention unit. The response to Vollmer's recommendations was limited, for it was not so much that his recommendations were shunned or disputed, it was simply a reality that during the Great Depression municipalities did not have the funds to implement any of the recommendations, and the report was relegated to the shelves to gather dust. Even the recommendation to improve police working conditions could not be maintained in his own police department; two months after his retirement, the city of Berkeley cut the pay of its police officers.

One of his first actions as a professor was to assist with the development of the first college-level training program in the country, not at the University of California, but at San Jose State College in San Jose, California. The program had actually developed out of an earlier collaboration with Earl Warren, in 1930. They had combined to create a police science training program. The first course began as an extension course taught at San Jose

Teachers College. At the time Vollmer became a professor, the program was moving toward becoming a two-year academic program, and Vollmer was called in to help develop the program. The program he helped create was very reflective of Vollmer's ideas of the well-educated police officer. According to Douthit:

> The first year requirements consisted of courses in police administration, physical education, psychology, English, chemistry, physical science, and political science with electives in commerce (typing and stenography) and physics. In the second year students took advanced courses in police administration, sociology, physical education (boxing and wrestling), introduction to psychiatry, bacteriology (micro-analysis), student health (first aid), political science, and American institutions, with electives in commerce, public health, and foreign languages. (1975, 116)

The curriculum leaned more broadly and away from police-specific classes, for as Vollmer explained, "After spending nearly a quarter of a century instructing policemen I have come to the conclusion that the mechanics of the profession are of less importance than a knowledge of human beings" (Douthit 1975, 117). The program was finally established in 1935 and was known as the San Jose State College Police School.

Vollmer's desire to create a program in higher education for police did not stop with the San Jose program, but continued with the program in which he was currently teaching. While it was more oriented toward concepts of administration and criminological theory, Vollmer envisioned a program that would consist of more police-specific courses, such as police science, that would ultimately lead police officers toward a bachelor's degree in policing. Vollmer was, however, also realistic about the prospects of that happening. He knew that a degree program tailored specifically to police was best left to the future. In the meantime, he focused his energies on professionalizing the police and training future police administrators.

In 1933, he was given the opportunity to make an assessment of police progress since the turn of the century by the *Journal of Criminal Law and Criminology*. He took on the task with relish and spoke at the end about the changes in policing, of which he had been an instrumental part, and what was beginning to be recognized as the police professionalization movement. Vollmer highlighted the fact in the article titled, "Police Progress in the Past Twenty-Five Years," when he explained that "in no other branch of government have such remarkable changes been made as those made in the field of police organization and administration during the last quarter of a century" (Douthit 1975, 110). He continued:

> One can scarcely believe that such great advances could be made in so short a time. It is a far cry from the old politically-controlled police department to the modern, scientifically-operated organization. Under the old system, police

officials were appointed through political affiliations and because of them. They were frequently unintelligent and untrained; they were distributed through the area to be policed according to the hit-or-miss system and without adequate means of communication; they had little or no record system; their investigation methods were obsolete; and they had no conception of the preventive possibilities of the service.

Vollmer would specifically cite advances in ten specific areas that, according to Samuel Walker, a leading police scholar, included five dealing "with internal administration and five dealing with scientific crime fighting" (Douthit 1977, 135). Walker pointed out that the article demonstrated a strong shift in Vollmer's thinking about policing. In just over a decade, Vollmer had left behind the rhetoric of the police officer as social worker and had moved to the more contemporary and conventional idea of the police officer as crime fighter. Thus, the application of bureaucratic principles to policing (the first five advances), combined with the latest technology (the second five advances), were all geared toward equipping the police with the proper organizational structure and tools to combat crime. The police professionalization movement was not only well entrenched, but it had also become well defined.

Over the ensuing years, between teaching and writing various articles and book reviews, Vollmer tackled the arduous chore of writing several books. The first major book at the time was coauthored with Alfred E. Parker, a local schoolteacher and friend of Vollmer's. The book was titled *Crime and the State Police* and was published in 1935. It was largely based on Vollmer's changing beliefs about policing. He had moved from advocating for the police officer to be a social worker to seeing the police officer as a professional crime fighter using all of the tools available to him, ranging from the latest in technology to the scientific study of criminals. In order to further the latter, Vollmer saw the centralization of police forces as a far more efficient means of effecting this professionalization. Writing to the president of the Los Angeles Bar Association in 1934, Vollmer explained that "it is my opinion that a single state police force which would eliminate all other police forces in the state would be much more efficient and economical than the multitudinous police units that are to be found in California" (Douthit 1975, 118). As Vollmer so succinctly declared, "we could wipe out of existence all constables, sheriffs, village marshals, municipal police forces, the state motor vehicle police force, and a number of other state forces that have police power, and substitute a carefully selected and well-trained body of men to do their work." One does have to wonder if Vollmer ever considered the fact that were this plan implemented, his beloved position of chief of the Berkeley Police Department would have been one of the positions eliminated.

Regardless, this new model of centralized control of police forces at the state level was the thrust of the new book. In the publication, Vollmer and Parker praised the efficiency of the European police forces, all of which were highly centralized and controlled. In particular, they singled out the Guardia Civil of Spain, which was a military-structured national police force, as being an exemplary agency.

Although Vollmer was serving as a professor during the early thirties, he still advocated for various programs that he had supported as a police chief. One such program was the centralized federal program of fingerprint records. In 1935, a new initiative was pushed by the Federal Bureau of Investigations (FBI), for all Americans to submit their fingerprints to the FBI's Civil Identification Division. Vollmer actually had advocated this same program in 1930 while still the police chief, but it was not part of a national campaign, rather simply an insider's request and one that Vollmer made to the citizens of Berkeley. More than two thousand citizens submitted their fingerprints to the FBI. In 1935, however, the FBI launched a national campaign and Professor Vollmer got behind the four-month campaign. To highlight the initiative, Robert G. Sproul, president of the University of California at Berkeley, posed for a photograph with Vollmer before submitting his own fingerprints at the university-based fingerprint station. The net result was more than fifty-two thousand sets of prints forwarded to the FBI's Civil Identification Division.

Perhaps Vollmer's greatest contribution to the research of policing, and what many see as his greatest contribution to policing overall, was the publication of his book *The Police and Modern Society* in 1936. The book was written in association with the Bureau of Public Administration, one of the grant recipients under which he was teaching at the University of California at Berkeley. The book presented a holistic treatment of Vollmer's views regarding the police role in society and its organizational structure. The book was divided into six major sections. The first looked at major crimes and the role of the police in relation to them. It is here that Vollmer's earlier notions of the police officer as a social worker had completely disappeared, for Vollmer clearly saw the proper role of the police officer as that of crime fighter. His second area was vice control. He argued the police were not the proper agency to deal with the problems of vice and that it was this type of enforcement that often led many departments into corruption and lawlessness. Vollmer advocated that other social institutions should be responsible for restraining such vices as gambling, prostitution, and alcoholism and that the police should only become involved when a crime had occurred.

The next area that Vollmer explored was the police role of controlling traffic. While Vollmer stated that it was a role and function of the police, he clearly was not an advocate of this role and found it a duty that was mostly beneath the professional crime-fighting police officer. The next area was general services, which Vollmer recognized as a necessary duty of the police officer, and, in the next chapter, he advocated heavily for the creation of crime prevention units, because he believed a true profession would work to prevent crime before it occurs. Finally, Vollmer focused on the proper means of recruiting, hiring, promoting, and organizing police personnel. His conclusions and recommendations for the future were once again highly reflective of Vollmer's passion, the education of the police. Vollmer truly believed that most of the problems with the police and all of the problems they faced could be overcome through education, training, and the application of scientific principles to all facets of policing.

RETIREMENT

Vollmer retired from the University at the end of the spring term in 1937. He moved all his papers and books into an office at his home on Euclid Avenue, where he took up writing about criminology and police administration. In his retirement, Vollmer limited his travels and tended to stay closer to home. In fact, wherever and whenever possible, he preferred to work entirely out of his home office. He conducted several seminars in his home on how to conduct police surveys with several of the senior officers of the Berkeley Police Department, through correspondence he consulted and advised police chiefs, many of whom were his former officers, from all over the country, and he engaged in other teaching and writing projects.

In 1939, Vollmer saw one of the things he had championed not only as a police chief, but as a professor, come to fruition: the establishment of his beloved police studies as a full major. After his retirement from academia, David Barrow, the chairman of the Political Science Department, and Professor A. M. Kidd attempted to keep Vollmer's ideas alive. It took more than a year, but they finally had gained the support of the university president, Robert Sproul, to create a freestanding department. Prior to this move, the university used the "group major" concept, which allowed for a major area of study to be housed within a host department of discipline. Hence, police studies had become the group major within the Department of Political Science. Now, however, it was rolled out from under political science to become its own department. As Morn explained, this move "was a significant development, and it testifies to the academic political skills of Vollmer" (1995, 37). Still further, with Vollmer's lobbying, O. W. Wilson, Vollmer's protégé, became the chair of the newly created department. Wilson moved to Berkeley in the summer of 1939, in advance of the program, beginning his own academic career in the fall of that year.

Vollmer continued to remain very active in terms of academic pursuits. In the early 1940s, he contacted the Charles C. Thomas Publishing Company and persuaded them to begin a book series on law enforcement. This line of books would become literally a reference shelf for police departments across the country on everything from patrol work and crime scene investigations to police administration. Also, popular at the time were books aimed at the young teen crowd that told true-life police stories. Pulp magazines were rife with these types of stories, and J. Edgar Hoover himself had written (with assistance) a number of these FBI crime file books. Vollmer agreed to write one with Alfred E. Parker, a former student at Berkeley who became good friends with August in the 1920s and would not only write books with Vollmer, but also several books about Vollmer after his death. The book was titled *Crime, Crooks, and Cops,* and was published in 1937. Vollmer did not look back favorably on this book's publication for he once reflected that the book was "in a class with Heine Faust pot-boilers—only much worse!" (Carte and Carte 1975, 81). Although these books remained very popular during the 1940s and 1950s, the book did little to enhance Vollmer's reputation.

As America entered World War II, several wars now removed from the Spanish-American War, Vollmer rendered his services once again. He became active in a group that went by the lengthy title of the Pacific Coast Committee on American Principles and Fair Play. The organization was aimed at reducing the hostility against the Japanese community living in America. After the surprise attack on the United States by Japan in Pearl Harbor, Hawaii, on December 7, 1941, the citizenry became very hostile toward all Japanese, and the government responded by relocating all Japanese to internment camps spread mostly throughout the American southwest. The committee, while not opposed to the relocation of the Japanese, attempted to alleviate the animosity toward the Japanese by placing the internment under civilian control. It was at the time under military control, where it would reside for the remainder of the war. In addition to the committee's attempts at changing the agency responsible for oversight, the group also "fought the efforts by some groups to pass legislation discriminatory against the Nisei, including efforts to remove their citizenship." The committee disbanded in 1945, upon the unconditional surrender of Japan to the United States.

Although the war had put Vollmer's ideas for a school of criminology at the University of California at Berkeley on the back burner, he continued to move forward with his advocacy of this academic field, especially as a means of educating police officers. Shortly after the attack on Pearl Harbor and America's entry into the war, Vollmer hosted a meeting in his home on Euclid Avenue to talk about the future of police education. The meeting was a group of powerful, although not necessarily like-minded, individuals interested in police education, including Benjamin W. Pavone, the chairman of the Peace Officers Training Division of San Francisco Junior College; William Wiltberger and Willard Schmidt from San Jose State; O. W. Wilson, University of California at Berkeley; and V. A. Leonard of Washington State College. There was much debate regarding the emphasis that should be placed on educating police officers: whether it should be more theoretical and academic in nature or if it should be more practitioner-oriented. While the debate was never fully settled and in many respects continues to this very day, those in attendance did agree that a society for the advancement of criminology should be formed. The decision was made to call it the Association of Heads of College Police Schools, and Vollmer was nominated to be the first president of the association. O. W. Wilson would serve as president the next year, a position he remained in for the next seven years, despite his own service in the military.

Part of the reason for this lengthy tenure had to do with the war, which interfered some with the plans for the society. In 1946, with the war over, a meeting was held in Berkeley, and the name of the society was changed to the Society for the Advancement of Criminology. The society continued to meet yearly in Berkeley until 1956, the year after Vollmer's death. The next year, the conference was held in Los Angeles and the name of the organization was once again changed to the name it still holds today: the American Society of Criminology (ASC). In 1959, the Society created the August Vollmer award, naming it for its founder, and it has been awarded annually to recognize outstanding research in the field of criminology.

Although the war had ended and America was entering a time of prosperity and hope, Vollmer's life was met with one of those inevitable tragedies; Pat, his most trusted companion, died. Vollmer was greatly affected by her passing for she truly was his life companion, but, as in the past, he busied himself by throwing himself into his work. It was at this point that he began the research and writing for his final book, perhaps his second most respected book. It was published in 1949 and was titled *The Criminal*. While his most renowned book, *Police and Modern Society,* was focused on police administration, this book was aimed at categorizing and dealing with the theoretical issues surrounding criminality. In his early years, Vollmer had constantly been in search of one theory to explain criminality. As he progressed in age he realized that there was not necessarily one theory to explain all crimes and that the nature of crime and criminality was vastly complex. The book, thus, became a compendium of various theories drawn from a number of disciplines. He divided the book into chapters on biological, physiological, psychological, sociopsychological, and pathological theories. Finally, at the end of the book he dealt with the various aspects of law enforcement and how it related to crime and criminality. Vollmer concluded that more research was needed, but he held out hope that medical science would be a significant contributor to understanding criminality and that the key to prevention remained in early childhood.

As Vollmer entered the new decade of the 1950s, he was able to witness one of his early endeavors finally come to fruition. In 1951, the University of California at Berkeley established the School of Criminology. This accomplishment was the result of his decades of working toward bringing a police education program to the college campus. His former police officer and student, O. W. Wilson, was appointed as the first dean of the new school.

Although Vollmer was now finally able to witness the establishment of what would become, in part, his legacy, he was now in his mid-seventies and beginning to suffer from Parkinson's disease. He was fast losing the ability to take care of himself and he was also losing his sight. Within several years he was diagnosed with cancer, and he confided to several close friends that "he would never become a bed patient, a person who would be helpless and a concern to other people" (Carte and Carte 1975, 82). He also did not want to take the numerous medications that he was prescribed. These feelings became so strong, that in the end, he committed suicide with the same revolver he had carried as the police chief of Berkeley. Vollmer died on November 4, 1955; he was seventy-nine. Despite having been married twice, he left behind no children, only a legacy that continues to reverberate through the years.

In the editorial pages of a brand new police journal, published shortly after Vollmer's death, the editors noted that "the Vollmer system of police administration attracted national attention, illuminating the way for an emerging profession and launching the American police services into a period of transition, the full implications of which are not yet generally understood" (Douthit 1975, 120). Since the time that was written, that has changed. The full breadth and depth of Vollmer's contribution to the police has not been lost on those scholars of policing, and in both the criminal justice and criminology disciplines, academicians continue to attribute much of the professionalization movement to Vollmer. Despite this fact, little has been written beyond the scholarly endeavors about his life.

In the early 1960s, Alfred E. Parker, Vollmer's friend and coauthor on several books, would begin the research to write a biography of Vollmer. Drawing on his previous conversations with Vollmer that had developed through both his professional and personal relationship, Parker was able to write the only true biography on Vollmer's life written to date. The book, while an adequate overview of Vollmer's early years and his time as a police chief, was written for the ten- to twelve-year-old crowd. Parker, as he reached his later years, once again picked up the idea of reviewing Vollmer's life through a book detailing the history of the Berkeley Police Department. This book, aimed toward the adult reader, did a good job of focusing on Vollmer's life, but was limited because of the fact the book attempted to be more about the police department, rather than its first police chief.

Thus, it would appear that Vollmer's legacy is one not forgotten in the field of criminal justice and especially in policing, but it is oddly lacking in a general historical sense. Nathan Douthit, writing in 1975, clearly stated that "it is certain that when historians set out to explore the development of police professionalism, one of the most important figures will be the man who served as the head of the police department in Berkeley, California, for over a quarter of a century—August Vollmer."

Gene and Elaine Carte, writing that same year on police professionalism, stated that "through his writings and teaching and by the example of his own department—probably the most effective and creative ever developed—Vollmer made the best case possible for the 'new policing'" (Carte and Carte 1975, 3). As they further explained, "in a field in which leadership abilities are traditionally preeminent, Vollmer was the outstanding leader of the first half of th[e twentieth] century, and his own skills were inextricably related to the image of policing that he created." As a police chief with a cadre of "college cops," he was able to leave a legacy through the numerous officers he educated, trained, and influenced, who left the Berkeley Police Department to become police chiefs in their own right. These included such notables as George Brereton, William F. Dean, Walter A. Gordon, John D. Holstrom (later a Berkeley police chief), V. A. Leonard, William Wiltberger, and, of course, O. W. Wilson. In terms of academia, as a professor, he again had the same kind of impact on the field through his protégés' creation of numerous college programs in police studies. These included Frank Boolsen, who helped create the University of Toledo's program; Oscar G. Olander, who pushed for the program at Michigan State College; George Brereton's program at San Jose State; V. A. Leonard's program at Washington State College; and, once again, O. W. Wilson's leadership in Vollmer's own program at Berkeley. In addition, two of these protégés, V. A. Leonard and O. W. Wilson, went on to write, like Vollmer, highly influential books, *A Theory of Police Administration* and *Police Administration,* respectively.

In terms of the program of police studies in higher education, Vollmer's legacy would perhaps reach the farthest. He helped to create a major in police studies and subsequently a School of Criminology at the University of California at Berkeley, and these types of programs were emulated far and wide across America. While Vollmer always envisioned them as a training mechanism for police officers, the dispute between the programs being practitioner-oriented or theoretically driven would grow, but would contribute greatly to Vollmer's legacy. While Vollmer helped create what would become the American Society of Criminology and served as its first president, the field of criminology came to focus more heavily on sociological theory by the 1960s as did the society. Those in the ASC who had felt, like Vollmer, that criminology should focus more on the police practitioner, broke away and created their own organization: The International Association of Police Professors (IAPP). As the focus on police, courts, and corrections developed in the 1960s and came to be known as "criminal justice," the IAPP changed its name to the Academy of Criminal Justice Sciences (ACJS), becoming the premier organization for analyzing the American system of justice. Although Vollmer was not there at its founding, it was clearly in line with his vision for higher education, and, thus, a part of his extensive legacy.

Vollmer left America an extensive legacy, one that continues to reverberate nearly a century later. Moving the police from the political era into the reform era, as it has been called, through his adherence to the professionalization movement, coupled with his devotion to educating the police, have largely been achieved. Moving police education from the realm of practitioner skill training to that of higher education is most evident today in the number of police officers with advanced degrees and the number of criminal justice and criminology programs across the United States, but perhaps his greatest vision for the future, that every police officer would be required to have a degree in the police sciences and that armed with this knowledge they would have the greatest ability to control crime and disorder, has not been achieved. Yet, it remains a goal for the future, a future born out of the innovative police reformer, August Vollmer.

NOTE

The author thanks Ronald "Chip" Burns of Texas Christian University for agreeing to give up his right to author this chapter on the life of August Vollmer. I also thank my graduate assistant, Hector Esparza, for his invaluable help on researching the life of August Vollmer. To both of you, I am most gratefully indebted.

FURTHER READING

Carte, Gene E., and Elaine H. Carte. 1975. *Police Reform in the United States: The Era of August Vollmer, 1905–1932.* Berkeley, CA: University of California Press.

Douthit, Nathan. 1975. August Vollmer, Berkeley's first chief of police, and the emergence of police professionalism. *California Historical Quarterly* 54:101–24.

Morn, Frank. 1995. *Academic Politics and the History of Criminal Justice Education.* Westport, CT: Greenwood Press.

Parker, Alfred E. 1961. *Crime Fighter: August Vollmer.* New York: Macmillan Company.

Parker, Alfred E. 1972. *The Berkeley Police Story.* Springfield, IL: Charles C. Thomas.

Vollmer, August. 1936. *The Police and Modern Society.* Berkeley, CA: University of California Press.

Vollmer, August. 1949. *The Criminal.* Brooklyn, NY: The Foundation Press.

Vollmer, August, and Alfred E. Parker. 1937. *Crime, Crooks, & Cops.* New York: Funk & Wagnalls.

Walker, Samuel. 1977. *A Critical History of Police Reform: The Emergence of Professionalism.* Lexington, MA: Lexington Books.

Wilson, O. W. 1953. August Vollmer. *The Journal of Criminal Law, Criminology, and Police Science* 44 (1): 91–103.

Courtesy of the Library of Congress

J. Edgar Hoover and the FBI

Kilby Raptopoulos and Jeffrey T. Walker

When one thinks of directors of government agencies in Washington, D.C., there is always one who comes to mind first for many—J. Edgar Hoover. He directed the FBI from 1924 until his death in 1972, surviving seven presidents of the United States and sixteen attorneys general. He has been called a master of politics, the Man, and the Power. Many thought of him as a bully who held too much power. He was answerable only to the president and the attorney general, neither of whom, in reality, had much power over him at all.

Hoover did become friends with a few presidents. Hoover and Richard Nixon became friends despite Nixon's rejection from the Bureau during an earlier job interview. Nixon once asked Hoover why he was not hired for the position; Hoover explained to Nixon that the Bureau's budgets were cut that year, forcing the Bureau to freeze all hiring. If Nixon had checked the Bureau budgets from 1937, he would have discovered that the Bureau's budget was actually increased that year by $825,000 from the previous year. Time, however, would prove that the friendship would disintegrate. By the time Nixon became president, he actively advocated removing Hoover from his position, but he could not bring himself to ask Hoover for his resignation. Hoover was not worried. He had outlasted the previous six presidents, and he was confident that this one posed no real threat.

EARLY LIFE OF HOOVER

John Edgar Hoover was born on January 1, 1895, to Dickerson and Annie Hoover, a middle-class family living in Washington, D.C., as the baby of four children. He came quickly after the death of their second daughter to diphtheria at the age of three. His father and grandfather worked for the U.S. Coast and Geodetic Survey. However, it was his mother who had the greater influence on Edgar, as she used to call him. Hoover's ancestors immigrated to America from Switzerland in the early 1800s. Annie came from this "Swiss stock"; her grandfather, Hoover's great-grandfather, was the first Swiss consul-general to the United States. His great-uncle was one of the Swiss stonemasons who worked on the Capitol.

Hoover grew up in their family home on Seward Square in Southeast Washington, D.C., and remained there until his death in 1972. The area was known to locals as "Pipetown." It was a two-story stone home in a middle-class neighborhood, surrounded by many other mid-level Washington bureaucrats' homes. Annie lived in the house with Hoover until her death; Hoover was forty-three when she died. Annie Hoover was a strict disciplinarian with very "old-fashioned virtues," which she impressed upon her children. She was a staunch Lutheran, which influenced Hoover at an early age. He attended Bible school religiously and sang in the church choir; he was even rewarded for not missing church once in fifty-two straight weeks.

Annie's attempts to mold her son into religion produced mixed results. After meeting a Presbyterian minister named Dr. Donald MacLeod, he joined the Presbyterian Church against his mother's wishes. Hoover even considered becoming a Presbyterian minister himself; however, he later abandoned this career path for another where he also believed his talent of being able to "distinguish between right and wrong" would be put to good use. Hoover did, however, hold close to his mother's teachings. He taught Sunday School for some time, and he even "served as assistant superintendent of the church's junior department" (Toledano 1973, 30).

Hoover began his education at Brent Public School, where he was known as a loner who read his Bible quite a bit. He never participated in neighborhood fights where the boys from Seward Square would fight the boys from other neighborhoods. He was a good, quiet student who loved sports, although he did not excel much at any. He was prevented from playing football because of his small size; however, he did make the baseball team for a few years.

As a young child, Hoover learned a hard work ethic and the value of a dollar. He created his first job at the age of twelve. Hoover began standing outside of the local grocery store advertising himself to carry groceries home for tips. His first employer paid him ten cents to carry two baskets of groceries for about two miles. He quickly learned the sooner he got back to the grocery store, the sooner he could start earning more money; thus, he would run back to the grocery store as quickly as possible. This resulted in some of his family and friends calling him "Speed." Young Hoover began working every day after school and all day on Saturday from 7 A.M. till 7 P.M. Hoover later stated, "I could earn as much as two dollars a day. In those times, that was a king's ransom." (Toledano 1973, 30).

Hoover showed his hard work and determination continuously throughout his youth. He created the *Weekly Review* at the age of eleven, a newspaper he wrote and edited himself about activities and observations on Seward Square. "The two page mimeographed handout told of life in Seward Square" (Hack 2004, 34), and it resulted in Hoover's meticulous journal entries about the daily activities and observations on his street. The weekly newspaper sold to neighbors for a penny apiece.

Hoover had a serious obstacle to overcome as a child: his stuttering problem. His father promised Hoover the disability would disappear with time; however, his mother was more concerned with the condition. She took him to several specialists to try to overcome the problem. One doctor suggested that he simply talk faster because the faster he talked the less opportunity there would be for him to stutter. Hoover practiced reading as fast as he could for many hours, and he was not only able to solve his stuttering problem but he also improved his reading level dramatically. Hoover not only overcame this disability but went on to lead his high school debate team successfully several years late. The team went undefeated for twelve straight matches.

Hoover chose not to attend the high school in his neighborhood. Instead, he chose to walk three miles one way every day to attend Central High School because it was a much bigger and better school. Although Central High was still a public school, they were geared more toward gifted students with a much more expanded curriculum. They offered foreign languages, classic literature, and advanced science in preparation for college. Hoover quickly became involved in the library club and the choir. After being cut from the football team before the first practice, he tried out and made the track team. He soon excelled and mastered the short sprints division.

One of Hoover's prized accomplishments at Central High School was his participation in the school cadet corps. Hoover progressed quickly, and by his senior year he had passed the ROTC officer's exam, made captain, and was given command of Company B, which he led down Pennsylvania Avenue at Woodrow Wilson's inaugural parade. He was later given command of Company A, which he would use as a pattern to organize the Bureau.

Hoover found it difficult to make friends in high school; thus, he stuck to studying. He took rigorous schedules, including accelerated classes in sciences such as chemistry, physics, Latin, and history. Hoover graduated with high honors from Central High School and was selected valedictorian of his class. He was offered a scholarship to attend the University of Virginia. Instead, he decided to stay at home and attend college at George Washington University, where he joined the Kappa Alpha Order and graduated with honors with a law degree in 1916. He went on to graduate a year later with his master's in law. During that time, Hoover worked in the Library of Congress to help put himself through school. He quickly advanced to clerk and began earning an annual salary of $840.

HOOVER'S EARLY CAREER

While studying at George Washington University, Hoover took a special interest in a U.S. postal inspector from New York City named Anthony Comstock, who was also one of the founders of an organization called the Society for the Prevention of Vice. Comstock was known for his relentless fight against "fraud and vice as well as pornography and information on birth control." It has been suggested that Hoover studied Comstock's techniques and later modeled his own crime-fighting techniques after them.

The year 1917 proved to be full of life-changing events for Hoover. Just as he was graduating from law school, the country was drawn into World War I. Hoover was criticized by many for not joining the war effort; however, it has never been decided whether or not he really was a "draft dodger." The facts could be interpreted either way. For example, Hoover's father, Dickerson, Sr., had a severe mental disorder that caused his mood to fluctuate between bouts of irritability and extreme sadness. He even spent several months in a sanatorium for the condition.

Literally a day before the United States declared war, he was forced to resign from his position from the U.S. Coast and Geodetic Survey without pension, where he had worked for the U.S. government for forty-two years. With their sister Lillian sick, it was left to both Hoover and his brother Dickerson, Jr., to support their family. It became necessary for Hoover to gain employment, and the Justice Department was hiring many young attorneys. Hoover's law clerk position with the Justice Department was draft-exempt, and it paid an annual salary of $990. However, Hoover has been criticized nonetheless because he did not apply for this new position with the Justice Department for three months after he graduated from law school, indicating that the money was not as necessary as one might think.

Hoover's career with the Justice Department took off rapidly. He was promoted after only three months and was again promoted after another three months. Now in charge of the Enemy Alien Registration Section, he was well on his way to making a name for himself at the department. He was quickly recognized for his hard work ethic by John O'Brian, special assistant to the attorney general, for his long hours, quick and efficient ability to get things done, and his habit of also working Sundays. Hoover was also known for his well-dressed appearance, his eagerness to complete even the smallest of tasks, and his pursuit of new duties.

As department head, Hoover led a team of fourteen individuals who were dedicated to keeping America safe from foreign threats. Because of World War I espionage and the threat of German spies, Hoover was given the challenge of sorting through raw intelligence collected by an amateur "spy hunting" organization called the American Protective League. The group developed out of a public fear of German infiltration into American society in an attempt to corrupt the war effort. This spy organization involved 250,000 members in six hundred cities. Their activities resulted in an immense amount of collected raw intelligence on friends and neighbors in their own communities. Although many of these reported suspicious activities ended up being nothing more than unfaithful husbands, Hoover and his team were given the task of sorting through the intelligence and determining any potential leads.

Hoover spent the next two years at this task, meticulously evaluating each case. This thoroughness did not go unnoticed. Hoover's supervisors continued to notice and acknowledge Hoover with raises in his annual salary and by giving him additional duties. By 1918 Hoover was allowed to hire his own secretary to keep his files and do all of his typing. Hoover's department began to develop and grow. They eventually began sending undercover agents out to investigate organizations who protested the war effort; thus began Hoover's focus on entrapping foreign "radicals" who opposed U.S. involvement in the war.

By the age of twenty-four, Hoover had risen to Special Assistant to the Attorney General, and, as of August 1, 1919, he received the break he needed to accelerate his career. It started with a terrorist ring that sent thirty-nine bombs to various political figures in Washington, D.C. One bomb exploded in front of Attorney General A. Mitchell Palmer's house, demolishing half of it. Luckily, the police recovered the rest of the bombs before anyone was seriously injured; however, the damage had already been done. In light of World War I and the "red scare," the threat of a communist invasion prompted the attorney general to appoint Hoover as the head of the General Intelligence Division.

Hoover's new tasks included "studying subversion in the United States and recommending ways and means to contain it." (Toledano 1973, 51). All special agents from the Bureau of Investigation, which would later be renamed the Federal Bureau of Investigation in 1935 by Hoover, were to report to Hoover with their intelligence so he could better conduct his research. Hoover condemned communism using two strategies: appealing to citizens' morals and their patriotism. Hoover claimed that communism was morally and ethically wrong, and he asserted it posed a threat to democratic freedoms. Hoover "traced the evolution of communism from the theories of Marx to the realities of Lenin and Trotsky...he cited extensively from Communist literature." (Nash 1972, 18–19).

In light of the progression of the war and the growing fear of communism, the government launched what became known as the "Palmer raids"—a complex, coordinated series of raids that took place in thirty-three cities within twenty-four hours. More than five thousand arrests were made, mostly immigrants participating in Communist Labor Party meetings or officers of the Federation of the Union of Russian Workers. Although the initial raids could be considered somewhat of a success, the aftermath quickly disintegrated into chaos and confusion. The local jails and police departments were unable to accommodate the large number of arrestees. The jails were too small, many officers could not communicate with the foreign-speaking arrestees, and warrants could not be written fast enough. Although quite a few were able to resist deportation, many immigrants were held in inhumane conditions and denied proper legal representation. The damage had been done; news of the raids leaked out and the public was outraged.

Hoover was assigned to help with the prosecution of Emma Goldman and Alexander Berkman, the two most notorious of the arrestees. The final victory came on December 2, 1919, as Emma and Alexander were boarded onto the *Old Buford* and set sail back to Russia. The deportation was just the beginning of a long battle that Hoover and the Bureau would wage against immigrants in their fight against communism. In 1920, Palmer commenced the "red raids"; investigators from the Bureau of Investigation stormed homes and businesses, arresting some twenty-five hundred illegal immigrants. The agents were instructed to report directly to Hoover himself.

The public again became outraged. Many agents took it upon themselves to use brutal force when making arrests, beating many of the immigrants. The public protested the raids, claiming many agents stormed the homes and businesses illegally without warrants. Many of the immigrants were again denied proper legal representation. Despite Palmer's unpopularity, Hoover remained unscathed.

Through his work in the General Intelligence Division, Hoover also developed a large index-card system as a means of cataloging individuals and organizations in radical movements. The cataloging system quickly accumulated entries and by 1921 contained 450,000 files on individuals from all over the country. Hoover ingeniously "cross-indexed" them by location so that if he needed to pull all the names from a specific location it could be accomplished quickly. Hoover also kept more detailed comprehensive files on the more significant radicals, which eventually grew into some 60,000 files. Hoover began amassing names for his cataloging system through American Protective League reports and seized membership lists from radical leaders such as Emma Goldman; however, Hoover wanted more. He sent out private detective agencies to gather their own lists of names and to work closely with special agents from the Bureau of Investigation. Hoover also had a team of bilingual translators scanning multiple foreign publications for anything radical pertaining to names or organizations.

HOOVER AS DIRECTOR

The year 1921 brought yet another significant promotion in Hoover's career. Newly elected president Warren G. Harding fired William J. Flynn, Director of the Bureau of Investigation, and hired William J. Burns on August 22. This change in leadership brought Hoover up to Assistant Director of the Bureau of Investigation and increased his salary to $4,000 a year. That same year, Hoover decided to change his name. He had discovered there was another man living in Washington, D.C., who also had the name John Edgar Hoover and who had accumulated quite a bit of debt. Hoover prided himself in paying all debts in a timely manner and felt it necessary to distinguish himself from the other John Edgar; thus, Hoover from then on became J. Edgar.

By 1921, the Bureau had become a haven for corruption. "It had become a cesspool of graft. Agents were appointed to their posts through political connections; with such immunity agents felt free to bribe and be bribed." (Nash 1972, 26). By 1923, President Harding had become ill and eventually died. Vice President Calvin Coolidge became president and immediately fired Attorney General Harry Daughtery and replaced him with Harlan Fiske Stone. Stone wanted to get rid of William J. Burns in an attempt to clean up the Bureau; however, he needed the right replacement. The president asked then Secretary of Commerce Herbert Hoover if he had any suggestions, and he, in turn, asked his aide Larry Richey. Richey suggested J. Edgar Hoover. Secretary Hoover went to Attorney General Stone with the suggestion, and on May 10, 1924, Stone named J. Edgar Hoover director of the Bureau of Investigation.

At the age of twenty-nine, Hoover was now in charge of the Bureau and set out quickly to improve it by making it more efficient and improving the quality of its special agents. Hoover created a complex fingerprint database, an idea he had for quite some time. He also bombarded his agents with memos on how they should conduct themselves personally. Hoover forbade them to drink alcohol and demanded they conduct themselves with "proper personal conduct." Hoover even fired a special agent from Denver who casually mentioned to an agent from the Washington office that they should go out for a drink after working on a long assignment. Two days later the Denver agent was released from his position with the Bureau.

Hoover promised the attorney general he would rid the Bureau of all politics; however, by 1931 Hoover had abandoned that promise entirely. By 1932 the national elections brought an overturn in power. The Republicans were voted out of office and the Democrats were voted in. In response to this change in power, Hoover fired more than a hundred well-trained and capable special agents and replaced them with agents recommended by the newly elected congress. This new birth of power led Hoover on a rampage over the next several decades, making himself one of the most feared men in Washington. Hoover investigated and accumulated information and files on politicians from the lowest ranks all the way up through the White House, and he used this "dirt" to his advantage. He claimed to many very innocently that this sensitive information had been delivered to him through the mail, his way of warning them not to cross the all-powerful director of the Bureau of Investigation. He not only simultaneously secured his position with the Bureau, he also secured the Bureau's position in politics.

Throughout the late 1920s and 1930s, Hoover and his G-men (a nickname for government men) gained national momentum, bringing down such criminal legends as Machine Gun Kelley, John Dillinger, Charles Arthur "Pretty Boy" Floyd, Frank Nash, and the Lindbergh kidnapper. Hoover loved public attention and never missed an opportunity to gloat on his agency's superior ability to "bring down the bad guys." This, however, was not always reality. For example, Hoover took all the credit for apprehending the primary suspect, Bruno Hauptmann, in the Lindbergh kidnapping. In reality, however, the big break came when a gas station attendant took down Hauptmann's license plate number on the five dollar bill that Hauptmann had used for a payment. The clerk at the bank saw the bill and called the Treasury Department to inquire if the bill was stolen. In fact, the bill was part of the ransom money paid by Lindbergh in hopes of getting his son back. The Treasury Department contacted the New York Police

Department who in turn tracked down the license plate number through the New York State Motor Vehicle Department. Hoover conveniently left out the part of the story where Charles Lindbergh ordered special agents out of his house in disgust at their inept inability to carry out their duties properly.

Amid the public triumph, Hoover came under attack during a senate hearing with Senator Kenneth D. McKellar, Chairman of the Senate Subcommittee for Appropriations. McKellar disputed Hoover's request for an additional $1,025,000 toward his annual budget, claiming Hoover was spending an excessive amount of money on advertising and publicity. The additional funding request seemed excessive to the appropriations committee, considering that Hoover only had a staff of less than seven hundred special agents plus some support staff. McKellar insinuated Hoover was trying to bolster the Bureau's public image by paying the media extraordinary sums of money for false press releases and advertisements with Hoover's face displayed during "G-men movies." Hoover denied the allegations. Although he denied having any hand in the making of this type of movie, he was unable to deny the fact that his face was displayed during advertisements that were shown throughout the movies. He also failed to disclose how he went to Baltimore to screen one of these movies before it was released in Washington. After McKellar asked Hoover "if any of the money appropriated by Congress for the Bureau's budget was ever used to promote the Bureau's image, Hoover quickly responded that not a penny had been appropriated to pay writers to build up the image of the Bureau" (Nash 1972, 53).

Hoover, in fact, had been working diligently to bolster the Bureau's public image. In addition to releasing constant press releases to the media and assisting in the making of such motion pictures, Hoover used several other tactics. Hoover assisted a Washington newspaper reporter with the creation of a radio program about G-men. Hoover also created a comic strip designed to "embellish" the Bureau that would be widely distributed via newspapers throughout the country. Author Courtney Ryley Cooper, whose book *Ten Thousand Public Enemies* praised Hoover and his special agents, was given a job at the Justice Department specifically to "publicize the division of investigation" (Cooper 1935). Even the Attorney General appointed Henry Soudam, chief Washington correspondent for the *Brooklyn Eagle*, to "build up the FBI's image of invincibility..., later turning Hoover into a household word within a year." (Nash 1972, 54).

McKellar also questioned Hoover's qualifications, stating that Hoover had never even made an arrest. Hoover referred to himself as a criminologist; however, when McKellar questioned him on this Hoover stated that he had never received any formal training in criminology nor had he ever attended his own National Police Academy. Hoover left the senate hearing embarrassed and humiliated, with a burning need to prove himself. Several weeks later he left for New Orleans to arrest personally "public enemy number one"—Alvin "Old Creepy" Karpis. In actuality Hoover waited in a nearby apartment building until federal agents had Karpis captured and then paraded out to lead him away in Bureau custody. By the time cartoonists McDayter and Drew released their version of the events, the public saw a mighty Hoover single-handedly manhandle Karpis out of his car and into the street subdued by a hammer lock as special agents watched in awe.

HOOVER AND ESPIONAGE

Despite the embarrassing McKellar hearings, President Roosevelt placed Hoover in charge of counterespionage in the United States. President Roosevelt requested that Hoover begin gathering information on not only communists but fascists as well. Roosevelt even brought Secretary of State Cordell Hull at Hoover's request to "make it legal." Hoover created the Special Intelligence Service (SIS) to conduct the Bureau's counterespionage investigations and immediately dispatched teams of agents to South America. Hoover had read a book published in 1911 that Germany would use South America as a springboard with which to push agents into the United States. Hoover became convinced that South America was swarming with Germans; however, his preoccupation with South America probably contributed to his lack of attention to other more imminent threats here on U.S. soil.

Although South America was important enough for Hoover to send many agents, apparently Hawaii was not. Hoover made a serious mistake by refusing to investigate Dr. Keuhn and his family, who played a major role in gathering intelligence for Japan in the bombing of Pearl Harbor. When the bombing occurred, Hoover was out of his office. Hoover was finally tracked down in New York City. His response was fast; he quickly began rounding up every Japanese American he and his agents could find.

Hoover eventually envisioned the Bureau as the chief counterintelligence agency in the United States; however, President Roosevelt had other visions. Roosevelt had instructed Major General William J. Donovan, Chief to the Office of Strategic Services (OSS), to create a "new worldwide intelligence service," thereby creating competition with Hoover. Donovan had had heroic successes with the OSS, even "shortening World War II by years because of his intelligence operations"—something that angered Hoover greatly. However, Hoover finally won this battle when he was able to persuade President Truman to disband the agency. Hoover quickly requested he pick up OSS's duties, although Truman never agreed to this. In desperation, Truman, plagued with increasingly complicated intelligence reports that were beginning to contradict one another, reluctantly created the Central Intelligence Agency (CIA) in 1947, much to Hoover's dismay.

With this move, Hoover had a new fight on his hands. He was determined to "dominate intelligence activities"; however, he found this increasingly difficult due to the fact that Allen Dulles, head of the CIA, had been granted "autonomous rule" of the intelligence community by Congress. In response, Hoover meticulously placed agents overseas and attached them to U.S. embassies in an attempt to continue his counterespionage investigations. The National Security Act of 1947 diminished Hoover's position greatly by moving the Bureau's intelligence division to the CIA's jurisdiction. Hoover found himself, as head of one of the federal government's intelligence-gathering agencies, answerable to the chairman of the board of the U.S. intelligence community—the director of the CIA.

Hoover, however, never went to great lengths to inform the CIA of anything. The Bureau reported as little as possible and only when demanded to do so. Hoover's unwillingness to share information with other intelligence agencies soon caught up to him. Hoover's Bureau was criticized by the Warren Commission in regards to JFK's assassination. The Bureau refused to share vital information with the Secret Service about Lee Harvey Oswald's communist background, his knowledge of the motorcade route, his job at the schoolbook depository, and lies he told the special agents during interrogation. The Dallas field office also ignored repeated threats that someone was going to kill Oswald. Despite the mounting evidence of the Bureau's negligence in the JFK assassination, Hoover still publicly claimed that the assassination was inevitable and that totally securing the president was impossible.

Hoover had lost credibility in the foreign intelligence community as a result of the assassination. Not recognizing Oswald as a real and potential threat was a severe blow. But to most in the underworld, this was no surprise. One spy who had worked in the United States for years stated after returning to Europe, "however efficient the FBI may be in pursuing gangsters and kidnappers, they are out of their depth when trying to deal with a sophisticated intelligence network. Most of their successes in this field have been due to information being handed to them on a plate by turncoats...he [Hoover] has a genius for publicity and an unrivaled capacity for extracting money from Congress." (Nash 1972, 130).

Despite Hoover's inability to gain credibility in the foreign intelligence arena, he did, however, convince Nixon to allow him to place special agents in twenty-five foreign cities, attached to foreign embassies. Nixon agreed to this without congressional approval or the public's knowledge. Nixon rationalized that it would be appropriate because of their expert ability to investigate American hostages. Hoover, however, had already placed special agents in at least twenty foreign cities several years prior to Nixon's approval.

Hoover's credibility was called into question again in another embarrassing situation, this time not only in regard to counterespionage but basic law enforcement criminal procedure. In 1949 Hoover received information from an FBI informant that a female employee of the Foreign Registration Office at the Justice Department was supplying the Soviet Embassy in Washington with top-secret documents. The Bureau immediately began following her. They meticulously monitored her every move for weeks, gathering a great deal of evidence. Her name was Judith Coplon, and according to the evidence, she was definitely working as a Soviet spy. Coplon eventually began requesting top-secret information from her supervisor, which she assured him was necessary for her to do her job properly. Hoover purposefully ordered her supervisor to start feeding her false information.

Within weeks special agents had caught her feeding false information to Soviets in New York City. Coplon, along with a Soviet spy, was arrested. This case also created problems for the Bureau. The trial required certain top-secret FBI files to be entered into evidence and brought forth in court to corroborate testimony. The Bureau was officially backed into a corner. To turn over the files would be disastrous because of the sensitive content. The files were full of evidence solely based on hearsay, rumors, gossip, and innuendos. However, to refuse to release the files would force the case to be dropped. In the end, the files were released, to the Bureau's public humiliation. The charges against Coplon were ultimately dropped anyway on a technicality. The arresting special agents failed to obtain an arrest warrant, thereby violating Coplon's civil rights and allowing her to walk away a free woman.

HOOVER AND THE KENNEDY BROTHERS

Hoover's fascination with the "red menace" stayed with him throughout his career. Throughout the 1930s, 1940s, and 1950s Hoover continued to investigate communist leaders and virtually ignored an increasing problem attacking America's urban cities—the Mafia. By the 1950s, organized crime was flourishing. Hoover believed this area of crime posed the greatest threat to his agents because they would be most susceptible to corruption; thus, he chose not to expose them to it. To put it simply, Hoover refused to acknowledge the Mafia as a problem. In 1959, Senator Robert Kennedy, then chief of the senate Labor Rackets Committee, attacked Hoover, stating that they needed to quit "pushing paper and start investigating more." At the time of the attack, Hoover had only four special agents in New York City investigating organized crime. The rest of the special agents, which numbered nearly four hundred, were focusing on communism. Hoover was therefore forced into the fight against organized crime, and he blamed Robert Kennedy for it.

Kennedy, consequently, was the only attorney general that Hoover could not manage his way around, and the White House was no help either. The attorney general's brother, President John F. Kennedy, agreed with Robert that organized crime was a serious issue. Despite Hoover and Kennedy's constant clash as to who should be dictating what the Bureau investigated,

Hoover publicly claimed responsibility for arresting famed mob leader Joseph Valachi after he was actually apprehended by federal narcotics officers. As a result, Hoover proclaimed to the American people the dangers that were arising from these "criminal cartels whose memberships seem to be Italian...who control major racket activities in metropolitan areas...who operate on a nationwide business...and who have until recent years carried out its activities in complete secrecy." (Nash 1972, 95–97).

On March 22, 1966, Hoover made another severe blunder. Chicago's underworld leaders gathered together at the Edgewater Beach Hotel for an honorary dinner for Fifi Buchieri, a well-known Mafia leader. The only law enforcement officer to cover the event was from the Northwest Indiana Crime Commission, who managed to gain access to the meeting. He reported on it the next day in the *Chicago Tribune*. When Hoover saw the paper the next morning, he was furious that none of his agents from the Chicago office had covered the event. Hoover demanded a full report on his desk within hours. A stunned and embarrassed Chicago office ran to the local police department to borrow and photocopy police reports. Hoover, not wanting to take the blame, quickly informed the media that his special agents were not allowed to perform undercover work.

Hoover considered the matter a shame because of his long-time friendship with Joseph Kennedy, father of John and Robert. Hoover, however, showed little mercy to the attorney general before JFK was shot, an event that probably saved Hoover's job. President Kennedy was said to have been within days of asking for Hoover's resignation because of conflicts with Robert Kennedy. The resignation would have been easy to get because the White House staff was going to have to submit a presidential proclamation to keep Hoover as active director because he had passed the mandatory retirement age—which JFK did not intend to do.

Hoover and Robert Kennedy butted heads for the rest of Robert's term. Robert would barge into Hoover's office, often unannounced, which usually irritated Hoover to no end. He would request Hoover's presence at staff luncheons, which Hoover refused to attend. Robert would often call field offices and talk to special agents without Hoover's permission, to the extent that agents were fearful Hoover would find out they were not following protocol.

After JFK died, Hoover continued to show no mercy to Robert. He called Robert the day of the assassination to inform him of the situation, and all he stated to him was "I have news for you, the President has been shot" and abruptly hung up. Robert got another call later from Hoover stating "The president is dead," and again abruptly hung up. From that point forward Hoover and Robert's relationship deteriorated rapidly. They hardly ever spoke. Hoover ordered the Bureau to discontinue the driving services they offered to Robert. Hoover quit reporting to Robert altogether and took his intelligence reports straight to President Johnson. The final fight came when

Robert requested Hoover start hiring more African American special agents. By the time Johnson became president and especially into Nixon's presidency, Hoover began to settle down into a more comfortable, unopposed position.

Robert Kennedy forced Hoover to begin investigating civil rights violations, and the first civil rights violator he wanted fixed was Hoover himself. Hoover claimed there were no problems with the Bureau, and he had plenty of black agents. Hoover's idea, however, of a black FBI agent was his chauffeur and personal receptionist. After Kennedy's inquiry, Hoover quickly called the Chicago office and demanded they go out and hire another African American agent. The supervising agent in Chicago asked the black janitor if he wanted to be made a special agent. Stunned, he nodded yes as the agents handed him a badge, credentials, and a much higher salary. By the end of the week he had been moved to a new position: chauffeur for the chief special agent of the Chicago office.

It was not until 1962 that the Bureau had an official African American special agent. Aubrey C. Lewis, a professional football player, was admitted into the FBI Academy at Quantico, Virginia. Hoover seized this opportunity to show the nation publicly that he was not a racist. Hoover had Lewis' photo published with himself, stating "We've paid no attention to race, creed, or color. This has been my strict FBI policy." (Nash 197, 152). When asked by the media exactly how many black agents the Bureau employed, Hoover commented that he could not divulge that information.

PROFILE OF HOOVER'S SPECIAL AGENTS

In fact Hoover's agents did fit a certain profile, and Hoover did not tolerate agents who strayed from this protocol. All were white males, had a clean-cut appearance and very neat trimmed hair; their socks and ties had to match, and they always wore dark suits. Hoover went to great lengths to ensure his agents fit the profile and that the profile fit the public's image of what a G-man should look like. Hoover went so far as to dismiss one of the recruits at the FBI academy after he had successfully completed all the requirements simply because his face was disfigured from his previous military combat. Hoover required strict education requirements as well. Only recruits from conservative schools were chosen for the academy. They had to have successfully completed an accredited law or accounting school and have at least three years of experience in the field. Hoover made sure his agents were well compensated for their accomplishments. FBI agents have generally been the highest paid federal law enforcement officers. Hoover justified this by persuading Congress that only a high salary would keep them free from bribery and corruption. Hoover also created a lucrative retirement package for all agents serving the Bureau for at least twenty years.

Hoover had little compassion for agents who even barely strayed from his profile. For example, Hoover once fired an agent for wearing a tie that was too loud. He threatened to fire an agent because Hoover found out he was reading *Playboy*. He also fired a man for marrying a woman of Arabian descent. Hoover's strict policies did not stop with the agents. Hoover expected his clerks to follow similar standards. Hoover fired a clerk from the Washington office in 1968 for "sleeping with young girls." The clerk sued Hoover; however, he did not win.

Hoover required a strict work ethic as well from his agents. They were expected to work overtime and to spend much of their time submitting meticulous progress reports to their superiors. Each agent was required to regularly submit a detailed progress report on every case, and depending on the type of case, to their agent in charge until the crime was solved. The agent in charge then forwarded all the progress reports to Hoover, who spent a great deal of his time reading through them. Hoover's clerical staff was also held to a high work ethic. They too had to submit regular progress reports on how many pages they typed each hour. They also had to abide by Hoover's handbook of conduct. They were subject to a very rigorous dress code and were forbidden from attending public political meetings. Two clerks from the Washington office helped organize an antiwar march through the National Peace Coalition, which resulted in their dismissal. They too sued Hoover through the American Civil Liberties Union; however, the suit came to nothing.

To ensure proper adherence of his rules, Hoover employed the Inspection Division of the Bureau to travel to different field offices unannounced to investigate the agents and ensure they were following proper protocol. The Inspection Division interrogated agents about why they had not solved certain cases. The agents, of course, would often comment that they did not have time because they were too busy writing lengthy memos about their every action. Agents were questioned about their personal life and reminded that they should always adhere to Hoover's strict code of conduct. Agents were also required to report all suspicious behavior of other agents that they might happen to witness. In so doing, Hoover created an elaborate spy ring within the Bureau, where no one was safe from being informed upon to Hoover.

Hoover also implemented a demerit system. Agents were given demerits for the smallest things. For example, agents were not allowed to take their coffee back to their desks, men were allowed to smoke on the job but women were not, agents were not allowed to leave their car windows down, and one agent was even given a demerit for dirty windows. If demerits were not enough punishment, Hoover always had the option of transferring them to another office in a remote region of the country. Agents were always fearful they would be transferred to some far away remote region such as Montana. As a result, the unspoken bureau motto quickly became "don't embarrass the Director." (Nash 1972, 171–75).

Despite Hoover's many faults as a director, there was one thing he mastered during his time at the Bureau: publicity. Although the Bureau claimed they "had no public relations office," there was, however, a Crime Records Division. This division had several duties. For example, they were required to handle all press inquiries and write press releases; they analyzed FBI crime statistics and prepared reports and wrote and published the nationwide *FBI Law Enforcement Bulletin* that was distributed to local and state police officers. Hoover's Bureau was also notorious for leaking information to a "leak man" who always worked for a "Hoover-approved" newspaper: the *Chicago Tribune,* the *New York Daily News,* and the *Washington Star.* Hoover never allowed information to be leaked to newspapers such as the *Wall Street Journal,* the *Washington Post,* the *National Observer,* and the *New York Times.* Hoover believed these newspapers were "anti-Bureau" and chose not to include them when he leaked material he wanted the public to read. Special agents also hand-picked certain reporters to accompany them on raids they knew would be a success, to ensure positive coverage the next day in the newspaper.

HOOVER'S FINAL YEARS

At the age of seventy-seven, despite criticism, Hoover had no intention of retiring. He planned to work until his eightieth birthday and then make his public announcement that he was stepping down. This, however, changed on May 2, 1972. Retired chauffeur James Crawford had come over to Hoover's home early that morning to help Hoover plant some rosebushes. Crawford arrived fifteen minutes early, as usual, and quickly got to work. A little later a worried Annie Fields, Hoover's longtime live-in cook and housekeeper, came out the back door of Hoover's home. She was concerned because Hoover had not risen from bed yet, and he rarely overslept. Crawford volunteered to go check. Several minutes later, he called down frantically for Annie to phone Hoover's personal physician, Dr. Robert Choisser, while he called Clyde Tolson, Hoover's long-time best friend and closest companion. Crawford found Hoover unconscious on the rug next to his bed.

Tolson had been Hoover's right-hand man for years, earning the nickname Junior. Hoover's chauffeur would come by and pick up Hoover, and then they would go by Tolson's place and pick him up as well. If weather permitted, the chauffeur would drop them off several blocks early so they could walk the rest of the way. They had a lot in common; both never married. They ate together, vacationed together, both loved sports, had no other real interests, and both were used to the "Washington bureaucracy." Tolson was initially hired by the Bureau as a special agent in 1928 and later became chief clerk of the Bureau in Washington. Two years later he rose to inspector, and only one year later assistant director. With time and patience, Tolson was finally promoted to the position in which he remained for the rest of his FBI career; he was named associate director of the Bureau in 1947, where he finally resigned after Hoover's death.

Hoover was laid to rest two days later in the congressional cemetery. His hour-long funeral, which took place at National Presbyterian Church, was broadcast live by all three networks. It was referred to as a "political event." Tolson, along with a few of Hoover's remaining relatives and a few of Hoover's closest office staff, were watching the funeral from a private section, shielded from the news cameras. The president gave the eulogy and the Army chorus sang. It was an event that ended a political era.

Three Areas of Law Enforcement Improvements Credited to Hoover

1. Personnel and management
   - appointments and promotions based on qualifications
   - agents must have degrees (law or accounting)
   - uniform discipline policy
   - agents must have character (even off-duty)
   - bureaucratic (hierarchical) organizational structure

2. Investigative practices
   - work ethic for agents = results oriented
   - agents to use technology and science to solve crime
   - forensic laboratory created
   - extensive intelligence files for investigative leads
   - specified investigative procedures put into policy to protect the rights of suspects

3. Law enforcement liaison and training
   - created FBI National Academy in 1935 (teaches management and investigation to state/local officials
   - *FBI Law Enforcement Bulletin* created
   - Fingerprint Identification division created to collect fingerprints from law enforcement around the country

Source: Herbert Johnson and Nancy Travis Wolfe, *History of Criminal Justice*, Cincinatti, OH: Anderson Publishing, 2003.

CREATION OF THE FBI

In 1908 Attorney General Charles Bonaparte created an executive order that did two things. First it banned the Justice Department, through "appropriation restrictions," from using the Secret Service as investigators for other governmental agencies, including their own. Through this executive order, Bonaparte, along with President Roosevelt, created the Bureau of Investigation, which sparked much controversy due to the rising concerns that a federal police force might abuse its newly granted powers. Now, with the removal of Secret Service investigators, the Department of Justice was left crippled. Second, Bonaparte was thus forced to create a new subdepartment under the Justice Department to be their investigative arm.

This new investigative force began with thirty-four special agents, nine of which were former Secret Service agents. The remaining agents were from special investigative committees from within the Justice Department. Needing congressional approval for the newly created Bureau of Investigation, Bonaparte assured Congress that the Bureau would only investigate "interstate commerce and anti-trust violations." Congressional approval finally came in January of 1909 (Theoharis and Cox 1998, 223).

The Bureau expanded its number of special agents and the number of crimes it investigated greatly over the next two decades due to several factors. During this time the federal government, under the Progressive Era, initiated such programs as the New Deal. The Bureau grew to 300 agents by World War I, and by 1920 the number of special agents had risen to 579—the largest the agency would be until 1936 when the number of agents would again start to increase dramatically.

In the beginning, the Bureau investigated fewer than twenty-five criminal statutes, ranging from violent crimes to "counterintelligence matters." However, in 1910, the White Slave Traffic Act, or the Mann Act as it is sometimes referred to, was passed, making the transportation of women across state lines for prostitution illegal. This made it a federal crime, adding it to the list of crimes investigated by the Bureau. This led the Bureau to divide itself into two units, allowing one unit to investigate illegal prostitution and one unit to tend to all other matters. The prostitution unit was headquartered in Baltimore, Maryland, while the main headquarters remained in Washington, D.C. The Bureau's powers were once again expanded with the Dyer Act of 1919, which made the transportation of stolen vehicles across state lines a federal crime. Between 1932 and 1934 crimes such as bank robbery, kidnapping, and extortion were federalized, again extending the Bureau's investigative powers to encompass an even wider range of enforceable crimes.

President Coolidge named J. Edgar Hoover FBI director in 1924, where he remained until his unexpected death in 1972. The President chose Hoover because he believed he could "reform and clean it up from its reputation as a haven for corruption." It was under his leadership that the name of the Bureau was changed in 1935 to the Federal Bureau of Investigation (FBI).

By the twenty-first century, the Bureau had spread out across the globe, with fifty-six field offices across the country and more than four hundred smaller satellite offices in all fifty states. It also has more than fifty international offices located in U.S. embassies worldwide. The FBI's headquarters are on Pennsylvania Avenue in Washington, D.C., in the J. Edgar Hoover FBI Building. The building was completed in 1975; however, it was named after its long-time director three years early, just two days after Hoover died. By March 2006, the FBI had grown to 12,515 special agents with 17,915 support staff. It now investigates "violations of more than 200 categories of federal law" (FBI Homepage). According to the FBI, these investigations include counterterrorism, counterintelligence, cyber crime, organized crime, civil rights violations, violent crimes, and theft.

FBI PRIORITIES

The FBI follows ten priorities grouped into two categories: national security and crime. The following ten priorities encompass a wide range of areas that not only focus on fighting crime and terrorism but also allow the agents to assist other law enforcement agencies in a cooperative effort. These priorities include "protecting the United States from terrorist attacks; protecting the United States against foreign intelligence operations and espionage; protecting the United States against cyber-based attacks and high-technology crimes; combating public corruption at all levels; protecting civil rights; combating transnational and national criminal organizations and enterprises; combating major white-collar crime; combating significant violent crime; supporting federal, state, county, municipal, and international partners; and upgrading technology to successfully perform the FBI's mission." (FBI Homepage).

CRIMES THE FBI INVESTIGATES

The FBI explains they investigate all federal crimes, clustered under its main two priorities of preserving national security and enforcing the federal criminal code. Special agents investigate crimes such as international and domestic terrorism and threats of possession of weapons of mass destruction, all of which directly relate to counterterrorism investigations. In regard to counterintelligence investigations, special agents investigate counterespionage and economic espionage along with counterproliferation. Special agents also investigate cybercrimes, for example, online sexual predation, Internet fraud, and computer intrusion.

According to the FBI's Web site, enforcing the federal criminal code requires special agents to investigate a wide range of federal laws. Special agents combat public corruption by investigating government and election fraud. They also investigate civil rights violations such as hate crimes and human trafficking. Investigating organized crime includes examining domestic terrorist organizations from all over the world. White-collar crime investigations include investigating bankruptcy fraud, health care fraud, money laundering, telemarketing fraud, identity theft, and insurance fraud. Special agents also investigate violent crimes and major thefts such as crimes against children, environmental crimes, Indian country crimes, gang violence, illegal narcotics, fugitives, art and jewelry theft, vehicle theft, and retail theft. In addition to investigating and enforcing foreign and domestic crimes, they also conduct background investigations and internal investigations within the FBI and assist local, state, and other federal law enforcement agencies.

QUALIFICATIONS TO BECOME AN FBI AGENT

According to the FBI's homepage, the first step in becoming a FBI special agent is obtaining a top-secret security clearance, which requires a thorough background investigation. Special agents must also be a U.S. citizen, must be between the ages of twenty-three and thirty-six, must obtain a bachelor's degree from an accredited college or university, must successfully complete several personal interviews, and must pass a written exam and an extensive medical examination. Traditionally the FBI has been interested in recruiting applicants who are specialized in law, accounting, or law enforcement; however, the FBI's interests are ever changing. Today the FBI is actively recruiting applicants who also specialize in foreign languages, computers, and the physical sciences.

TRAINING PROGRAM

Once hired by the FBI, all special agents are required to complete a seventeen-week training program at the Marine Corps base at Quantico, Virginia. The complex is home to a complete training facility including dorms and dining services, classrooms, indoor and outdoor firing ranges, a gymnasium, a pursuit/defensive driving course, a chapel, an auditorium, and a mock town known as Hogan's Alley. Quantico is also home to the Drug Enforcement Administration's special agent training facility. During the program training, agents are exposed to more than 640 hours of teaching focused in four primary areas: "academics, firearms, operational skills, and the integrated case scenario." (FBI Homepage).

Special agents are tested through nine comprehensive examinations in seven areas where they must score at least 85 percent. The seven areas of study include "law, forensic science, behavioral science, interviewing, ethics, interrogation, and basic and advanced investigative techniques." (FBI

Homepage). In addition to academics, special agents are required to pass a physical fitness test that is administered upon entry into the academy, at week 14, and again at week 17. Special agents are also required to pass a defensive tactics course and qualify on two handguns and a shotgun with an 80 percent or higher score.

Hogan's Alley is another unique feature of the FBI training academy. Hogan's Alley allows special agents to apply what they have learned in practical settings, allowing them to practice surveillance techniques and handling dangerous situations involving firearms and hostage situations. Hogan's Alley opened in 1972. It is structured to look and feel like a real town. Behind the imitation restaurants and businesses are classrooms and surveillance rooms that assist new agents in applying their newly learned tactical skills in a real-life practical setting.

OTHER ENTITIES AT QUANTICO

The FBI academy is not the only FBI-run operation at Quantico. According to the FBI homepage, Quantico is also home to several research institutions that provide FBI special agents and other law enforcement agencies with support services and training. For example, Quantico houses the Behavioral Science Unit, a division of Training and Development that focuses on training new special agents and providing the Bureau with a research arm to help special agents stay abreast of current criminological trends. Although the instructors are mostly experienced officers and agents who hold higher degrees in either criminology, psychology, or sociology, they also employ forensic psychologists, research and management analysts, and technical information specialists. The Behavioral Science Unit trains special agents in such areas as "domestic terrorism, death investigations, gangs, criminal behavior, counterterrorism, and applied criminology" (FBI Homepage). The unit's primary research focus is the criminal offender and his or her "behaviors and motivations." Currently the Behavior Science Unit is researching various topics including "hate crimes, use of deadly force, juveniles, religion and crime, and gang violence." For interested students, the Behavioral Science Unit offers several internships, which can be accessed through the FBI's Web page.

Quantico also houses the FBI National Academy. This is a specialized program that allows law enforcement leaders and managers to take undergraduate and graduate-level college classes specializing in "law, behavioral sciences, forensic sciences, leadership, development, communication, and health/fitness" (FBI Homepage). The academy is held four times a year, with around 250 individuals in each class. The academy is by invitation only. Attendees are selected from all levels of government, all fifty states, and from all over the world. Once an officer has completed the academy he or she is asked to join the FBI National Academy Associates, an organization committed to raising standards of professionalism in law enforcement by "developing higher levels of competency, cooperation, and integrity" (FBI Homepage). This organization has some 15,000 members from all over the country, all committed to excellence in law enforcement.

The Technology Service Unit, which is also located at Quantico, is part of the FBI Academy. This specialized unit is located in Hogan's Alley, specifically to assist special agents training at Quantico and to provide "FBI Academy students and staff with the technological resources and support they need to improve their ability to access, store, retrieve, and exchange information via a computer and to do it in a timely, cooperative and supportive manner" (FBI Homepage). This unit also assists special agents with their audiovisual, graphics, information technology, photography, and video needs. In addition to assisting special agents and training agents, they also support a distance-learning program that provides FBI personnel and other law enforcement agencies worldwide with enforcement training and education. They distribute material globally via the Internet and also in CD-ROM format, as well as assisting with live and prerecorded productions for the Law Enforcement Television Network.

The FBI Laboratory, located at the FBI headquarters in Washington, D.C., is another division of the FBI, providing special agents with the forensic technical assistance needed to collect, process, and preserve critical evidence. The FBI lab is one of the largest in the world, and its assistance is offered to not only special agents with the FBI but other federal, state, and local law enforcement agencies at no charge. The laboratory processes evidence such as DNA analysis, explosives, computer analysis, firearms, hazardous materials, latent prints, material analysis, and trace evidence, just to name a few. The laboratory also operates CODIS (the Combined DNA Index Analysis), a nationwide DNA index system that catalogs DNA from local, state, and federal violent offenders.

The FBI Laboratory established the Forensic Science Research and Training Center at Quantico in 1981, which is a division of the FBI Laboratory. It provides newly hired special agents with forensic science training. FBI lab technicians and other personnel from local, state, and other federal law enforcement agencies are also able to continue their forensic training and learn new advanced methods in forensic analysis. The Forensic Science Research and Training Center also provides law enforcement agents with a continuing education program that offers in-service hours to help agents continue their training and knowledge to keep up with the ever-changing trends and new advanced methods. Cost-free training to law enforcement personnel is provided in areas such as "latent fingerprint identification, DNA analysis, hairs and fibers examination, firearms and toolmarks identification, document examination, bomb disposal, polygraph testing, shoe prints and tire tread analysis, and artist sketching" (FBI Homepage).

CRIMINAL JUSTICE INFORMATION SERVICES

The Criminal Justice Information Services (CJIS) is the largest division of the FBI. It is located in Clarksburg, West Virginia. The CJIS serves not only the FBI but the entire law enforcement community as well. It was created in 1992 to merge several other smaller departments within the Bureau into one large information services division. Several departments located at the CJIS complex are the National Crime Information Center (NCIC), Integrated Automated Fingerprint Identification System (IAFIS), National Instant Criminal Background Check System (NICS), the Uniform Crime Reporting (UCR), and the National Incident-Based Reporting System (NIBRS).

The FBI's National Crime Information Center 2000 (NCIC 2000) is an updated extension of the previous NCIC, originally established in 1967. It is a nationwide information system that is linked not only with federal law enforcement agencies but state and local agencies as well. It even allows mobile access for patrol cars, thus linking local patrol officers with other local, state, and federal agencies, allowing immediate access and sharing of files. It is currently linked to all fifty states, Washington, D.C., Canada, the Virgin Islands, and Puerto Rico.

The NCIC 2000 provides several services vital to fighting crime. For example, it contains an online sex offender database that allows law enforcement offers to obtain and share immediate access to violent sexual offenders' records. It also stores mugshots and other identifying photos, life scars, or tattoos. It has an advanced name search, so officers can not only search a specific name but all other phonetically similar names as well. It contains the SENTRY file, a complete database of all incarcerated federal prisoners and their location. Officers are able to search fingerprints and offenders currently on probation and/or parole. These features makes NCIC 2000 unique in that it allows law enforcement agencies of all levels immediate access and shared information from all over the country, making it much easier to track down or investigate offenders traveling across the country.

The Integrated Automated Fingerprint Identification System (IAFIS), which began operations in 1999, is a complex database that stores fingerprints and criminal records of offenders from all over the country. The "Criminal Master File" contains 47 million offenders' fingerprints and criminal histories that correspond to the prints. They gather data on a voluntary basis from federal, state, and local law enforcement agencies nationwide, which is submitted electronically. This electronic submission allows agencies to give and retrieve information in record time. Officers are able to retrieve information from IAFIS within two hours of their initial request.

The NICS performs background checks for federal firearm licensees in accordance with the Brady Handgun Violence Prevention Act (1993). Without the successful completion of a background examination, federal licensees are unable to obtain their firearm. The Uniform Crime Reports (UCRs) are also prepared at the CJIS complex. These reports help law enforcement agencies of all levels measure and analyze crime all over the country. More than 17,000 agencies nationwide contribute data. The NIBRS was created to improve the collection methods and analysis techniques to ensure greater quantity and quality of data.

NATIONAL SECURITY BRANCH

The National Security Branch of the FBI was created in 2005 to enhance the Bureau's ability to combat terrorism. This branch combined the counterterrorism, counterintelligence, and intelligence divisions all under one FBI director, who then reports to the National Director of Intelligence. This division has recently added a fourth department known as the Weapons of Mass Destruction Division. The National Security Branch is located at the National Counterterrorism Center (NCTC) in the Washington, D.C., area. The NCTC allows the Bureau's intelligence departments to better share information and coordinate with the federal intelligence community.

STRATEGIC INFORMATION AND OPERATIONS CENTER

In addition to the Headquarters in Washington, D.C., the FBI Academy in Quantico, Virginia, the CJIS in Clarksburg, West Virginia, and the National Security Branch in the Washington, D.C., area, the FBI has a Strategic Information and Operations Center (SIOC) that houses a permanently staffed round-the-clock crisis management team. The SIOC was designed as a command post where the FBI could run two crisis management teams simultaneously. Two of the major crises and their investigations that were managed at the SIOC were the Oklahoma City bombing and the 9/11 attacks. The structure itself is 40,000 square feet, with theaters for large briefings, a watch floor with a control room, and a twenty-four-hour watch post.

Conclusion

Hoover's reign over the FBI stretched for forty-eight years and resulted in one of the largest and most elite law enforcement agencies in the world. After quickly rising through the Justice Department, Hoover became director at the age of only twenty-nine and soon after started transforming the FBI into his model agency. With Hoover's leadership, it has grown from a small field office in Washington, D.C., to a multicountry intelligence agency that stretches all across the globe. With Hoover's masterful ability to bolster images and enhance dramatic truths, he managed to mold the FBI into a powerful intelligence agency that is now the largest law enforcement agency in the country. Throughout his career, he devoted endless amounts of time investigating communism and avidly pursued placing the FBI at the forefront of the intelligence arena. He demanded the utmost adherence to FBI policy from not only special agents but support staff as well and held both men and women to a strict disciplinary code. One can only wonder how proud Hoover would be now if he had the opportunity to come back and sit once more in the director's chair.

FURTHER READING

Cooper, Courtney Riley. *Ten Thousand Public Enemies*. Boston: Little-Brown and Co., 1935.
Federal Bureau of Investigation. Homepage. http://www.fbi.gov (May 6, 2007).
Fox, J. F., Jr. Unique unto itself: The records of the Federal Bureau of Investigation: 1908 to 1945. *Journal of Government Information* 30 (2004): 470–81.
Gentry, Curt. *J. Edgar Hoover: The Man and the Secrets*. New York: W. W. Norton & Company, 1991.
Hack, Richard. *Puppetmaster: The Secret Life of J. Edgar Hoover*. Beverly Hills: New Millennium Press, 2004.
Nash, Jay Robert. *Citizen Hoover*. Chicago: Nelson Hall, 1972.
Theoharis, Athan, and John Stuart Cox. 1988. *The Boss: J. Edgar Hoover and the Great American Inquisition*. Philadelphia: Temple University Press.
Toledano, Ralph de. 1973. *J. Edgar Hoover: The Man in His Time*. New Rochelle, NY: Arlington House.

Courtesy AP Images

Thomas Dewey

Clarrisa Breen

Thomas E. Dewey was born on March 24, 1902, to Annie Thomas and George Martin Dewey of Owosso, Michigan, in rooms above his maternal grandfather's store. His youth was spent around the same store and in the garden his grandfather planted behind the store. He was a Boy Scout, raised chickens (a job he hated), was a printer's devil for the local paper, and later did volunteer farm work during World War I. Dewey was close to his mother and would consult with her even during his years as special prosecutor and governor of New York.

When he started at the University of Michigan in 1919, he paid for his first year from wages earned as a sales agent for the *Saturday Evening Post*. The *Post* was offered in Owosso through the Curtis Publishing Company, and Dewey's first taste of the courts came when he was asked to testify at a hearing of a federal antitrust suit against this company.

Despite his aunt's ruminations that he should be a lawyer, he began his studies at the University of Michigan in literature and music. He excelled, performing in operas and with the Glee Club. He also wrote as a reporter for the Michigan Daily, covering events occurring at the Law School and reviewing concerts. He pledged the Phi Mu Alpha Sinfonia fraternity, an organization that, as a lawyer, he would later advise in legal and tax matters.

In the summer of 1923, when he finished his first year in Michigan's School of Law, Dewey went to Chicago where he split his time clerking in the law firm of Litzinger, Healy, and Reid—Reid being his mother's cousin—and studying voice with a scholarship to the Stephens Studio. It was here that he met a young mezzosoprano named Frances Hutt, who would later become his wife. At the end of the summer, he decided to follow the Stephens Studio (and Miss Frances Hutt) back to New York City and to complete his legal education at Columbia Law School.

Dewey grew his signature mustache during a trip to Europe after his third year of law school. He and friend, Ward Jenks, challenged each other to see who could grow a mustache first; he kept his for life. The fate of Jenks' mustache is unknown.

Dewey referred to his time at Columbia as one of the happiest of his life, in which he lived in two worlds at once, those of music and the law. In regard to music, he sang as the bass soloist for St. Matthew's and St. Timothy's Episcopal Church, earning just enough each Sunday ($15) to cover his weekly voice lessons with the Stephens Studio. After a year at Columbia and a disastrous bout of laryngitis, Dewey gave up on music and turned his full attention to his legal studies.

Upon graduation and passing the bar in 1926, Dewey went to work for Larkin, Rathbone, and Perry, a Wall Street law firm. Dewey's early practice consisted of relatively simple matters: adoptions and estates, amounts owed, insurance claims, negligence, and income tax returns, when taxes paid may have amounted to as little as ten dollars and Dewey's fee, half as much.

It was a fellow lawyer who introduced Dewey to politics in New York City. Sewell Tyng, who would later assist Dewey as special prosecutor, was a volunteer captain of the Tenth Assembly District. With his encouragement, the next year, Dewey became the captain of a two-block district between 10th and 11th streets, one block east and one west of 5th Avenue.

He held this position for three years and called on every voter he could find, encouraging straight-ticket Republican voting. If he failed to get a voter to agree with the entire Republican ticket, he would pitch support for the district's assembly candidate. As a district captain, Dewey first encountered the corruption and sophistication of Tammany Hall. On election day, gangsters employed by Tammany Hall would create diversions that allowed an abundance of bogus votes to be cast for their candidates.

In 1928, Dewey served as a special assistant attorney general in charge of supervising the polls at the 110th Street School in Harlem. It was this position that brought Dewey into alignment with what would be the pursuit of his life. There he witnessed the flooding of the polling place with armed members of the Dutch Schultz mob.

As soon as these individuals were in place, unregistered voters would swarm into the polling place and cast votes for the mob's preferred candidate. Dewey and his associates attempted to hold the unregistered voters for fraud, but the police did nothing. Dewey's fellow poll supervisors experienced similar events, and many were injured as they attempted to fulfill their supervisory duties; one was pushed down a flight of stairs, and others were beaten and thrown out of the polling places.

At this time, Tammany Hall had the tightest hold on politics in New York City. Dewey observed that citizens were disillusioned with their political situation but believed that nothing could be done, that it was not only unwise, but dangerous to fight city hall. Tammany Hall commanded loyalty and subjugation through violence and threats against merchants, but also through the disbursement of turkeys at Thanksgiving and free buckets of coal and other handouts around the hollidays to the poor and to immigrants, ensuring their gratitude and cooperation.

It was in response to these early experiences with New York politics and Tammany Hall that Dewey joined the Young Republicans in 1928. At the time, the Young Republicans in New York City was composed mostly of fellow Wall Street lawyers; they conducted research on political concerns at the local, state, and national levels. The associations Dewey made in this group would stay with him for the rest of his career. The group would meet and dine together often, especially in winter, from the 1930s through the 1960s.

Though he was now active in the political sphere, Dewey continued his legal practice, beginning his trial work with mostly pro bono work and a few cases of technical violations by corporate clients. In June of 1928,

Dewey married Frances Hutt, who was by this point a well-known professional mezzosoprano under the stage name of Eileen Hoyt. After the stock market crash of 1929, Dewey, who had moved on to the firm of McNamara and Seymour, first came into contact with George Z. Medaille, considered at the time the best trial lawyer at the New York bar.

Dewey's involvement with Medaille began with a case where a woman sued a corporate client of McNamara and Seymour's after she lost money in the October 1929 crash. Dewey did not believe, though he had done the research for the case, that he could adequately try the case, because of his limited trial experience, and recommended Medaille to his firm. During the course of this case, Medaille was called on to become the U.S. Attorney for the Southern District of New York. Upon accepting the position, Medaille requested that Dewey provide him with the names of young lawyers from the Young Republican Club and downtown law offices who could infuse new life into the staff.

Medaille offered Dewey a place on his staff the day he took his oath of office. Dewey refused because he was making $8,500 a year, an impressive sum for the Depression, and taking the position Medaille offered would mean a decrease in pay. Medaille offered a second time, a week later. This time he offered Dewey the chief assistant U.S. attorney position, and after discussions with his boss at McNamara and Seymour and with his wife, Dewey accepted and Medaille made the appropriate political maneuvers to make certain the appointment was approved. Dewey was twenty-eight years old.

As chief assistant U.S. attorney, Dewey held to the strict policies put in place by Medaille:

1. No assistant could conduct an outside law practice.
2. No photographs were permitted of an assistant and a defendant.
3. No public announcements of investigations, except announcements necessary to court procedure such as indictments or arraignments.
4. No leaking of information.
5. Absolutely no trials by newspaper.
6. No discussion of office work outside of the office.

Medaille believed that "the walls had ears, and so had the elevators." He identified some of those ears as the bail bondsmen who waited in the halls. Considering them a danger to witnesses, Medaille had them cleared from the halls. Medaille encouraged his staff to conduct mock versions of the trials they were to pursue in the office, while he sat as judge.

Of their purpose Medaille stated: "We are not sludges or political hacks, like the state prosecuting offices. We have the benefit of the Federal Bureau of Investigation, the Intelligence Service of the Treasury, the Post Office inspectors, the Secret Service, the Narcotics Squad, and all the other federal agencies. Many of them are superb. However there are limits to what they can do alone, while together we can do a great job" (Smith, 1982).

Dewey and Medaille worked very well together. In fact Dewey picked up many of Medaille's habits, including that of juggling coins. The first case assigned to Dewey by Medaille in 1931 came from the Seabury investigation, aimed at disrupting Tammany Hall. It was named the Seabury investigation after Judge Seabury.

This case was the income tax evasion case of a New York City vice squad police officer named James Quinlivan. The income in question was an estimated $80,000 worth of graft. The case was a sensational one and Dewey was uncertain of how he would do, because he still possessed little actual trial experience and this case had drawn the attention of newspapers and radio.

Dewey's key witness was a petty thief who had served as an informant and pickup man for Quinlivan. Over the course of his testimony he informed the court of how he had over the years provided Quinlivan with the passwords for brothels and speakeasies and later that Quinlivan and his partner William O'Connor sent him to similar locations as well as gambling establishments to collect payoffs.

He testified that those places that did not pay were subjected to what Quinlivan called an observation sale. For those locations, Quinlivan would go to the Federal Court and submit an affidavit that he witnessed an unknown person making a purchase of alcohol at that location, allowing Quinlivan to acquire a warrant that allowed him to go back with a prohibition agent for an arrest.

To corroborate the thief's testimony, Dewey called witnesses who would be viewed as more respectable by the jury, to testify to the house and cars bought by Quinlivan. At a time when a police officer's salary was $2,500 a year, a $16,500 house would certainly raise some eyebrows. Even though approximately a thousand cases of extortion, bribery, and obstruction of justice had been identified through the course of the investigation leading to his indictment, these charges were not pursued by the state and did not fall under federal jurisdiction. Quinlivan was convicted solely on income tax evasion and sentenced to three years in an Atlanta penitentiary.

Within a year from its beginning, the Seabury investigation lead to corruption charges being filed against Mayor Walker of New York City, resulting in Walker's resignation in the midst of his hearing before Governor Franklin D. Roosevelt. Dewey turned his attention to Arthur "Dutch Schultz" Flegenheimer, Irving "Waxey Gordon" Wexler, and Jack "Legs" Diamond. This investigation required that ordinary citizens come forth with information, something Dewey would stress in later radio addresses as special prosecutor.

Over the course of the investigations into Schultz and Gordon, Dewey and his associates employed a variety of techniques to gain information: wiretaps, reports from special agents, names of witnesses, grand jury subpoenas of bank records, and so forth. However, it was a frequent revelation that witnesses engaged in obstruction. Dewey worked to gain power within the court to employ valid sanctions for obstruction in the case of witnesses.

The first witness who became a test case for this scenario was a bank clerk named Frederick Lang. Lang controlled accounts for Waxey Gordon and his suspected brewery. Though he was repeatedly called before the grand jury and given the option of protection if he was afraid of reprisals, Lang refused to talk and was cited for contempt. He served ninety days and maintained his silence, even after Waxey Gordon was indicted. Though contempt citations were a useful tool in Dewey's arsenal, he and his associates were careful in how they were employed, because of the importance of public opinion and the desire to prevent the witnesses who kept silent up to and including the point of contempt from being viewed as sacrificial victims.

> **How a Beer Empire Operated During Prohibition**
>
> Part of the testimony used against Waxey Gordon was an explanation of how breweries continued to operate during prohibition. The federal government permitted what was called "near beer," a substance made by removing the alcohol from real beer. Breweries developed for the creation of near beer had to be licensed with the federal government. This application had to be filed by a corporation whose owners and officers were real, living, and respectable.
>
> The federal government required books that could be regularly inspected to show the amount of near beer made, with a ledger of sales. Although these breweries also produced real beer, prohibition brewers kept the real beer off the books. In the case of Waxey Gordon's brewery, near beer accounted for only 1 percent of his operation. The real beer was piped out of the brewery through an underground series of pipes and hoses running through the sewers beneath the brewery. From there, the beer was piped into the garage where it would be poured into prepared barrels. If the brewery wanted to hide its involvement with real beer after a garage was discovered, a new garage could be purchased within the area and more hose added to the underground system to move the beer to the new location.
>
> In the case of Waxey Gordon's product, the quality was likely rather suspect. Gordon's brewmaster (a man with thirty-three years of legal brewing experience) testified that good beer took six to eight weeks to make and should be allowed to sit in the vats for as much as three months, depending on season, demand, and weather. Gordon's beer sat for no more than forty-eight hours before being sent through the pipelines to the trucks.

Legs Diamond was originally charged with kidnapping and torturing a farmer for refusing to divulge the location of a still in what Diamond considered his territory; however, he was acquitted because of lack of a connection between himself and the actual event. Dewey followed this acquittal with a charge of operating a still, while he and his office continued to investigate Diamond for income tax evasion.

An unfortunate element of the Diamond case was the fact that Medaille had been retained by Diamond years earlier to represent him in a murder case. Although the indictment was dismissed because of lack of evidence and the case never went to trial, the ethics of the situation prompted concern as a possible point of appeal because of Medaille's signature on the still operation indictment.

Medaille, in the interest of the case, went on vacation for the duration, leaving Dewey as acting U.S. Attorney for the Southern District of New York. Diamond was convicted and sentenced to four years imprisonment and a fine of $11,000 for operating the still. Associates of Diamond's tried at the same time received slightly lesser sentences. However, Diamond was released on bail at the request of his counsel pending appeal. Diamond was shot dead within a few days of his release.

Further cases during his tenure as chief assistant U.S. attorney included the "Cupid of City Hall" case against deputy clerk James McCormick, who after mumbling the words of the marriage ceremony would open a drawer full of money and fumble with the marriage certificate until the bride or groom gave him a "gift" for performing the ceremony. McCormick was indicted for tax evasion for failing to pay income tax on these "gifts." Upon the testimony of sixty witnesses over the course of a four-day trial, McCormick was convicted and sentenced to four months and a fine of $15,000. McCormick was the first of the Tammany Hall leaders to be removed from office by Dewey and his associates. That fall, 1932, Dewey's first son, Thomas E. Dewey, Jr., was born.

Following the birth of his son, Dewey did not decrease his case load but made certain to be the one to feed his son each morning at 6 A.M. before heading to the office. Dewey tried Patrick Commerford, boss of Local 125 of the International Union of Operating and Hoisting Engineers and vice president of the New York Building Trades Council. Members of the union brought evidence to Dewey in this case, mostly of strikes conducted without discernable reasons and ended just as quickly with no change in treatment or pay. Each strike or walk out was orchestrated to acquire payoffs from companies to Commerford and other Tammany Hall politicos. He was convicted and sentenced to a year and a day in prison, as well as a fine of $2,000.

While still in pursuit of Dutch Schultz and Waxey Gordon, Dewey's team indicted and won a conviction for income tax evasion against Joseph Castalado, who ran a racket on artichokes. If vegetable dealers did not get their artichokes through Castalado, he would make certain the artichokes they did order through others did not make it to market before they spoiled; other dealers were robbed and/or beaten until all acquiesced, and his racket was established.

Among the multitude of cases, one that influenced a change in federal policy related to a code-writer whose services were no longer deemed necessary with the end of WWI. Herbert Yardley had at one time been responsible for the creation of the State and War department's joint code and cipher office, referred to as the "Black Chamber." However, the Black Chamber and Yardley were denied funding by Secretary of State, Henry Stimson, who considered the activities of the Chamber inappropriate and closed the office.

Yardley, without a job or outlet and with limited funds, went on to publish a series of books about codes and code writing in the United States, which were translated into several languages and eventually raised concerns about national security, both in the United States and in other nations. Dewey brokered a deal with Yardley to prevent the publication of further books by convincing the new Secretary of State, Cordell Hull, to sign a letter of apology.

This case resulted in Dewey and his staff drafting a bill signed into law by President Franklin Roosevelt in 1933 that provided criminal sanctions against leaks of codes or encryptions between foreign powers and their ambassadorial mission in the United States. Subsequently in December 1943, Yardley sent an encrypted Christmas card to Dewey that decoded to read: "Real Merry Christmas we send to you H. O. Yardley and Frank Ochs too New name upon the White House Door, Thomas E. Dewey Elected in Forty Four." (Herbert O. Yardley, personal communication, 1943).

By 1933, Dewey had frequently engaged grand juries to hear cases against various rackets. These grand juries, though complimentary to Dewey, often remarked about the long hours and the abundance of witnesses that they were called to endure, sometimes as many as five hundred per session. These grand juries marveled over the lack of quality and the fear present in the witnesses, especially in the victims of racketeers. During the winter of that year, Dewey and his staff were able to assemble enough evidence to indict Schultz and Gordon for income tax evasion.

The Schultz case was exceedingly difficult to build. Many involved in Schultz's operation were subpoenaed and questioned before grand juries without providing any information; many were cited for contempt and imprisoned, and others ignored their subpoenas and also served time. Schultz himself stayed in hiding until Medaille, Dewey, and their associates were no longer in office. Dewey and his associates were, however, able to arrest Waxey Gordon. The case against Gordon was also a difficult one to build, as Dewey and his staff raced to acquire records and materials from banks and offices before Gordon's men could remove them.

Other books and records were simply rewritten to remove mention of Gordon's name or his brewery. The investigation employed handwriting analysis by Scott Leslie, who helped Dewey identify the false identities of Gordon's associates and sort out changes in books and records. Politicians also attempted to dampen Dewey's case against Gordon.

The district attorney of New York County, a long-time Tammany Hall supporter, announced he would be conducting his own investigation of

Waxey Gordon, one that ended shortly thereafter with the announcement that "no witness was brave enough to testify against Waxey Gordon" (Smith 1982). This announcement resulted in many of Dewey's witnesses promptly forgetting what they had told Dewey and his staff.

During this time, as Dewey collected telephone records, bank accounts, toll slips, and other bits and pieces to assemble his case against Gordon, Waxey Gordon was in hiding because of rumors of a gang war raging in New York City. He was found at his summer home on White Lake in the Catskills and surrendered without violence.

Gordon's holdings were extensive, including two breweries; at least sixty trucks outfitted for the hidden transport of beer; warehouses; hotel suites; offices; and a complete automobile repair shop. However, before the case began, Medaille, anxious to return to private practice, resigned and Dewey served in his stead until President Roosevelt could appoint a successor.

Upon leaving, Medaille said of Dewey, "Mr. Dewey is young, but he has the head of a veteran on his shoulders. He is a very good trial lawyer and a great administrator." In taking the office until Roosevelt could appoint a successor for Medaille, Dewey was the youngest to hold the office at the age of thirty-one.

The trial began on November 20, 1933. The trial was based in the testimony of those not scared off by Gordon and his mob, including a restaurant operator named Helen Dellbeck, considered by Dewey and his staff as the heroine of the trial. She operated a small restaurant across from the garage where barrels were loaded onto trucks. She had sought out Gordon to send some of his men to eat at her restaurant, since business was poor. When the men did come they rang up large telephone bills that Gordon advised her to give to him and he would pay them. Her testimony was essential in linking Gordon to an organized mob.

Roosevelt appointed Medaille's permanent replacement, Martin T. Conboy, on November 25, 1933. On December 27, Thomas E. Dewey was appointed special assistant to the attorney general specifically for the case against Irving Wexler. Dewey rested his case, in which he used 131 witnesses and 939 exhibits to show the volume of Gordon's net income, which from beer alone was estimated to be $1,338,000 in 1930. This was compared to his reported net income of $8,100 for the same year, on which he had paid income tax totaling $10.76. At this time the Gordon case was considered the biggest racket case to have occurred in the East.

The defense put forth witnesses attempting to prove that Gordon was a poor man, stating that his house was purchased with money he had borrowed and money made when his wife asked him to sell her jewelry, saying that she would prefer a nice house to jewelry that she never wore. They ascribed his brewery and all its accoutrements to two men who had been assassinated in gangland fashion years before and two other men who were considered fugitives at the time of the trial.

In his summation, Dewey reminded the jury, "This is not a beer case, it is not a murder case, it is not a case of any kind except an income tax case. I said that to you with all sincerity and clarity at my command at the beginning of this case, and I repeat it. This is a prosecution of the most flagrant violation and the most flagrant conspiracy to violate the revenue laws of your government which has ever been committed in the history of the United States and I believe that that statement can stand uncontradicted." (Dewey 1974).

The jury took fifty-one minutes to convict Waxey Gordon, and he was sentenced to ten years imprisonment and a fine of $20,000. Among his last actions as acting U.S. attorney, Dewey indicted public officials and also those who identified and counseled officials to take bribes. He issued hundreds of warrants for illegal voter registration and dispatched U.S. Marshals to polling places and campaigned against voter tampering.

Of his work for the U.S. Attorney's office, Dewey believed, "We had all done a useful job. Among other things, the underworld had learned it was dangerous not to pay its income taxes. It was established that with manpower and enough patience and skill the biggest criminal enterprises could be broken up. We had pioneered what we considered to be new techniques of combining investigative and legal skills in criminal investigation with new, investigative accounting procedures and extensive use of grand jury examination of hostile witnesses." (Dewey 1974).

In 1934, Dewey left the U.S. Attorney's office for the Southern District of New York and resumed private practice, though he maintained his position as special assistant to the attorney general, specifically for the case against Irving Wexler because of appeals in the Waxey Gordon case. Gordon lost those appeals by the summer of 1935, and Dewey resigned from the position on July 13, 1935, submitting a bill for $1,200 for his time and services rendered.

In 1934, mostly free of work with the U.S. attorney's office, Dewey also became chairman of the Committee of Criminal Courts Law and Procedure of the city bar association. He advocated for a shift away from defendant's protection by the law including:

1. The grant of authority for a prosecutor to comment on a defendant's failure to testify in his own defense.
2. The presumption of ownership for firearms found in vehicles.
3. The establishment of a central felony court.
4. The acceptance of a majority verdict of ten of twelve jurors.
5. The creation of laws forbidding lawyers to advise in the operation of criminal enterprises.
6. The denial of bail for individuals with two convictions.

None of these suggestions were adopted and some were considered unethical by the bar. During this time, one of the investigators from the Seabury investigations, Irving Ben Cooper, announced that seventy-seven bail bondsmen continuously perjured themselves in order to claim funds from Dutch Schultz for assisting his numbers runners. Public outcry resulted in the empanelling of a grand jury, but internal squabbles in the district attorney's office seemed to bring the investigation to a halt.

The foreman of this grand jury, Lee Thompson Smith, stated that "We have labored under the most difficult handicaps. Every conceivable obstacle has been put in our path" (Smith 1982). He and the rest of the jury, refused to quit, but subsequently refused the admittance of any assistant to the district attorney's office, subpoenaing witnesses on their own, and publically demanding that District Attorney William Copeland Dodge appoint a special prosecutor of their choosing. They were dubbed the "runaway grand jury" (Smith 1982).

The district attorney, who appointed a man of his own choosing, sending the grand jury into another deadlock, refused the runaway grand jury's suggestions for a special prosecutor. Meanwhile, further allegations were being brought in front of the grand jury including charges against the district attorney as being involved in a poultry racket. The grand jury stepped down with a demand that then Governor Lehman appoint a special prosecutor, a demand that was supported by many civic groups in New York.

In 1935, Dewey was not the first choice for special prosecutor after the demands made by the runaway jury. Four other lawyers were identified and offered the job: Charles Hughes, Jr., George Medaille, Charles Tuttle, and Thomas Thacher; however, as a group they refused and offered Dewey's name instead.

Even with this support, the governor was reluctant to appoint Dewey to the position. When he did, he referred to Dewey as relatively unknown, but competent. Dewey accepted a position as special prosecutor for the county of New York, appointed to investigate concerns of vice and graft in the county (F. W. Adams, correspondence, 1935).

In his position as a U.S. attorney, Dewey relied upon the support of the federal government, as special prosecutor, he himself admitted that he was on his own. Further, when District Attorney Dodge referred to Dewey's position, he stated that Dewey had accepted a position as deputy assistant district attorney, the lowest rank in the district attorney's office.

An anonymous letter to the attorney could be posted for two cents, and at this time, anonymity was the norm. Letters with tips and information about cases bore signatures of assumed names, ambiguous organizations, or simply nameless concerned citizens. In his first weeks as special prosecutor,

> *"I am confident that with your help we can stamp out racketeering in New York. We can make this city too dangerous for organized crime. To what extent this investigation succeeds, is largely in your hands. Your cooperation is essential. Your confidence will be respected. Your help will be kept secret and your persons protected. If you have evidence of organized crime, of whatever kind, however large or small, bring it to us. The rest is our job. We will do our best."*
> —Thomas E. Dewey radio address, July 30, 1935, on stations WABC, WOR, and WMCA

Dewey picked Acting Deputy Chief Inspector John Lyons to head the detectives who would report directly to his office.

During Dewey's tenure as special prosecutor, dinner for twelve, with drinks, cost $67; dinner was $2 a plate and a telephone call was 10 cents. The bulk of the bill was incurred over mixed drinks and scotch. After the Criminal Courts Committee attended such a dinner at Dewey's club, Dewey sent a note to those in attendance that the cost came to $6.70 per person, and if they had enjoyed the party, they were to send him a check for the same.

Lyons assembled an investigative staff of seventy-six. He began with a dozen veteran police officers, from undercover units and the alien and bomb squads. Other officers were selected as they finished their training at the police academy; these officers would make the bulk of what became known as the "grand jury squad." These men were chosen based on their education and lack of political associations and bad habits. Lyons' men were to be loyal to him and to Dewey and not be jaded by precinct routine. Added to these men were men with backgrounds in pharmacology, photography, and stenography.

Lawyers selected to work with Dewey were to be paid between $1,500 and $4,000 a year. These numbers were to increase over Dewey's years of service as special prosecutor, but the original staff consisted of nineteen men and one woman, ranging in age from twenty-five to forty. Most were distinguished graduates, young lawyers with varying political and educational backgrounds. Many were members of Phi Beta Kappa, and stories are told that the prevalence of Phi Beta Kappa keys on the watch chains of Dewey's staff convinced some defense attorneys to argue that they should be removed as potential weapons.

Both the legal and support staff of Dewey's office were chosen with great care, to be beyond reproach and trustworthy, mainly to prevent leaks of information to the press and to those who would report back to organized crime and political figures under investigation. Some lawyers picked to work with Dewey's staff were paid only a dollar a day, but were selected with as much care and consideration as those who received the highest salary his office could offer.

One of these dollar-a-day lawyers, Manuel Robbins, remarked of the experience and of Dewey: "He had an air of inspiration about him that certainly got carried on to his staff. It was a crusade, and we were all young enough to be very ardent crusaders…we were battling the whole, organized underworld of New York City, and we were the forces of decent living" (Smith 1982)

Dewey ran his office under the same rules as Medaille had during his tenure as U.S. attorney. However, Dewey's position as Special Prosecutor was not without troubles. He could not maintain Medaille's rule against discussing investigations with the press. Publicity and a good relationship with the press were essential to Dewey's work as special prosecutor and with maintaining his legitimacy in that office, especially since the press, when not given information by Dewey, were inclined to focus on gossip and rumors about problems and rackets not investigated by Dewey and with speculation regarding possible ongoing investigations.

He had to convince the police that he was not a politician or someone who talked a good game without accomplishing anything. To do this, Dewey made certain that he consistently highlighted the activities of Lyons and the other detectives who worked for the special prosecutor's office on rackets investigations in press releases and public speeches, praising their efforts and establishing his relationship with the police as a partnership, rather than treating the police as his subordinates.

His biggest problems arose, however, when his request for appropriations to fund his salary and that of his staff was the subject of an injunction against the comptroller, seeking to prevent Dewey from receiving any payment at all. Arguments were made before the Supreme Court of New York and in the *Daily News* against Dewey's appointment and his salary (Letter to City Editor, July 30, 1935).

In order to prosecute organized crime figures in New York, it was necessary for Dewey and his staff to draft a new bill for the New York state legislature. Dewey submitted the proposed bill in 1935, as investigations into loan sharking and prostitution rackets were initiated in the special prosecutor's office.

Up to this point it was necessary to file separate indictments for each offense. In this case, there were ninety indictments, some of which rested on the testimony of a single witness, whose cooperation and survival were not guaranteed. The bill Dewey and his staff sent to the state legislature mirrored one in place on the federal level, allowing for a joinder of felonies. It was passed just days before Dewey submitted his first racket indictment.

Dewey's office's first rackets investigation targeted loan sharks, considered by Dewey to be "one of the most vicious rotten rackets that ever plundered our city" (Dewey 1974). This first investigation led to the arrest of twenty-two loan sharks, all with ties to organized crime and within a month, the conviction of twenty-one, one escaping on a technical violation made by a young assistant in Dewey's office. Over the course of these trials more were arrested, bringing the total to thirty-six convictions.

Loan-sharking investigations led to targeted investigations of political corruption and graft, as well as other elements of organized crime. Dewey indicted Edward S. Moran, Jr., in 1937 for receiving bribes as a member of the legislature. Moran accepted funds upward of $8,500 from taxicab operation organizations for influence over his votes and authority in the assembly to prevent unfavorable legislation against taxicab services and organizations. As special prosecutor, Dewey won convictions in seventy-two of seventy-three cases.

Included in those cases were racketeering investigations regarding Louis Lepke Buchalter, Dutch Schultz, and Charles "Lucky" Luciano, as well as Tammany Leader James Hines, who lost his hold over the 11th District when LaGuardia was elected in 1937 with Dewey as district attorney. Of those, Lepke was sentenced to death in the electric chair after Dewey resigned his position as special prosecutor.

The phrase United We Stand has gained modern recognition as the motto of the war on terror after the events of September 11, 2001. During Dewey's investigation of Schultz and Luciano, similar signs were frequently seen in restaurants and cafeterias, displaying images of an American eagle with its wings spread over the skyscrapers of New York City. These signs identified establishments as part of Dutch Schultz's restaurant extortionist racket.

Dutch Schultz was tried and acquitted for income tax evasion in the small town of Malone, on the New York/Canadian border. Schultz returned to New York City, where Dewey attempted to prepare an indictment against Schultz for charges of failing to file an income tax return not covered in the Malone trial.

Dewey was the recipient of continual death threats by this time. His wife, pregnant with their second child, received repeated crank calls requesting that she come to the morgue to identify Dewey's body. J. Edgar Hoover sent Dewey letters warning him that his life was in danger. The price on his head was $25,000. Dewey employed a bodyguard, who also served as his chauffeur.

The biggest threat to Dewey was Dutch Schultz himself, who considered Dewey a personal nemesis. It was Schultz's desire to see Dewey assassinated that ultimately led to his own death by gangland assassination in October of 1935. Lepke and Luciano were concerned about Schultz's intention to have Dewey assassinated, despite their refusal to be involved and warnings against such an occurrence, because they believed it could be the catalyst for a "national crusade against organized crime." (The Herlands Report 1954).

Schultz had purportedly planned Dewey's assassination for October 25, 1935, seven days after the birth of Dewey's second son. Lepke is credited with ordering the assassination of Schultz in the men's room of the Palace Chop House on October 23, 1935. Schultz succumbed to his wounds on October 26th.

Charles "Lucky" Luciano was considered a major organizing force in the criminal underworld of 1920s and 30s New York. He was called "Lucky" partly because of his survival of an assassination attempt by rival narcotics sellers and partly because of a tattoo on his right arm. The horseshoe tattooed on his arm was pointed out by Luciano himself, as a reason for the nickname. The case made against him by Dewey was based on charges of running prostitution rings.

World War II and Charles "Lucky" Luciano

Born Salvatore Lucania in Sicily in 1897, Lucky Luciano was instrumental in the organization of crime in America. He immigrated illegally and is considered responsible for loan sharking, drug trafficking, and protection rackets for prostitution. He was tried for his involvement with prostitution, narcotics, and racketeering in 1936. He was sentenced to thirty to fifty years in prison.

Of Dewey, Luciano said, "Dewey was such a...racketeer himself, in a legal way, that he crawled up my back with a frame and stabbed me." (The Herlands Report 1954). As World War II escalated, Meyer Lansky brokered a deal for Luciano to be transferred to Great Meadow to be of easier access to Naval Intelligence. Luciano's influence was employed to secure cooperation with other members of organized crime and among unions and dock workers to rout out spies, communists, and saboteurs.

It was highlighted in the Herlands Report that without Luciano's say-so, it would have been impossible for Lansky or others to convince dockworkers that it was "all right for them to cooperate." Through Luciano, Lansky and others were allowed to introduce naval personnel as "okay, regular guys," allowing them more access and less interference on the docks. Luciano was particular about his involvement, especially when his influence was used to generate contacts with the Mafia in Sicily.

Luciano stated, "When I get out—nobody knows how this war will turn out—whatever I do, I want it kept quiet, private, so that when I get back to Italy I'm not a marked man." (The Herlands Report 1954). Luciano was well aware of his imminent return to Italy, because a warrant of deportation was already lodged against him. His collaboration with naval intelligence was corroborated by the district attorney's office, whose wire taps on known organized crime locations picked up naval intelligence work.

Among the specific actions taken under Luciano's advisement was the determination of the location where antiwar and anti-American literature was being printed in Harlem and the avoidance of the organization of longshoremen by Harry Bridges.

The Herlands Report closed with the findings that: "No practical purpose would be served by debating the technical scope of Luciano's aid to the war effort." Over and beyond any precise rating of his contribution is the crystal clear fact that Luciano and his associates and contacts during a period when "the outcome of the war appeared extremely grave" were responsible for a wide range of services that were considered "useful to the Navy."

Luciano's body was returned to the United States after his death of a heart attack in 1962. He is buried in a New York cemetery.

Dewey and his investigators moved against the prostitution racket in January 1936 in a raid that covered eighty brothels, of which forty were inexplicably unsuccessful. However, this fact was never fully investigated because Dewey found it necessary to commandeer taxi cabs to transport the sheer number of people picked up in the successful raids back to his offices and to local jails.

> **Eunice Carter**
>
> Eunice Carter was the only female and the only African American attorney in Dewey's original special prosecutor's office and was also distinguished as the first African American woman in the New York district attorney's office. She also sat as secretary of LaGuardia's Committee on Conditions in Harlem in the mid-1930s. She was the wife of a Harlem dentist and a graduate of Smith College and Fordham University Law School. Carter was instrumental in identifying the prostitution racket that led to the prosecution of Charles "Lucky" Luciano.
>
> Carter was active in the magistrate's court, often when campaigns against prostitution were at their peak. Carter identified that no prostitute represented by Attorney Abe Karp was ever sentenced to a prison term. Though Dewey was not inclined to investigate prostitution as a racket, convinced it was more a social rather than criminal concern, Carter and another lawyer in Dewey's employ, Murray Gurfein, convinced Dewey that organized crime was definitely involved in prostitution.
>
> Along with others in Dewey's employ, Carter, who conducted most of the interviews with prostitutes in preparation for the case, was highlighted for her untiring efforts in bringing about the conviction of Luciano. Dewey later appointed her as head of the Special Sessions Bureau of the district attorney's office with another veteran of his staff, Sol Gelb, a position she held until 1945. Carter entered into private practice after that and worked as an activist as a charter member of the National Council of Negro Women and with the United Nations.

It was the scope of the raids that convinced three of the madams in custody that Dewey must have arrested the entire mob. Those madams decided, unlike others who swore they were simply housewives and their girls were students, models, artists, or telephone operators, that they would cooperate in order to get the mob out of their business. Dewey was disappointed by this initial cooperation, three of one hundred arrested prostitutes was hardly the beginnings of a successful prosecution, but others were swayed as Dewey and his staff informed them, "We are not in the business of prosecuting prostitutes and madams and pimps and heels in this business. We are here in an effort to get the big shots" (Dewey 1974).

Further, they asked those they arrested, the prostitutes held on bail set at $10,000 each and gangsters, a much higher rate, that they simply provide information, whether they wanted or were willing to testify or not. Those who were willing to testify were granted immunity. Over the course of four months, after placing Frank Hogan in charge of the women and as they were gradually weaned off drugs and treated for diseases picked up in the brothels, many were convinced to talk. The medical records of each girl were kept to corroborate their standing as prostitutes, as some continued to swear that they were only students or had legitimate jobs.

Once it became apparent that Dewey was convincing those prostitutes he had in custody to give up information, despite warnings and threats, others associated with the business began to talk: bookers (men who convinced women to enter brothels), thieves who had worked as collectors of protection money, and pimps. These men assisted in creating the clearest links between prostitution and Luciano.

Luciano's primary involvement with the prostitution racket was in establishing a cut of the profits of each brothel. He would send enforcers, such as Tommy "the Bull" to convince, through threats and violence, madams to pay fees for protection. If they refused to do so, their establishments were trashed and girls and madams were hospitalized. Further links were established when employees of the hotels where Luciano kept suites identified leaders of the prostitution racket as frequent visitors of those rooms. These witnesses were crucial, as they were among a handful of individuals not involved in criminal activities who could be called to testify.

Luciano was arrested on April Fool's Day 1936, in a casino in Hot Springs, Arkansas; he was jailed, but shortly was released on $5,000 bond. A second warrant for his arrest was issued, as it was imperative to keep him in jail until he could be extradited to New York. This time his bail was set at $200,000, and Luciano was transferred to a jail in Little Rock, Arkansas, to await extradition. Bribes were offered to the attorney general of Arkansas to allow Luciano to escape, and politicians and lawyers advocated for his release. They failed to have an effect, and Luciano was extradited to New York. Once in New York, Luciano was held under the highest level of bail ever set in New York at that time, the sum of $350,000.

> *"You cannot convict the men at the very top of a criminal enterprise, who deal with criminal subordinates, who deal through criminal subordinates beneath them, except upon the testimony of the people who are their associates, their subordinates, or their intimates. There is not any other way known to the law under the system of jurisprudence ... we cannot get bishops; we cannot get clergymen; we cannot get bankers, or business men to testify about gangsters, pimps and prostitution. They just don't happen to be available as witnesses... We have to use as witnesses such of the associates of these defendants as we can compel to tell the truth."*
> —Thomas E. Dewey, summation, trial of Charles "Lucky" Luciano

As the trial began, attempts were made by the defense to distance Luciano from the charges, identifying him as being involved in race tracks and gambling, but not prostitution. The defense swore that Luciano was not acquainted with his codefendants and that none had ever worked for him. Cross-examinations of prostitutes by the defense was brutal, and many were questioned about why they had decided to cooperate with Dewey's office.

This line of questioning, however, led to the downfall of the defense, when prostitute Thelma Jordan detailed torture methods, such as being burned by cigars or having one's tongue split, used by Luciano's organization to prevent and punish prostitutes for talking. Her testimony provided further assistance to Dewey, when she stated that she testified because of her faith in the special prosecutor's office.

Frequent objections were made, especially when witnesses, such as booker Al Weiner was asked by the defense what Dewey had promised in return for his testimony. To this question, Weiner replied: leniency and placement in "a jail where I won't be murdered" (Dewey 1974). Problems arose for Dewey when respectable and criminal witnesses alike backed out of their testimony, and some even swore that they had lied in previous statements given in Dewey's office. Others claimed a failure of memory.

Luciano took the stand in his own defense. Under cross-examination by Dewey, he admitted to as much as he believed Dewey might be able to prove. He admitted to involvement in bookmaking, race tracks, narcotics, bootlegging, gambling, lying about his occupation on gun permits, and failure to pay state income tax. He denied involvement with prostitution, other than hiring prostitutes for his personal use, despite the testimony of fifty prostitutes and madams contrary to that fact. He was found guilty and sentenced to thirty to fifty years in prison.

In 1938, as district attorney, Dewey filed an indictment leading to the arrest of arguably the most powerful Democrat in New York State. James J. Hines was arrested on May 25, 1938, and charged with running a numbers racket. Dewey received substantial negative publicity for his initial persecution of Hines, his opponents in the courtroom and politics believing the indictment was a political maneuver to assist Dewey in establishing himself as a gubernatorial nominee.

Dewey did not back down, however, and began the prosecution's case by establishing the link between Hines and the late Dutch Schultz, as well as how former District Attorney Dodge assisted Hines in controlling the maneuvers of police and judges throughout New York City. Witnesses for the prosecution included the fire chief of Troy, New York, Schultz's former lawyer, and other key members of Tammany Hall, as well as principal numbers runners within the racket.

This case had its roots in the original information given to the runaway grand jury that had established the need for a special prosecutor. In those sessions, the police commissioner had testified that Hines protected slot machine and poultry rackets. However, points raised by the defense allowed for a mistrial to be declared when a member of the runaway grand jury was called to testify. Hines was released on bail as Dewey prepared for a new trial.

The second trial occurred a year later on January 26, 1939, after Dewey made a failed run for governor. His popularity had not diminished with this failure to win the election, and he received an abundance of anonymous support. Letters were sent with Dewey's photograph from the newspaper in place of an address and still were delivered, many without postage or with the district attorney's office as the return address.

The first blow to the case, however, came when a key prosecution witness, George Weinberg, committed suicide over his fears of being subject to retribution for his involvement in the case as state's evidence. Judge Nott, who sat on the bench for the trial, permitted Weinberg's testimony from the first trial to be read into evidence, after he had informed the jury of Weinberg's suicide. New witnesses were brought forward, including a bartender who established the connection between Hines and Dutch Schultz, citing frequent meals he had witnessed between the two.

The jury agreed with Dewey about connections between Hines and Schultz, as well as Hines' involvement in widespread political corruption and abuse of his political power. After seven hours of deliberation, they found Hines guilty on all thirteen counts of the indictment. Hines was granted leniency because of his age and was sentenced to four to eight years imprisonment. Hines appealed the case until 1940, but the conviction was upheld and Hines served four years in Sing Sing Prison.

Dewey's perseverance in the Hines prosecution made him a popular figure in political cartoons and commentary. As the Brooklyn Dodgers drastically improved their standing in baseball in 1939, it was remarked by sports caster Fred Allen that "if the team won two more games that season, Dewey would investigate them" (Smith 1982). Streets were named after him and he was a prominent figure in movie newsreels. Friends remarked that he received more publicity in 1940 than Hitler.

In the numerous speeches made by Dewey in closing remarks and the aftermath of successful convictions, it was not uncommon for him to draw attention and give credit to his staff, but he focused also on juries and

> "Whispers concerning racial and religious preferences have been injected into both sides. The man or woman who votes for a candidate because of his race or religion, or votes against him for such a reason, is a disgrace to American citizenship. I condemn and despise any support that is based on racial or religious prejudices. There are some things more important than being elected governor and one is the spirit of religious and racial good will. I would rather go down to defeat than be elected by votes based on race or religion."
> —Handwritten note attached to letter from Thomas E. Dewey to Walter White, secretary of the NAACP, June 21, 1939

witnesses. He spoke of these people as breaking the unspoken law of "Thou shalt not squeal" and standing up to the most dangerous men of their age.

He spoke of their courage and of their perseverance, whether they themselves were members of the defendant's criminal network or ordinary citizens. Among the stories told of Thomas E. Dewey is one of a ten-year-old girl who was disappointed over an abundance of rain. She told her father that if the rain did not stop, she was going to sue God. When her father replied that she was unlikely to win such a suit, she replied, "I could if Dewey was my lawyer" (Smith 1982).

After his work as special prosecutor, Dewey returned to private practice and did well. He ran for governor on the Republican ticket in 1942 and won. World War II resulted in a very different role for Dewey, not only as district attorney, but also as an outspoken opponent of discrimination based on race and nationality.

As governor, he was faced with petitions for leniency and pardon from some of the individuals he had sought to prosecute and had himself prosecuted during his tenure as special prosecutor. Among them was Louis Lepke Buchalter, who was prosecuted in Federal Court on narcotics charges and in Brooklyn on charges of murder, related to his mob involvement. He petitioned Dewey for clemency, but Dewey refused. Lepke was executed by electric chair in March 1944. Of him, Dewey stated "No man deserved it more" (Smith 1982).

Dewey did pardon another mob figure from his past, however. Because of his assistance to the Allies in WWII, Dewey pardoned Charles "Lucky" Luciano, who was then deported to his native Italy. The Herlands Report, detailing not only Luciano's career in crime but also his service to the allies, was instrumental in his pardon.

In 1944 and 1948 Dewey ran for president on the Republican ticket. The Gallup poll for the 1948 presidential election predicted Dewey would win the presidential election, resulting in erroneous headlines of "Dewey Beats Truman." However, Dewey lost, with Truman claiming 303 votes in the Electoral College and a margin of two million popular votes.

In running for president, Dewey had avoided outright condemnation of communism in his political campaign for the 1948 election, a point many believe may have cost him the election. Dewey, however, was not an extremist, like Senator McCarthy and others from the heyday of the red scare. He accepted America's role in defending the world against the threat of communism, but he did not pursue communism in the same fashion that he sought out graft and racketeers during his tenure as special prosecutor.

Dewey continued to be involved in politics with the Republican Party; his assistance and support were considered vital for nominations and political primaries, and he also worked to recruit new members, especially among young voters. Yet, after his failed presidential runs, Dewey settled into a life of private law practice. He also engaged in an active friendship with FBI director J. Edgar Hoover. The two were voluminous correspondents, sending newspaper clippings of interest and books back and forth. When Hoover was tapped to examine racial tension and riots in the mid- to late 1960s, Dewey became the silent author of the final report. His involvement in the project was hoped, by President Johnson, to be a moderating factor, reigning in Hoover's reputed extremist tendencies.

Dewey, however, turned out to be the more radical of the two, although he had hoped his involvement would assist in creating a compromise between ideas of welfare and warfare, so much so that some have argued that his response to growing concerns held racist undertones. This would be in direct contrast with Dewey's writings, speeches, and actions on the subject. As governor, he had enacted the first state law forbidding discrimination in employment based on race or religion. During World War II he made speeches cautioning against racial discrimination and the alienation of immigrants and citizens whose heritage stemmed from the AXIS powers.

His decision not to seek a third run for president was considered by some to be a sign that he was turning his back on his civic duty to the American people; however, Thomas E. Dewey was above all else a patriot. He believed in his country. Anything that threatened the core ideals of America was suspect in his eyes, be it corrupt politicians, organized crime figures, communism, or extremist groups. The strongest defense against such factors, he believed, was the power of the American people to be actively involved in their government and in the legal process.

This view was best summed up by Dewey in a state address made during his run for governor in 1942. "It is for us, in the face of a totalitarian world to declare our faith in democracy by taking the time to register and vote... Failure to perform your duty to register to vote causes your right to vote to become weaker. And never forget that when you fail to vote others who do vote are exercising your rights for you. Power residing in the people tends to wither away by so much as they do not use that power. Someone will always exercise the power of government. In America, that power must forever rest with the people. But it will be kept by the people only if they use it." (Private papers of Thomas E. Dewey).

Dewey died March 16, 1971, and is buried in Pawling cemetery in Duchess County, New York.

FURTHER READING

There are three key volumes of note on Thomas E. Dewey.

Richard Norton Smith's biography details Dewey's political career and his influence in Republican politics.

Smith, Richard Norton. 1982. *Thomas E. Dewey and His Times. The First Full Scale Biography of the Maker of the Modern Republican Party.* New York: Simon & Schuster.

Thomas E. Dewey's autobiography was a key resource in writing this chapter and contains an abundance of trial transcripts as well as Dewey's reminiscences of his work prior to becoming governor.

Dewey, Thomas E. 1974. *Twenty against the Underworld. An Autobiography of a District Attorney and His Fight against Organized Crime.* Edited by Rodney Campbell. New York: Doubleday.

Another great source of information regarding Dewey is the following:

Stohlberg, Mary. 1995. *Fighting Organized Crime Politics: Justice and the Legacy of Thomas E. Dewey.* Boston: Northeastern University Press.

The greatest source of information about Thomas E. Dewey is the collection of private papers, case files, scrapbooks, photographs, and multimedia materials held in the Rare Books Division of the University of Rochester Library in Rochester, New York. The following were used in writing this chapter:

1. General Private Papers, unspecified; Series 1, Box 89, Folder 1.
2. Envelope attached to the letter to Lawyers Bar Association from a few tenants of 115 East 130, Series 1, Box 89, Folder 1.
3. General Private Papers, Series 1, Box 4; specifically, file 6: private law cases through 1924: Henry M. Carrere, tax returns.
4. The people of the state of New York against Edward S. Moran, Jr., Grand Jury indictment, Private Papers, Series 1, Box 4, Folder 2.
5. The people of the state of New York against Charles H. Mullens and William Solomon, Grand Jury indictment, Private Papers, Series 1, Box 4, Folder 2.
6. Letter from the Department of Justice dated December 27, 1933 to Thomas E. Dewey, Private Papers, Series 1, Box 11, Folder 1.
7. In general, Private Papers, Series 1, Box 10, Folder 6: private law cases through 1934: Irving Wexler, alias Waxey Gordon.
8. Letter from Thomas E. Dewey dated July 13, 1935, to Col. C. E. Stewart, Private Papers, Series 1, Box 11, Folder 1.
9. Letter from F. W. Adams dated July 1, 1935, to Thomas E. Dewey, Private Papers, Series 1, Box 11, Folder 1.
10. Klein letter to City Editor July 30th, 1935; B.C.L. Company v. Frank J. Taylor; BCL Company v. LaGuardia; letters between Henry Klein and John Langel, July to August 1935, Private Papers, Series 1, Box 89, Folder 12.
11. In general, statements by Thomas E. Dewey, re: discrimination in employment vs. Italians; for the Pittsburgh *Courier* re: African Americans; Private Papers, Series 1, Box 88, Folders 4 and 5.
12. Personal correspondence: first term X-Y Series 4, Box 203; Christmas card from Herbert O. Yardley, December 20, 1943.
13. Private Papers, J. Edgar Hoover correspondence; post-governor correspondence, Series 8, Box 21, Folder 9.

The Herlands Report (1954), the official report of William Herlands, the New York State Commissioner of Investigation, detailed the agreements made between U.S. Naval Intelligence and the Mafia leaders of

Thomas Dewey

New York. The following items in the report are from the private papers in the Dewey collection at the University of Rochester.

14. The Herlands Report, September 17, 1954, Series 13, Box 16, Folder 2.
15. Governor Dewey's commutation: pp. 2, 9, and 10.
16. Transfer to Great Meadow for Naval Intelligence: pp. 6, 7, 49, and 51–53.
17. Luciano file for executive clemency: May 8, 1945, pp. 8 and 99.
18. Why Naval intelligence used criminals: pp. 14, 15, and 18.
19. Why Luciano was brought in: pp. 8 and 39.
20. What Luciano did: p. 68, secured cooperation of others; p. 69, "all right for them to cooperate"; p. 70, allow for introductions of naval personnel as okay, regular guys, allowing them more access and less interference; pp. 86, 87, and 90, contacts with the Mafia in Sicily.
21. Luciano on "it": p. 61, "When I get out—nobody knows how this war will turn out—whatever I do, I want it kept quiet, private, so that when I get back to Italy I'm not a marked man." (because a warrant of deportation was lodged against him).
22. DA's office wiretaps picked up naval intelligence work: p. 72, Harlem literature printing; p. 73, union cards; pp. 73 and 74, avoidance of organization of longshoremen by Harry Bridges.
23. Findings: p. 94, "No practical purpose would be served by debating the technical scope of Luciano's aid to the war effort. Over and beyond any precise rating of his contribution is the crystal clear fact that Luciano and his associates and contacts during a period when "the outcome of the war appeared extremely grave" were responsible for a wide range of services which were considered "useful to the Navy."

Courtesy of the Library of Congress

Robert Kennedy: The Enforcer Within

J. Scott Granberg-Rademacker

In an address at the University of Georgia Law School on May 6, 1961, Robert "Bobby" Francis Kennedy (RFK) said: "We know that it is law which enables man to live together, that creates order out of chaos. We know that the law is the glue that holds civilization together." (Guthman and Allen 1993). This simple statement summed up Kennedy's sober belief in upholding the law. It was this sacred belief in the law that drove him to take on some of the most notorious gangsters, racketeers, and hoodlums and later drove him to take on Southern racism by enforcing civil rights legislation in the newly desegregated South.

Robert Kennedy had a distinguished career as a public servant, serving as a lawyer on the staff of the Senate Permanent Subcommittee on Investigations, of which Senator Joseph McCarthy was the chair. He also served as counsel for the Senate Select Committee on Improper Activities in the Labor or Management Field, otherwise known as the "Rackets Committee," and as U.S. Attorney General during the Kennedy (John) and Johnson administrations. RFK was elected to the senate in New York and was a presidential candidate during the 1968 election. The career of Robert Kennedy was in many ways like a light bulb: it burned bright and constant, it illuminated some of the darkest corners of the criminal underworld, and it burned out unexpectedly and prematurely.

To fully understand Robert Kennedy the crime fighter it is helpful to understand his roots. Kennedy's upbringing and personality contributed greatly to his effectiveness in public life. This chapter is divided into four sections. The first section expounds on RFK's early life and how his family dynamics and upbringing forged his tenacious personality. The second section details RFK's role on the Rackets Committee, and the third section explores Kennedy's tenure as attorney general, with a special emphasis on civil rights and the battle against organized crime. The fourth section reflects on Bobby Kennedy's contribution as a crime fighter.

THE YOUNG BOBBY

Robert Kennedy was born on November 20, 1925, in Brookline, Massachusetts. He was the seventh of nine children born to Rose Fitzgerald and Joseph Patrick Kennedy, Sr. Growing up in the Kennedy house was a Darwinian experience. Joe Kennedy, Sr., was intensely competitive and constantly pushed the children to improve. With such a large family, the competition for Joe Sr.'s attention was fierce, and the older children had an advantage because of their age. Young Bobby lived in the shadow of his older siblings—not having the athleticism of his older brother Joe Jr., the wit of his older brother Jack, or the grace of his older sister Kathleen.

These three older children (dubbed by the other siblings as the "golden trio") received the lion's share of their father's attention. To Joe Sr., these were the children most likely to be successful. He paid little attention to young Bobby, who was not very tall, athletic, or witty. At dinnertime, Joe Sr. would sit with Joe Jr., Jack, and Kathleen at one end of the table and talk politics, while Bobby would sit at the other end of the table with Rose. As Evan Thomas notes, this was the wrong end of the table to be on in the Kennedy family. Despite his mother's affection, RFK desperately sought his father's approval.

In an effort to toughen him up, young Robert Kennedy was enrolled in boxing lessons.

—Thomas, 2000

However, obtaining his approval was difficult. RFK was a mediocre student and was mercilessly teased by his older siblings. In family games or debates, young Bobby seldom won. This was difficult for him because his father's approval and attention were usually showered on those who were "winners." Joe Sr.'s own words to his children are telling: "We don't want any losers around here. In this family we want winners...Don't come in second or third—that doesn't count—but win" (Kennedy 1974). In an effort to overcompensate for his lack of athleticism, young Bobby developed a fiery personality and a dogged determination, both of which served him well later in life.

During World War II, RFK fell in love with the gallant notion of fighting for one's country. Both of his older brothers were in the service and fighting overseas, and Bobby was anxious to join the fight. John was stationed on a PT boat and tasted battle firsthand when a Japanese destroyer severed the boat. The *New York Times* praised JFK for his bravery in battle. Joe Jr. (not wanting to be outdone by JFK in terms of bravery) volunteered for a high-risk mission to fly a bomber filled with explosives into a secret German base. The plan was to crash the bomber directly into the base, where it would explode, and Joe Jr. would parachute out before detonation. Unfortunately, the bomber exploded and killed Joe Jr. before reaching the target.

Bobby Kennedy: "What I remember most vividly about growing up was going to a lot of different schools, always having to make new friends, and that I was very awkward. I dropped things, and fell down all the time. I had to go to the hospital a few times for stitches in my head and my leg. And I was pretty quiet most of the time. And I didn't mind being alone."

—Newfield, 1969

Despite aspirations to get his wings and fly, RFK flunked his flight school exam and resigned from officer training to enlist in the Navy. To add further humiliation to his already battered ego, the destroyer that Bobby served on was named the *Joseph P. Kennedy Jr.*, after his heroic older brother (his father pulled strings at the Pentagon to get the ship named after his eldest son). Robert Kennedy finally shipped out for duty in February 1946—when the war was all but over. Disappointed by the lack of action and the boredom of life at sea, Kennedy was honorably discharged from the navy nearly four months later.

Though young, RFK was also developing a sense of personal integrity. The death of Joe Jr. meant that Bobby had increasing importance in the family. This was especially evident as he played the role of peacemaker between his father and his brother Jack. Bobby had also learned the value of hard work: he had learned that through hard work and determination he could compensate for his own personal shortcomings.

During his brother Jack's congressional campaign for the 11th Congressional District, Bobby Kennedy was enlisted by his father to help JFK get elected. He was assigned the difficult task of campaigning in East Cambridge—an area where JFK had little support. This working-class neighborhood saw the Kennedy family as snobbish and aristocratic. To relax, Bobby used to go across the street from the campaign headquarters in East Cambridge and play softball with local kids in the park, and although JFK didn't carry East Cambridge, a local Cambridge politician noted that Bobby Kennedy's softball playing did more to win the hearts of the people of East Cambridge than all of the other campaigning.

It was during the campaign in East Cambridge that Bobby Kennedy met his future wife Ethel Skakel. Ethel was in many ways very similar to RFK's sisters. She was athletic, witty, and always quick with a joke or pranks. She also had a competitive spirit worthy of a Kennedy and was a devout Catholic (like Bobby). What Ethel gave to Bobby was something that he never before had in his life—unconditional love and devotion. Ethel's love gave Bobby a stable family foundation and helped him to grow his confidence.

Robert and Ethel Kennedy would frequently entertain guests at their Hickory Hill estate. Sometimes, they would bring in top academics to host seminars on various topics; other times they would host rowdy soirees where it was not uncommon for guests to be pushed into the pool.

—Schlesinger, 1978

After graduating from the University of Virginia Law School in the summer of 1951, Robert Kennedy took up the task of managing his brother's 1952 senate campaign. RFK's strength was not his organizing ability—which was dubious during his brother's campaign. In fact, Bobby found managing the campaign to be much more burdensome than simply doing campaign work. He was accustomed to knocking on doors and distributing leaflets, but RFK was not very good at planning effective events. Often he did not grasp the complexities of micro-managing large-scale campaign events, and it was up to the campaign staff to tell Bobby that some of his ideas simply were not feasible. RFK's real contribution as campaign manager came from his ability to be the "bad guy." He rolled up his sleeves and conducted a lot of the dirty work of the campaign behind the scenes and in doing so saved his brother from such unpleasant dealings. This allowed JFK to appear as though he were above politics, and his movie-star image remained intact. This was important because it was Robert Kennedy who was the one making enemies—not John Kennedy. Bobby rebuffed incumbent Governor Paul Dever and the Massachusetts Democratic party bosses by declining their help because he saw them as political dinosaurs on the verge of extinction. He also had no tolerance for loitering patronage seekers around the campaign office and frequently threw them out.

The management skills that Robert Kennedy learned while running his brother's campaign were a precursor to the way that he ran the Justice Department later on. During his brother's run for the senate, Bobby had a vision for the campaign. He saw it not as "politics as usual" (the back-slapping wheeling-and-dealing that he despised), but "politics as *unusual*." He wanted to portray his brother as a strong and handsome candidate who was above the dirty game of politics. To do so, he knew that he had to be the enforcer and the bearer of bad news. Further complicating matters was the fact that JFK was quite sickly throughout the campaign and often relied on Bobby to help him disguise the extent of his ailments on the campaign trail (John Kennedy had been diagnosed with Addison's disease and was receiving cortisone treatments). This kind of determination and assistance made Bobby invaluable to JFK's senate victory.

> *One of Bobby Kennedy's dubious campaign ideas during JFK's Senate campaign: "Let's have a tea for five hundred people tomorrow in Worcester."*
> —Thomas, 2000

RFK was also a tremendous motivator and led by his own example. Young activists for the Kennedy senate campaign were inspired by his tireless determination and relentless work ethic. No task was too small or unimportant for Bobby. He worked long and hard hours for his brother, often going canvassing door-to-door on his own after work hours. This brand of leadership-by-example was later realized by Bobby at the Justice Department as well.

After his successful bid for the senate, JFK realized that he had perhaps been wrong about Bobby in the past. His brother was no longer the awkward young boy who always got picked on by his siblings. Instead, it became obvious that when Bobby put his mind to something, he became a force to be reckoned with. Even Joe Sr. admired Bobby's hard work and determination, once remarking to a reporter that Bobby was "the most determined person" he had known (Schlesinger 1978, 97). Still, while talking nice about Bobby to others, Joe Sr. gave his son a cruel reality check after the campaign, as recalled by O'Brien (1974, 41–42):

> "Well, what are you going to do now?"
> "What do you mean?" asked Bobby.
> "You've got to get to work. You haven't been elected to anything," stated Joe Sr.

In an effort to help Bobby find a job, Joe Sr. called Senator Joseph McCarthy (R-Wisconsin) in December 1952 to inquire whether he would be able to find work in his office for RFK. In January 1953, Robert Kennedy assumed the role of assistant counsel on the Senate Permanent Subcommittee on Investigations of which McCarthy was the chair. This proved to be a useful assignment for RFK, as it taught him investigative and adversarial techniques that would be invaluable when cross-examining labor racketeers and mobsters in the future. The work of the committee also appealed to RFK's moral code, where right and wrong were clearly distinguishable and middle ground was largely nonexistent. RFK had only drafted one report for the subcommittee on the subject of trade with communist countries, which was widely accepted to be one of the best reports produced by the committee, when a personal (and mutual) dislike for McCarthy's lead counsel, Roy Cohn, curtailed Bobby Kennedy's effectiveness. The situation became so bad that Bobby warned McCarthy that Roy Cohn was leading him and the subcommittee toward disaster. After only six months as assistant counsel, Kennedy quit.

Joseph McCarthy was a family friend of the Kennedy's and had even dated two of Robert Kennedy's sisters.

—Steel, 2000

Shortly thereafter, Robert went to work as an assistant to his father on a governmental reform committee that was headed up by former president Herbert Hoover. RFK found the work exceedingly dull and was glad to return to work as minority counsel on the Senate Permanent Subcommittee on Investigations. By this point, McCarthy had overplayed his hand and his enemies were becoming more unified against him. Accusations of being unpatriotic for opposing him no longer had sufficient traction, and Democrats on the subcommittee had stripped McCarthy of his sole ability to appoint the staff of the subcommittee. With unifying opposition against McCarthy, the Democrats on the committee offered RFK the job as minority counsel.

Robert Kennedy, recounting a conversation he had with Senator McCarthy: "I told him that I thought he was out of his mind and was going to destroy himself."

—Hilty, 1997

RFK took his role as minority counsel as a chance to get back at Roy Cohn. Bobby seemed to have no interest in making McCarthy look bad; he wanted to embarrass his old rival instead. During one exchange between McCarthy and Senator Henry Jackson (D-Washington), Jackson was asking McCarthy about a plan put forward by Cohn and another staffer. Bobby—who was well versed on the details of the plan—fed questions to Senator Jackson that completely picked the plan apart and made it almost laughable. The line of questioning was so upsetting to Cohn that he angrily stomped over to Kennedy after the hearing and took a swing at him. The two men were separated, and RFK remained calm, casting only a mocking smile at Roy Cohn. It was not long afterward that McCarthy fell from public grace. When the Democrats regained control of the Senate during the midterm election of 1954, Robert Kennedy went from minority counsel on the Senate Permanent Subcommittee on Investigations to chief counsel.

> The morning headline on the *New York Daily News* after the altercation between Robert Kennedy and Roy Cohn read: "COHN, KENNEDY NEAR BLOWS IN 'HATE' CLASH."
> —Schlesinger, 1978

THE TOUGH BOBBY

During his time as chief counsel on the Subcommittee on Investigations, Bobby Kennedy earned a name for himself by going after mobsters and corrupt union leaders. RFK was aware that the Committee, now in Democratic control, still needed to at least appear to be interested in rooting out communists so that they didn't get shown up politically by Republicans on the issue. All the same, Kennedy envisioned a change of course for the committee toward its original intent: weeding out fraud and corruption in government, labor, and management.

However, it was not until the summer of 1956 that Bobby got a clear idea of the direction that he wanted to take the Investigations Subcommittee. Investigative journalists began writing stories about mob infiltration and corruption in unions, and Kennedy was intrigued. As chief counsel, he was in a position to probe this issue. Going after mobsters and corrupt union leaders fed into RFK's black-and-white sense of moralism. He also saw the chance to score some political points for his brother while pursuing his own interest. Joe Sr. advised Bobby against moving the subcommittee in that direction. He was worried that by antagonizing unions—a stalwart of Democratic support—Bobby might jeopardize JFK's chances at the presidency in the future. Bobby didn't see it that way though. In his mind, rooting out corrupt union leaders would actually benefit the rank-and-file union members. He had made up his mind.

Bobby solicited the help of Carmine Bellino, a former FBI accountant who had experience working as a consultant on several congressional committees. In Kennedy's own words, Bellino was an "accounting and investigative genius." They took a trip to the West Coast to investigate allegations that the Teamster's Union had been infiltrated by mobsters who wanted to get their hands on the Teamster's $250 million pension fund. RFK was horrified by the stories of harassment and strong-arm tactics he heard while in Los Angeles. Kennedy recounts one particularly graphic and troubling occurrence (Kennedy 1960, 8):

> There was a union organizer from Los Angeles who traveled to San Diego to organize juke-box operators. He was told to stay out of San Diego or he would be killed. But he returned to San Diego. He was knocked unconscious.

When he regained consciousness the next morning he was covered with blood and had terrible pains in his stomach. The pains were so intense that he was unable to drive back to his home in Los Angeles and stopped at a hospital. There was an emergency operation. The doctors removed from his backside a large cucumber. Later he was told that if he ever returned to San Diego it would be a watermelon. He never went back.

Stories like this one led Kennedy and Bellino to dig further. They began to ask union officials about instances of violence, corruption, and mob activity. Early on in the investigation, Kennedy recounted that he never suspected that Teamster president David Beck was corrupt. He suspected that the corruption—while widespread—was generally a local or regional problem. When the investigative duo began asking difficult questions to Teamster officials, they were usually less than helpful, occasionally stonewalling or providing names of rival union members as the "real bad guys." While in Seattle, Kennedy met up with an anonymous tipster who provided concrete information that the corruption in the Teamster's Union went all the way to David Beck. An associate of Beck's named Nathan Shefferman had told RFK that he had been paid by the Teamsters for work he had done on the West Coast, though the president of the Western Conference of Teamsters, Frank Brewster, indicated that Shefferman had never done any work for the Teamsters that he was aware of and had never been an employee. This seemed to indicate a misuse of Teamster funds, because "if Beck was paying money to Nathan Shefferman from Western Conference funds, as our information indicated, it was not apparently for any legitimate work Shefferman did for the union" (Kennedy 1960, 13).

Kennedy and Bellino also uncovered more damaging information about David Beck when they learned that a contractor had done work on Beck's house and had been paid out of Teamster funds. The evidence seemed to be mounting against Beck. However, when the Teamster vice presidents were subpoenaed before the committee, they began taking the Fifth Amendment on the grounds that the committee did not have jurisdiction. To combat this problem, a select committee was temporarily formed with the specific charge of investigating corruption in labor-management relations. The committee was staffed with four Democratic senators: McClellan (the chair), Kennedy (Robert's brother), McNamara, and Ervin, and four Republican senators: McCarthy, Mundt, Goldwater, and Ives. The McClellan Committee solved the jurisdictional question, but now a new problem arose: David Beck had fled the country. The committee had no jurisdiction to subpoena Beck while he was overseas, but in Beck's absence RFK did manage

---

Bobby Kennedy's address to the American Trucking Association in 1959: "The theft of millions of dollars of union funds by men like Dave Beck, James R. Hoffa, James Cross, and others is a grievous enough crime, but at best it is only a symptom of other more serious and underlying problems. A number of men in important union positions have come to regard unions as their own personal possessions."

—Guthman and Allen, 1993

to get some pretty damaging testimony from Western Conference Teamster President Frank Brewster. Brewster testified that he had no knowledge about what David Beck was doing with the money he was withdrawing from the Western Conference Teamster's account and that he was never informed by David Beck that these withdrawals were loans to Beck himself. This seemingly harmless bit of testimony laid out a subtle but snaring trap for David Beck. RFK correctly suspected that Beck was going to claim that the money taken from the Western Conference Teamsters account was a loan—a claim that could now be refuted with Brewster's testimony.

When Beck finally returned to the United States, young Bobby Kennedy was eager to get him on the stand. RFK's sharp questioning about the misappropriation of Union funds utterly destroyed Beck on the stand, forcing him to plead the Fifth Amendment every time he was pinned down on an issue. For Bobby, the painstaking financial digging that he and Bellino had done paid large dividends. As Beck took the stand, RFK recalled: "…I looked at him [Beck], and realized that here was a major public figure about to be utterly and completely destroyed before our eyes. I knew the evidence we had uncovered would be overwhelming. It would make him an object of disgust and ridicule" (Kennedy 1960, 29). RFK then mercilessly chipped away at Dave Beck's shady "loan" with no past misstep too small to be divulged:

> Mr. Kennedy: Do you feel that if you gave a truthful answer to this Committee on your taking of $320,000 of Union funds that that might tend to incriminate you?
> Mr. Beck: It might.
> Mr. Kennedy: Is that right?
> Mr. Beck: It might.
> Mr. Kennedy: You feel that yourself?
> Mr. Beck: It might.
> Mr. Kennedy: I feel the same way.
> Chairman: We will have order, please.
> Mr. Kennedy: I want to know, breaking that money down, Mr. Beck, did you use Union funds to purchase five dozen diapers for some of your friends at $9.68?

Even after Dave Beck's memory was "refreshed" under oath by the associate who had made these illicit purchases for him, he still refused to answer any questions. Shortly thereafter, Dave Beck was indicted and convicted of larceny and income tax evasion.

Dave Beck was pardoned by President Gerald Ford in 1975.

Dave Beck's fall left a power vacuum at the top of the Teamster's Union. Emerging to fill the void was a short, robust man named James "Jimmy"

Riddle Hoffa. Mr. Hoffa had been marketed to the Teamster rank-and-file as a reformer. Kennedy was skeptical; he had heard rumors about Hoffa's connection with the criminal underworld. In an effort to allay RFK's fears, Hoffa invited him to dinner at his friend Eddie Cheyfitz's house. Six days before their scheduled dinner, Bobby received a telephone call from a lawyer in New York named John Cye Cheasty, indicating that he had "...information that will make your hair stand on end" (Kennedy 1960, 33). At Kennedy's request, he came to visit RFK in Washington, D.C., the next day. He laid a large amount of money on Kennedy's desk and promptly blurted out that this money was offered to him by Jimmy Hoffa as a "down payment" if he could get a job as an investigator on Kennedy's staff and then pass committee information along to Hoffa. The total amount of the down payment was $1,000 in cash, and Hoffa also offered him $2,000 a month as retainer for this shady service. Kennedy was deeply shocked that anyone would have the audacity to try to influence the work of the committee in this way.

Instead of seeing Hoffa's bribe of Cheasty as a threat, RFK saw it as an opportunity. He decided (with Cheasty's approval) to use Cheasty's special "position" with Hoffa as a chance to spring a trap. He gave Cheasty the names of witnesses who would soon be subpoenaed before the committee—information that only those working for the committee would have known. Cheasty was to pass this information along to Jimmy Hoffa under FBI surveillance—which he did. He learned that the "handoff" had been made just before departing for dinner with Hoffa and Cheyfitz.

At dinner, Hoffa admitted to Kennedy that he had issued Teamster charters in the state of New York to friends of a notorious character named Johnny Dio. The trouble with these charters was that they existed only on paper because the locals they were issued to had no members—they were "paper locals." It was later uncovered that these paper locals were issued to rig the election of the New York Joint Council president, though that evening Hoffa told RFK they were issued to protect the Teamster local membership from being co-opted by the AFL-CIO when the two unions merged.

Jimmy Hoffa to Robert Kennedy: "I do to others what they do to me, only worse." Kennedy's response: "Maybe I should have worn my bulletproof vest."
—Kennedy, 1960

As for Cheasty, he had been doing a marvelous job of laying out the trap for Jimmy Hoffa. He continued to feed information to Hoffa about the committee and then report back to RFK about what information Hoffa was interested in obtaining. The FBI had been monitoring the transactions between Cheasty and Hoffa for over three weeks. On March 13, 1957, FBI agents arrested James Riddle Hoffa at the DuPont Plaza Hotel with sensitive committee documents in his possession. Indeed they were the very documents that Bobby had supplied Cheasty to give to Hoffa.

Before the trial, Kennedy firmly believed that Jimmy Hoffa would be convicted on bribery charges. However, the trial soon became a spectacle that highlighted the great lengths Hoffa was willing to undertake to win. Before the trial was underway, Hoffa hired Edward Bennett Williams to defend him. Ed Williams was one of the best defense attorneys of the day. Hoffa also hired the law partner of the judge's brother and two prominent African American attorneys to join his defense team. This issue of race was an important consideration all throughout the trial. During the jury selection phase of the trial, Ed Williams used his preemptory challenges to dismiss only white jurors—so that the jury consisted of eight African Americans and four Caucasians. Williams believed that African American jurors would be more likely to sympathize with organized labor than with the government. The Teamsters also paid for the legendary former boxing champion Joe Louis (who himself was an African American) to attend the trial for two days and to embrace Hoffa publicly. Mr. Williams even suggested during cross-examination that Cheasty had once investigated the National Association for the Advancement of Colored People (NAACP)—a claim that Cheasty vehemently denied. The trial verdict rendered was in Hoffa's favor.

Hoffa's acquittal was a stunning blow to Kennedy, but his time in the courtroom was far from over. Later that same year Hoffa went on trial in New York for wiretapping the personal telephones of some Teamster members. The jury deadlocked, and when the case was retried in 1958, Hoffa escaped with another acquittal. Hoffa's legal victories only further strengthened RFK's resolve against him.

> *When asked by a reporter what he would do if Jimmy Hoffa was acquitted, Kennedy retorted: "I'll jump off the Capitol."*
> —Kennedy 1960, 56

By the time Hoffa was subpoenaed before the Rackets Committee, both he and Kennedy had learned some necessary survival skills. When questioning witnesses before the committee, Kennedy was usually over-prepared. Just like his days growing up with such hotly competitive siblings, RFK's coping mechanism was dogged determination. He collected documents and records by the bundle and would often spend long nights going over Teamster payrolls and bank accounts. Always, he was searching for the "smoking gun" that would bring down Jimmy Hoffa and rid the Teamsters of their underworld rulers. As time went on, RFK's basement office became more and more cluttered with papers. Realizing that he was unable to keep up with the mounting documentation that was accumulating, he began taking speed-reading classes. The long nights of poring over documents continued for Bobby. One late night RFK was driving home and noticed that the lights were still on at the Teamster's headquarters. Not to be outdone, Kennedy turned his car around and headed back to the office. When Jimmy Hoffa

> *Jimmy Hoffa: "You never can tell with a jury, like shooting fish in a barrel."*
> —Kennedy, 1960

heard about this, he started leaving the lights on when he left the office for the evening.

Still, the Robert Kennedy work ethic had an electric effect on his office staff. Investigators found him to be very approachable and accessible. The office culture was to call people by their first names, and it was not unusual for RFK to invite investigators out to his Hickory Hill estate to talk about cases or witnesses while tossing the football around. His informal, lead-by-example style eventually won for Bobby Kennedy the largest congressional staff at the time (over one hundred) and kept the Rackets Committee actively pursuing the agents of corruption and violence.

> At the beginning of the Rackets Committee hearings, Jimmy Hoffa would often playfully address RFK as "Bobby." As the hearings wore on and Hoffa became less amused, he would speak to Robert Kennedy as "Mr. Kennedy." Over time, Jimmy Hoffa would not address RFK at all and would address his answers to Bobby's questions to Senator McClellan.
>
> —Kennedy, 1960

When it came to interrogating witnesses sworn in before the committee, Robert Kennedy eventually developed a hard-nosed style all his own. He learned how to read witnesses and over time became very adept at pushing their buttons. On one occasion, the notorious (but well-dressed) gangster Momo Salvatore "Sam" Giancana was subpoenaed before the committee. Sam Giancana was known to be the heir to Al Capone's syndicate, and it was believed at the time that Giancana was the top boss of organized crime in Chicago. Giancana was a man who had stuffed people into the trunks of cars and hung people on meat hooks, but while Giancana was on the stand, Bobby ridiculed the Mafia Don of Chicago (Schlesinger 1978, 165; Senate Select Committee 1959, 18672–81):

> Mr. Kennedy: Would you tell us if you have opposition from anybody that you dispose of them by having them stuffed in a trunk? Is that what you do, Mr. Giancana?
> Mr. Giancana: I decline to answer because I honestly believe my answer might tend to incriminate me.
> Mr. Kennedy: Would you tell us anything about any of your operations or will you just giggle every time I ask you a question?
> Mr. Giancana: I decline to answer because I honestly believe my answer might tend to incriminate me.
> Mr. Kennedy: I thought only little girls giggled, Mr. Giancana.

On another occasion after a union boss swore at him under oath, Kennedy egged him on further, taunting him when the microphone was off: "You're full of shit" (Thomas 2000, 83). Kennedy even wore Jimmy Hoffa down. On one occasion, Hoffa lost his cool and sneered at Bobby: "You're sick! That's what's the matter with you—you are sick."

Despite losing his temper on a couple of occasions, Hoffa adapted his strategy as the hearings went on. At first, he was charming and friendly with the committee—even to the point of humor, but as the hearings wore on, it became clear to Hoffa that he could not charm his way off of the committee's radar. He had always prided himself on being the underdog, and he continued to play that role out while on the stand. As RFK circled like a shark smelling blood, Jimmy Hoffa often tried to juxtapose his blue-collar background with Bobby's affluent background in an effort to put political pressure on the committee to back off (portraying that he was being "picked on" by Bobby and the committee). As the hearings wore on, RFK's withering questioning got to him. He appeared beaten and tired on the stand—but he had another strategy up his sleeve that worked very well for him (and created a great deal of frustration for Kennedy and the rest of the committee).

Hoffa knew that if he invoked his Fifth Amendment right against self-incrimination on the stand, he would jeopardize his standing as the Teamster president. So instead he developed a series of tactics that essentially stonewalled the committee. One strategy when under tough questioning was to give long and rambling answers with no substance. On one occasion, Robert Kennedy asked Jimmy Hoffa about a sweetheart deal he had made with the Riss and Company trucking corporation. Specifically, the drivers employed by Riss wanted to own their own trucks. Richard Riss, the company president, wanted the Teamster drivers to purchase the trucks from the company. He met with Jimmy Hoffa and the alleged agreement that was made was that Riss would pay money into the Teamster's pension and welfare fund (which was little more than a slush fund), and Hoffa would force the drivers to purchase the trucks from Riss. Riss ordered the trucks for about $13,000 each. They then filed a claim with General Motors that the trucks were defective and worth only about $3,500 each. General Motors settled by reimbursing Riss $3,000 for each truck. Riss then turned around and sold these "defective" trucks to their own drivers for $14,800—a full $1,800 more than what he originally paid for them. When the Teamster drivers began to file grievances, Jimmy Hoffa reorganized all of the drivers (regardless of where they lived) into his own Detroit-based Local 299. By placing the drivers in his own local, Hoffa could stop the drivers from filing grievances against the company. When RFK asked Hoffa about this corrupt little deal, he successfully obscured the issue before the committee with the following reply (Kennedy 1960, 153):

> Mr. Hoffa: No, sir, let me explain that. Riss and Company does not operate equipment. TM&E operates the equipment…Under the law when you lease a piece of equipment other than driver–owners as such, you cannot, and if you try to read our contract we specifically accepted in here, you cannot take and have two checks for drivers who are not driver–owners as such, but where you have a fleet operation and it is in here, sir, right in here—
> Mr. Kennedy attempts to interrupt.

Senator McClellan: Let him finish.

Mr. Hoffa: Let me read it to you, without reading it all. It starts: "owner–operator section 1," at the bottom it states: "Note where the owner–driver is used in this article it means owner–operator only and nothing in this article shall apply to any equipment leased except where owner is also used as a driver." This means, sir, where there is a fleet operation, and TM&E is an equipment fleet operation, it does not come within the scope of this contract where you have to do equipment checks. If we can get the employer voluntarily to do it, fine, but if we try legally to enforce the issues we have been advised that we can find ourselves in a problem, as Mr. Goldwater stated a while ago, of antitrust and monopoly. We recently went all the way to the United States Supreme Court on this particular provision and the United States Supreme Court ruled after we had lost in all the lower courts that this was a legal provision in our contract because we recognized our inability to negotiate for a profit return and rather only the basic minimum returns to operate a piece of equipment and that the drivers' earnings were protected. This was the United States Supreme Court ruling out of Ohio, ACEF I believe is the case.

Responses such as this one were not uncommon for Jimmy Hoffa and often successfully moved the discussion of the committee away from the original question and toward trying to decipher Hoffa's clouded responses.

Another stall tactic that Jimmy Hoffa used when under pressure was to conveniently forget important facts and information. This saved him the trouble of having to plead the Fifth Amendment. Kennedy recalled one such occasion when he was asking Hoffa about his plan to have Teamster officials wear tiny recording devices called Minifons into the grand jury room so that there would be a record of the evidence (Kennedy 1960, 78–80):

Mr. Hoffa: What did I do with them? Well, what did I do with them?
Mr. Kennedy: What did you do with them?
Mr. Hoffa: I am trying to recall.
Mr. Kennedy: You could remember that.
Mr. Hoffa: When were they delivered, do you know? That must have been quite a while.
Mr. Kennedy: You know what you did with the Minifons and don't ask me.
Mr. Hoffa: What did I do with them?
Mr. Kennedy: What did you do with them?
Mr. Hoffa: Mr. Kennedy, I bought some Minifons and there is no question about it, but I cannot recall what became of them.

After going around on this issue for a while, RFK asked Hoffa if he had ever worn a Minifon, to which he replied:

Mr. Hoffa: You say "wear." What do you mean by "wear"?
Mr. Kennedy: I have done as much to refresh your memory as I know how to do. If you cannot recall it from that, and you want to leave the record that way, if you want to think that this committee is so stupid and that the public is so stupid that they will believe that you could not remember having done a thing like that, you leave the record that way.

On several occasions Hoffa's selective memory could not be refreshed despite direct evidence and testimony that made the answer painfully obvious. It was one of Hoffa's ploys to keep from admitting anything incriminating while avoiding the stigma of pleading the Fifth, though RFK went out of his way to make Hoffa look silly for his poor memory.

Hoffa also learned how to take the Fifth Amendment by proxy. His strategy was to claim that he had no knowledge regarding the issue at hand and would refer questioning to one of his henchmen. When questioned, those individuals would then plead the Fifth, saving Hoffa from having to do it himself. Jimmy Hoffa used this strategy numerous times to get himself out of trouble. Generally, his subordinates obliged Hoffa in this scheme because they knew that they had a lot to lose if Hoffa was no longer the International Teamster president. This coupled with the fact that Jimmy Hoffa never kept documentation for anything, never wrote checks, and dealt only in cash meant that the trail of money was difficult to follow and nearly impossible to ascertain when Hoffa was hiding behind his men on the stand.

Despite the long nights, the frustrating witnesses, and the political maneuvering, RFK did not prevail against Jimmy Hoffa during the life of the Rackets Committee (though Hoffa was convicted of jury tampering and mail fraud later). However, Bobby's work on the committee was valuable both to him and to the country. For Bobby Kennedy, working on the Rackets Committee gave him valuable experience supervising cases and investigators. Over time, he developed a managing style all his own—it was informal in culture but professional in task. He learned how to handle difficult personalities and political interference while managing a large staff. He learned from his position as chief counsel the importance of hard work and self-discipline. He led by example, and he expected those around him to work no less hard than he did.

His clashes with Jimmy Hoffa and other shady figures forged his toughness and determination. It further crystallized his stark view of right and wrong. After thrashing some of the most feared underworld figures on the stand, he made it his mission to try to root out the dark influences of criminals and gangsters from institutions like the Teamsters. On a personal note, Robert Kennedy was a little disappointed that he was not able to unearth enough incriminating evidence against Jimmy Hoffa, but it was those clashes with Hoffa that made him stronger. It was a strength Bobby would come to rely on in his career at the Justice Department.

Robert Kennedy wrote a book about his experience on the Rackets Committee entitled *The Enemy Within*. For a short time, it was a national bestseller.

—Thomas, 2000

The work of the committee frequently grabbed headlines and was often in the spotlight. The media paid close attention when notable underworld figures or prominent union or business leaders testified. This media attention helped place the problem of union corruption in the public eye. Although the committee was not able to get Jimmy Hoffa, more than twenty prominent labor leaders, business managers, and mobsters were tried and convicted as a result of the work done by Bobby Kennedy and the Rackets Committee. Dave Beck was toppled, Jimmy Hoffa's days were numbered, and the American public began to realize just how far the arms of organized crime could reach.

THE JUST BOBBY

After Bobby Kennedy's resignation as chief counsel of the Senate Rackets Committee in September of 1959, he took up the duty of running his brother Jack's 1960 presidential campaign. It was just taken for granted (even by Bobby himself) that he would be JFK's campaign manager. The campaign was chaotic and unbalanced, but it did have a winning strategy. The plan was to win the Democratic nomination by side-stepping political bosses such as Richard Daley and David Lawrence initially and appealing to the grassroots voters. If they could win enough votes on their own, the political bosses would then have no choice but to support Kennedy for president.

Shortly after resigning from the Rackets Committee, RFK took a trip to Texas to visit Lyndon Baines Johnson (LBJ). Johnson was a forceful Senate majority leader and was a much bigger threat to JFK's presidential bid than Hubert Humphrey. Bobby wanted to know whether or not LBJ was going to launch his own presidential bid in 1960. He also wanted to know if Johnson would try to stop JFK from becoming president at the convention. Johnson (in his patronizing way) assured Bobby that he was not going to run and that he would not be an obstacle to JFK's presidential bid. Bobby left LBJ's ranch satisfied that Johnson was going to remain on the sidelines, but Johnson's promise of neutrality was a doublecross that Robert Kennedy would always hold against LBJ as perfidious.

At the Democratic convention, LBJ began doing everything he could to discredit Kennedy. His strategy was to let Kennedy and Humphrey beat each other up on the campaign trail and then to arrive at the convention as the party's savior. Johnson incorrectly overestimated the importance of the political bosses in the 1960 election, and he didn't realize that JFK already had enough delegates at the convention to win the nomination on the first ballot. Given the deceit by Johnson, it came as quite a shock to Bobby that Jack was considering LBJ as vice president. JFK saw past Johnson's betrayal and examined the upside to having him on the ticket. First of all, he was well connected in the Senate, so he could help get JFK's legislative agenda passed. More immediately it would be advantageous to have a Southern, non-Catholic on the ballot to help win Southern sympathy. Last (and most important), Jack Kennedy knew that LBJ could deliver the state of Texas on election night. Much to Bobby Kennedy's chagrin, the general election ticket was JFK–LBJ.

One of the defining moments of the election (and for years to come) came when JFK and RFK both made telephone calls on behalf of Martin Luther King, Jr. Dr. King had been thrown in jail and refused bail for a questionable misdemeanor traffic offense. He was sentenced to four months hard labor in a rural Georgia penitentiary. Coretta King was genuinely concerned that she might never see her husband again. Distressed, she telephoned the Kennedy campaign to intervene. Jack Kennedy called Coretta King back, and news of this telephone call was soon picked up by the press. RFK was cagey at first, concerned that news of JFK's call to Mrs. King would jeopardize his electoral fortunes in southern states, but RFK was also bothered by the fact that a judge would deny bail for a measly traffic ticket. In the end, RFK decided (with his brother's blessing) to telephone the judge and ask for King's release. The judge agreed to release Dr. King at Bobby's request. This single phone call, which King learned about, was the beginning of an often turbulent relationship between RFK and the famed civil rights leader.

Robert Kennedy's telephone call to Judge Mitchell in DeKalb County, Georgia, was believed by historians to have been made in the heat of moral outrage over the imprisonment of Dr. King. It was later revealed that Georgia Governor Ernest Vandiver (who was officially a segregationist) called Bobby and asked him to telephone the judge about securing King's release.
—Thomas, 2000

After John F. Kennedy had won the election, Bobby didn't want to be a cabinet member in his brother's administration. He was looking to strike out on his own and make a name for himself on the political scene. He briefly considered a run for the governor of Massachusetts, and he also toyed with the idea of getting into private law practice. These adventures, however, would have to wait as his father kept bending his and Jack's ears with a request that sounded more like a demand: Jack should appoint Bobby to be attorney general. Both of the Kennedy brothers were skeptical. They knew that the press would, in Jack's words, "kick our balls off", and a flurry of articles charging nepotism would follow (Thomas 2000, 110). They also knew that there were political risks to appointing Bobby to be the nation's top lawyer when he had never practiced law before. Still Kennedy's father was unrelenting. "Nobody is better qualified," Joe Sr. told a doubtful Jack Kennedy. Eventually JFK yielded to his father and agreed to appoint Bobby to the top post in the Justice Department.

Public reaction in the mainstream press was pretty much what was expected—cries against nepotism. But the newly elected JFK was able to placate the press enough by pointing out that Bobby

---

Eunice Shriver: "Bobby we'll make Attorney General so he can throw all the people Dad doesn't like into jail. That means we'll have to build more jails."
— Fay, 1966

Kennedy knew a lot about both communists and organized crime, and when asked about Bobby's lack of experience in the courtroom Jack retorted, "The basic requirement for the job is not that at all. It is the ability to administer a great department." (Schlesinger 1978, 236).

When selecting his Justice Department staff, Robert Kennedy wanted heady young lawyers who were not too political. Young, hungry talent was the basic qualification for working in RFK's Justice Department. RFK offered the job of deputy attorney general to Bryon White, who was a close family friend. It proved to be a good selection, as Bryon White had connections and knew the kind of lawyers that Bobby was looking for: assistant attorney generals like Burke Marshall (Civil Rights Division) and Nicholas Katzenbach (Office of Legal Counsel). Bobby also recruited long-time friend John Seigenthaler and newspaper reporter Edwin Guthman to be his administrative assistant and public relations specialist, respectively. These two men helped shield the department from political pressure and media criticism. As a tip of the hat to Republicans, Kennedy appointed Republican Herbert "Jack" Miller to head the Criminal Division.

> *Long-time Justice Department lawyer Patricia Collins jokingly said of Bobby Kennedy: "We never had an attorney general who had that close personal relationship with the staff. He always said that he'd been here himself, he'd been an attorney down in the Criminal Division, and nobody had every paid any darn attention to him, and he was going to fix that."*
>
> —Demaris, 1975

The mood at the Justice Department was one of hope and optimism. Kennedy's management style was one of informality and team building. He encouraged everyone to call each other by their first names—something relatively uncommon at the time. He also made a number of quaint changes to the décor in his office, such as hanging up his children's drawings. All of this was done to loosen the mood in the department. He wanted his lawyers to be happy and excited. He trusted them to handle cases and gave them lots of independence, and he didn't want any impediments to interoffice communication. This type of environment was exciting to many of the young attorneys recruited to join the Kennedy New Frontier. In many ways, they had the best of both worlds—they could engage in work that was seen as important and meaningful, and they were part of a team that allowed them to get the job done their own way.

> It was not uncommon for Robert Kennedy to drop in on lawyers working in the Justice Department unannounced and quiz them on the cases they were working on.
>
> —Schlesinger, 1978

Kennedy wanted to expand the reach of the Justice Department into two important areas: organized crime and civil rights. However, the department relied on the Federal Bureau of Investigation (FBI) for much of its intelligence information. Neither of these two areas of law enforcement was of particular interest to FBI director J. Edgar Hoover at the time. Hoover was still fixated on rooting out communists at the beginning of the Kennedy administration. To Kennedy, spending time and resources hunting communists in the country was ridiculous. To him the real menace to America was the "enemy within": organized crime and corruption. This infuriated Hoover who had to this point ignored and even scoffed at the idea that organized crime was widespread. This was most likely because catching mobsters was much more dangerous and time consuming than catching communists. Still, Kennedy tried—often unsuccessfully—to placate Hoover enough to get him to cooperate.

Regardless of what Hoover thought about organized crime, Bobby Kennedy plunged the Justice Department on in that direction. He vastly expanded the number of lawyers investigating organized crime, and he urged them to be resourceful—much like his Rackets Committee staff. If they couldn't get help from the FBI, they were instructed to see if other federal, state, or local agencies would lend assistance, and if help was still not forthcoming, they were instructed to investigate matters themselves.

When asked about the Communist Party in the United States, RFK responded: "It couldn't be more feeble and less of a threat, and besides its membership consists largely of FBI agents."
—Schlesinger, 1978, 262

Ronald Goldfarb recounts one such instance in 1962. United Auto Workers (UAW) Local 12 was led by a man named Richard Gosser at the time. The IRS had reported to the Justice Department that it was conducting an investigation into reports of widespread gambling at the automobile manufacturing plant in Toledo, Ohio. Investigations of this sort were relatively commonplace, but they had learned through the course of the investigation that confidential files related to the investigation were being leaked to a local hoodlum who was subsequently turning them over to Gosser. This was allowing Gosser to keep tabs on the IRS investigation. The leaker of the documents turned out to be one of the IRS' own employees. With the help of the Justice Department lawyers, Gosser was caught, convicted of conspiring to defraud the government, and sentenced to three years in prison. Further adding to the intrigue of this case was the fact that Gosser had organized northeastern Ohio for Kennedy during the 1960 election, and his conviction demolished the Democratic Party organization in that area. Despite the political pressure that RFK might have felt about going after a political ally like Gosser, he instructed his lawyers to prosecute fairly and not to pull any punches for Gosser. It was political integrity and the fair pursuit of justice such as this that endeared RFK to many of the young Justice Department lawyers.

> Bobby Kennedy's Justice Department indicted five Democratic mayors, three Democratic judges, and two Democratic members of Congress.
> —Schlesinger, 1978

In fact, RFK's Department of Justice scarcely let family connections or political loyalty get in the way of prosecution. Robert Kennedy brought bribery charges against New York state Supreme Court Judge Vincent Keogh despite the fact that Judge Keogh's brother Eugene Keogh was instrumental in helping JFK win the presidency. Bobby also authorized pursuing a breach of contract case against Matt McCloskey, who was the ambassador to Ireland, and had LBJ's close personal advisor Bobby Baker indicted and convicted on tax evasion and fraud charges. RFK also kept his own conscience clean when he properly recused himself from the consideration as to whether or not to bring tax evasion charges against close family friend James Landis (who was ultimately convicted). RFK was never one to pull punches when it came to his job.

Criminal Division lawyer Ronald Goldfarb: "The top political animals in the Kennedy administration helplessly watched Robert Kennedy's organized crime drive knock off politician after politician around the country."
—Goldfarb, 1974

Young lawyers reveled in finding new and inventive ways to prosecute notorious mobsters. Joseph "Doves" Aiuppe, longtime member of the Chicago Mafia and Al Capone's personal driver, was convicted of illegally transporting mourning doves across state lines in violation of the Migratory Bird Act. Larry Gallo, brother of notorious "Crazy Joe" Gallo and member of the Profaci crime family, was snagged by the Justice Department for falsifying information on a Veteran's Administration home mortgage loan application.

Other members of the criminal underworld proved more elusive to RFK. Infamous Chicago mobster Sam Giancana remained untouchable throughout Kennedy's tenure at Justice because all the evidence on him (he admitted to murder and bribery among other offenses) was obtained through illegal wiretaps. Giancana's girlfriend, Judith Exner, had an affair with JFK during the 1960 presidential campaign, and news like this in the mainstream press would have generated an enormous headache for the President.

The most satisfying prize for RFK was the conviction of Jimmy Hoffa on the charge of jury tampering. It began with an indictment of Hoffa in Nashville, Tennessee, for taking payoffs from an employer in violation of the Taft-Hartley Act. The trial began in October 1962, and after a few days, a Hoffa aid named Ed Partin came forward and contacted Walter Sheridan at the Justice Department. He offered to be an informant for the government, and Bobby Kennedy agreed. Partin's job in Hoffa's entourage was to stand guard at Jimmy Hoffa's hotel room door. Hoffa and several others boasted to Partin that they had paid off one of the jurors and were trying to get in with several others. Partin relayed this information to Sheridan, who took it back to Bobby. After a lively discussion, it was decided to move ahead with the prosecution of Hoffa on the charge of jury tampering. Ed Partin was the prosecution's star witness and provided devastating testimony against Jimmy Hoffa. Hoffa was convicted on two counts and sentenced to eight years in prison.

On the heels of his jury tampering conviction, Jimmy Hoffa went on trial in Chicago for defrauding the Teamster's pension and welfare fund. The idea was to use wire and mail fraud legislation to convict Hoffa of his scheme to load $20 million from the Central States Pension Fund so that the high finder's fees could be diverted to Hoffa's creditors to pay off some of his debts. Hoffa was convicted and sentenced to five years in prison on top of the eight-year conviction for jury tampering. James Riddle Hoffa began serving his sentence on March 7, 1967, in the Lewisburg, Pennsylvania, penitentiary. Robert Kennedy lived out the short remainder of his life believing that Jimmy Hoffa would remain safely behind bars. On December 23, 1971, President Richard Nixon commuted Hoffa's sentence on the condition that he not engage in labor-related activities for ten years.

By the end of Robert Kennedy's time at the Justice Department, there had been 201 indictments against Teamster officials, and his staff had won 126 convictions. While RFK believed the Teamsters were especially corrupt, attention was paid to the illegal activities of other unions as well. Table 1 details a partial list of the pursuits of Kennedy's Justice Department against corrupt organized labor.

Table 1. Robert Kennedy's war on corrupt labor during his time at the Justice Department

Labor union	Corrupt activities pursued by the Kennedy Justice Department
Amalgamated Workers Union	Taft-Hartley violations
American Guild of Variety Artists	Kickbacks
Building Service Employees Union	Company payoffs
Independent Brotherhood of Production, Maintenance and Operating Employees Union	Embezzlement
Industrial Workers of America	Embezzlement
International Longshoremen's Association	Embezzlement
International Union of Electrical, Radio, and Machine Workers	Filing false records, embezzlement
Iron Workers Union	Company payoffs
New Jersey Plumbers Union	Company payoffs
Plumbing and Pipefitting Union	Rigging bids to fix prices
Seafarers' International Union	Obstruction of justice
United Mine Workers	Coal company kickbacks, illegal payoffs, embezzlement

Source: Goldfarb (1995, 201–202).

To be sure, Robert Kennedy tried to maintain the fight against organized crime and corrupt labor while at the Justice Department. With his brother as the president, it would seem that RFK had a free hand to pursue the real criminals—the real "enemy within." However, his effectiveness in fighting organized crime was often hampered by those around him: FBI director J. Edgar Hoover and his very own brother Jack. Hoover's lackadaisical approach toward organized crime slowed Bobby's pursuit of underworld figures and was a drag on the overall prosecutorial effectiveness of the Justice Department in bringing mobsters to justice. As JFK's presidency continued, he came to rely more often on Bobby as his most trusted advisor. Bobby was intimately involved in the disastrous Bay of Pigs invasion and the Cuban missile crisis. Such weighty affairs were a distraction to RFK's pursuit of corrupt labor officials and gangsters and required him to focus on political, diplomatic, or military affairs in ways that no previous attorney general had ever had to do.

> *Robert Kennedy: "... all people are created equal. Logically it follows that integration should take place today everywhere ... other people have grown up with totally different backgrounds and mores, which we can't change overnight."*
> —Schlesinger, 1978

Through the late 1950s and early 1960s, the civil rights movement was coming into full bloom. The historic 1954 Supreme Court case *Brown v. Board of Education* ordered the integration of public schools and spelled the beginning of the end of segregation in the Deep South. The Montgomery bus boycotts in 1955–1956 instilled a sense of confidence in African Americans that they could change the status quo. The late 1950s also saw the rise of a talented young Baptist minister and civil rights leader—Martin Luther King, Jr. In 1957 and 1960, Civil Rights acts were passed in an effort to ensure suffrage rights for African Americans living in the South. Unfortunately, Eisenhower's administration enforced these laws with indifference and lassitude. By 1960, sit-ins at "whites only" counters were occurring in cafés and restaurants across the South; protests were becoming more common as time went on.

For Bobby Kennedy, civil rights was a new policy area that he was not all that familiar with. "I won't say that I stayed awake nights worrying about civil rights before I became attorney general," Bobby told writer Peter Maas (Schlesinger 1978, 286). In many ways, his approach toward civil rights was influenced by two competing factors: his moral sense of decency and the political realities of enforcing the law. The synthesis of these two forces amounted to an incremental approach toward civil rights that made almost no one involved happy. Southern segregationists and politicians reviled any intervention by the federal government to enforce the law, and civil rights activists believed RFK's Justice Department was stuck in low gear.

Inside the civil rights division, Justice Department lawyers focused on enforcing voter registration laws. This had a positive political benefit because most of the African Americans who were newly registered to vote were Democrats. However, civil rights activists wanted more. They strove for true racial equality and showed fearless resolve in an effort to achieve that end.

On May 4, 1961, a young cadre of seven African Americans and six white protesters with high ideals, dubbed the "Freedom Riders," set out on a bus ride across Dixie country to test the integration of interstate transportation facilities. Ten days later outside of Anniston, Alabama, their bus was torched and they were viciously beaten by an angry mob of white southerners. Though this kind of violence startled the young attorney general, he (and his brother) believed deep down that the Freedom Riders had brought these troubles on themselves. Still, he felt that he had a duty to protect them if possible. He sent his administrative assistant, John Seigenthaler, to Alabama to try to help them obtain safe passage and to keep trouble from finding them.

However, getting the Freedom Riders out of Alabama was another problem because the Greyhound Bus Company could not find a driver willing to continue the dangerous journey. Bobby was incensed and took it upon himself to intervene by telephoning George Cruit, a Greyhound superintendent (Schlesinger 1978, 296):

Mr. Cruit: Drivers refuse to drive.
Mr. Kennedy: Do you know how to drive a bus?
Mr. Cruit: No.
Mr. Kennedy: Well, surely somebody in the damn bus company can drive a bus, can't they?...I think you should—had better be getting in touch with Mr. Greyhound or whoever Greyhound is and somebody better give us an answer to this question. I am—the Government—is going to be very much upset if this group does not get to continue their trip....Under the law they are entitled to transportation provided by Greyhound....Somebody better get in the damn bus and get it going and get these people on their way. Mr. Cruit, I think that if some of your people would just sit down and think for a few minutes that somebody would be able to drive a bus 80 or 90 miles.

Greyhound eventually found a driver, and the Freedom Riders were once again on their way. However, more trouble lay ahead of them. As the bus pulled into Montgomery, Alabama, an angry mob carrying clubs and chains descended on the bus. Deputy Assistant Attorney General John Doar happened to be across the street and witnessed the entire spectacle. "It's terrible. It's terrible," Doar exclaimed to Kennedy over the phone. "There's not a cop in sight. People are yelling 'Get 'em, get 'em.' It's awful." (Guthman 1971, 170–71). John Seigenthaler had been circling the bus station in his car and tried to rescue one of the freedom riders when he was hit in the back of the head and knocked unconscious himself. All the while, FBI agents were watching and keeping careful tabs on what was happening, but were ordered by Hoover not to intervene.

> While John Seigenthaler was hospitalized after trying to rescue a Freedom Rider in Montgomery, Alabama, Bobby called him and jokingly thanked him for helping to win the black vote. Seigenthaler retorted to Bobby that he should probably give up any aspirations of being governor of Alabama.
>
> —Thomas, 2000

Shortly thereafter, Martin Luther King, Jr., arrived in Montgomery, Alabama, to speak at the First Baptist Church. RFK sent a force of five hundred federal marshals under the command of Bryon White. A large crowd of more than fifteen thousand jammed into the First Baptist Church to hear Dr. King speak. Outside of the church, trouble was brewing. A menacing mob of white southerners was gathering—evidently intent on burning the church and everyone inside. Dr. King called Bobby at the Justice Department and apprised him of the troubling situation. RFK tried to allay King's fears by assuring him that the federal marshals were on their way. In an effort to try to lighten the mood, Bobby suggested that so long as Dr. King was in a church, he might say a prayer for the Kennedy family. King did not find the attempt at humor amusing. When the marshals arrived at the church, it was not altogether clear that they would be able to hold off the rowdy mob. Finally, reinforcements from the Alabama state patrol and the National Guard helped drive back the angry mob.

Kennedy wanted to get the Freedom Riders out of Alabama and out of the South as soon as possible, but this was unacceptable to the Freedom Riders. They insisted on continuing their journey to Jackson, Mississippi, which worried Bobby immensely given the grim reception that had been rolled out for them in Alabama. Bobby called his old friend, Mississippi senator Jim Eastland for advice. Senator Eastland said that he would see to it that there was no violence, but he also added that the Freedom Riders would be promptly arrested once they reached Jackson—and they were.

Still, segregation at bus terminals existed in the South. The Interstate Commerce Commission (ICC) was the governing body with jurisdiction to issue regulations requiring the terminals be integrated, but they were an independent commission and not subject to presidential directives. As attorney general, Bobby decided to petition them to issue a new regulation ending segregation at interstate bus terminals. The ICC issued the regulation, and within a year and a half systematic segregation in interstate transportation had come to an end.

Education was a second front that opened up in the battle for civil rights. A spirited and civic-minded young African American named James Meredith applied for admission to the all-white University of Mississippi ("Ole Miss") in Oxford, Mississippi. After a series of legal battles and attempts by the university to stall, the Fifth Circuit Court ruled in 1962 that there could be no more delays in denying Meredith admission to the university. Three days later, Mississippi's segregationist Governor Ross Barnett went on television and defiantly stated that Mississippi "...will not surrender to the evil and illegal forces of tyranny" (Lord 1965). Despite a federal ruling to the contrary, the governor delayed. RFK tried to get him to capitulate by having him held in contempt and fined $10,000 each day for defying a federal court order. Barnett continued to resist.

The stage was set for a showdown between the state of Mississippi and the federal government, and Bobby expected trouble. He spoke to Governor Barnett several times in the following days, attempting to work out a peaceful way to register Meredith. Barnett proposed a far-flung solution that bordered on theatrics. Barnett would stand in the doorway to the administration building (the Lyceum) and the federal marshals escorting Meredith would draw their guns and push the governor aside. This would give Barnett the political cover he needed while still allowing Meredith to be registered. Barnett also agreed to keep law and order. RFK reluctantly agreed to this deal, but as Meredith was about to arrive on the Ole Miss campus, pickup trucks full of angry white men from the countryside, bearing rifles and coolers of beer, began arriving on the Ole Miss campus in droves. Governor Barnett called Kennedy to tell him the deal was off—there was no way for him to control the unruly mob that was gathering.

> Bobby Kennedy had secretly tape-recorded each conversation with Mississippi Governor Ross Barnett so that he could declare publicly that he had been double-crossed by the Governor if James Meredith was not registered at Ole Miss.
> —Schlesinger, 1978

Barnett proposed another idea—to sneak him onto campus. Left with few options, Bobby agreed, and it was arranged to have Meredith sneak onto the Ole Miss campus and hide out in an abandoned dormitory. A command post was set up at the Lyceum. Near nightfall, the angry rabble outside became more violent. The state troopers who were supposed to maintain law and order were mysteriously ordered to withdraw from campus. The situation became grim as university students began hurling rocks, bricks, and Molotov cocktails at the federal marshals surrounding the Lyceum. The marshals fought back with tear gas. Then around dusk,

> When he learned about the Soviet missiles in Cuba, Bobby Kennedy remarked: "Can they hit Oxford, Mississippi"?
> —Schlesinger, 1978

gunshots rang out, hitting several of the federal marshals. The students dispersed and the men from the countryside took over the siege. RFK learned that Meredith's dormitory was being stormed as well.

Bobby was on the telephone with Ed Guthman, who was in the Lyceum, to get an update on the situation (Guthman 1971, 204–5):

Mr. Guthman: Pretty rough. It's getting like the Alamo.
Mr. Kennedy: Well, you know what happened to those guys.

Oddly enough, RFK's gallows humor raised the morale of those in the Lyceum and got them through the long and dangerous night.

The decision was finally made to bring in an overwhelming number of federal troops to lift the siege. The army began airlifting the force in from Memphis, Tennessee, at a painfully slow pace. Tense minutes ticked by on campus as federal marshals stood their ground and heroically followed orders not to return fire. Law and order were finally restored when reinforcements for federal troops arrived, though a high price had been paid—160 federal marshals had been wounded during the night. Meredith was registered that morning and later became a graduate of Ole Miss.

Despite the diversion into the areas of transportation and education, the issue of voting rights was in RFK's mind the quintessential crux of the civil rights issue. If southern African Americans could be registered (and allowed) to vote, they could then use their votes to further political action and bring about sweeping change in other areas. Civil rights activists were reticent about this strategy. Many of them (including Martin Luther King, Jr., for a time) saw this strategy as a way to take the wind out of the sails of the civil rights movement. Still, Bobby pushed on and in February 1963, President Kennedy sent a voting rights bill that RFK largely authored to Congress for consideration. It was relatively modest in scope and was met with indifference and inaction on Capitol Hill.

On May 2, Martin Luther King, Jr., organized a movement to have roughly a thousand African American children visit segregated department stores and sit at segregated lunch counters. Bobby warned Dr. King that this was a bad idea—not only was he putting children in harm's way, but Birmingham's police force was headed up by Sheriff Eugene "Bull" Connor. King rebuffed Kennedy's caution and went ahead with the demonstration. Kennedy's fears were well founded. Sheriff Connor pulled out all the stops, unleashing vicious attack dogs on the helpless children. He also authorized his officers to use fire hoses and had many of the children arrested and thrown into jail with the general prison population. It would take more than a week for Kennedy's Justice Department to broker an agreement with the city of Birmingham to get the children released from prison.

The tragic events in Birmingham were plastered in all of the newspapers. Horrible pictures of children recoiling from police dogs and being pinned down with fire hoses were everywhere. RFK realized that the best route to real change was a sweeping new piece of civil rights legislation, but he needed a pretext to give his brother political cover. That cover came when Alabama Governor George Wallace vowed to see to it personally that no African American students were allowed at the University of Alabama.

With visions of Oxford, Mississippi, on his mind, RFK began to determine if there was a way to diffuse Governor Wallace's racial bomb without bloodshed. Several scenarios were rehearsed, including pushing the governor aside or dragging him away—but Bobby worried that a physical confrontation might spark violence reminiscent of Ole Miss. Instead, it was agreed that Wallace would be allowed to posture for the cameras and a general from the Alabama National Guard would order the governor to step aside. This is exactly what happened, and the students were registered without any violence.

RFK's victory at the University of Alabama gave JFK the courage to back Bobby's sweeping civil rights bill. Unfortunately, JFK was never to see the passage of this bill. Shortly after John F. Kennedy's death, President Lyndon Johnson sent a revised version of Kennedy's civil rights bill to Capitol Hill, which resulted in the famous Civil Rights Act of 1964.

THE TRAGIC BOBBY

After resigning as attorney general in September of 1964, Bobby Kennedy launched a successful senatorial bid in the state of New York. By this time, RFK had learned many life lessons: He had worked for the McCarthy and McClellan committees. He had gone toe-to-toe with notorious mobsters and corrupt labor leaders. He had helped his brother get elected to the presidency and had been a forceful attorney general. He had been intimately involved in the Bay of Pigs disaster, the Cuban missile crisis, and the Vietnam conflict. He had also taken on the complex issues of civil rights and racial justice at one of the most volatile times in American history. He had gone through a great deal.

As a senator, RFK's attitude had changed. No longer was he the enforcer of the laws—he now took on the role of lawmaker. Despite his frustrations in the Senate, Bobby worked to further the lives of the poor and underprivileged. He was largely responsible for orchestrating the launch of the Bedford-Stuyvesant Restoration Corporation in New York, which was a serious attempt at revitalizing a very poor section of Brooklyn, and tirelessly worked to improve the plight of poor people in New York City. He also vigorously spoke out against the escalation of the war in Vietnam. He traveled extensively to Africa, Asia, and Central America and educated himself and others on the terrible conditions of the poor in those countries.

RFK was growing tired of the Senate; he saw that his ability to do good depended too much on others. He decided to launch his presidential bid in 1968. Two feelings fueled this decision. The first was his sense of compassion and duty to the poor. He felt that he could do much more good for them in the Oval Office than on Capitol Hill. The second was his deeply rooted hatred for Lyndon Johnson. Bobby's presidential campaign got off to a roaring start. His first speech at Kansas State University was a tidal wave of enthusiasm. With Johnson's poll numbers slipping, Bobby's stock rose.

Still, RFK was attempting to do something nearly unheard of—unseat an incumbent president in the primaries. He knew that about half of the party delegates would be controlled by big labor or would come from the South—both of which seemed unlikely to support him. After it became clear to Johnson that he was going to lose in Wisconsin, he announced that he was going to discontinue the bombing in Vietnam and would not run for reelection. This threw the race wide open, but the road still looked difficult. Vice President Hubert Humphrey had the backing of LBJ, and Eugene McCarthy posed a potential challenge as well.

Kennedy took his message to the people as few other candidates had ever done. He insisted on driving through the poor parts of town and gave impromptu speeches on the tops of cars. The frenzied crowds followed him like a rock star. They would mess up his hair and try to rip off his clothing. His appeal was to the poor and the young—those not necessarily plugged into the political scene. The air was electric wherever Bobby Kennedy visited, but sobriety and tragedy once again touched the nerve of America.

On April 4, 1968, Dr. Martin Luther King, Jr., was shot in Memphis, Tennessee. Bobby was in Indianapolis, Indiana, and he appealed to the hope and goodness of the American spirit. RFK's own words would have been nearly as applicable at the time of his own death scarcely two months later (Guthman and Allen 1993, 356–57):

> ...What we need in the United States is not division; what we need in the United States is not hatred; what we need in the United States is not violence or lawlessness; but love and wisdom, and compassion toward one another, and a feeling of justice toward those who still suffer within our country, whether they be white or black.
>
> So I shall ask you tonight to return home, to say a prayer for the family of Martin Luther King, that's true, but more importantly to say a prayer for our own country, which all of us love—a prayer for understanding and that compassion of which I spoke.
>
> We can do well in this country. We will have difficult times; we've had difficult times in the past; we will have difficult times in the future. It is not the end of violence; it is not the end of lawlessness; it is not the end of disorder.
>
> But the vast majority of white people and the vast majority of black people in this country want to live together, want to improve the quality of our life, and want justice for all human beings who abide in our land.
>
> Let us dedicate ourselves to what the Greeks wrote so many years ago: to tame the savageness of man and make gentle the life of this world.
>
> Let us dedicate ourselves to that, and say a prayer for our country and for our people.

Bobby Kennedy's own life was cut short on June 6, 1968, when he was shot in the head by Sirhan Sirhan at the Ambassador Hotel in Los Angeles. That evening should have been one of his greatest triumphs, as he had just declared victory in California. It is often tempting to look to the past and ask "what if?" What if Bobby Kennedy had not been killed? But that is probably not the most appropriate question—a better question might be to ask how we can help make America the place of Bobby Kennedy's—and our—dreams.

FURTHER READING

Allison, Graham, and Philip Zelikow. 1999. *Essence of Decision: Explaining the Cuban Missile Crisis.* New York: Longman.

Beran, Michael Knox. 1998. *The Last Patrician: Bobby Kennedy and the End of American Aristocracy.* New York: St. Martin's Press.

Branch, Taylor. 1988. *Parting the Waters: America in the King Years, 1954–1963.* New York: Simon & Schuster.

Demaris, Ovid. 1975. *The Director: An Oral Biography of J. Edgar Hoover.* New York: Harper's Magazine Press.

Fay, Paul B. 1966. *The Pleasure of His Company.* New York: Harper & Row.

Goldfarb, Ronald. 1974. Politics at the Justice Department. In *Conspiracy*, ed. John C. Raines, New York: Harper & Row.

Goldfarb, Ronald. 1995. *Perfect Villains, Imperfect Heroes: Robert F. Kennedy's War against Organized Crime.* Sterling, VA: Capital Books.

Guthman, Edwin O. 1971. *We Band of Brothers.* New York: Harper & Row.

Guthman, Edwin O., and Richard C. Allen, eds. 1993. *RFK: Collected Speeches.* New York: Viking.

Hersh, Seymour M. 1997. *The Dark Side of Camelot.* Boston: Little, Brown.

Hilty, James W. 1997. *Robert Kennedy: Brother Protector.* Philadelphia: Temple University Press.

Kennedy, John F. 1964. *Profiles in Courage.* New York: Harper & Row.

Kennedy, Robert. 1960. *The Enemy Within.* New York: Harper & Brothers.

Kennedy, Robert. 1967. *To Seek a Newer World.* Garden City, NY: Doubleday.

Kennedy, Robert. 1969. *Thirteen Days: A Memoir of the Cuban Missile Crisis.* New York: Norton.

Kennedy, Rose. 1974. *Times to Remember.* Garden City, NY: Doubleday.

Lord, Walter. 1965. *The Past that Would Not Die.* New York: Harper & Row.

Mahoney, Richard D. 1999. *Sons & Brothers: The Days of Jack and Bobby Kennedy.* New York: Arcade.

Mollenhoff, Clark, R. 1965. *Tentacles of Power: The Story of Jimmy Hoffa.* Cleveland, OH: World.

Navasky, Victor. 1971. *Kennedy Justice.* New York: Atheneum.

Newfield, Jack. 1969. *Robert Kennedy: A Memoir.* New York: Dutton.

O'Brien, Lawrence F. 1974. *No Final Victories: A Life in Politics—from John F. Kennedy to Watergate.* Garden City, NY: Doubleday.

O'Donnell, Kenneth P., and David F. Powers, with Joseph McCarthy. 1972. *Johnny, We Hardly Knew Ye: Memories of John Fitzgerald Kennedy.* Boston, Little & Brown.

Schlesinger, Arthur M., Jr. 1978. *Robert Kennedy and His Times.* Boston: Houghton Mifflin.

Senate Select Committee. 1959. *Hearings.* 86th Congress, 1st Session.

Sheridan, Walter. 1972. *The Rise and Fall of Jimmy Hoffa.* New York: Saturday Review Press.

Steel, Ronald. 2000. *In Love with Night: The American Romance with Robert Kennedy.* New York: Simon & Schuster.

Thomas, Evan. 2000. *Robert Kennedy: His Life.* New York: Simon & Schuster.

Courtesy AP Images

Jim Garrison

Elvira M. White

Depending on one's age, it is possible that many people are not familiar with the colorful and controversial former district attorney of New Orleans who became both famous and infamous for his dogged conspiracy theories regarding the assassination of President John F. Kennedy in 1962. Jim Garrison is both criticized and revered for his pursuit and ultimate prosecution of the one and only person tried for a role in the Kennedy assassination. Similar to the current controversy regarding former North Carolina District Attorney Mike Nifong's relentless prosecution of some Duke lacrosse team members in an allegation of rape, Garrison stubbornly pursued the case of Clay Shaw. Shaw was ultimately found not guilty, yet Garrison remained unapologetic to his death regarding his belief that he had been correct in his pursuit of the case. There have been more than two thousand books and articles written about the Kennedy assassination, and many have been written about Jim Garrison and his pursuit of a conspiracy plot in the death of President Kennedy. Garrison added to the volume of work in this regard by penning his own books including *On the Trail of the Assassins,* published in 1988. He also authored *The Star Spangled Contract* and *A Heritage of Stone.* Garrison died with a mixed reputation; some found him crazy, others judged him crooked, but there were certainly those who considered him correct in his assertions. The public ultimately will decide which version to believe.

JIM GARRISON—THE PERSON

Jim Garrison was born Earling Carothers Garrison in Knoxville, Iowa, on November 20, 1921, but grew up in New Orleans. Though little has been written regarding his early childhood years, Garrison wrote that height—he was 6 feet 7 inches tall—was an inherited trait in his family as was the profession of being a lawyer. His grandfather and his father were both lawyers, and his grandfather was more than 7 feet tall. Garrison became acquainted with famous trial attorney Clarence Darrow through his grandfather's working relationship with Darrow. Garrison was so impressed with Darrow's ability as a trial attorney and passion for justice that he named one of his own children Darrow.

Garrison's father drank heavily, thus causing a family breakup and the ultimate divorce of his parents, but not before his father kidnapped him when he was six years old. Garrison's mother hired a private investigator who re-kidnapped Jim Garrison and returned him to his mother. Jim Garrison never saw his father again. In later years, if Jane Garrison deigned to mention her husband, it was always in disparaging tones. Garrison never stopped yearning for his father, and he would become overly trusting of slightly older men, men who more often than not betrayed him. Over the course of his life, Garrison mentioned often how he missed not having had a father. Meanwhile, Jane Garrison became obsessed by this son who so came to resemble her that in later years her granddaughter Virginia would describe her as

"Daddy in drag." Garrison's mother was so obsessed with him that she moved to Oklahoma when he was stationed there while in the Army.

Garrison entered the army at age nineteen, one year before Pearl Harbor. He prided himself on being a patriot and considered the Army his surrogate family. He was commissioned a second lieutenant and volunteered for training as a pilot to fly planes for observation of enemy troops. He was trained in Fort Sill, Oklahoma and subsequently flew combat missions over the front lines in France and Germany. Garrison went on to serve eighteen years as a field artillery officer in the National Guard after his five years of active duty in the Army.

Following his active Army duty, Garrison followed his family tradition and went to law school at Tulane. Shortly thereafter, he joined the FBI as a special agent in Seattle and Tacoma. His career with the bureau was short, as Garrison became bored with his assignment of conducting background checks of prospective employees for a defense plant and returned to the practice of law.

Garrison's rise to district attorney in New Orleans in 1961 came as a surprise to many people, including Garrison. Although he had experience as an assistant district attorney, he threw his hat in the ring like many others dissatisfied with the services of then district attorney Richard Dowling. With very little politicking beyond television appearances, and given no chances of winning, Garrison won the election after a runoff with the sitting district attorney. It was the first time in New Orleans history that any public official had ever been elected citywide without support from any political organization. While Garrison was pursuing a professional career, he also was building a family. Garrison and his wife had five children. When Garrison lost the election to Harry Connick in 1973, he went on to become a Louisiana State District Court judge for the 4th Circuit Court of Appeals from 1978 to 1991.

GARRISON—THE PROSECUTOR

Garrison took office on March 3, 1962. Because he had won election as an independent, the assistant district attorneys he hired were the top graduates from neighboring law schools, what he considered the best of the city's bright young trial lawyers. He bragged that there was not one single political appointment, and that allowed his office to operate without obligation to outside influences.

Upon entering office, Garrison brought charges in a number of high-profile cases including that of his predecessor. Garrison indicted the former district attorney Dowling and one of his assistants for criminal malfeasance. The charges were subsequently dismissed for lack of evidence. He also was proud of the almost nightly vice raids that he authorized in the French Quarter. Sometimes, it is reported, he led the raids carrying a pistol. Still, the raids failed to produce any tangible results. Soon, Garrison became embroiled in conflicts with local criminal court judges, with Garrison accusing the judges of racketeering and conspiring against him. The judges fired back, charging Garrison with misdemeanor criminal defamation. Garrison was convicted in January 1963. The U.S. Supreme Court, in *Garrison v. Louisiana*, 379 U.S. 64 (1964), overturned Garrison's conviction, deciding that his conviction for criticizing the official conduct of public officials was unconstitutional. Garrison simultaneously indicted Judge Bernard Cocke with criminal malfeasance. In two trials personally prosecuted by Garrison, Judge Cocke was acquitted. Garrison charged nine policemen with brutality but dropped the charges two weeks later. During the same period, in a press conference he accused the state parole board of accepting bribes but failed to obtain grand jury indictments. Further, he accused the state legislature of accepting bribes and was unanimously censured by the legislature.

Despite the faulty prosecutions, Garrison earned a good reputation with the people in New Orleans during the first two years of his tenure. He was equally proud to report that his office had not lost a homicide case in three years. In 1965, Garrison ran for reelection against Judge Malcolm O'Hara and won with 60 percent of the vote. Thus it appeared that he still had the confidence of the voters of New Orleans, and that Garrison was on target for a long successful career as New Orleans prosecutor, until one day in 1966.

In November of 1966, Garrison told a journalist that he had important information on the assassination of President Kennedy. This began the erosion of his political career and indeed life as he had come to know it. Garrison lost the election to Harry Connick in 1973, ending his career as a prosecutor.

THE INVESTIGATION OF THE ASSASSINATION OF A PRESIDENT

Many Americans remember exactly what they were doing at the moment they heard that President John F. Kennedy was killed on November 22, 1963. Jim Garrison was no different than other people and thus remembered where he was and what he was doing at that same moment. According to Garrison, he was working in his office in New Orleans when his chief assistant rushed into Garrison's office to announce the shooting of the president. After processing the news and having subsequent in-depth discussions, it appeared to Garrison and members of his staff that there was a connection between the reported suspected assassin, Lee Harvey Oswald, and David Ferrie, a New Orleans figure who had a chance encounter with Garrison shortly after he won the election. (According to Garrison, Ferrie had rushed up to him in a rather bizarre manner to congratulate him on winning the district attorney race.) Two days later Garrison met with key members of his staff. One of his assistants reported that Ferrie had made a trip to Texas forty-eight hours before—on the day of the assassination. Thus began Garrison's probe of a conspiracy theory in the assassination of President Kennedy.

Garrison reported the contents of his preliminary investigation to the FBI. As a former member of the bureau and as a law enforcement arm of the government, Garrison reported that he was confident that the federal government would conduct a thorough investigation. The FBI questioned and released Ferrie with such speed that it both startled and surprised Garrison, and he began to lose faith and confidence in the agency where he had previously been employed. As Garrison remarked at the time, he had mistakenly assumed both he and the federal government were on the same page. But this setback did not deter Jim Garrison from his continued inquiry into a possible conspiracy in the assassination of the president.

Garrison's investigation explored the possibility of a connection between another New Orleans figure, Clay Shaw, and Lee Harvey Oswald.

THE INVESTIGATION AND THE MEDIA

After investigating the assassination, Garrison, with the assistance of his staff, was convinced that a group of right-wing activists including David Ferrie, Carlos Bringuier, and Clay Shaw were involved in a conspiracy with the Central Intelligence Agency (CIA) to kill President Kennedy. Garrison suggested that such a plot was in retaliation for the president's attempts to obtain a peace settlement in both Cuba and Vietnam. It was at this time that Garrison's relationship with media outlets such as *Newsweek* and *Life* magazine took a turn for the worse. In the ordinary course of political life, in a district attorney's office, the media is usually welcomed, because it is the vehicle by which the prosecutors inform the public of activity within the office. When Garrison shared his conspiracy theory with a *Life* magazine reporter, he originally was told that top management of the magazine supported him and would provide technical support that would result in a mutual exchange of information. Subsequently, *Newsweek* published an article critical of Garrison. In May 1967, *Newsweek* questioned Garrison's connection to the mob and organized crime. (Subsequent diaries belonging to Tom Bethell confirmed that conversations had occurred.)

Undaunted, Garrison continued his pursuit of the conspiracy theory. Three years after the assassination of President Kennedy, Garrison had a conversation with U.S. Senator Russell Long of Louisiana. According to Garrison, Long stated that the participants of the Warren Commission were wrong in their conclusions of how the president was killed. The Warren Commission was an investigatory body established by President Lyndon B. Johnson through executive order to investigate all circumstances concerning the assassination. After the conversation with Senator Long, Garrison ordered the entire set of the Warren Commission volumes. While waiting for the volumes to arrive, Garrison researched the biographical information of all commission members, wanting to determine who the individuals were who were making one of the most profound conclusions in the nation's recent history. The commission had officially concluded that President Kennedy's murder was accomplished by one man shooting from behind the president, but Garrison, after a review of the documents, determined that the Warren Commission report was wrong in its conclusion. Thus, the Jim Garrison controversy began.

THE TRIAL

Garrison's investigation into a possible conspiracy theory led him and those trusted members of his staff to investigate Oswald's activities while he was in New Orleans during the summer of 1963. Garrison concluded that there was a connection between Oswald and intelligence agents, including the FBI. He authorized questioning of other persons whom he determined could have been involved in the plot. Garrison concluded that he had enough evidence to try Clay Shaw, a person who had supplied the CIA with information on numerous occasions. Garrison also concluded that there was a real substantiated connection between Oswald, Jack Ruby, and Shaw. By 1966, Garrison considered the two major suspects in the murder of President Kennedy as Clay and David Ferrie. Ferrie had been a CIA contract employee. Ferrie had made a strong anti-Kennedy speech at a meeting of the New Orleans Civic Club in 1961, and the speech was so controversial that some persons walked out. On the basis of information he had found, Garrison concluded that Shaw had connections to Lee Harvey Oswald, while the federal government concluded that Garrison was on a witch hunt, a grand jury in New Orleans had indicted Shaw.

To assure the public that he had evidence to support the indictment and prosecution of Shaw, Garrison took the unusual step of holding a preliminary hearing where a judge would decide if there was sufficient evidence to move forward with a trial. The judge determined that Garrison could move forward. Prior to the trial, Garrison escaped prosecution himself when it was suggested that he had personal involvement with a known homosexual. He believed that the FBI was behind the potential set-up. Garrison also claimed that his home and office phones were "bugged." Garrison was concerned that with the intensity of the federal government's opposition to his investigation, his ability to fairly prosecute the case would be compromised. (In later years, it was determined that the federal government may have planted agents in Garrison's office to gather information on his activities and report back.)

By the time Shaw's trial began, Garrison's case had been weakened. Several prominent witnesses had either been killed, died mysteriously, or were relocated to states that would not honor Garrison's extradition requests. "Circus" became a description of the Shaw trial. By the time Garrison went to court, his list of plotters and conspiracies had grown longer and wilder. They included Minutemen, oil millionaires, munitions exporters, White Russians, the Dallas police, members of the Dallas establishment, and unidentified elements of the "invisible Nazi substructure." Garrison's witnesses were weirder still. One of them showed up wearing a toga and identifying himself as "Julius Caesar." The star in the state lineup admitted that the conspiratorial meeting he was supposed to have recalled under hypnosis might really have been "an inconsequential bull session." The testimony of another witness, a New York businessman named Charles Speisel, who claimed he had been at a Shaw party where criticisms of the president had turned into talk of ways to kill him, disintegrated under cross-examination. Among other things, Speisel said he had been hypnotized fifty or sixty times. When asked how he knew this, Speisel replied: "When someone tries to get your attention—catch your eye. That's a clue right off." By the end of the trial, the jury took less than one hour to find Shaw not guilty.

The negativity regarding Garrison continued. James Phelan of the *Saturday Evening Post*, among others, in an article titled, "Rush to Judgment in New Orleans," suggested that Garrison's prosecution was a rush to prosecute someone after he had created so much fanfare regarding his ability to solve the Kennedy assassination case. Moreover, it was suggested that the private side of Garrison reflected a homophobic slant in that he waged an almost obsessive vendetta against the New Orleans homosexual community. Before the trial and during the investigation Garrison had suggested that the assassination was a "homosexual thrill killing." Clay Shaw had been rumored to be a homosexual, thus providing a reason Garrison antagonists suggested that he pursued the case against Clay with such vigilance.

AFTER THE TRIAL—THE MOVIE

Despite the fact that several witnesses from Garrison's office came forth and agreed to be interviewed and gave less than flattering comments regarding the prosecution of Shaw, Oliver Stone was not deterred in his efforts to produce a movie based on the Jim Garrison saga. According to some authors, there was an overwhelming sense of lunacy unleashed, which was the pervasive atmosphere in which the late Clay Shaw was wrongfully indicted and brought to trial in New Orleans by the late Jim Garrison, the district attorney for some thirty years. Stone's movie produced even more controversy and discussion of Garrison's pursuit of the "real" Kennedy assassin.

Oliver Stone was accused of chasing fiction and that *JFK* did not reflect all of the more controversial avenues that Garrison pursued in his quest to solve the assassination case. Stone suggested that he had never paid much attention to the details of the JFK assassination at the time it occurred. Moreover,

Stone suggested that when the media coverage was high regarding Garrison, he had been in Vietnam. The filmmaker indicated that he had a renewed interest in the case as a result of reading Garrison's book, *On the Trail of the Assassins*. Stone suggested that Garrison's book read like a "Dashiell Hammett whodunit" (Stone and Sklar 1972). Stone subsequently met with Garrison at the time he became a judge on the Louisiana Circuit Court of Appeals, and according to Stone's account, he was deeply impressed. But Stone was accused of taking Garrison's assertions at face value and failing to follow up any inconsistencies in Garrison's version of events.

Stone accepted Garrison's version that the FBI failed to investigate fully numerous leads, including the connection between Ferrie, Oswald, Clay, and other characters alleged to have been involved in the conspiracy to kill President Kennedy. Yet official district attorney files in 1967 showed that there was no evidence that a conspiracy had ever existed in New Orleans or that any New Orleans resident was involved in a conspiracy to kill the president, and Stone was accused of ignoring facts when he directed the movie. Stone saw a different man in Garrison than others did.

Stone indicated that when he read Garrison's book, *On the Trail of the Assassins*, he saw the soul of a gem. He was impressed with Garrison the man, a World War II veteran who had served in Korea, a family man, a prosecutor, and someone who believed in the American way. As a prosecutor, Stone suggested that Garrison had a duty to pursue a crime if he believed that one had taken place. Stone had a difficult time understanding why there was so much opposition to Jim Garrison.

Authors such as Anthony Summers later answered Stone's questions of opposition by suggesting that serious scholars and researchers believed that Garrison's investigation was a misdirected shambles and an abuse of the justice system. Others suggested that after months of highly publicized promises of what he would present at trial, Garrison produced no witnesses to suggest a CIA involvement in an assassination conspiracy and seemed only to be obsessed with Clay Shaw. Stone was further accused of playing loosely with the facts and choosing to make Garrison the hero of the movie. In order to make Garrison the hero in the movie, Stone had to make Clay Shaw guilty.

Stone did not have to abide by the rules of evidence nor did he have to be concerned about defamation, Clay Shaw had died before the movie opened, giving Stone greater creative ability when he made the movie. Garrison was seen as the prism through which Stone viewed the entire series of investigative events. Views that seemed to confirm Garrison were embraced, and views that were different from Garrison's were dismissed as misinformation or government propaganda. Stone did not bow to pressure. As late as 1992, in a speech before the National Press Club in Washington, D.C., Stone, amid much criticism, defended Garrison. He indicated that he had heard all of the criticism regarding Garrison and none held up to investigation. Further he challenged the detractors to show him evidence that Garrison had

Report of the President's Commission on the Assassination of President Kennedy (aka "Warren Commission Report"), September 24, 1964

Chapter 1: Summary and Conclusions

The assassination of John Fitzgerald Kennedy on November 22, 1963, was a cruel and shocking act of violence directed against a man, a family, a nation, and against all mankind. A young and vigorous leader whose years of public and private life stretched before him was the victim of the fourth Presidential assassination in the history of a country dedicated to the concepts of reasoned argument and peaceful political change. This Commission was created on November 29, 1963, in recognition of the right of people everywhere to full and truthful knowledge concerning these events. This report endeavors to fulfill that right and to appraise this tragedy by the light of reason and the standard of fairness. It has been prepared with a deep awareness of the Commission's responsibility to present to the American people an objective report of the facts relating to the assassination.

Narrative of Events

At 11:40 A.M., c.s.t., on Friday, November 22, 1963, President John F. Kennedy, Mrs. Kennedy, and their party arrived at Love Field, Dallas, Tex. Behind them was the first day of a Texas trip planned 5 months before by the President, Vice President Lyndon B. Johnson, and John B. Connally, Jr., Governor of Texas. After leaving the White House on Thursday morning, the President had flown initially to San Antonio where Vice President Lyndon B. Johnson joined the party and the President dedicated new research facilities at the U.S. Air Force School of Aerospace Medicine. Following a testimonial dinner in Houston for U.S. Representative Albert Thomas, the President flew to Fort Worth where he spent the night and spoke at a large breakfast gathering on Friday.

Planned for later that day were a motorcade through downtown Dallas, a luncheon speech at the Trade Mart, and a flight to Austin where the President would attend a reception and speak at a Democratic fundraising dinner. From Austin he would proceed to the Texas ranch of the Vice President. Evident on this trip were the varied roles which an American President performs—Head of State, Chief Executive, party leader, and, in this instance, prospective candidate for reelection.

The Dallas motorcade, it was hoped, would evoke a demonstration of the President's personal popularity in a city which he had lost in the 1960 election. Once it had been decided that the trip to Texas would span 2 days, those responsible for planning, primarily Governor Connally and Kenneth O'Donnell, a special assistant to the President, agreed that a motorcade

(continued)

through Dallas would be desirable. The Secret Service was told on November 8 that 45 minutes had been allotted to a motorcade procession from Love Field to the site of a luncheon planned by Dallas business and civic leaders in honor of the President. After considering the facilities and security problems of several buildings, the Trade Mart was chosen as the luncheon site. Given this selection, and in accordance with the customary practice of affording the greatest number of people an opportunity to see the President, the motorcade route selected was a natural one. The route was approved by the local host committee and White House representatives on November 18 and publicized in the local papers starting on November 19. This advance publicity made it clear that the motorcade would leave Main Street and pass the intersection of Elm and Houston Streets as it proceeded to the Trade Mart by way of the Stemmons Freeway.

By midmorning of November 22, clearing skies in Dallas dispelled the threat of rain and the President greeted the crowds from his open limousine without the "bubbletop," which was at that time a plastic shield furnishing protection only against inclement weather. To the left of the President in the rear seat was Mrs. Kennedy. In the jump seats were Governor Connally, who was in front of the President, and Mrs. Connally at the Governor's left. Agent William R. Greer of the Secret Service was driving, and Agent Roy H. Kellerman was sitting to his right.

Directly behind the Presidential limousine was an open "follow-up" car with eight Secret Service agents, two in the front seat, two in the rear, and two on each running board. These agents, in accordance with normal Secret Service procedures, were instructed to scan the crowds, the roofs, and windows of buildings, overpasses, and crossings for signs of trouble. Behind the "follow-up" car was the Vice-Presidential car carrying the Vice President and Mrs. Johnson and Senator Ralph W. Yarborough. Next were a Vice-Presidential "follow-up" car and several cars and buses for additional dignitaries, press representatives, and others.

The motorcade left Love Field shortly after 11:50 A.M., and proceeded through residential neighborhoods, stopping twice at the President's request to greet well-wishers among the friendly crowds. Each time the President's car halted, Secret Service agents from the "follow-up" car moved forward to assume a protective stance near the President and Mrs. Kennedy. As the motorcade reached Main Street, a principal east-west artery in downtown Dallas, the welcome became tumultuous. At the extreme west end of Main Street the motorcade turned right on Houston Street and proceeded north for one block in order to make a left turn on Elm Street, the most direct and convenient approach to the Stemmons Freeway and the Trade Mart. As the President's car approached the intersection of Houston and Elm Streets, there loomed directly ahead on the intersection's northwest corner a seven-story, orange brick warehouse and office building, the Texas School Book Depository. Riding in the Vice President's car, Agent Rufus W. Youngblood of the Secret Service noticed that the clock atop the building indicated 12:30 P.M., the scheduled arrival time at the Trade Mart.

The President's car which had been going north made a sharp turn toward the southwest onto Elm Street. At a speed of about 11 miles per hour, it started down the gradual descent toward a railroad overpass under which the motorcade would proceed before reaching the Stemmons Freeway. The front of the Texas School Book Depository was now on the President's right, and he waved to the crowd assembled there as he passed the building. Dealey Plaza—an open, landscaped area marking the western end of downtown Dallas—stretched out to the President's left. A Secret Service agent riding in the motorcade radioed the Trade Mart that the President would arrive in 5 minutes.

Seconds later shots resounded in rapid succession. The President's hands moved to his neck. He appeared to stiffen momentarily and lurch slightly forward in his seat. A bullet had entered the base of the back of his neck slightly to the right of the spine. It traveled downward and exited from the front of the neck, causing a nick in the left lower portion of the knot in the President's necktie. Before the shooting started, Governor Connally had been facing toward the crowd on the right. He started to turn toward the left and suddenly felt a blow on his back. The Governor had been hit by a bullet which entered at the extreme right side of his back at a point below his right armpit. The bullet traveled through his chest in a downward and forward direction, exited below his right nipple, passed through his right wrist which had been in his lap, and then caused a wound to his left thigh. The force of the bullet's impact appeared to spin the Governor to his right, and Mrs. Connally pulled him down into her lap. Another bullet then struck President Kennedy in the rear portion of his head, causing a massive and fatal wound. The President fell to the left into Mrs. Kennedy's lap.

Secret Service Agent Clinton J. Hill, riding on the left running board of the "follow-up" car, heard a noise which sounded like a firecracker and saw the President suddenly lean forward and to the left. Hill jumped off the car and raced toward the President's limousine. In the front seat of the Vice-Presidential car, Agent Youngblood heard an explosion and noticed unusual movements in the crowd. He vaulted into the rear seat and sat on the Vice President in order to protect him. At the same time Agent Kellerman in the front seat of the Presidential limousine turned to observe the President. Seeing that the President was struck, Kellerman instructed the driver, "Let's get out of here; we are hit." He radioed ahead to the lead car, "Get us to the hospital immediately." Agent Greer immediately accelerated the Presidential car. As it gained speed, Agent Hill managed to pull himself onto the back of the car where Mrs. Kennedy had

(continued)

climbed. Hill pushed her back into the rear seat and shielded the stricken President and Mrs. Kennedy as the President's car proceeded at high speed to Parkland Memorial Hospital, 4 miles away.

At Parkland, the President was immediately treated by a team of physicians who had been alerted for the President's arrival by the Dallas Police Department as the result of a radio message from the motorcade after the shooting. The doctors noted irregular breathing movements and a possible heartbeat, although they could not detect a pulse. They observed the extensive wound in the President's head and a small wound approximately one-fourth inch in diameter in the lower third of his neck. In an effort to facilitate breathing, the physicians performed a tracheotomy by enlarging the throat wound and inserting a tube. Totally absorbed in the immediate task of trying to preserve the President's life, the attending doctors never turned the president over for an examination of his back. At 1 P.M., after all heart activity ceased and the Last Rites were administered by a priest, President Kennedy was pronounced dead. Governor Connally underwent surgery and ultimately recovered from his serious wounds.

Upon learning of the President's death, Vice President Johnson left Parkland Hospital under close guard and proceeded to the Presidential plane at Love Field. Mrs. Kennedy, accompanying her husband's body, boarded the plane shortly thereafter. At 2:38 P.M., in the central compartment of the plane, Lyndon B. Johnson was sworn in as the 36th President of the United States by Federal District Court Judge Sarah T. Hughes. The plane left immediately for Washington, D.C., arriving at Andrews AFB, Md., at 5:58 P.M., e.s.t.. The President's body was taken to the National Naval Medical Center, Bethesda, Md., where it was given a complete pathological examination. The autopsy disclosed the large head wound observed at Parkland and the wound in the front of the neck which had been enlarged by the Parkland doctors when they performed the tracheotomy. Both of these wounds were described in the autopsy report as being "presumably of exit." In addition the autopsy revealed a small wound of entry in the rear of the President's skull and another wound of entry near the base of the back of the neck. The autopsy report stated the cause of death as "Gunshot wound, head" and the bullets which struck the President were described as having been fired "from a point behind and somewhat above the level of the deceased."

At the scene of the shooting, there was evident confusion at the outset concerning the point of origin of the shots. Witnesses differed in their accounts of the direction from which the sound of the shots emanated. Within a few minutes, however, attention centered on the Texas School Book Depository Building as the source of the shots. The building was occupied by a private corporation, the Texas School Book Depository Co., which distributed school textbooks of several publishers and leased space to representatives of the publishers. Most of the employees in the building worked for these publishers. The balance, including a 15-man warehousing crew, were employees of the Texas School Book Depository Co. itself.

Several eyewitnesses in front of the building reported that they saw a rifle being fired from the southeast corner window on the sixth floor of the Texas School Book Depository. One eyewitness, Howard L. Brennan, had been watching the parade from a point on Elm Street directly opposite and facing the building. He promptly told a policeman that he had seen a slender man, about 5 feet 10 inches, in his early thirties, take deliberate aim from the sixth-floor corner window and fire a rifle in the direction of the President's car. Brennan thought he might be able to identify the man since he had noticed him in the window a few minutes before the motorcade made the turn onto Elm Street. At 12:34 P.M., the Dallas police radio mentioned the Depository Building as a possible source of the shots, and at 12:45 P.M., the police radio broadcast a description of the suspected assassin based primarily on Brennan's observations. When the shots were fired, a Dallas motorcycle patrolman, Marrion L. Baker, was riding in the motorcade at a point several cars behind the President. He had turned right from Main Street onto Houston Street and was about 200 feet south of Elm Street when he heard a shot. Baker, having recently returned from a week of deer hunting, was certain the shot came from a high-powered rifle. He looked up and saw pigeons scattering in the air from their perches on the Texas School Book Depository Building. He raced his motorcycle to the building, dismounted, scanned the area to the west and pushed his way through the spectators toward the entrance. There he encountered Roy Truly, the building superintendent, who offered Baker his help. They entered the building, and ran toward the two elevators in the rear. Finding that both elevators were on an upper floor, they dashed up the stairs. Not more than 2 minutes had elapsed since the shooting.

When they reached the second-floor landing on their way up to the top of the building, Patrolman Baker thought he caught a glimpse of someone through the small glass window in the door separating the hall area near the stairs from the small vestibule leading into the lunchroom. Gun in hand, he rushed to the door and saw a man about 20 feet away walking toward the other end of the lunchroom. The man was empty handed. At Baker's command, the man turned and approached him. Truly, who had started up the stairs to the third floor ahead of Baker, returned to see what had delayed the patrolman. Baker asked Truly whether he knew the man in the lunchroom. Truly replied that the man worked in the building, whereupon Baker turned from the man and proceeded, with Truly, up the stairs. The man they encountered had started working in the Texas School Book Depository Building on October 16, 1963. His fellow workers described him as very quiet—a "loner." His name was Lee Harvey Oswald.

(continued)

Within about 1 minute after his encounter with Baker and Truly, Oswald was seen passing through the second-floor offices. In his hand was a full Coke bottle which he had purchased from a vending machine in the lunchroom. He was walking toward the front of the building where a passenger elevator and a short flight of stairs provided access to the main entrance of the building on the first floor. Approximately 7 minutes later, at about 12:40 P.M., Oswald boarded a bus at a point on Elm Street seven short blocks east of the Depository Building. The bus was traveling west toward the very building from which Oswald had come. Its route lay through the Oak Cliff section in southwest Dallas, where it would pass seven blocks east of the roominghouse in which Oswald was living, at 1026 North Beckley Avenue. On the bus was Mrs. Mary Bledsoe, one of Oswald's former landladies who immediately recognized him. Oswald stayed on the bus approximately 3 or 4 minutes, during which time it proceeded only two blocks because of the traffic jam created by the motorcade and the assassination. Oswald then left the bus. A few minutes later he entered a vacant taxi four blocks away and asked the driver to take him to a point on North Beckley Avenue several blocks beyond his roominghouse. The trip required 5 or 6 minutes. At about 1 P.M. Oswald arrived at the roominghouse. The housekeeper, Mrs. Earlene Roberts, was surprised to see Oswald at midday and remarked to him that he seemed to be in quite a hurry. He made no reply. A few minutes later Oswald emerged from his room zipping up his jacket and rushed out of the house.

Approximately 14 minutes later, and just 45 minutes after the assassination, another violent shooting occurred in Dallas. The victim was Patrolman J. D. Tippit of the Dallas police, an officer with a good record during his more than 11 years with the police force. He was shot near the intersection of 10th Street and Patton Avenue, about nine-tenths of a mile from Oswald's roominghouse. At the time of the assassination, Tippit was alone in his patrol car, the routine practice for most police patrol officers at this time of day. He had been ordered by radio at 12:45 P.M. to proceed to the central Oak Cliff area as part of a concentration of patrol car activity around the center of the city following the assassination. At 12:54 Tippit radioed that he had moved as directed and would be available for any emergency. By this time the police radio had broadcast several messages alerting the police to the suspect described by Brennan at the scene of the assassination—slender white male, about 30 years old, 5 feet 10 inches and weighing about 165 pounds.

At approximately 1:15 P.M., Tippit was driving slowly in an easterly direction on East 10th Street in Oak Cliff. About 100 feet past the intersection of 10th Street and Patton Avenue, Tippit pulled up alongside a man walking in the same direction. The man met the general description of the suspect wanted in connection with the assassination. He walked over to Tippit's car, rested his arms on the door on the right-hand side of the car, and apparently exchanged words with Tippit through the window. Tippit opened the door on the left side and started to walk around the front of his car. As he reached the front wheel on the driver's side, the man on the sidewalk drew a revolver and fired several shots in rapid succession, hitting Tippit four times and killing him instantly. An automobile repairman, Domingo Benavides, heard the shots and stopped his pickup truck on the opposite side of the street about 25 feet in front of Tippit's car. He observed the gunman start back toward Patton Avenue, removing the empty cartridge cases from the gun as he went. Benavides rushed to Tippit's side. The patrolman, apparently dead, was lying on his revolver, which was out of its holster. Benavides promptly reported the shooting to police headquarters over the radio in Tippit's car. The message was received shortly after 1:16 P.M.

As the gunman left the scene, he walked hurriedly back toward Patton Avenue and turned left, heading south. Standing on the northwest corner of 10th Street and Patton Avenue was Helen Markham, who had been walking south on Patton Avenue and had seen both the killer and Tippit cross the intersection in front of her as she waited on the curb for traffic to pass. She witnessed the shooting and then saw the man with a gun in his hand walk back toward the corner and cut across the lawn of the corner house as he started south on Patton Avenue.

In the corner house itself, Mrs. Barbara Jeanette Davis and her sister-in-law, Mrs. Virginia Davis, heard the shots and rushed to the door in time to see the man walk rapidly across the lawn shaking a revolver as if he were emptying it of cartridge cases. Later that day each woman found a cartridge case near the home. As the gunman turned the corner he passed alongside a taxicab which was parked on Patton Avenue a few feet from 10th Street. The driver, William W. Scoggins, had seen the slaying and was now crouched behind his cab on the street side. As the gunman cut through the shrubbery on the lawn, Scoggins looked up and saw the man approximately 12 feet away. In his hand was a pistol and he muttered words which sounded to Scoggins like "poor dumb cop" or "poor damn cop."

After passing Scoggins, the gunman crossed to the west side of Patton Avenue and ran south toward Jefferson Boulevard, a main Oak Cliff thoroughfare. On the east side of Patton, between l0th Street and Jefferson Boulevard, Ted Callaway, a used car salesman, heard the shots and ran to the sidewalk. As the man with the gun rushed past, Callaway shouted "What's going on?" The man merely shrugged, ran on to Jefferson Boulevard and turned right. On the next corner was a gas station with a parking lot in the rear. The assailant ran into the lot, discarded his jacket and then continued his flight west on Jefferson.

In a shoe store a few blocks farther west on Jefferson, the manager, Johnny Calvin Brewer, heard the siren of a police car moments after the radio in his

(continued)

store announced the shooting of the police officer in Oak Cliff. Brewer saw a man step quickly into the entranceway of the store and stand there with his back toward the street. When the police car made a U-turn and headed back in the direction of the Tippit shooting, the man left and Brewer followed him. He saw the man enter the Texas Theatre, a motion picture house about 60 feet away, without buying a ticket. Brewer pointed this out to the cashier, Mrs. Julia Postal, who called the police. The time was shortly after 1:40 P.M.

At 1:29 P.M., the police radio had noted the similarity in the descriptions of the suspects in the Tippit shooting and the assassination. At 1:45 P.M., in response to Mrs. Postal's call, the police radio sounded the alarm: "Have information a suspect just went in the Texas Theatre on West Jefferson." Within minutes the theater was surrounded. The house lights were then turned up. Patrolman M. N. McDonald and several other policemen approached the man, who had been pointed out to them by Brewer.

McDonald ordered the man to his feet and heard him say, "Well, it's all over now." The man drew a gun from his waist with one hand and struck the officer with the other. McDonald struck out with his right hand and grabbed the gun with his left hand. After a brief struggle McDonald and several other police officers disarmed and handcuffed the suspect and drove him to police headquarters, arriving at approximately 2 P.M.

Following the assassination, police cars had rushed to the Texas School Book Depository in response to the many radio messages reporting that the shots had been fired from the Depository Building. Inspector J. Herbert Sawyer of the Dallas Police Department arrived at the scene shortly after hearing the first of these police radio messages at 12:34 P.M. Some of the officers who had been assigned to the area of Elm and Houston Streets for the motorcade were talking to witnesses and watching the building when Sawyer arrived. Sawyer entered the building and rode a passenger elevator to the fourth floor, which was the top floor for this elevator. He conducted a quick search, returned to the main floor and, between approximately 12:37 and 12:40 P.M., ordered that no one be permitted to leave the building.

Shortly before 1 P.M. Capt. J. Will Fritz, chief of the homicide and robbery bureau of the Dallas Police Department, arrived to take charge of the investigation. Searching the sixth floor, Deputy Sheriff Luke Mooney noticed a pile of cartons in the southeast corner. He squeezed through the boxes and realized immediately that he had discovered the point from which the shots had been fired. On the floor were three empty cartridge cases. A carton had apparently been placed on the floor at the side of the window so that a person sitting on the carton could look down Elm Street toward the overpass and scarcely be noticed from the outside. Between this carton and the half-open window were three additional cartons arranged at such an angle that a rifle resting on the top carton would be aimed directly at the motorcade as it moved away from the building. The high stack of boxes, which first attracted Mooney's attention effectively screened a person at the window from the view of anyone else on the floor.

Mooney's discovery intensified the search for additional evidence on the sixth floor, and at 1:22 P.M. approximately 10 minutes after the cartridge cases were found, Deputy Sheriff Eugene Boone turned his flashlight in the direction of two rows of boxes in the northwest corner near the staircase. Stuffed between the two rows was a bolt-action rifle with a telescopic sight. The rifle was not touched until it could be photographed. When Lt. J. C. Day of the police identification bureau decided that the wooden stock and the metal knob at the end of the bolt contained no prints, he held the rifle by the stock while Captain Fritz ejected a live shell by operating the bolt. Lieutenant Day promptly noted that stamped on the rifle itself was the serial number "C2766" as well as the markings "1940" "MADE ITALY" and "CAL. 6.5." The rifle was about 40 inches long and when disassembled it could fit into a handmade paper sack which after the assassination, was found in the southeast corner of the building within a few feet of the cartridge cases.

As Fritz and Day were completing their examination of this rifle on the sixth floor, Roy Truly, the building superintendent, approached with information which he felt should be brought to the attention of the police. Earlier, while the police were questioning the employees, Truly had observed that Lee Harvey Oswald, 1 of the 15 men who worked in the warehouse, was missing. After Truly provided Oswald's name, address, and general description, Fritz left for police headquarters. He arrived at headquarters shortly after 2 P.M. and asked two detectives to pick up the employee who was missing from the Texas School Book Depository. Standing nearby were the police officers who had just arrived with the man arrested in the Texas Theatre. When Fritz mentioned the name of the missing employee, he learned that the man was already in the interrogation room. The missing School Book Depository employee and the suspect who had been apprehended in the Texas Theatre were one and the same—Lee Harvey Oswald.

The suspect Fritz was about to question in connection with the assassination of the President and the murder of a policeman was born in New Orleans on October 18, 1939, 2 months after the death of his father. His mother, Marguerite Claverie Oswald, had two older children. One, John Pic, was a half-brother to Lee from an earlier marriage which had ended in divorce. The other was Robert Oswald, a full brother to Lee and 5 years older. When Lee Oswald was 3, Mrs. Oswald placed him in an orphanage where his brother and half-brother were already living, primarily because she had to work.

In January 1944, when Lee was 4, he was taken out of the orphanage, and shortly thereafter his mother moved with him to Dallas, Tex., where the older boys joined them at the end of the school year. In May of 1945

(continued)

Marguerite Oswald married her third husband, Edwin A. Ekdahl. While the two older boys attended a military boarding school, Lee lived at home and developed a warm attachment to Ekdahl, occasionally accompanying his mother and stepfather on business trips around the country. Lee started school in Benbrook, Tex., but in the fall of 1946, after a separation from Ekdahl, Marguerite Oswald reentered Lee in the first grade in Covington, La. In January 1947, while Lee was still in the first grade, the family moved to Fort Worth, Tex., as the result of an attempted reconciliation between Ekdahl and Lee's mother. A year and a half later, before Lee was 9, his mother was divorced from her third husband as the result of a divorce action instituted by Ekdahl. Lee's school record during the next 5 and a half years in Fort Worth was average, although generally it grew poorer each year. The comments of teachers and others who knew him at that time do not reveal any unusual personality traits or characteristics.

Another change for Lee Oswald occurred in August 1952, a few months after he completed the sixth grade. Marguerite Oswald and her 12-year-old son moved to New York City where Marguerite's oldest son, John Pic, was stationed with the Coast Guard. The ensuing year and a half in New York was marked by Lee's refusals to attend school and by emotional and psychological problems of a seemingly serious nature. Because he had become a chronic school truant, Lee underwent psychiatric study at Youth House, an institution in New York for juveniles who have had truancy problems or difficulties with the law, and who appear to require psychiatric observation or other types of guidance. The social worker assigned to his case described him as "seriously detached" and "withdrawn" and noted "a rather pleasant, appealing quality about this emotionally starved, affectionless youngster." Lee expressed the feeling to the social worker that his mother did not care for him and regarded him as a burden. He experienced fantasies about being all-powerful and hurting people, but during his stay at Youth House he was apparently not a behavior problem. He appeared withdrawn and evasive, a boy who preferred to spend his time alone, reading and watching television. His tests indicated that he was above average in intelligence for his age group. The chief psychiatrist of Youth House diagnosed Lee's problem as a "personality pattern disturbance with schizoid features and passive-aggressive tendencies." He concluded that the boy was "an emotionally quite disturbed youngster" and recommended psychiatric treatment.

In May 1953, after having been at Youth House for 3 weeks, Lee Oswald returned to school where his attendance and grades temporarily improved. By the following fall, however, the probation officer reported that virtually every teacher complained about the boy's behavior. His mother insisted that he did not need psychiatric assistance. Although there was apparently some improvement in Lee's behavior during the next few months, the court recommended further treatment. In January 1954, while Lee's case was still pending, Marguerite and Lee left for New Orleans, the city of Lee's birth.

Upon his return to New Orleans, Lee maintained mediocre grades but had no obvious behavior problems. Neighbors and others who knew him outside of school remembered him as a quiet, solitary, and introverted boy who read a great deal and whose vocabulary made him quite articulate. About 1 month after he started the 10th grade and 11 days before his 16th birthday in October 1955, he brought to school a note purportedly written by his mother, stating that the family was moving to California. The note was written by Lee. A few days later he dropped out of school and almost immediately tried to join the Marine Corps. Because he was only 16, he was rejected. After leaving school Lee worked for the next 10 months at several jobs in New Orleans as an office messenger or clerk. It was during this period that he started to read communist literature. Occasionally, in conversations with others, he praised communism and expressed to his fellow employees a desire to join the Communist Party. At about this time, when he was not yet 17, he wrote to the Socialist Party of America, professing his belief in Marxism.

Another move followed in July 1956 when Lee and his mother returned to Fort Worth. He reentered high school but again dropped out after a few weeks and enlisted in the Marine Corps on October 1956, 6 days after his 17th birthday. On December 21, 1956, during boot camp in San Diego, Oswald fired a score of 212 for record with the M-1 rifle—2 points over the minimum for a rating of "sharpshooter" on a marksman/sharpshooter/expert scale. After his basic training, Oswald received training in aviation fundamentals and then in radar scanning.

Most people who knew Oswald in the Marines described him as a "loner" who resented the exercise of authority by others. He spent much of his free time reading. He was court-martialed once for possessing an unregistered privately owned weapon and, on another occasion, for using provocative language to a noncommissioned officer. He was, however, generally able to comply with Marine discipline, even though his experiences in the Marine Corps did not live up to his expectations.

Oswald served 15 months overseas until November 1958, most of it in Japan. During his final year in the Marine Corps he was stationed for the most part in Santa Ana, Calif., where he showed marked interest in the Soviet Union and sometimes expressed politically radical views with dogmatic conviction. Oswald again fired the M-1 rifle for record on May 6, 1959, and this time he shot a score of 191 on a shorter course than before, only 1 point over the minimum required to be a "marksman." According to one of his fellow marines, Oswald was not particularly interested in his rifle performance, and his unit was not expected to exhibit the usual rifle proficiency. During this period he expressed strong admiration for Fidel Castro

(continued)

and an interest in joining the Cuban army. He tried to impress those around him as an intellectual, but his thinking appeared to some as shallow and rigid.

Oswald's Marine service terminated on September 11, 1959, when at his own request he was released from active service a few months ahead of his scheduled release. He offered as the reason for his release the ill health and economic plight of his mother. He returned to Fort Worth, remained with his mother only 3 days and left for New Orleans, telling his mother he planned to get work there in the shipping or import-export business. In New Orleans he booked passage on the freighter SS Marion Lykes, which sailed from New Orleans to Le Havre, France, on September 20, 1959.

Lee Harvey Oswald had presumably planned this step in his life for quite some time. In March of 1959 he had applied to the Albert Schweitzer College in Switzerland for admission to the Spring 1960 term. His letter of application contained many blatant falsehoods concerning his qualifications and background. A few weeks before his discharge he had applied for and obtained a passport, listing the Soviet Union as one of the countries which he planned to visit. During his service in the Marines he had saved a comparatively large sum of money, possibly as much as $1,500, which would appear to have been accomplished by considerable frugality and apparently for a specific purpose.

The purpose of the accumulated fund soon became known. On October 16, 1959, Oswald arrived in Moscow by train after crossing the border from Finland, where he had secured a visa for a 6-day stay in the Soviet Union. He immediately applied for Soviet citizenship. On the afternoon of October 21, 1959, Oswald was ordered to leave the Soviet Union by 8 P.M. that evening. That same afternoon in his hotel room Oswald, in an apparent suicide attempt, slashed his left wrist. He was hospitalized immediately. On October 31, 3 days after his release from the hospital, Oswald appeared at the American Embassy, announced that he wished to renounce his U.S. citizenship and become a Russian citizen, and handed the Embassy officer a written statement he had prepared for the occasion. When asked his reasons, Oswald replied, "I am a Marxist." Oswald never formally complied with the legal steps necessary to renounce his American citizenship. The Soviet Government did not grant his request for citizenship, but in January 1960 he was given permission to remain in the Soviet Union on a year-to-year basis. At the same time Oswald was sent to Minsk where he worked in radio factory as an unskilled laborer. In January 1961 his permission to remain in the Soviet Union was extended for another year. A few weeks later, in February 1961, he wrote to the American Embassy in Moscow expressing a desire to return to the United States.

The following month Oswald met a 19-year-old Russian girl, Marina Nikolaevna Prusakova, a pharmacist, who had been brought up in Leningrad but was then living with an aunt and uncle in Minsk. They were married on

April 30, 1961. Throughout the following year he carried on a correspondence with American and Soviet authorities seeking approval for the departure of himself and his wife to the United States. In the course of this effort, Oswald and his wife visited the U.S. Embassy in Moscow in July of 1961. Primarily on the basis of an interview and questionnaire completed there, the Embassy concluded that Oswald had not lost his citizenship, a decision subsequently ratified by the Department of State in Washington, D.C. Upon their return to Minsk, Oswald and his wife filed with the Soviet authorities for permission to leave together. Their formal application was made in July 1961, and on December 25, 1961, Marina Oswald was advised it would be granted.

A daughter was born to the Oswalds in February 1962. In the months that followed they prepared for their return to the United States. On May 9, 1962, the U.S. Immigration and Naturalization Service, at the request of the Department of State, agreed to waive a restriction under the law which would have prevented the issuance of a United States visa to Oswald's Russian wife until she had left the Soviet Union. They finally left Moscow on June 1, 1962, and were assisted in meeting their travel expenses by a loan of $435.71 from the U.S. Department of State. Two weeks later they arrived in Fort Worth, Tex.

For a few weeks Oswald, his wife and child lived with Oswald's brother Robert. After a similar stay with Oswald's mother, they moved into their own apartment in early August. Oswald obtained a job on July 16 as a sheet metal worker. During this period in Fort Worth, Oswald was interviewed twice by agents of the FBI. The report of the first interview, which occurred on June 26, described him as arrogant and unwilling to discuss the reasons why he had gone to the Soviet Union. Oswald denied that he was involved in Soviet intelligence activities and promised to advise the FBI if Soviet representatives ever communicated with him. He was interviewed again on August 16, when he displayed a less belligerent attitude and once again agreed to inform the FBI of any attempt to enlist him in intelligence activities.

In early October 1962 Oswald quit his job at the sheet metal plant and moved to Dallas. While living in Forth Worth, the Oswalds had been introduced to a group of Russian-speaking people in the Dallas-Fort Worth area. Many of them assisted the Oswalds by providing small amounts of food, clothing, and household items. Oswald himself was disliked by almost all of this group whose help to the family was prompted primarily by sympathy for Marina Oswald and the child. Despite the fact that he had left the Soviet Union, disillusioned with its government, Oswald seemed more firmly committed than ever to his concepts of Marxism. He showed disdain for democracy, capitalism, and American society in general. He was highly critical of the Russian-speaking group because they seemed devoted to American concepts of democracy and capitalism and were ambitious to improve themselves economically.

(continued)

In February 1963 the Oswalds met Ruth Paine at a social gathering. Ruth Paine was temporarily separated from her husband and living with her two children in their home in Irving, Tex., a suburb of Dallas. Because of an interest in the Russian language and sympathy for Marina Oswald, who spoke no English and had few funds, Ruth Paine befriended Marina and, during the next 2 months, visited her on several occasions.

On April 6, 1963, Oswald lost his job with a photography firm. A few days later, on April 10, he attempted to kill Maj. Gen. Edwin A. Walker (retired, U.S. Army), using a rifle which he had ordered by mail 1 month previously under an assumed name. Marina Oswald learned of her husband's act when she confronted him with a note which he had left, giving her instructions in the event he did not return. That incident, and their general economic difficulties, impelled Marina Oswald to suggest that her husband leave Dallas and go to New Orleans to look for work.

Oswald left for New Orleans on April 24, 1963. Ruth Paine, who knew nothing of the Walker shooting, invited Marina Oswald and the baby to stay with her in the Paines' modest home while Oswald sought work in New Orleans. Early in May, upon receiving word from Oswald that he had found a job, Ruth Paine drove Marina Oswald and the baby to New Orleans to rejoin Oswald.

During the stay in New Orleans, Oswald formed a fictitious New Orleans Chapter of the Fair Play for Cuba Committee. He posed as secretary of this organization and represented that the president was A. J. Hidell. In reality, Hidell was a completely fictitious person created by Oswald, the organization's only member. Oswald was arrested on August 9 in connection with a scuffle which occurred while he was distributing pro-Castro leaflets. The next day, while at the police station, he was interviewed by an FBI agent after Oswald requested the police to arrange such an interview. Oswald gave the agent false information about his own background and was evasive in his replies concerning Fair Play for Cuba activities. During the next 2 weeks, Oswald appeared on radio programs twice, claiming to be the spokesman for the Fair Play for Cuba Committee in New Orleans.

On July 19, 1963, Oswald lost his job as a greaser of coffee processing machinery. In September, after an exchange of correspondence with Marina Oswald, Ruth Paine drove to New Orleans and on September 23, transported Marina, the child, and the family belongings to Irving, Tex. Ruth Paine suggested that Marina Oswald, who was expecting her second child in October, live at the Paine house until after the baby was born. Oswald remained behind, ostensibly to find work either in Houston or some other city. Instead, he departed by bus for Mexico, arriving in Mexico City on September 27, where he promptly visited the Cuban and Russian embassies. His stated objective was to obtain official permission to visit Cuba, on his way to the Soviet Union. The Cuban Government would not grant his visa unless the Soviet Government would also issue a visa permitting his entry into Russia. Oswald's efforts to secure these visas failed, and he left for Dallas, where he arrived on October 3, 1963.

When he saw his wife the next day, it was decided that Oswald would rent a room in Dallas and visit his family on weekends. For 1 week he rented a room from Mrs. Bledsoe, the woman who later saw him on the bus shortly after the assassination. On October 14, 1963, he rented the Beckley Avenue room and listed his name as O. H. Lee. On the same day, at the suggestion of a neighbor, Mrs. Paine phoned the Texas School Book Depository and was told that there was a job opening. She informed Oswald, who was interviewed the following day at the Depository and started to work there on October 16, 1963.

On October 20 the Oswalds' second daughter was born. During October and November Oswald established a general pattern of weekend visits to Irving, arriving on Friday afternoon and returning to Dallas Monday morning with a fellow employee, Buell Wesley Frazier, who lived near the Paines. On Friday, November 15, Oswald remained in Dallas at the suggestion of his wife who told him that the house would be crowded because of a birthday party for Ruth Paine's daughter. On Monday, November 18, Oswald and his wife quarreled bitterly during a telephone conversation, because she learned for the first time that he was living at the rooming house under an assumed name. On Thursday, November 21, Oswald told Frazier that he would like to drive to Irving to pick up some curtain rods for an apartment in Dallas. His wife and Mrs. Paine were quite surprised to see him since it was a Thursday night. They thought he had returned to make up after Monday's quarrel. He was conciliatory, but Marina Oswald was still angry.

Later that evening, when Mrs. Paine had finished cleaning the kitchen, she went into the garage and noticed that the light was burning. She was certain that she had not left it on, although the incident appeared unimportant at the time. In the garage were most of the Oswalds' personal possessions. The following morning Oswald left while his wife was still in bed feeding the baby. She did not see him leave the house, nor did Ruth Paine. On the dresser in their room he left his wedding ring which he had never done before. His wallet containing $170 was left intact in a dresser-drawer.

Oswald walked to Frazier's house about half a block away and placed a long bulky package, made out of wrapping paper and tape, into the rear seat of the car. He told Frazier that the package contained curtain rods. When they reached the Depository parking lot, Oswald walked quickly ahead. Frazier followed and saw Oswald enter the Depository Building carrying the long bulky package with him.

(continued)

During the morning of November 22, Marina Oswald followed President Kennedy's activities on television. She and Ruth Paine cried when they heard that the President had been shot. Ruth Paine translated the news of the shooting to Marina Oswald as it came over the television, including the report that the shots were probably fired from the building where Oswald worked. When Marina Oswald heard this, she recalled the Walker episode and the fact that her husband still owned the rifle. She went quietly to the Paine's garage where the rifle had been concealed in a blanket among their other belongings. It appeared to her that the rifle was still there, although she did not actually open the blanket.

At about 3 P.M. the police arrived at the Paine house and asked Marina Oswald whether her husband owned a rifle. She said that he did and then led them into the garage and pointed to the rolled up blanket. As a police officer lifted it, the blanket hung limply over either side of his arm. The rifle was not there.

Meanwhile, at police headquarters Captain Fritz had begun questioning Oswald. Soon after the start of the first interrogation, agents of the FBI and the U.S. Secret Service arrived and participated in the questioning. Oswald denied having anything to do with the assassination of President Kennedy or the murder of Patrolman Tippit. He claimed that he was eating lunch at the time of the assassination, and that he then spoke with his foreman for 5 to 10 minutes before going home. He denied that he owned a rifle and when confronted, in a subsequent interview, with a picture showing him holding a rifle and pistol, he claimed that his face had been superimposed on someone else's body. He refused to answer any questions about the presence in his wallet of a selective service card with his picture and the name "Alek J. Hidell."

During the questioning of Oswald on the third floor of the police department, more than 100 representatives of the press, radio, and television were crowded into the hallway through which Oswald had to pass when being taken from his cell to Captain Fritz' office for interrogation. Reporters tried to interview Oswald during these trips. Between Friday afternoon and Sunday morning he appeared in the hallway at least 16 times. The generally confused conditions outside and inside Captain Fritz' office increased the difficulty of police questioning. Advised by the police that he could communicate with an attorney, Oswald made several telephone calls on Saturday in an effort to procure representation of his own choice and discussed the matter with the president of the local bar association, who offered to obtain counsel Oswald declined the offer, saying that he would first try to obtain counsel by himself. By Sunday morning he had not yet engaged an attorney.

At 7:10 P.M. on November 22, 1963, Lee Harvey Oswald was formally advised that he had been charged with the murder of Patrolman J. D. Tippit.

Several witnesses to the Tippit slaying and to the subsequent flight of the gunman had positively identified Oswald in police lineups. While positive firearm identification evidence was not available at the time, the revolver in Oswald's possession at the time of his arrest was of a type which could have fired the shots that killed Tippit.

The formal charge against Oswald for the assassination of President Kennedy was lodged shortly after 1:30 A.M., on Saturday, November 23. By 10 P.M. of the day of the assassination, the FBI had traced the rifle found on the sixth floor of the Texas School Book Depository to a mail order house in Chicago which had purchased it from a distributor in New York. Approximately 6 hours later, the Chicago firm advised that this rifle had been ordered in March 1963 by an A. Hidel for shipment to post office box 2915, in Dallas, Tex., a box rented by Oswald. Payment for the rifle was remitted by a money order signed by A. Hidell. By 6:45 P.M. on November 23, the FBI was able to advise the Dallas police that, as a result of handwriting analysis of the documents used to purchase the rifle, it had concluded that the rifle had been ordered by Lee Harvey Oswald.

Throughout Friday and Saturday, the Dallas police released to the public many of the details concerning the alleged evidence against Oswald. Police officials discussed important aspects of the case, usually in the course of impromptu and confused press conferences in the third-floor corridor. Some of the information divulged was erroneous. Efforts by the news media representatives to reconstruct the crime and promptly report details frequently led to erroneous and often conflicting reports. At the urgings of the newsmen, Chief of Police Jesse E. Curry, brought Oswald to a press conference in the police assembly room shortly after midnight of the day Oswald was arrested. The assembly room was crowded with newsmen who had come to Dallas from all over the country. They shouted questions at Oswald and flashed cameras at him. Among this group was a 52-year-old Dallas nightclub operator—Jack Ruby.

On Sunday morning, November 24, arrangements were made for Oswald's transfer from the city jail to the Dallas County jail, about 1 mile away. The news media had been informed on Saturday night that the transfer of Oswald would not take place until after 10 A.M. on Sunday. Earlier on Sunday, between 2:30 and 3 A.M., anonymous telephone calls threatening Oswald's life had been received by the Dallas office of the FBI and by the office of the county sheriff. Nevertheless, on Sunday morning, television, radio, and newspaper representatives crowded into the basement to record the transfer. As viewed through television cameras, Oswald would emerge from a door in front of the cameras and proceed to the transfer vehicle. To the right of the cameras was a "down" ramp from Main Street on the north. To the left was an "up" ramp leading to Commerce Street on the south.

(continued)

The armored truck in which Oswald was to be transferred arrived shortly after 11 A.M. Police officials then decided, however, that an unmarked police car would be preferable for the trip because of its greater speed and maneuverability. At approximately 11:20 A.M. Oswald emerged from the basement jail office flanked by detectives on either side and at his rear. He took a few steps toward the car and was in the glaring light of the television cameras when a man suddenly darted out from an area on the right of the cameras where newsmen had been assembled. The man was carrying a Colt .38 revolver in his right hand and, while millions watched on television, he moved quickly to within a few feet of Oswald and fired one shot into Oswald's abdomen. Oswald groaned with pain as he fell to the ground and quickly lost consciousness. Within 7 minutes Oswald was at Parkland Hospital where, without having regained consciousness, he was pronounced dead at 1:07 P.M.

The man who killed Oswald was Jack Ruby. He was instantly arrested and, minutes later, confined in a cell on the fifth floor of the Dallas police jail. Under interrogation, he denied that the killing of Oswald was in any way connected with a conspiracy involving the assassination of President Kennedy. He maintained that he had killed Oswald in a temporary fit of depression and rage over the President's death. Ruby was transferred the following day to the county jail without notice to the press or to police officers not directly involved in the transfer. Indicted for the murder of Oswald by the State of Texas on November 26, 1963, Ruby was found guilty on March 14, 1964, and sentenced to death. As of September 1964, his case was pending on appeal.

Conclusions

This Commission was created to ascertain the facts relating to the preceding summary of events and to consider the important questions which they raised. The Commission has addressed itself to this task and has reached certain conclusions based on all the available evidence. No limitations have been placed on the Commission's inquiry; it has conducted its own investigation, and all Government agencies have fully discharged their responsibility to cooperate with the Commission in its investigation. These conclusions represent the reasoned judgment of all members of the Commission and are presented after an investigation which has satisfied the Commission that it has ascertained the truth concerning the assassination of President Kennedy to the extent that a prolonged and thorough search makes this possible.

1. The shots which killed President Kennedy and wounded Governor Connally were fired from the sixth floor window at the southeast corner of the Texas School Book Depository. This determination is based upon the following:

- Witnesses at the scene of the assassination saw a rifle being fired from the sixth floor window of the Depository Building, and some witnesses saw a rifle in the window immediately after the shots were fired.
- The nearly whole bullet found on Governor Connally's stretcher at Parkland Memorial Hospital and the two bullet fragments found in the front seat of the Presidential limousine were fired from the 6.5-millimeter Mannlicher-Carcano rifle found on the sixth floor of the Depository Building to the exclusion of all other weapons.
- The three used cartridge cases found near the window on the sixth floor at the southeast corner of the building were fired from the same rifle which fired the above-described bullet and fragments, to the exclusion of all other weapons.
- The windshield in the Presidential limousine was struck by a bullet fragment on the inside surface of the glass, but was not penetrated.
- The nature of the bullet wounds suffered by President Kennedy and Governor Connally and the location of the car at the time of the shots establish that the bullets were fired from above and behind the Presidential limousine, striking the President and the Governor as follows:
  1. President Kennedy was first struck by a bullet which entered at the back of his neck and exited through the lower front portion of his neck, causing a wound which would not necessarily have been lethal. The President was struck a second time by a bullet which entered the right-rear portion of his head, causing a massive and fatal wound.
  2. Governor Connally was struck by a bullet which entered on the right side of his back and traveled downward through the right side of his chest, exiting below his right nipple. This bullet then passed through his right wrist and entered his left thigh where it caused a superficial wound.
- There is no credible evidence that the shots were fired from the Triple Underpass, ahead of the motorcade, or from any other location.

2. The weight of the evidence indicates that there were three shots fired.
3. Although it is not necessary to any essential findings of the Commission to determine just which shot hit Governor Connally, there

(continued)

is very persuasive evidence from the experts to indicate that the same bullet which pierced the President's throat also caused Governor Connally's wounds. However, Governor Connally's testimony and certain other factors have given rise to some difference of opinion as to this probability but there is no question in the mind of any member of the Commission that all the shots which caused the President's and Governor Connally's wounds were fired from the sixth floor window of the Texas School Book Depository.

4. The shots which killed President Kennedy and wounded Governor Connally were fired by Lee Harvey Oswald. This conclusion is based upon the following:

- The Mannlicher-Carcano 6.5-millimeter Italian rifle from which the shots were fired was owned by and in the possession of Oswald.
- Oswald carried this rifle into the Depository Building on the morning of November 22, 1963.
- Oswald, at the time of the assassination, was present at the window from which the shots were fired.
- Shortly after the assassination, the Mannlicher-Carcano rifle belonging to Oswald was found partially hidden between some cartons on the sixth floor and the improvised paper bag in which Oswald brought the rifle to the Depository was found close by the window from which the shots were fired.
- Based on testimony of the experts and their analysis of films of the assassination, the Commission has concluded that a rifleman of Lee Harvey Oswald's capabilities could have fired the shots from the rifle used in the assassination within the elapsed time of the shooting. The Commission has concluded further that Oswald possessed the capability with a rifle which enabled him to commit the assassination.
- Oswald lied to the police after his arrest concerning important substantive matters.
- Oswald had attempted to kill Maj. Gen. Edwin A. Walker (Retired, U.S. Army) on April 10, 1963, thereby demonstrating his disposition to take human life.

5. Oswald killed Dallas Police Patrolman J. D. Tippit approximately 45 minutes after the assassination. This conclusion upholds the finding that Oswald fired the shots which killed President Kennedy and wounded Governor Connally and is supported by the following:

- Two eyewitnesses saw the Tippit shooting and seven eyewitnesses heard the shots and saw the gunman leave the scene with revolver in hand. These nine eyewitnesses positively identified Lee Harvey Oswald as the man they saw.
- The cartridge cases found at the scene of the shooting were fired from the revolver in the possession of Oswald at the time of his arrest to the exclusion of all other weapons.
- The revolver in Oswald's possession at the time of his arrest was purchased by and belonged to Oswald.
- Oswald's jacket was found along the path of flight taken by the gunman as he fled from the scene of the killing.

6. Within 80 minutes of the assassination and 35 minutes of the Tippit killing, Oswald resisted arrest at the theater by attempting to shoot another Dallas police officer.
7. The Commission has reached the following conclusions concerning Oswald's interrogation and detention by the Dallas police:

    - Except for the force required to effect his arrest, Oswald was not subjected to any physical coercion by any law enforcement officials. He was advised that he could not be compelled to give any information and that any statements made by him might be used against him in court. He was advised of his right to counsel. He was given the opportunity to obtain counsel of his own choice and was offered legal assistance by the Dallas Bar Association, which he rejected at that time.
    - Newspaper, radio, and television reporters were allowed uninhibited access to the area through which Oswald had to pass when he was moved from his cell to the interrogation room and other sections of the building, thereby subjecting Oswald to harassment and creating chaotic conditions which were not conducive to orderly interrogation or the protection of the rights of the prisoner.
    - The numerous statements, sometimes erroneous, made to the press by various local law enforcement officials during this period of confusion and disorder in the police station would have presented serious obstacles to the obtaining of a fair trial for Oswald. To the extent that the information was erroneous or misleading, it helped to create doubts, speculations, and fears in the mind of the public which might otherwise not have arisen.

8. The Commission has reached the following conclusions concerning the killing of Oswald by Jack Ruby on November 24, 1963:

(continued)

- Ruby entered the basement of the Dallas Police Department shortly after 11:17 A.M. and killed Lee Harvey Oswald at 11:21 A.M.
- Although the evidence on Ruby's means of entry is not conclusive, the weight of the evidence indicates that he walked down the ramp leading from Main Street to the basement of the police department.
- There is no evidence to support the rumor that Ruby may have been assisted by any members of the Dallas Police Department in the killing of Oswald.
- The Dallas Police Department's decision to transfer Oswald to the county jail in full public view was unsound. The arrangements made by the police department on Sunday morning, only a few hours before the attempted transfer, were inadequate. Of critical importance was the fact that news media representatives and others were not excluded from the basement even after the police were notified of threats to Oswald's life. These deficiencies contributed to the death of Lee Harvey Oswald.

9. The Commission has found no evidence that either Lee Harvey Oswald or Jack Ruby was part of any conspiracy, domestic or foreign, to assassinate President Kennedy. The reasons for this conclusion are:

- The Commission has found no evidence that anyone assisted Oswald in planning or carrying out the assassination. In this connection it has thoroughly investigated, among other factors, the circumstances surrounding the planning of the motorcade route through Dallas, the hiring of Oswald by the Texas School Book Depository Co. on October 15, 1963, the method by which the rifle was brought into the building, the placing of cartons of books at the window, Oswald's escape from the building, and the testimony of eyewitnesses to the shooting.
- The Commission has found no evidence that Oswald was involved with any person or group in a conspiracy to assassinate the President, although it has thoroughly investigated, in addition to other possible leads, all facets of Oswald's associations, finances, and personal habits, particularly during the period following his return from the Soviet Union in June 1962.
- The Commission has found no evidence to show that Oswald was employed, persuaded, or encouraged by any foreign government to assassinate President Kennedy or that he was an

agent of any foreign government, although the Commission has reviewed the circumstances surrounding Oswald's defection to the Soviet Union, his life there from October of 1959 to June of 1962 so far as it can be reconstructed, his known contacts with the Fair Play for Cuba Committee and his visits to the Cuban and Soviet Embassies in Mexico City during his trip to Mexico from September 26 to October 3, 1963, and his known contacts with the Soviet Embassy in the United States.

- The Commission has explored all attempts of Oswald to identify himself with various political groups, including the Communist Party, U.S.A., the Fair Play for Cuba Committee, and the Socialist Workers Party, and has been unable to find any evidence that the contacts which he initiated were related to Oswald's subsequent assassination of the President.
- All of the evidence before the Commission established that there was nothing to support the speculation that Oswald was an agent, employee, or informant of the FBI, the CIA, or any other governmental agency. It has thoroughly investigated Oswald's relationships prior to the assassination with all agencies of the U.S. government. All contacts with Oswald by any of these agencies were made in the regular exercise of their different responsibilities.
- No direct or indirect relationship between Lee Harvey Oswald and Jack Ruby has been discovered by the Commission, nor has it been able to find any credible evidence that either knew the other, although a thorough investigation was made of the many rumors and speculations of such a relationship.
- The Commission has found no evidence that Jack Ruby acted with any other person in the killing of Lee Harvey Oswald.
- After careful investigation the Commission has found no credible evidence either that Ruby and Officer Tippit, who was killed by Oswald, knew each other or that Oswald and Tippit knew each other.

Because of the difficulty of proving negatives to a certainty the possibility of others being involved with either Oswald or Ruby cannot be established categorically, but if there is any such evidence it has been beyond the reach of all the investigative agencies and resources of the United States and has not come to the attention of this Commission.

10. In its entire investigation the Commission has found no evidence of conspiracy, subversion, or disloyalty to the U.S. government by any federal, state, or local official.

(continued)

11. On the basis of the evidence before the Commission it concludes that Oswald acted alone. Therefore, to determine the motives for the assassination of President Kennedy, one must look to the assassin himself. Clues to Oswald's motives can be found in his family history, his education or lack of it, his acts, his writings, and the recollections of those who had close contacts with him throughout his life. The Commission has presented with this report all of the background information bearing on motivation which it could discover. Thus, others may study Lee Oswald's life and arrive at their own conclusions as to his possible motives. The Commission could not make any definitive determination of Oswald's motives. It has endeavored to isolate factors which contributed to his character and which might have influenced his decision to assassinate President Kennedy. These factors were:

- His deep-rooted resentment of all authority which was expressed in a hostility toward every society in which he lived;
- His inability to enter into meaningful relationships with people, and a continuous pattern of rejecting his environment in favor of new surrounding;
- His urge to try to find a place in history and despair at times over failures in his various undertakings;
- His capacity for violence as evidenced by his attempt to kill General Walker;
- His avowed commitment to Marxism and communism, as he understood the terms and developed his own interpretation of them; this was expressed by his antagonism toward the United States, by his defection to the Soviet Union, by his failure to be reconciled with life in the United States even after his disenchantment with the Soviet Union, and by his efforts, though frustrated, to go to Cuba.

Each of these contributed to his capacity to risk all in cruel and irresponsible actions.

12. The Commission recognizes that the varied responsibilities of the President require that he make frequent trips to all parts of the United States and abroad. Consistent with their high responsibilities Presidents can never be protected from every potential threat. The Secret Service's difficulty in meeting its protective responsibility varies with the activities and the nature of the occupant of the office of President and his willingness to conform to plans for his safety. In appraising the performance of the Secret Service it

should be understood that it has to do its work within such limitations. Nevertheless, the Commission believes that recommendations for improvements in Presidential protection are compelled by the facts disclosed in this investigation.

- The complexities of the Presidency have increased so rapidly in recent years that the Secret Service has not been able to develop or to secure adequate resources of personnel and facilities to fulfill its important assignment. This situation should be promptly remedied.
- The Commission has concluded that the criteria and procedures of the Secret Service designed to identify and protect against persons considered threats to the president, were not adequate prior to the assassination.
  1. The Protective Research Section of the Secret Service, which is responsible for its preventive work, lacked sufficient trained personnel and the mechanical and technical assistance needed to fulfill its responsibility.
  2. Prior to the assassination the Secret Service's criteria dealt with direct threats against the President. Although the Secret Service treated the direct threats against the President adequately, it failed to recognize the necessity of identifying other potential sources of danger to his security. The Secret Service did not develop adequate and specific criteria defining those persons or groups who might present a danger to the President. In effect, the Secret Service largely relied upon other federal or state agencies to supply the information necessary for it to fulfill its preventive responsibilities, although it did ask for information about direct threats to the President.
- The Commission has concluded that there was insufficient liaison and coordination of information between the Secret Service and other federal agencies necessarily concerned with Presidential protection. Although the FBI, in the normal exercise of its responsibility, had secured considerable information about Lee Harvey Oswald, it had no official responsibility, under the Secret Service criteria existing at the time of the President's trip to Dallas, to refer to the Secret Service the information it had about Oswald. The Commission has concluded, however, that the FBI took an unduly restrictive view of its role in preventive intelligence work prior to the assassination. A more carefully coordinated treatment of the Oswald case by the FBI might well have resulted in bringing Oswald's activities to the attention of the Secret Service.

(continued)

- The Commission has concluded that some of the advance preparations in Dallas made by the Secret Service, such as the detailed security measures taken at Love Field and the Trade Mart, were thorough and well executed. In other respects, however, the Commission has concluded that the advance preparations for the President's trip were deficient.

    1. Although the Secret Service is compelled to rely to a great extent on local law enforcement officials, its procedures at the time of the Dallas trip did not call for well-defined instructions as to the respective responsibilities of the police officials and others assisting in the protection of the President.
    2. The procedures relied upon by the Secret Service for detecting the presence of an assassin located in a building along a motorcade route were inadequate. At the time of the trip to Dallas, the Secret Service as a matter of practice did not investigate, or cause to be checked, any building located along the motorcade route to be taken by the President. The responsibility for observing windows in these buildings during the motorcade was divided between local police personnel stationed on the streets to regulate crowds and Secret Service agents riding in the motorcade. Based on its investigation the Commission has concluded that these arrangements during the trip to Dallas were clearly not sufficient.

- The configuration of the Presidential car and the seating arrangements of the Secret Service agents in the car did not afford the Secret Service agents the opportunity they should have had to be of immediate assistance to the President at the first sign of danger.
- Within these limitations, however, the Commission finds that the agents most immediately responsible for the President's safety reacted promptly at the time the shots were fired from the Texas School Book Depository Building.

Recommendations

Prompted by the assassination of President Kennedy, the Secret Service has initiated a comprehensive and critical review of its total operations. As a result of studies conducted during the past several months, and in cooperation with this Commission, the Secret Service has prepared a planning document dated August 27, 1964, which recommends various programs considered necessary by the Service to improve its techniques and enlarge its resources. The Commission is encouraged by the efforts taken by the Secret Service since the assassination and suggests the following recommendations.

1. A committee of Cabinet members including the Secretary of the Treasury and the Attorney General, or the National Security Council, should be assigned the responsibility of reviewing and overseeing the protective activities of the Secret Service and the other Federal agencies that assist in safeguarding the President. Once given this responsibility, such a committee would insure that the maximum resources of the federal government are fully engaged in the task of protecting the President, and would provide guidance in defining the general nature of domestic and foreign dangers to Presidential security.

2. Suggestions have been advanced to the Commission for the transfer of all or parts of the Presidential protective responsibilities of the Secret Service to some other department or agency. The Commission believes that if there is to be any determination of whether or not to relocate these responsibilities and functions, it ought to be made by the Executive and the Congress, perhaps upon recommendations based on studies by the previously suggested committee.

3. Meanwhile, in order to improve daily supervision of the Secret Service within the Department of the Treasury, the Commission recommends that the Secretary of the Treasury appoint a special assistant with the responsibility of supervising the Secret Service. This special assistant should have sufficient stature and experience in law enforcement, intelligence, and allied fields to provide effective continuing supervision, and to keep the Secretary fully informed regarding the performance of the Secret Service. One of the initial assignments of this special assistant should be the supervision of the current effort by the Secret Service to revise and modernize its basic operating procedures.

4. The Commission recommends that the Secret Service completely overhaul its facilities devoted to the advance detection of potential threats against the President. The Commission suggests the following measures.

- The Secret Service should develop as quickly as possible more useful and precise criteria defining those potential threats to the President which should be brought to its attention by other agencies. The criteria should, among other additions, provide for prompt notice to the Secret Service of all returned defectors.
- The Secret Service should expedite its current plans to utilize the most efficient data-processing techniques.
- Once the Secret Service has formulated new criteria delineating the information it desires, it should enter into agreements with each federal agency to insure its receipt of such information.

5. The Commission recommends that the Secret Service improve the protective measures followed in the planning and conducting of Presidential

(continued)

motorcades. In particular, the Secret Service should continue its current efforts to increase the precautionary attention given to buildings along the motorcade route.

6. The Commission recommends that the Secret Service continue its recent efforts to improve and formalize its relationships with local police departments in areas to be visited by the President.

7. The Commission believes that when the new criteria and procedures are established, the Secret Service will not have sufficient personnel or adequate facilities. The Commission recommends that the Secret Service be provided with the personnel and resources which the Service and the Department of the Treasury may be able to demonstrate are needed to fulfill its important mission.

8. Even with an increase in Secret Service personnel, the protection of the President will continue to require the resources and cooperation of many federal agencies. The Commission recommends that these agencies, specifically the FBI, continue the practice as it has developed, particularly since the assassination, of assisting the Secret Service upon request by providing personnel or other aid, and that there be a closer association and liaison between the Secret Service and all federal agencies.

9. The Commission recommends that the President's physician always accompany him during his travels and occupy a position near the President where he can be immediately available in case of any emergency.

10. The Commission recommends to Congress that it adopt legislation which would make the assassination of the President and Vice President a federal crime. A state of affairs where U.S. authorities have no clearly defined jurisdiction to investigate the assassination of a President is anomalous.

12. The Commission has examined the Department of State's handling of the Oswald matters and finds that it followed the law throughout. However, the Commission believes that the Department in accordance with its own regulations should in all cases exercise great care in the return to this country of defectors who have evidenced disloyalty or hostility to this country or who have expressed a desire to renounce their American citizenship and that when such persons are so returned, procedures should be adopted for the better dissemination of information concerning them to the intelligence agencies of the government.

13. The Commission recommends that the representatives of the bar, law enforcement associations, and the news media work together to establish ethical standards concerning the collection and presentation of information to the public so that there will be no interference with pending criminal investigations, court proceedings, or the right of individuals to a fair trial.

Note: The full report is available at the National Archives Web site: http://www.archives.gov/research/jfk/warren-commission-report/.

been wrong in his criminal pursuit of the JFK assassination. Lambert, in her book, *False Witness*, attempted to do just that, refute the movie version. According to written sources, Stone has refused to read or comment on Lambert's work.

Stone's movie was produced in the United States. It was filmed in Dallas, Texas, New Orleans, Louisiana, and Washington, D.C. When it was released in 1991, it grossed $69,741,131 from the U.S. market. There is a lack of credible information regarding the amount of money that it has made over the years in after-market sales. However a perusal of Web sites suggests that people are still watching the movie today and weighing in on the controversial Jim Garrison.

CONCLUSION

Biographer Joan Mellen met New Orleans District Attorney Jim Garrison in 1969. His relentless search for the truth about what happened to President Kennedy made a deep impression on her. In 1997, Mellen started to work on the story of Garrison's life. Her biography turned into the story of Garrison's investigation and then into a new investigation of the assassination itself. In 2005, Mellon published *A Farewell to Justice*. Mellon revisited the entire Garrison investigation, uncovered new evidence, and established the intelligence agencies' roles in both the president's assassination and its cover-up. Moreover, she relied on a Gallup Poll that suggested that twice as many people believed that the CIA was responsible for the assassination as believed that Oswald, a man without a known motive, acted alone.

Thus the question remains today, was Garrison a misguided irrational man on a mission without substance or was he a prosecutor who truly believed that he could and did solve the case of the assassination of President John F. Kennedy? Ultimately the public will decide if Garrison's conspiracy theory was correct, even if he prosecuted the wrong individual. In either case, Jim Garrison is an icon of crime fighting. Perhaps it is fitting that since his death in New Orleans in October 1992, his headstone reads, "Let justice be done though the heavens fall."

FURTHER READING

Brener, Milton, E. 1969. *The Garrison Case*. New York: Clarkson N. Potter.
Davy, William. 1999, *Let Justice Be Done: New Light on the Jim Garrison Investigation*. Reston: Jordan Publishing.
Garrison, Jim. 1988. *On the Trail of the Assassins*. New York: Warner Books.
History Channel Special on Patricia Lambert's book. August 16, 2000.
http://mcadams.posc.mu.edu/bethell1.htm (accessed on August 22, 2007).
http://movies.yahoo.com/movie/1800341652/details.

http://www.archives.gov/research/jfk/warren-commission-report.
http://www.chron.com/content/chronicle/special/jfk/theory/garrison.html.
Hurt, Henry. 1985. *Reasonable Doubt*. New York: Henry Holt.
Lambert, Patricia. 1998. *False Witness: The Real Story of Jim Garrison's Investigation and Oliver Stone's Film JFK*. New York: M. Evans.
Lane, Mark. 1992. *Fact or Fiction? The Movie-Goers Guide to the Film* JFK. Rush to Judgment. New York: Thunder's Mouth.
Look. 1968. "The Persecution of Clay Shaw." August 26.
Marrs, Jim. 1989. *Crossfire: The Plot That Killed Kennedy*. New York: Carroll & Graf.
Mellen, Joan. 2005. *A Farewell to Justice: Jim Garrison, JFK's Assassination, and the Case That Should have Changed History*. Dulles, VA: Potomac Books.
Phelan, James. 1967. Rush to judgment in New Orleans. *The Saturday Evening Post*, May 6.
Riordan, James. 1995. *Stone*. New York: Hyperion.
Stone, Oliver, and Zackery Sklar. 1992. *JFK: The Book of the Film*. New York: Applause.
Summers, Anthony. 1989. *Conspiracy*. New York: Paragon House.
Washington Post. 1992. p. 12. May 19.

© Getty Images

Buford Pusser

Jacob Rodriguez

In a politically correct America, criminologists have proposed that law enforcement officials should not view themselves as "crime fighters," but instead, should think of themselves as "social peacekeepers" or "peace officers." However, in a time when there is no peace to be maintained, law enforcement officials had no choice but to resort to their crime-fighting techniques. The crime-fighting model of policing was developed by few but was often recognized by many through the media. These few crime fighters include robust men such as Wyatt Earp, Frank Hamer, and of course, who can forget about the legendary sheriff of McNairy County, Tennessee, Buford Hayes Pusser (1937–1974)?

Sheriff Department Facts: Reported by the U.S. Department of Justice, Bureau of Justice Statistics

Personnel

- As of June 2003, the 3,061 sheriffs' offices in the United States had about 330,000 full-time employees, including about 174,000 sworn personnel. This represented an increase of about 9,500 sworn and 26,900 nonsworn employees since 2000.
- Racial and ethnic minorities comprised 18.8% of full-time sworn personnel in 2003, up from 13.4% in 1987. Women were 12.9% of officers in 2003, about the same as in 1987 (12.6%).
- From 2000 to 2003 the number of black or African American officers increased by 1,990, or 13%; Hispanic or Latino officers by 1,960, or 20%; officers from other minority groups by 500, or 20%, and female officers by 960, or 5%.
- Sixty-nine percent of sheriffs' offices had officer separations during the 12-month period ending June 30, 2003. Overall, about 13,500 officers separated, including 7,900 resignations, 2,700 retirements, and 1,200 dismissals.
- Seventy-one percent of sheriffs' offices hired new officers during the 12-month period ending June 30, 2003. Overall, about 13,900 officers were hired, including 11,300 entry-level hires, and 2,200 lateral transfers/hires.
- During the 12-month period ending June 30, 2003, 31% of sheriffs' offices had full-time sworn personnel called up as full-time military reservists. Overall, about 2,800 officers were called up.

Operations

- A quarter of sheriffs' offices, including more than half of those serving 1 million or more residents, used foot patrol routinely. An estimated

- 10%, including nearly two-thirds of those serving 1 million or more residents, used bicycle patrol on a regular basis.
- In 2003, 94% of sheriffs' offices, employing 93% of all officers, participated in a 9-1-1 emergency system compared to 28% and 53% in 1987. In 2003, 71% of sheriffs' offices, employing 83% of all officers, had enhanced 9-1-1, compared to 8% and 23% in 1987.
- Thirty-six percent of sheriffs' offices had officers assigned full time to a special unit for drug enforcement, with about 4,000 officers assigned nationwide. Nearly half of sheriffs' offices had officers assigned to a multi-agency drug task force, with about 3,500 officers assigned full time nationwide.
- Ninety-eight percent of sheriffs' offices were responsible for serving civil process, 94% for providing court security, and 76% for operating a jail.
- Fifty-two percent of sheriffs' offices had drug asset forfeiture receipts during 2002, including more than 80% of those serving 500,000 or more residents. Nationwide, receipts totaled about $178 million, or $992 per officer.

Budget and Pay

- Sheriffs' offices had total operating budgets of $22.3 billion during fiscal 2003, 18% more than in 2000 after adjusting for inflation. Expenditures in 2003 averaged $124,400 per officer, and $82 per resident.
- In 2003 starting salaries for entry-level deputies ranged from an average of about $23,300 in the smallest jurisdictions to about $38,800 in the largest.

Source: http://www.ojp.usdoj.gov/bjs/pub/pdf/so03.pdf.

LIFE-CHANGING EXPERIENCE

At the tender age of sixteen years, Buford Pusser witnessed a life-altering experience that arguably led him to a life of crime fighting. For weeks, a few of Pusser's high school classmates had been harassing him to join them on an excursion to a notorious gambling den, located just inside Tennessee's southern border. Deep down inside, Pusser wanted to go, especially because his curiosity grew while listening to the tales of his classmates. Stories were often told about brawls, gambling, drinking, and easy women. He also knew that just a decade earlier, men from a nearby camp found excitement and, more often, trouble in the cheap joint less than twenty miles away. One evening, in December 1953, the curiosity was more than he could handle; the hunger for excitement and action had taken charge. Pusser, his best friend, and several classmates journeyed to the White Irish Club. As they approached the run-down structure, Buford suddenly felt "eerie" about the whole situation and knew he should not have gone. Although Pusser had no business visiting a bar at sixteen, he witnessed corruption first hand.

After making their way through several drunken patrons who cluttered the dance floor, Pusser and his friends found a vacant table in one corner of the establishment and tried to hide their innocence by trying to look like seasoned veterans of the joint. The environment was so loud that drunken shouts rose above the sad country music, and during brief lulls between record changes, the steady clatter of dice mingled with the tinkling of ice cubes. The boys bought several beers without once being questioned about their age. Buford felt nervous but he could not quite put his finger on why; he just felt something bad was going to happen that evening. Buford thought to himself, "What are we doing here?" While sipping their beers, loud shouts erupted near a back room, where a sailor wearing his neatly pressed uniform loudly accused a slender, red-faced man of cheating at dice. Pusser wondered what was going on. Suddenly, a short, stocky brunette lady, Louise Hathcock, drew a claw hammer from her apron and yelled, "What's going on here?" The employee stated that the sailor had accused him of cheating. Louise Hathcock yelled, "I'll teach this son-of-a-bitch a lesson he won't forget!" From behind, Louise struck the sailor in the head with a crunching blow. The sailor stumbled backward and then fell to the floor. Louise yelled at him to get up, but the sailor was bleeding profusely and struggled to his knees as he headed for the door. Louise continued her attack, repeatedly smashing his head while screaming profanity. (Louise Hathcock and her husband, Jack, had risen from the backwash of poverty to the top of the criminal ladder. They were considered the overlords of the "State Line Mob." Together they ran a restaurant and hotel, both of which were booming businesses. The couple would later divorce, and Jack was eventually killed by Louise's new lover, Carl Douglas "Towhead" White.) At first Buford and his friends were paralyzed with disbelief, and then Buford ordered his friends to get out of the club as quickly as possible. The boys worked their way out of the White Irish Club while glancing through the cluster of people to see the bleeding sailor lying in his own pool of blood. However, before they could get to the door, it opened and a deputy sheriff entered. At first it was a sign of relief, but as the sheriff entered the club, he took one last draw of his cigar, ground it with his shoe, and looked at the fallen sailor. His first and only question in his thorough investigation was, "What in the world happened here, Louise?" The smirk on the deputy's face was closely observed by Pusser. Louise declared, "The bastard just died of a heart attack," as the crowd erupted in laughter. The sheriff only commented that if she said so, then it must have been true. He then ordered a beer as he proceeded to call an ambulance. Buford and his friends quickly ran out the door, relieved to be out of such a hostile environment and into the cool and refreshing air. Pusser and his friends were still in disbelief and had repeatedly exclaimed that she had beaten the sailor to death with a claw hammer. The boys knew that the deputy and Louise were in "cahoots" and that the sheriff and his deputies were probably getting paid off by the Hathcock's establishment. Pusser felt disgusted, and in that moment he knew that nobody in the county was safe with those types of criminal incidents going on.

This had been Pusser's first encounter with the infamous "State Line Mob," which sources indicated was affiliated with a loosely organized network of local crime syndicates called the Dixie Mafia. The Dixie Mafia was a criminal organization that operated primarily in the southern part of the United States. It was particularly well known for committing violent acts such as rape, assault, and murder. It is believed that the organization is still operating today but on a much smaller and clandestine scale. It was known by the locals that the state line was an area where major league criminals hid out between jobs. Louise and her kin were often hospitable to these criminals. This encounter would not be the first with Louise Hathcock, and Pusser's strong sense of justice, which had been displayed from his childhood years, continued to grow.

EARLY YEARS

Helen Pusser gave birth to her third child on December 12, 1937. Buford Hayes Pusser was born in Finger, Tennessee, to Carl and Helen Pusser. Carl and Helen struggled to survive as Depression-era farmers while caring for their three children. In addition to his farm work, Carl Pusser worked part-time as a barber and later in the local sawmill.

As a boy Buford was strongly attached to his mother. His father, Carl, felt that he needed to outgrow the attachment if he were to ever get anywhere in life. Buford was also timid and would follow his mother around everywhere. Buford was so attached to his mother that she would often accidentally step on him while working around the house. This would upset her and she would often reprimand Buford for not playing outside with the other youngsters. Buford could not understand his mother's point of view about playing outside or her explanation for him going to school, for that matter. Helen would often explain to her son that education was important, but Buford begged his mother not to send him, "Please, Mommy, I don't want to go to school." His first few years of school were harsh; he had to repeat the first grade because he fell behind in his studies. As big as Buford was, he was also often picked on and ridiculed for being shy. Even at the age of eleven he avoided school functions so he would not have to ride the school bus for fear of being picked on or getting lost. By the time he was twelve he had his first job at the general store in Adamsville. Buford loved to work and had already proved himself to be a hard worker.

When work was slow, he enjoyed going to town with his mother, because his father was often working out of town. In one incident in the summer of 1951 on a Saturday afternoon, Buford and his mother decided to drive into town for a horse show that had been going on. Buford persuaded his mother to let him drive the old Hudson car that Carl had left behind because of the lack of gasoline money. As Buford approached the city limit, he was driving well over seventy miles per hour. His mother shouted for him to slow the car down and that he was going to kill them both. Buford slowed the vehicle down to about fifty miles per hour, but his mother continued to insist he was still driving way too fast. This was the first time Buford had demonstrated his love for speeding, and it was this type of recklessness that would ultimately lead to his fate.

TEENAGER IN ADAMSVILLE, TENNESSEE

In early 1952 the Pussers moved to Adamsville, Tennessee, when Buford was fourteen. Pusser maintained average grades in school and graduated from Adamsville Elementary School. Immediately after graduation Pusser went to work full-time at the general store. Buford enjoyed work so much that he often contemplated giving up school for work, which was bad to bring up around his mother because it would stir up the hornets' nest at home. Consequently, he entered high school that year and for the first time he found something he really enjoyed about school: athletics. Buford quickly got the attention of the coaches as he impressed them with his athletic ability. Buford was especially keen about football; he loved the camaraderie and the rough physical contact it offered. Pusser found a new way of life in sports, and he became an instant star. He would later discover basketball as well. Sports made the first two years of high school much more tolerable.

Early in his junior year, Buford was beginning to run into problems with his school work. Buford was failing two subjects, history and biology. So after a few weeks he decided to drop out of school to go work full-time at a pipeline in Wynnewood, Oklahoma. His mother was extremely disappointed, but she knew he was growing up and reluctantly gave him permission. Buford wrote his mother every day about his job and new friends, but especially about the Native Americans he had encountered. He seemed to be intrigued by the Creek Indians and took several snapshots with several Creek Indian youths. However, the venture to Oklahoma was short-lived, and Pusser returned to Adamsville High School within two months.

During this time Pusser's life grew increasingly dangerous and unwholesome, in part because of developments around the area. Phenix City, Alabama, a small town that adjoins Columbus and Fort Benning, Georgia, had long been a haven for the underworld. Phenix City had undergone a modest transformation throughout Buford's childhood. Officials in Phenix City made efforts to rid the town of bootleggers, prostitutes, and vice crime. Much of the vice activity and accompanying criminal element migrated northwest to McNairy County, Tennessee, and to McNairy's bordering county, Alcorn County (Corinth), Mississippi. These counties became hotbeds for bootlegging, prostitution, and gambling. Pusser saw life in his community at its most unsavory when he was sixteen, when he witnessed the life-altering experience that some argue ultimately led him into a life of law enforcement.

Buford struggled through the rest of eleventh grade, while he continued to work at the general store. By his senior year in high school he was much more focused on his studies, and despite missing his junior year of football he continued to excel. A number of college scouts came out to see him play. Buford received three scholarships in football, including a very tempting one from Florida State University, and four scholarships to play basketball. Buford, in the privacy of his room, would often admire the seven athletic scholarships he had received and dreamed of headlines about the fullback from Adamsville on sports pages. As many people know, headlines were in store for Buford, but not for sports.

A YOUNG MAN

Buford Pusser was now becoming a young man. In 1956 he graduated from high school and turned down the athletic scholarships in order to join the Marines that August. However, fortuitous circumstances led him to a medical discharge after only four months because of an asthma condition. Pusser returned to Adamsville, where his father Carl had become the police chief. His father swelled with pride when Buford spoke highly of his accomplishment of being chief. During this time, in November 1956, Buford was in a horrific car accident that nearly took his life. He injured his back to the point that the pain was sometimes more than he could bear. This was the first of several car accidents Buford was involved in throughout his lifetime.

In early 1957, while recovering from injuries he had received in the automobile accident, Buford decided to cross the Mississippi line to Corinth and went to the Plantation Club, which was owned by W. O. Hathcock, Louise Hathcock's brother-in-law. Before he arrived, Buford drove around town looking for someone to accompany him. Unfortunately, everyone else had something better to do that night. When he arrived at the Plantation Club, he witnessed a man and a woman in the front seat of a vehicle having sex; Buford was disgusted by the thought and wondered why they wouldn't go to the old hotel. As he walked into the club, a woman grabbed him and tried to pull him onto the dance floor; he refused and instead requested a table. Pusser had about seventy dollars on him that evening, and he wondered if he could double his money by gambling. He got up from his table and approached the gambling area where he decided to play dice. Early in the game he noticed that the dice had been changed by the handlers. Pusser immediately claimed that he was being cheated. Four good-sized men grabbed him and pulled him away from the table. They beat him repeatedly with their fists and when he was on the floor, they continued to kick him. When they were finished with him, they threw him out the back door and left him in the pouring rain. All Pusser could think about, in that very instant, was that these people were going to pay him back for every ounce of blood they spilled. He was beaten severely enough to require 192 stitches. Buford swore to get even.

Pusser came to the realization that he needed to leave his small town so that he could make some real money. He felt he needed to get away and move into a big city. Pusser moved to Chicago in August 1957 to take a job with the Union Bag Company. A year later, in 1958, Pusser began wrestling professionally to supplement his pay. Before one match, he ran squarely into a petite blonde lady, Pauline Mullins. Pauline Mullins was a twenty-four-year-old divorcee with two children, and he instantly fell in love with her and her children. Pusser and Pauline married on December 5, 1959. Less than a month after their marriage, the Pusser's newlywed period was rudely interrupted on January 4, 1960, when Pusser was arrested on a warrant from Corinth, Mississippi, and charged with the December 13, 1959, armed robbery and attempted murder of W. O. Hathcock. The arrest stemmed from the beating he had received at the Plantation Club years earlier. Hathcock alleged that Pusser had gone to the Plantation Club to get his money back and also to deliver some payback for the beating he had received. At the trial, Pusser claimed that he was in Illinois on the day of the assault. He was acquitted, in large measure because the jury placed little credence in the testimony of Pusser's accusers, who included Hathcock and some of Corinth's disreputable police officers. The armed robbery incident officially became Case Number 8954, and the intent to commit murder charge was tagged Case Number 8955. Pusser pleaded not guilty, and the judge allowed him to post bond. The courtroom where the trial took place was packed with people from all walks of life. Everyone listened intently as the trial progressed, and the tension could be felt across the room. Because of Pusser's witnesses and the evidence presented by his counsel, Buford was found not guilty of armed robbery and charges were later dropped on the intent to commit murder.

The happy days of making money and living a better life in Chicago were starting to look gloomy. During this time his job at Union Bag Company was beginning to irritate him, and his wrestling career was keeping him away from his family. The only thing that kept him truly happy that year was that Pauline had announced that he was going to be a father. Pusser's only natural child, Dwana Aitoya Pusser, was born during this stage of his life, on January 9, 1961. Pusser was a natural at being a father, but was still unhappy about being in Chicago. In 1962, he decided to relocate his family back to Tennessee. Pusser resumed his wrestling career in Tennessee but traveled mostly around the South. Most of his matches were in small west Tennessee towns, and he once won $50 at a county fair for wrestling a bear.

LAW ENFORCEMENT CAREER BEGINS

In 1962, Buford's father, Carl Pusser, retired as Adamsville police chief. Carl had a bad leg that had been bothering him for a while from an accident he was involved in. Carl had enough influence to get his twenty-four-year-old son appointed as his successor. Buford was voted in unanimously by the city council. Shortly thereafter, in September 1962, Buford decided to seek his first elected office with the constables. The constable position he was seeking was a part-time job that would not interfere with his current position as police chief. Buford beat the incumbent by more than 115 votes and was elected Third District constable. Pusser worked long hours patrolling the streets of Adamsville; there were some days when he would only get three hours of sleep in a twenty-four-hour period.

In November 1962, Pusser received a tip about an illegal whiskey operation in his district and immediately checked out the information. Buford went to the location alone and witnessed three men standing around a large homemade distillery along with sacks of sugar, hundreds of gallon jugs, stacks of hickory wood, and several fifty-gallon barrels. There was also a blackened steam boiler going full blast. This was Buford's first experience in dealing with moonshiners, and he knew he couldn't pull off the raid by himself. Pusser returned to his office and phoned two federal revenue agents. Two days later the agents arrived and went over detailed plans on how to go about the raid. Pusser and the agents completed the raid successfully, arresting three men and blowing up the boiler. Pusser, along with two federal agents, had just participated in the first of what would be many moonshine raids in Buford's county. Under normal circumstances, Pusser would have notified the McNairy County Sheriff James Dickey, but Pusser did not trust him. Pusser suspected Sheriff Dickey of being bought by the moonshiners and the "State Line Mob," and therefore Pusser did not notify him in advance of the raid. This was a public slap in Dickey's face that further exacerbated an already existing rivalry between the two. Dickey had done nothing to slow down the criminal activity in the area, and because he was still bitter about the incident with the Hathcocks, Buford was determined to get rid of the state line criminal element. He felt that the only way he could possibly accomplish this was to acquire the top law enforcement seat in the county, that of sheriff. Buford brought the notion to his father Carl who not only approved the idea but was also very excited. Carl knew Buford could easily beat Dickey in the next election, so Carl became his campaign manager. Carl, who was an old hand at politics, quickly persuaded the mayor to raise $500 for the campaign; however, Buford was beginning to feel apprehensive about the whole thing. It wasn't that he was afraid of the criminal element along the state line, but he was afraid that the citizens of the county would not vote for him. Either way, he felt that he had to at least try for the good citizens of McNairy County.

Pusser ran for sheriff of McNairy County in 1964 as a Republican. Pusser's pledge was his famous words, "If you elect me, I will clean up the corruption and violence that has made the state line notorious. I'll make McNairy County a decent place to live and raise a family." Buford campaigned day and night, determined to reach all 18,000-plus residents of McNairy County. He went to large and small towns, even those that were predominately Democratic. Most people remembered Pusser as the black bear wrestler. Because of this, they pledge to vote for him, but Buford would not take these pledges seriously. Pusser knew that talk was cheap and that only the polls could determine if his constituents were serious. Louise Hathcock had heard rumors of Pusser's likely victory and immediately sent word that she would pledge $600 for his campaign. All he had to do was pick it up at the hotel; however, Pusser would not have anything to do with her, especially not her money. The campaign went smoothly until right before the election. His rival, Sheriff Dickey was found dead two weeks before the August 1964 election, in an automobile accident. Speculation arose that criminals of the State Line Mob were afraid that Dickey's knowledge of their activities would be used against them, so they set up his death to make it look like an accident. The suspicions were never confirmed. The suspicious timing of Dickey's death cast a shadow over the election. In spite of his death, a large number of voters cast ballots for Dickey. However, when the votes were tallied, Pusser won by three hundred votes. Pusser, the youngest sheriff in Tennessee history, was sworn in on September 1, 1964, at the age of twenty-six. Carl Pusser served as his son's only deputy, tending the county jail.

Buford often got bruises, cuts, and small scrapes while doing his job, but at this point he had not experienced anything too serious. However, not long after becoming sheriff, Pusser suffered his first serious injury at the hands of a law breaker, being stabbed by a hitchhiker in November 1964. Pusser picked up the hitchhiker in his unmarked police unit. As the hitchhiker stepped into the vehicle, he quickly stabbed Buford twice in the chest. Pusser drove himself to the hospital and was kept for twenty-four hours for observation. Buford thought that this was a once-in-a-lifetime incident and was not too worried about it, but his wife Pauline did not have the same sentiments. She was scared for her husband's life. The assailant was never caught, and Buford theorized that the assailant was a wanted man and became frightened upon recognizing that Buford was a law enforcement officer. Less than two months later, Buford was called to a rural house fire. He quickly noticed a suspicious old Dodge vehicle with the back nearly touching the ground. He went over to ask the person what was in the trunk. The individual responded that there was only the usual stuff like a tire, jack, and some tools. As Buford stood in front of the vehicle to write down the license plate, the driver of the vehicle turned the ignition on and proceeded to drive the car forward, nearly running over Buford. Buford barely had enough time to jump on the trunk, spread eagle, trying to take the keys from the ignition. The driver stabbed Buford five times on his back, and the passenger hit him over the head with a sledge hammer. Pusser fell from the car and rolled onto the rough gravel. In the background someone could be heard asking why Pusser wasn't killed by such a vicious attack. Buford was rushed to McNairy County Memorial Hospital. The attackers' car was found not far away, and in it was thirty-one gallons of "white whiskey." The license plates of the vehicle were stolen, and the identities of the suspects were never known. Pusser recovered from his injuries at a remarkable speed and was back on the job two weeks later. Pusser's biggest part of the job was busting up and arresting moonshiners in McNairy County. He conducted forty-two raids during his first year in office. Even though Buford was keen on shutting down the moonshiner businesses, he exhibited compassion toward some of the bootleggers; he gave several of them Christmas away from jail if they promised to return and give him no trouble later on. He knew where they all lived and would arrest them later if they failed to return. His relationship with the local underworld, however, became increasingly combative. On several occasions he arrested Louise Hathcock. Hathcock repeatedly tried to give money to Pusser to leave her alone, starting with $500 monthly payments and later increasing the offer to $1000 per month, but Pusser would not cooperate. He insisted that she was not going to buy him, and the feud continued. Pusser's feuds were not only with the local underworld, but extended to other law enforcement agencies as well. In 1965, Pusser began receiving complaints about Tennessee state troopers who would force accident victims to use one wrecker service. According to the complaints, victims were forced to use Bob Hertz at Selmer to tow all wrecked vehicles, regardless of what the owners wanted. Pusser demanded that troopers stop the practice and use rotating wrecker services instead of giving all calls to one company. Buford wanted the wrecker companies to rotate on a weekly basis. Instead of rotating the wrecker services immediately, the troopers retaliated by setting up road blocks and arresting McNairy County citizens. During one court appearance Pusser and the trooper captain got into an argument, which led to Pusser's grabbing the captain by the collar and pushing him up against the wall. The two argued for a bit, and Buford then wasted no time leaving the facility. A week after the public feud between Pusser and the troopers, Pusser succeeded in having most of the troopers transferred to other parts of the state. As the end of Buford Pusser's two-year term neared, he announced his candidacy for reelection.

SECOND TERM

During his second term, Pauline could no longer support him. She was too fearful that he might get hurt or even killed. After all that she had already experienced with Buford, Pauline wanted Buford to settle down and live an ordinary life. She knew, however, that his mind was set and there was nothing she could do to change it. Buford had pledged that he was going to clean up the state line and believed that a man was no better than his word.

Buford won the sheriff's election by a three-to-one margin, against a Democrat who had already been sheriff once. The county's people had confidence in Buford Pusser, and he had started to put down some of the illegal activities. They knew that he would continue in his pursuits to put the hoodlums out of business or into an early grave.

The long-standing feud with Louise Hathcock continued in his second term as well, and on February 1, 1966, at approximately 10:15 A.M., it came to a head. Pusser and his deputies headed to the motel where they were about to serve two warrants against Mrs. Hathcock, one for theft and the other for possession of whiskey. Upon arriving at the motel, a wiry looking man and his wife stood outside the motel and told Buford and his deputies that they were the ones who called about the theft. The Illinois couple was checking out of Hathcock's hotel when she told the man to empty his wallet. The couple accused Hathcock of stealing $125 from them. Pusser told the man to sign the theft warrant, and he and his deputies then entered the hotel office. It was determined by Buford that Louise was drunk, and he speculated that she had not stopped drinking from the previous night. Louise denied the allegations and repeatedly called the couple "liars." While searching the Hathcock residence, Pusser found a half-case of Yellow Stone whiskey. Hathcock insisted that she had an explanation for that and asked Buford to talk to her in her private quarters. As the two entered Louise's room, she tried to shut the door, but several articles of clothing were caught between the lock and the catch. Slowly, she reached into her pocket and withdrew a .38 caliber pistol, while she held a mixed drink in her left hand. Mrs. Hathcock pulled the trigger twice; the second time was a misfire; he returned fire, shooting her once in the left shoulder and the second time striking her under the right arm. The second shot tore a hole in Louise's heart and lung, killing her. This was the first time but certainly not the last time Buford was forced to take a human life. Investigations proved that Buford Pusser was justified in his actions. The district attorney, however, still presented it to a grand jury, which wasted no time in announcing that the killing was justified and the case was immediately closed. Shortly after Hathcock's death, Carl Pusser received an anonymous phone call from a man who stated that the local underworld had placed a $10,000 bounty on Buford's head and that he was going to collect it. Carl responded in an angry voice, "Go ahead and collect it, you son of a bitch, if you think you're man enough," and then slammed down the receiver.

Pauline often received similar threats. She was told on several occasions that her children were going to have their heads cut off and thrown into the river to give it some color, and others said that Buford was going to die as Louise did, full of bullets. However, there was nothing the Pussers could do but wait until someone acted on the threats. It appears that someone may have acted on the threats on January 2, 1967. Pusser stopped a speeding car. As he approached the car, he was shot twice; the suspects sped away as he struggled to his car. Buford managed to drive himself to McNairy County Hospital. Two suspects were eventually questioned but were never charged, and the case was never solved. Law enforcement authorities focused on Carl Douglas "Towhead" White, a close friend of Louise Hathcock. White, a well-known criminal entrepreneur in northern Mississippi and western Tennessee, was imprisoned at Fort Leavenworth, Kansas, at the time Pusser was shot. White was never linked to the shooting but even Pusser believed he had something to do with it. Reliable reports indicated that White was plotting to get Buford because he had dared to meddle with his kingdom and his woman. The worst was yet to come for the Pussers.

AUGUST 12, 1967

The tragedy that made Pusser famous occurred around 5:00 A.M. on August 12, 1967. Pusser received a call that trouble was brewing on the Mississippi state line and he was needed to check it out. For reasons still unclear, Pauline went along for the ride. She sensed something different about this particular phone call, and she didn't want Buford to be alone. Little did she know what was waiting for them at the site. He drove out of Adamsville west on Highway 64 at about ninety miles per hour. He then drove off U.S. 64 onto Gilcreast-Stantonville Road, which stretched six miles onto U.S. 57. While driving to the troubled area, they talked about how excited they were about heading to Pauline's family reunion. Buford then turned off Gilcreast-Stantonville Road and onto U.S. 57. Buford then glanced at his automatic shotgun and instinctively felt the holstered .41 magnum pistol at his side. Pusser was so focused he did not hear a black car approaching behind him. Suddenly, while driving on Highway 57, they heard the roar of the black car's engine. Fire then belched out of a .30 caliber carbine, and a window in Pusser's car shattered. The shots missed him but the particles of glass entered his face. Unfortunately, the same shots managed to hit Pauline in the head. Pauline moaned and grabbed Buford by the arm as she slumped down the seat. Buford knew his only chance was to escape so he could find help for Pauline. He continued to drive two more miles down the road; thinking he had escaped the assailants, he stopped the car. Pusser gently placed his wife's head on his lap and became frightened and enraged when he saw the gaping hole in her head. Buford prayed aloud, "Oh, God, please don't let her die! Please, God, don't let her die!" (Morris 1971, 131). The shooter then returned, shooting Pauline again and shooting Buford in the face. This second time the car was sprayed by scores of bullets at point-blank range. Pusser was hit twice in the lower jaw by slugs. His entire chin dropped to his chest held only by a flap of skin. He fell to the floorboard as another bullet ripped through the metal door and shattered Pauline's skull. The ambushers sped away thinking that Pusser and Pauline were dead. Buford then gripped the steering wheel and pulled himself to the driver's seat. He looked at Pauline and knew immediately she was dead. For the first time in his life, Buford Pusser felt helpless. At that moment he pledged to Pauline that he would avenge her death and he told her he loved her.

He next drove himself to an abandoned grocery store on U.S. Highway 45. He tried repeatedly to lift the microphone, but it kept slipping because of all the blood. He finally managed to grab the microphone and pushed the transmitter, but his messages were incoherent. Buford wondered why he could not talk. When he looked at the mirror, it became clear. Buford's effort to call for help was hampered by the rural location, by the darkness, and by his inability to speak coherently because a 30-30 slug had blown off his chin. Carl was the only dispatcher who immediately recognized his voice. The only thing Carl could understand was "45"; he immediately thought of U.S. Highway 45 and the state line. Carl immediately sent for help on both the county and state police radios. The first officer on the scene quickly realized that Pauline was dead and that Pusser could not talk about the incident because he had been shot in the jaw, so the police on the scene made Buford as comfortable as possible. The Selmer police chief arrived shortly thereafter, followed by an army of police officers from the surrounding area. Several officers made comments about how it was pretty much over for Buford.

Carl assigned the preparation of breakfast for the inmates to a "trustee" and quickly phoned his wife. Helen was about to call Pauline to tell her the bad news, but remembered that she had already been upset about Buford's line of work. Helen decided that someone else could break the news. Helen had no idea Pauline was already dead. Carl was waiting at the hospital when Buford arrived; after seeing his son's disfigured face and blood, Carl cursed himself. He did not think his son would live. As the paramedics pulled Buford into the hospital, the manager of the local funeral parlor pulled up and asked Carl what he wanted him to do with the body. Carl asked, "What body?" Carl did not know Pauline was dead, and when he heard the news, it felt like a giant fist had just hit him. He saw Pauline's body and asked the funeral parlor manager to take her away. Most likely, Pauline Pusser was not a target, but was simply in the wrong place at the wrong time. Helen arrived shortly and asked how Buford was doing, Carl told her he did not know and that Pauline had been with him and now was dead. Helen had a chance to see Buford before they transferred him to another hospital. Pusser was transferred to Baptist Hospital in Memphis, where a team of specialists was waiting to work on him. Fearing that the criminals might strike again, he was guarded by Shelby County police officers.

A few hours after the ambush, rumors spread like wildfire across the county. Rumors circulated, such as that Buford had murdered his wife and covered it up by shooting himself. The rumors became worse in the local beer joints. However, after a thorough investigation by several law enforcement agencies, including the FBI, it was found that evidence proved beyond a reasonable doubt that Buford Pusser could not have engineered the crime. The investigators also concluded that the ambush was motivated by Pusser's campaign to clean up the illegal activities in the area. The officers then launched a full-scale search for the assassins, and even the governor of Mississippi ordered his state's highway patrol to aid in the investigation. The Tennessee governor, at the request of the district attorney, offered a $5,000 reward, and the owner of the local Walgreen's drug store headed a fund drive to raise an additional $2,500. The money still sits there today. Pauline was buried shortly thereafter, and it was reported that there were approximately three hundred people at the services. Contrary to popular belief Pusser did not attend the funeral; he was still at Baptist Memorial Hospital fighting for his own life. After eighteen days and several surgeries, Buford finally went home. He underwent sixteen operations on his face. Recovering from his physical wounds was only part of the battle. Pusser was emotionally frightened.

The sheriff was more than sure that Towhead White had masterminded the whole thing, even though he was not the one to pull the trigger. White was in prison at the time, but Buford speculated that he had issued a contract to kill him. Unfortunately, White was never charged. Pusser, however, did have other suspects that he was ready to hunt down even if it took him the rest of his life. He traced his first suspect, a man named Carmine Raymond Garliardi, to Boston, Massachusetts. Before Pusser could gather any evidence to arrest him, Garliardi was killed and his body was dumped in Boston harbor. Another suspect was Kirksey Nix, Jr., of Oklahoma. Nix was the head of the Dixie Mafia, a shadowy confederation of criminal organizations that had long dominated vice crime throughout the South, especially along the Mississippi Gulf Coast. At the time of the incident, Nix was also serving a life sentence for robbery and murder, but Pusser suspected Nix nonetheless.

Wanting to appear less conspicuous, Buford changed his style of dress. He began wearing tailored suits, colorful ties, and immaculate white shirts. He also traded cars so often the townspeople had a hard time keeping up with the model and color of his vehicle. He did this especially to keep the criminal element guessing. Pusser also vowed to carry a gun the rest of his life; he armed himself to meet any situation. Buford replaced the automatic 12-gauge shotgun with an AR-15, retired his old .41 caliber magnum, and holstered a new .357 magnum. Buford also became suspicious to the point of obsession, taking no chances and trusting no one outside his circle. He began to live daily in the shadow of darkness and often alternated between periods of depression and obsessive fear. For example, in one incident, while getting ready to have a few drinks with a newspaper reporter, Buford became suspicious of the bottle he was about to pour his drinks from. He asked the reporter if the bottle had been opened and examined the seal closely. He then sniffed the bottle several times and told the reporter that "you can't ever tell." This was only one of many things that he now did differently; his lifestyle would never be the same.

THIRD TERM

Pusser was reelected for a third term in 1968 by a two-to-one margin. Pusser's efforts to rid the area of many of the dives and gambling houses also gained ground. He managed to close down or burn down many of the illegal houses and activities in McNairy County. At one point, even White was beaten severely by Pusser and left in the swamp, but he did not die at Pusser's hands. White would be killed later on April 2, 1969, while trying to rob a hotel. The effort to silence Buford Pusser had backfired; he became more popular than ever, while many of his enemies died or were put out of business.

Several events made 1969 another notable year in Pusser's life; this time Pusser did not need a campaign speech. His actions spoke louder than words, especially in the fattened county treasury department. The new revenue had provided Pusser with a $10,000 salary, plus expenses, and a new vehicle. Buford slowly seemed to be getting back to his old self, until an incident occurred at a local apartment complex. In 1969, he received a call about a man being drunk out of his mind who was threatening to kill several people. Buford knew the perpetrator well; he was an ex-con who had already served time for killing several people, including his wife. As Buford arrived at the scene, he adjusted his weapon and knocked on the door of the apartment where the incident was taking place. A overly polite voice from inside the apartment told Buford to come in. When he opened the apartment door, bullets came flying through, one streaking across Buford's abdomen, a second by his head, a third chipping the handle of his holstered weapon, and two more slamming into the wall next to him. Pusser reacted quickly, drawing his weapon and firing. Luckily, Buford hit the shooter between the eyes, and the bullet tore through the back of his head. Buford Pusser had killed the second and last person in his lifetime. The case was turned over to the grand jury, and they concluded that Buford Pusser killed the man in self-defense.

Later that same year Pusser was in another life-threatening car accident. While driving at a speed of about one hundred miles per hour, he fell asleep at the wheel from a long thirty hours of work. The vehicle went off the shoulder of the road and the right fender struck an embankment. The car then shot in the air and flipped over as it crashed on its top. Buford was trapped in his vehicle. As he lay there almost bleeding to death, he heard a voice saying, "Not again!" The person at the scene had realized it was Sheriff Pusser and quickly left the scene to call for help. Buford then heard the sound of an ambulance approaching; the noise reminded him of that hot summer day in August. He was filled with emptiness, as when he immediately knew his wife was dead. Shortly thereafter, he heard noises around him: people talking, a wrecker unwinding cable wire, and metal being pulled apart as he felt the pressure lift off his body. He was put on a stretcher and into the ambulance. He felt the rear wheels of the ambulance spin before they caught traction, and the vehicle jumped onto the highway heading toward McNairy County Memorial Hospital.

Upon arrival at the hospital, the doctor immediately realized that he had lost a lot of blood and needed to be taken to the Baptist Hospital in Memphis. As they drove to Memphis, the doctor checked Pusser's pulse from time to time but said nothing. While Buford lay there in pain, he began to have many thoughts of his childhood, his daughter Dwana, Pauline, and even Louise Hathcock and the man he had recently killed in the apartment. He then pulled his thoughts together and suddenly heard strange hissing sounds coming from the engine. Then there was a loud piercing noise and a cloud of smoke coming from the front of the ambulance. The doctor asked the driver what was wrong. The ambulance was over-heating. The driver thought he needed to get back to the service station to get water quickly. As they arrived at the station an attendant quickly brought out a water hose. However, the attendant knew that putting water into the radiator was not going to work; it was too hot and the water pump had broken. The driver of the ambulance called the local funeral home so that they could send an ambulance. As Buford lay in the ambulance in pain, he wondered if it was really the end. At that moment he realized that life seemed to have been a stacked deck from the start. Then the second ambulance finally arrived; the doctor knew they had lost a lot of time and told the new driver to get them there fast. The driver sped off and seldom touched the brakes while weaving through traffic. Suddenly the ambulance stopped. The back door of the vehicle opened and Buford's dark brown eyes squinted against the unwanted daylight. The sounds of the city could be heard as Memphis was beginning to awake, but for Pusser, sleep waited somewhere beyond the antiseptic walls of the emergency room. Thoughts and visions once again entered and left his mind, and at last he slept. Pusser would live to see another day, but how many more days was the question. Buford was released from the hospital and returned to work. He went about his daily duties as usual, but he had no idea that his days were finally numbered.

DEATH

It had been obvious since childhood that Pusser had a history of driving fast, having had several accidents in his lifetime, but his notoriety and position as a law enforcement officer had gotten him out of several traffic tickets.

However, they would not save his life. On August 21, 1974, Buford was returning from a press conference in Memphis, Tennessee. On his way home he decided to stop by the McNairy County Fair and Livestock show. While at the fair and show he decided to have a few beers. He left the fair and livestock show and headed for home. It was approximately six miles on Highway 64, west of his home in Adamsville, while driving more than one hundred miles per hour, that Buford's Corvette left the highway and smashed into an embankment. On impact he was thrown from the vehicle and died at the scene. It was discovered that Pusser's blood alcohol content was .18, almost twice the legal limit. There were often rumors about his death that brought about unscrupulous conspiracy theories, at least one of which succeeded in conning the Pusser family out of a considerable amount of money.

MEDIA AND PUBLIC PERCEPTION

Buford's wife's murder made him one of the most famous law enforcement officers in the United States. One of the first persons to capitalize on the Pusser tragedy was Eddie Bond, an occasional country singer, disc jockey, and record company owner. Bond paid tribute to the legendary Sheriff Pusser with a song called "The Ballad of Buford Pusser," which Bond cowrote with Jim Climer in 1968. The record enjoyed enormous popularity in western Tennessee and northern Mississippi. Buford's father, Carl Pusser, sold copies of the record from the jail. Record sales were brisk. Pusser and Bond began to realize profits from their business venture. This brought them to become intimate friends. Buford even made Eddie Bond a deputy sheriff. "The Ballad of Buford Pusser" began opening big doors for the McNairy lawman. Also that year the Tennessee House of Representatives named Pusser an honorary sergeant-at-arms, and he was also named national police officer of the month by a New York detective magazine.

Buford's term was set to expire in 1970. He was barred by a county ordinance from seeking another term as sheriff, but he was elected Third District constable again. Pusser had also established a friendship with a fellow Tennessean and writer named W. R. Morris. Morris teamed with up with Eddie Bond in furthering the Pusser image and penned a 1971 biography about Pusser titled *The Twelfth of August: The Story of Buford Pusser*.

Another big opportunity for Pusser came when Mort Brisken, a Hollywood scriptwriter and television producer heard the Pusser song during a thirty-minute news special over the Columbia Broadcasting System's network. Brisken was much impressed with the song, so the writer-producer flew to Memphis, Tennessee, rented a car, and drove to Adamsville to talk to Buford Pusser. Shortly thereafter, Buford signed an agreement with Brisken giving him exclusive rights to produce a movie and television saga on his life. Brisken informed Buford that Bing Crosby Productions would film the motion picture and the American Broadcasting Company would film the television series. Brisken then collected all of Buford's scrapbooks and headed back to Hollywood. Part of the deal was also that Pusser would serve as a technical advisor for the movie. Three months later, Brisken mailed Buford a copy of the movie script. His first criticism of the movie was its script. Pusser complained that the violence was toned down too much and he felt that being sheriff of McNairy County was far from glamorous. However, he did not object to other inaccuracies, the most prominent of which wrongly portrayed Pusser wielding a huge stick to mete out street justice. McNairy County citizens were miffed that *Walking Tall* was filmed in their neighboring counties, and some officials disliked glorifying Pusser's violent behavior.

Shortly after the movie deal, while serving as constable, he encountered legal troubles of his own, again stemming from his propensity to violence. In 1972 Pusser was charged with assault with a deadly weapon for beating a man he claimed pointed a gun at him. The charges were later dismissed when the accuser mysteriously did not appear in court.

For some reason there was also a growing animosity toward Pusser from the citizens of McNairy County, which seemed to be getting stronger as time went by. He was defeated in his bid for sheriff in 1972. Pusser blamed his loss on the movie, *Walking Tall*, which to the surprise of the producer had flopped. McNairy County citizens laughed at Pusser because of the inaccuracies in the movie, especially the portrayal of Pusser carrying a huge stick, which became the movie's trademark. Pusser had never rammed his car into a saloon, and he never designated the courthouse bathroom as the local judge's chambers, as was depicted in the movie.

Stung by *Walking Tall*'s failure, Bing Crosby Productions redid the movie's promotional trailer, and the impact this time was tremendous. It surprised everyone; *Walking Tall* became one of the top box office draws of 1972 and 1973. *Variety* called it the year's best sleeper. *Photoplay* magazine named it the motion picture of the year. The movie starred Joe Don Baker in the role of Buford Pusser. Baker and Pusser became good friends, and Baker vowed to make the people of McNairy County sorry for rejecting Buford Pusser.

According to Pusser, *Walking Tall* was about 70 percent fiction, but by this time the public did not care. Pusser's character had become larger-than-life; he had become America's new hero. The movie contained graphic violence (for its time), which naturally the public enjoyed immensely. Pusser was portrayed as a bold, incorruptible one-man crime-fighting machine. He unhesitatingly used his huge stick to wallop the bad guys. Buford fought judicial ineptitude and corruption, and he did his best to make the sheriff's office representative of the population by hiring an African American deputy, which was another fiction captured on film.

Buford Pusser became one of the most sought-after public figures in the nation. CBS produced a documentary about Pusser. Governor Winfield Dunn declared October 21, 1973, Buford Pusser Day in Tennessee. Pusser began to receive money just for his appearances. In some instances he would receive $1,000 to $2,500 for personal appearances. Pusser also lived the high life, rubbing shoulders with the elite of Nashville's country music establishment. It was also rumored that Buford began a romantic relationship with Anne Galloway, a Miss Tennessee pageant winner. In his public appearances, Pusser would say that *Walking Tall* did not result in any increased public sympathy toward law enforcement. It merely reinforced existing beliefs about the proper role of law enforcement. In addition it was replete with violence—always a drawing card for American movie buffs.

However, as time went on, Pusser's fame began to experience a negative shift once more. His brashness and violent tendencies made him many enemies among some of Tennessee's most influential people. Some individuals began to question whether Pusser was the upstanding individual portrayed in *Walking Tall*. There was an incident where his stepdaughter bashed him in a newspaper. In an interview with an Ohio newspaper, Pusser's stepdaughter said Pusser was responsible for Pauline's death; it was thought that this accusation was made more out of bitterness than fact.

Another issue brought to the forefront was that it had been ironic that one of Pusser's claims to fame was his penchant for busting moonshiners because he was a drinker himself. He found even more time for bar hopping after the release of *Walking Tall*. Rumors began to surface, such as the time when in a local Moose Lodge a man accused Pusser of accepting money while he was sheriff so the man and his wife could sell illegal alcohol. An argument ensued, and Pusser beat the man so severely that the man literally defecated in his pants.

Pusser's friendships with some of the people who had made him famous soured as well. He had a falling out with Republican Party officials after backing Democrat Ray Blanton in the 1974 gubernatorial race. His friendship with the actor Joe Don Baker, who starred as Pusser in *Walking Tall*, went south as well. Pusser, a Republican, had serious political disagreements with Baker, a Democrat. Baker called Pusser a fascist pig who would do anything to support the existing political establishment. Pusser called Baker a "conceited bastard" and claimed that Baker owed his career to him.

Bing Crosby Productions wanted to film a sequel to *Walking Tall,* but after the clash between Baker and Pusser, negotiations with Baker proved fruitless. Pusser had done a screen test and was awarded the part of playing himself. Filming was scheduled to start on September 20, 1974, in Jackson, Tennessee. Obviously, Buford Pusser did not live to play himself in the movie, nor did he live to become commissioner of public safety, the promise made by Ray Blanton in exchange for his support in the governor's race.

Two more *Walking Tall* movies were made, but neither enjoyed the critical commercial success of the first movie. A CBS television movie was also made featuring Brian Dennehy as the legendary Buford Pusser. Dwana,

Pusser's daughter, maintains an Web site devoted to Buford Pusser, complete with saleable items that capitalize on Pusser's name. Pusser's former home has also become a museum.

During the life of Buford Pusser he received as much praise as he did criticism. Either way, he is a crime-fighting icon who will not soon be forgotten. His legacy will live on because his family lives on, and he has made his mark on the American criminal justice system.

TIMELINE

1937 Born in Finger, Tennessee.
1942 Buford's first day of school.
1948 Buford often avoids school bus rides, for fear of getting lost.
1950 Fist job at the general store in Adamsville.
1951 Demonstrates his desire for driving fast while attending a horse show.
1952 The Pusser family moves to Adamsville, Tennessee.
1953 First encounter with the infamous "State Line Mob" and police corruption.
1956 Buford graduates from high school with seven athletic scholarships and has his first encounter with death.
1957 Moves to Chicago to work for Union Bag Company, becomes a wrestler, and meets his future wife.
1959 Buford Pusser and Pauline Mullins get married, and Buford gets arrested for armed robbery and intent to commit murder.
1961 Buford's first and only natural child, Dwana Aitoya Pusser, is born.
1962 Returns to Tennessee from Chicago, becomes police chief of Adamsville, is elected as constable in the Third Civil District, and along with two federal agents conducts his first moonshine raid.
1964 Runs for McNair County Sheriff for the first time at age twenty-six.
1965 Feud with Tennessee State Troopers.
1966 Buford Pusser kills Louise Hathcock while serving a search warrant.
1967 Is shot twice and left for dead in a routine traffic stop. Pauline and Buford respond to trouble at the state line, but it is a set-up to kill both of them. Pauline dies at the scene.
1968 Is elected to a third term by a two-to-one margin. Eddie Bond and Jim Climer write "The Ballad of Buford Pusser."
1969 Kills the second person in his lifetime. Second car accident, ambulance overheats.
1970 Is barred from seeking reelection as sheriff, but as is reelected as Third District constable.
1971 W. R. Morris writes the biography of Buford Pusser, *The Twelfth of August: The Story of Buford Pusser*. Movie deal with Hollywood for *Walking Tall*.

1972 *Walking Tall* becomes one of the top box office draws of 1972 and 1973.
1974 Dies in a car accident coming home from McNairy County Fair and Livestock Show.
2004 Third *Walking Tall* movie is released starring Dwayne "The Rock" Johnson.

FURTHER READING

Grigg, William Norman. 2004. "One man against the mob: A legend in the mold of Davy Crockett, Sheriff Buford Pusser reclaimed Tennessee's McNairy County from the murderous 'State Line Mob.'" *The New American* magazine, Appleton, WI.

Jones, Mark. 2005. *Criminal Justice Pioneers in U.S. History.* New York, Pearson Education.

Kleinig, John. 1996. *The Ethics of Policing.* New York, Cambridge University Press.

Morris, W. R. 1971. *The Twelfth of August: The Story of Buford Pusser.* Nashville, TN: Aurora Publishing.

Morris, W. R. 1990. *The State Line Mob.* Nashville, TN: Rutledge Hill Press.

Courtesy of Photofest

Eddie Egan and Sonny Grosso

Ellen Leichtman

There is a point, of course, where a man must take the isolated peak and break with all his associates for clear principle; but until that time comes he must work, if he would be of use, with men as they are. As long as the good in them overbalances the evil, let him work with them for the best that can be obtained.

Theodore Roosevelt
Former Police Commissioner of New York City

Every cop understands that the nature of the job is to break the law in order to protect society and then to lie about it in order to maintain society's illusions...and also to accept the fact that if he's caught lying, he's going to get locked up, in order to maintain society's illusions.

David Milch
Producer of *NYPD Blue*, *Hill St. Blues*, and *Deadwood*

In the 1960s, drugs were fast becoming a major area of national concern. As a result, the interdiction of drugs was becoming a central focus within both the New York City Police Department and the Federal Bureau of Investigation (FBI). It was also the main concern of two New York City cops, detective first-grade Edward "Eddie" Egan and detective second-grade Salvatore "Sonny" Grosso, who were assigned to the New York City Police Department's Narcotics Bureau. Unknown to them, the case that was to make them famous was about to unfold. It was a Saturday night, and after being on duty for twenty-seven consecutive hours, Egan and Grosso decided to go to the Copacabana, a famous nightspot in Manhattan, to relax.

Drug Enforcement Administration (DEA) Fact Sheet: Heroin

Overview of Heroin

Heroin is an illegal, highly addictive drug. It is both the most abused and the most rapidly acting of the opiates. Heroin is processed from morphine, a naturally occurring substance extracted from the seed pod of certain varieties of poppy plants. It is typically sold as a white or brownish powder or as the black sticky substance known on the streets as "black tar heroin." Although purer heroin is becoming more common, most street heroin is "cut" with other drugs or with substances such as sugar, starch, powdered milk, or quinine. Street heroin can also be cut with strychnine, fentanyl, or other poisons. Because heroin abusers do not know the actual strength of the drug or its true contents, they are at risk of overdose or death. Heroin also poses special problems because of the transmission of HIV and other diseases that can occur from sharing needles or other injection equipment. First synthesized from morphine in 1874, heroin was not extensively used in medicine until the early 1900s. Commercial production of the new pain remedy was first started in 1898. It initially received widespread acceptance from the medical profession, and physicians remained unaware of its addiction potential for years. The first comprehensive control of heroin occurred with the Harrison Narcotic Act of 1914. Today, heroin is an illicit substance having no medical utility in the United States.

Heroin can be injected, smoked, or sniffed/snorted. Injection is the most efficient way to administer low-purity heroin. The availability of high-purity heroin, however, and the fear of infection by sharing needles has made snorting and smoking the drug more common. National Institute on Drug Abuse (NIDA) researchers have confirmed that all forms of heroin administration are addictive.

Street Names

Smack, thunder, hell dust, big H, nose drops.

Short-term Effects

Intravenous users typically experience the rush within 7 to 8 seconds after injection, whereas intramuscular injection produces a slower onset of this euphoric feeling, taking 5 to 8 minutes. When heroin is sniffed or smoked, the peak effects of the drug are usually felt within 10 to 15 minutes. In addition to the initial feeling of euphoria, the short-term effects of heroin include a warm flushing of the skin, dry mouth, and heavy extremities.

Long-term Effects

Chronic users may develop collapsed veins, infection of the heart lining and valves, abscesses, cellulites, and liver disease. Pulmonary complications, including various types of pneumonia, may result from the poor health condition of the abuser, as well as from heroin's depressing effects on respiration. In addition to the effects of the drug itself, street heroin may have additives that do not really dissolve and result in clogging the blood vessels that lead to the lungs, liver, kidneys, or brain. This can cause infection or even death of small patches of cells in vital organs.

One of the most significant effects of heroin use is addiction. With regular heroin use, tolerance to the drug develops. Once this happens, the abuser must use more heroin to achieve the same intensity or effect that they are seeking. As higher doses of the drug are used over time, physical dependence and addiction to the drug develop.

Withdrawal, which in regular abusers may occur as early as a few hours after the last administration, produces drug craving, restlessness, muscle and bone pain, insomnia, diarrhea and vomiting, cold flashes with goose bumps ("cold turkey"), kicking movements ("kicking the habit"), and other symptoms. Major withdrawal symptoms peak between 48 and 72 hours after the last dose and subside after about a week. Sudden withdrawal by heavily dependent

(continued)

> users who are in poor health is occasionally fatal, although heroin withdrawal is considered less dangerous than alcohol or barbiturate withdrawal.
>
> **Trafficking Trends**
>
> Four foreign source areas produce the heroin available in the United States: South America (Colombia), Mexico, Southeast Asia (principally Burma), and Southwest Asia (principally Afghanistan). However, South America and Mexico supply most of the illicit heroin marketed in the United States. South American heroin is a high-purity powder primarily distributed to metropolitan areas on the East Coast. Heroin powder may vary in color from white to dark brown because of impurities left from the manufacturing process or the presence of additives. Mexican heroin, known as "black tar," is primarily available in the western United States. The color and consistency of black tar heroin result from the crude processing methods used to illicitly manufacture heroin in Mexico. Black tar heroin may be sticky like roofing tar or hard like coal, and its color may vary from dark brown to black.
>
> Pure heroin is rarely sold on the street. A "bag" (slang for a small unit of heroin sold on the street) currently contains about 30 to 50 milligrams of powder, only a portion of which is heroin. The remainder could be sugar, starch, acetaminophen, procaine, benzocaine, or quinine, or any of numerous cutting agents for heroin. Traditionally, the purity of heroin in a bag ranged from 1 to 10 percent. More recently, heroin purity has ranged from about 10 to 70 percent. Black tar heroin is often sold in chunks weighing about an ounce. Its purity is generally less than South American heroin and it is most frequently smoked, or dissolved, diluted, and injected.
>
> **Arrests and Sentencing**
>
> Between October 1, 2004, and January 11, 2005, there were 391 federal offenders sentenced for heroin-related charges in U.S. courts. Approximately 97.4 percent of the cases involved trafficking. Between January 12, 2005, and September 30, 2005, there were 1,279 federal offenders sentenced for heroin-related charges in U.S. courts. Approximately 97.8 percent of the cases involved trafficking.
>
> Source: http://www.usdoj.gov/dea/concern/heroin.html.

The two men were both good-looking six footers, although that's where the physical likeness stopped. Egan was a thickset, florid, red-headed Irishman, while Grosso was a dark-haired, wiry, pale skinned Italian who worried. He was also a black-belt in karate.

Egan was dating the hat-check girl. The two men knew the headwaiter and were shown to a table way in the back, on one of the raised terraces.

They ordered drinks and were settling in when Grosso pointed out a crowded, noisy table below them. While the two detectives watched, they saw at least two drug pushers they knew. The "host" at the table was called Patsy. Egan and Grosso observed them for an hour and a half, until the floor show ended, at which time Patsy and the rest of his party got up and left. Egan and Grosso decided to follow him. That was the beginning of what was later dubbed The French Connection.

The 1961–1962 New York case was the largest drug bust in history up to that time, with 112 pounds of heroin, worth $32 million on the street, confiscated. Although many cops and federal agents worked on the case, Egan and Grosso were the names associated with it. The two men attained national prominence later, first from the 1969 best-seller *The French Connection* by Robin Moore and then from the 1971 five-time Academy Award winning movie of the same name directed by William Friedkin, starring Gene Hackman and Roy Scheider. Both Egan and Grosso played small parts in the movie, Egan as his own boss Walt Simonson and Grosso as Bill Klein, an FBI agent.

The movie became a pivotal point in both of their lives as it became an entry for both men into movies and television by giving them experience in many aspects of film making, especially as advisors and actors. It may also have been instrumental in splitting them up as partners because of jealousy in the upper ranks of the New York City Police Department. Egan later went to Hollywood, where he had a successful acting career for several decades. Grosso has gone on to become an influential producer in the firm Grosso-Jacobson Productions. Some of his best known productions are the movie *Trackdown: Finding the Goodbar Killer* with George Segal; *Out of the Darkness: Finding the Son of Sam* with Martin Sheen; the TV movie and series *Counterstrike* with Christopher Plummer; the TV movie and series *A Family for Joe* with Robert Mitchum; and the TV series *Cop Talk* for Tribune Entertainment, which Grosso hosted. Another major television production, which got critical reviews was *A Question of Honor*, based on Grosso and Rosenberg's book *Point Blank*. Among other accomplishments, Grosso was the technical advisor and acted in *The Godfather* and made such television shows such as *Top Cops*, *Truck 1*, and *The Big Easy*, and several other made-for-television movies, such as *All-American Girl: The Mary Kay Letourneau Story* and the adaptations of several books by Mary Higgins Clark, including *Moonlight Becomes You*, *Let Me Call You Sweetheart*, and *While My Pretty One Sleeps*.

Robin Moore's book went into great detail about the actual surveillance and detective work Egan, Grosso, and others put in from October 7, 1961, to February 24, 1962, and then described the aftermath of the case. It details the lengthy boredom and occasional excitement of police work and uses the actual names of the people involved. The movie, however, moved beyond the workings of the case. In *The Poughkeepsie Shuffle*, a BBC documentary on the making of the movie, which is included in the thirtieth anniversary DVD of the movie, director William Friedkin discusses why he took liberties with the actual events of the case. The movie needed more action than the book supplied, so he decided to include how Egan and Grosso (with their names changed to Doyle and Russo) normally worked "the street." He found the two "hilarious" with "an approach to law enforcement [he] felt had just the right touch for the time. It was like a game for them." In order to give the director, cast, and others a working understanding of what being a cop in New York was all about, Egan and Grosso took them on ride-alongs and sometimes raids. The two detectives let Friedkin and the actors go with them so that the movie would have the flavor of the street. According to Grosso, "Whatever we said, somebody would write it down, and then it would show up in the movie."[1] Thus a book about an actual police action was changed into a movie about the way Egan and Grosso worked. Many of the movie scenes that dealt with the street lives of James "Popeye" Doyle and Buddy "Cloudy" Russo came from the real-life experiences of Eddie "Popeye" Egan and Sonny "Cloudy" Grosso.

THE EARLY YEARS

Edward "Eddie" Egan was born on January 3, 1930, and grew up in the Queens neighborhoods of Woodside and Hollis where his main ambition was to be a major league baseball player. He was always independent and considered himself self-sufficient from the age of twelve, perhaps because he never knew his father and was not close with his firefighter stepfather. When his mother died, shortly before he graduated from parochial school, he moved in with his grandparents. There was a lot of friction in the house, however, possibly because of his temper, and at the age of seventeen he left high school to get away from his grandmother. He enlisted in the Marines for two years, where he became a drill instructor.[2]

After the Marines, Egan played service ball and was offered a small contract by the Washington Senators. He then was traded to the New York Yankees Class B Norfolk farm team, where he played center field. According to Egan, at that time the Yankees were looking for a replacement for Joe DiMaggio, who was getting on in years and he, Egan, was being considered, along with a shortstop from Oklahoma, Mickey Mantle. But while he was waiting and hoping to move from the Class-B to the Class-A team, he was recalled by the Marines. This was when Egan began to give up his dreams of playing professional ball. At the same time, the Marine doctors found that Egan had broken his arm during his enlistment period and were undecided about whether to deploy him. Instead they kept him on hold and told him to be ready to be called up again within three months.[3]

Egan had never considered being a cop, but during this period of uncertainty he took and passed the exam to become a member of the police force of the Port Authority of New York. The three months went by, but there was no further word from the Marines. This meant that Egan had to make a decision, whether to try out at the Yankees' Florida training camp or stay with the Port Authority. He decided to stay in New York, which proved fortuitous. A few months later the Yankees signed Mantle. Egan stayed with the Port Authority for four more years. The Marines never recalled him.[4]

By 1955, Egan was getting frustrated with the lack of available advancement at the Port Authority. He had joined when it was a new organization, which meant that senior officers were years away from retirement. After passing the sergeant's exam twice without advancing, Egan turned to the New York City police and took their entrance exam. He placed 361st of almost 60,000.[5]

Egan was very ambitious, a trait he said was evident from the day he entered the Police Academy. Moore records Egan's first day. He reported an hour early to the gym in Flushing Meadows Park, Queens, where he found and captured three girls hiding in the bushes. They turned out to be escaped prisoners with a total of thirteen felony charges against them. This impressed Police Commissioner Stephan P. Kennedy, who gave Egan the weekend off, both to acknowledge Egan's actions and to set an example for other recruits. From that time on, Egan tried to get every weekend off. His arrest record while he was a recruit was so high, ninety-eight arrests, that he was taken out of training early and assigned to a special unit of veteran detectives who covered Times Square. He was not promoted to detective, however. Subsequently, he was returned to the academy when he refused to become a "shoofly" (a cop who spies on other cops). Egan always believed that cops should not spy on other cops. After he graduated, he was sent to Harlem. Within the first two weeks he made thirty-seven arrests, including that of singer Billie Daniels, which led to Daniels's indictment and conviction in a shooting incident. In the summer of 1956, almost exactly a year after he joined the police, Egan received his gold shield.[6]

Egan's personal interest was to work in narcotics. As he related to Moore, his ambition was linked to a family incident that occurred while he was a beat cop in Harlem. One day his six-year-old niece came home from school a little late and found that her friends had already gone roller-skating without her. Wanting to join them and in a hurry, she asked her mother, who was sitting on the front stoop waiting for her, if it would be all right for her to go. Her mother said yes and told her she could go upstairs by herself and get her skates. They lived on the sixth floor of a walk-up, so the little girl charged up the six flights of stairs, entered the apartment, threw her book bag on the kitchen table, and ran into her bedroom. There she found "four dark, Spanish-looking men," one holding her piggy bank. Two of the men grabbed her, while a third got her skates and proceeded to beat her around the face and head with them. They then ran out with the piggy bank and left her bleeding and semiconscious on the floor. Her mother, wondering what was taking her daughter so long, came upstairs and found her. Nearly hysterical, she called her brother, Egan, who came rushing to Brooklyn. Enlisting the help of the local precinct, he tore through the neighborhood, rounding up anyone ever suspected of criminal or deviant behavior. He found the four within two hours. Thus, while Egan was always an ambitious man, this incident gave focus to his career. Egan worked in the Narcotics Bureau for three years before he was teamed up with Sonny Grosso.[7]

Salvatore "Sonny" Grosso was one of four children, the eldest and only son. He grew up in a warm, welcoming, ethnic Italian neighborhood in East Harlem, a place where everyone knew everyone else and everyone else's business. It was a safe place, where families were large and kids played on the street. His mother, whom he describes as gentle and hardworking, would go out for a quart of milk and not return for two hours because she would stop and talk with everyone on the route. Grosso's father, a truck driver, died young, at thirty-six, which thrust Sonny into the role of head of the household at the age of fourteen with his beautiful, devoted mother at thirty-three years of age trying to survive.[8]

The family then moved to the west side of Harlem, to an Irish neighborhood called "Vinegar Hill." Sonny found his place in the new community even though, as a dark Italian, he visibly stood out from his new neighbors. Robin Moore described Grosso as introverted, withdrawn, and stern, but added that that might be partly because he has a "sad, heavy-lidded Mediterranean face." Normally, according to Moore, Grosso wore his feelings on his face, except when he got angry. Then all expression left. In *Murder at the Harlem Mosque,* however, Grosso describes himself as having been an organizer of basketball, softball, and stickball teams. Grosso did not date much and did not have a serious relationship, unlike Egan, who rarely met a woman he didn't like.[9]

After high school, at the beginning of the Korean War, Grosso was drafted into the army. He served two years, working as a radio operator. He also boxed. In 1952, however, he injured his knee and was discharged. He then got a job with the post office and drove a mail truck for two years, mainly in the midtown section of Manhattan around Times Square. He was still the main support for his mother and three sisters.[10]

Then, in 1954, he took the Civil Service Police Academy exam and, like Egan, scored in the top three hundred of a pool of around fifty thousand. After the Police Academy, he was assigned, by chance, to his old neighborhood of East Harlem, the 25th Precinct. What he found was a vastly changed place. Instead of the close Italian neighborhood of his early years, he now found a vicious ghetto, ruled by a minority of people through force and intimidation. The major source of trouble was the sale and use of illegal drugs. Grosso was especially repulsed by the ravages of heroin and what it was doing to the Puerto Ricans and blacks who had moved in. Although he was originally from the neighborhood, his return as a cop was often greeted with derision and mistrust. However, it wasn't in Sonny's nature to respond in kind. Instead, as he told Robin Moore, he understood the situation as a response to the current plight of the city. While he believed that drugs were a major problem, he did not really comprehend the enormity of that problem. Then, after a short time in Harlem he saw how drugs destroyed lives. Joining the Narcotics Bureau, he centered his focus on drug pushers and dealers.[11]

Grosso rose from the uniformed division to first-grade detective in only three years. He received his promotion from second to first grade in late summer of 1963 based on his work in The French Connection. This was the fastest rise of any detective in the history of the NYPD.[12] When Grosso retired in 1976, after twenty years on the force, he held the record for the most arrests made during his career.[13]

THEIR WORKING RELATIONSHIP

Egan saw the world in opposites, black and white, right and wrong. By "right" he meant adhering to the morals and values of his lower-middle-class, conservative, Queens, Irish Catholic background, which were forged in the 1940s and 1950s. His sister, Maureen Massett, a Dominican nun, described him as a "passionately by-the-book moralist" and in many ways a "very old fashioned" man, "a product of his time." For example, she said, he believed that nuns should always wear habits and always would almost interrogate her if he caught her not wearing one. He believed he stood for what was right and because of that, he would always win. Even at the end of his life, when he was fighting incurable colon cancer, he believed he would beat it—all he needed was his sister's prayers. He believed that he had lived his life adhering to the correct morals and values and that, in the end, he would be taken care of.[14]

Those who knew Egan described him as someone who would do what he thought was right, regardless of what the law said. He was theatrical, bigger-than-life, stubborn, egocentric, moralistic, and headstrong. He would declaim in front of judges during testimony, argue with defense attorneys, and play to juries. He often testified that he witnessed drug deals going down, even though that meant he would have had to be able to see around or through buildings or extremely long distances in the dark. He loved to be on stage, whether that stage was a courtroom or a bar where he was arresting suspects.[15]

Egan saw himself as central to ridding the city of drugs. He knew that junkies were breaking the law and causing a drug epidemic throughout America's inner cities. On a larger scale, he believed that mankind was inherently "dirty" and that everyone was guilty of something. By this Egan meant that people were inherently weak, not that all people broke the law. It may have been this self-understanding of his own failings that led him to be able to spot shortcomings in others and be able to exploit them, and he was the best at that game.[16]

Egan wanted people to fear him. One way to do that was to make people think he was crazy. This is illustrated in the Santa Claus scene in *The French Connection,* especially when he interrogates a man about picking his feet in Poughkeepsie. This nonsense sentence was classic Egan and one he used often during interrogations. He also liked to antagonize people. As Grosso said, Egan always did things the hard way.[17]

Grosso always felt that Egan was a good partner, but he was also excessively egocentric. In an interview with the BBC, Grosso said: "Nobody would fool around with us, nobody would fool with Eddie. If Eddie said '"Hold it,' they held it. If he said, 'Put your hands on your head,' they'd do it. I don't know what would happen today, but in those days they had a lot of respect for us."[18] But when Roy Scheider, who played Russo in the movie, asked Grosso what it was like to work with Egan, Grosso replied: "If I don't like him, who will?" No one wanted to work with him. Scheider said that gave him an insight into how to handle the role of Russo (Grosso).[19]

Egan was not an easy person to like; even his few friends agreed. Egan worked best with a partner who would let him have his way and stand to the side. According to Grosso: "With Eddie it was all I, I, I, me, me, me. But I was a lot safer with Egan. We were. We felt a lot better about ourselves because of cops like Egan." Egan liked to be the center of attention. Grosso says that Egan also had a reputation of being insensitive to all people who broke the law. Quoting Sonny Grosso, "Eddie didn't just challenge minorities, he challenged everyone. He had to prove he was tougher and crazier than everybody else, to make people fear him."[20] Grosso usually made excuses for Egan's behavior, even to the point of trying to explain Egan's behavior when Grosso took him to Grosso's favorite New York restaurant, Rao's, an old landmark Italian restaurant in Grosso's old neighborhood. Egan will always be remembered for ruining the steak the restaurant prided itself on with mounds of ketchup, driving the chef nuts.[21]

Egan's nickname while he was a beat cop was "Bullets." He said he got it because as a beat cop he had been known to wear an extra cartridge belt.[22] However, according to Grosso, "Eddie was also good with his hands, and he was good with his mouth, and back then cops had to back up what they said. We had no radios, you were out there by yourself, and to be in control you had to assume that control. But with a gun Eddie couldn't hit that fucking car if we stood in front of it." The real story about the nickname came from the number of bullets he expended, because he used so many of them in target practice on the range. Again from Grosso, "The truth of the matter, and he wore it well, is that accuracy on the range was something he did not excel in."[23]

However, Egan's code name changed to Popeye when he joined the Narcotics Bureau because he was a womanizer. Egan liked to "popeye around," eyes bulging, looking at and chasing girls.[24] Possibly because of this trait,

Egan failed in relationships. Always the optimist in this department, however, he was engaged to a fourth woman at the time of his death in 1995.[25] Perhaps because of his unhappy childhood, he had problems with family and commitment issues. Instead, he found his home in the comfort of male institutions like the Marines, the Yankees, and finally the New York Police Department, which everyone agreed "was the one true love of his life."[26] In the end, however, it was not true to him.

Egan always believed he was destined to be a star and went about making that dream a reality. He sought the society of reporters, writers, and people from Hollywood who were interested in cops and in telling cops' stories. Grosso retells the story of how the book got to be written. In 1968, while he and Egan were on patrol, they were contacted by the Chief of Detectives' office to go to Toots Shor's restaurant and meet with author Robin Moore, who wanted to write a book about the case. Grosso's supervisors in the NYPD were worried about how Egan would present the case to Moore and cautioned Grosso to "make sure that hole-in-the-head doesn't say anything stupid to Moore that gets the department into trouble."[27] At the table, sitting with Moore, Grosso saw his two idols, John Wayne and Joe DiMaggio, with Toots Shor. While Grosso sat there in shock, Egan took over, telling everyone about his exploits, how many busts he and Grosso had made, and how the two of them led the Narcotics Bureau in arrests. Egan was already picturing a movie and was deciding who would play him. He decided on Paul Newman, with Ben Gazzara playing Grosso. Moore's book centers around Egan and Grosso with a large cast of characters.[28]

Egan also got director William Friedkin interested in the story and made sure he and anyone else involved in the production got firsthand experience in whatever they needed, included going on raids and, in the case of Hackman, actually arresting someone. Egan also pushed to have the movie made and then made sure Friedkin centered the movie around Detective Jimmy "Popeye" Doyle.[29]

The book and the movie made the two nationally known and kept them in the news. Their cases were given special attention, describing some of the "crazy gimmicks" they used to make arrests. Grosso relates one story where he and Egan had just apprehended someone for a half kilo of heroin. They brought him to the station, but before they could process him, a reporter was there asking Grosso how he felt when Egan lowered him into a sewer to get the key to the lockerbox. Grosso was taken aback, because this hadn't happened. But holding up his end of the partnership, he looked the reporter straight in the eye and answered, deadpan, "I don't know, let me think about that." When Grosso questioned Egan about that later, Egan replied that his made-up stories were really of no consequence. The only thing that was important was that the public knew that they were bringing in the bad guys and arresting the dope dealers. Then he told Grosso that the only thing to worry about was getting the job done. The stories were just a little icing on the cake, for the papers, so people coming to work in the morning could read about New York's finest.[30]

THE FRENCH CONNECTION

The French Connection, the book, so named because several of the major characters were Frenchmen who shipped heroin into the United States from Marseilles, became a best-selling police-procedural about the investigation. It was published in 1969. Egan and Grosso were broken up as a team in 1968, after working together for a decade. Egan was assigned to the 81st Precinct in the Bedford-Stuyvesant section of Brooklyn, and Grosso was sent to the 28th Precinct in Harlem.[31] Egan felt that one of the major reasons the two were reassigned was jealousy from the higher echelon in the police department over the book and the newspaper coverage. However, if he was correct in his reasoning, that jealousy only grew with the release of the movie in October 1971. The case, which already was a legend within the police department, now grew to national proportions.

The movie *The French Connection*, which garnered five Oscars, including best picture, best actor (Gene Hackman), and best director (William Friedkin), was based less on the procedure of the case worked by Egan and Grosso than their modus operandi on the street.

The second scene in the movie, which is supposed to take place in Brooklyn (the exteriors are Brooklyn), is based on the way the two partners would conduct a raid. In the movie, the two are staking out a bar. Based on an actual case, Popeye Doyle is wearing a Santa Claus suit, while Cloudy Russo is behind a pushcart. Popeye looks into to window of the bar at several black men, played by actual petty crooks, junkies, and others from the streets of Harlem. As Grosso said, "We rounded up a bunch of guys we knew, guys we had busted for using and selling and gave them a chance to be in a movie with us. And they loved it."[32]

The scene progressed the way Egan and Grosso worked. They would rush through the front door, in order to panic everyone into dumping whatever illegal substances they had or into trying to get away. Egan loved that type of action. He thrived on confrontation and confusion, as it gave him a way both to use his theatrical personality and to make people afraid of him. Grosso hated the confrontations and was uncomfortable with them, but played his role as the enforcer. "Eddie would be yelling, 'Get up against the wall! Get over here! Do this! Do that! Hey, what the fuck did I just say? You fuck, you want me to break that arm?'"[33] While Egan acted like a drill sergeant, Grosso was the straight man. "All right, you heard what he said, get over here." That was how they achieved their incredible numbers of narcotic arrests. They would arrest anyone in the bar who threw drugs on the floor.[34]

Egan and Grosso also had a substantial influence on the final characterizations of both Gene Hackman and Roy Scheider. As Grosso writes:

> We took them on our rounds with us, Friedkin too. We could never do all of that today. We taught them how to be cops, how to act like cops, and to some extent how to think like cops. Gene Hackman says that he was never quite so scared in his life as he was in some of those first days. I think he thought he might get killed out there. And I guess that was always a real possibility for us all. We taught him how to enter a place, how to frisk, and how to arrest. We took him to shooting galleries (where heroin deals are made and where the junkies could be found shooting up) and flophouses. Having those guys with us got to be so commonplace that when we'd enter the shooting galleries, the junkies would calmly turn around and ask if this was for real or if this was for the movies. The line between "real" and "reel" definitely got blurred.[35]

NEW YORK REFORM

The French Connection case took place at the beginning of the 1960s, a time of great unrest, when the police became "the pigs" to many middle-class urban students, who became involved in the civil rights movement and then the anti-Vietnam War movement. It was a time when a generation of college students experimented with drugs and their motto was Timothy Leary's catchy "Turn On, Tune In, Drop Out." It was a time when young people saw the hypocrisy of their elders, who spouted the morals and values of the 1950s but did not fulfill them. It was a time when people were beginning to see the world in shades of gray, rather than in black and white. Many grew up on television shows such as "Father Knows Best" and "Leave It To Beaver," which depicted American life as white, middle-class, Protestant, and suburban. Urban reality was quite different, with people from different ethnicites, races, and religions living in proximity, not together, but in a patchwork-quilt type[36] of urban pattern. The divorce rate was soaring, and women were entering the workforce in droves. The police themselves, like Egan and Grosso, came from these ethnic neighborhoods.

On May 21, 1970, Mayor John Lindsay, who was running for president, appointed Judge Whitman Knapp to head an independent, five-person panel to investigate corruption in the New York City Police Department. This was brought about as a response to a six-month investigation by *The New York Times*, spearheaded by information given to reporter David Burnham by Patrolman Frank Serpico and Sergeant David Durk, when these two New York City police officers uncovered corruption in the police department. The commission's panel consisted of five members, one of whom was New York Police Commissioner Howard Leary, who was often at loggerheads with the other members. Leary felt the police were under unfair attack and took umbrage at the charges, saying that most police officers were not corrupt and that he welcomed any and all investigations. However, he suddenly resigned his position effective October 1, 1970, not explaining why. His action took Lindsay by surprise, as he had not expected Leary to leave. Lindsay immediately looked for a successor and found Patrick V. Murphy, who was then the police commissioner of Detroit.[37]

Murphy, a major police reformer, took over the position of commissioner on October 1, 1970. Among his first projects to initiate in high-crime areas were to disband some special squads so that decision-making would shift to the local precincts; to encourage police to know the community in which they worked in order to cut down on violence against police, a strategy now called "community policing"; to increase the number of minority police officers; and to raise education standards so that the force would become college-educated. Under Murphy, police corruption was drastically cut, but tension between those on patrol and those in administration increased dramatically. Officers were so afraid of being charged with accepting bribes that they began to refuse even a free cup of coffee. As one officer said: "The men hate him, but right now a cop would lock up his partner—with all the pressure that's on him."[38]

This was during the time of the Knapp Commission, when Frank Serpico and Robert Leuci were working against the police, routing out police corruption. Serpico had always fought corruption in the police department. Leuci, however, had been a corrupt cop in the Special Investigations Unit (SIU) of the Narcotics Bureau, the same bureau out of which Egan and Grosso had worked, whom internal affairs and the federal government turned and used as a spy in the early 1970s to find other corrupt officers. Grosso had little fondness for those kinds of guys.

In the 1960s, the reputation of the police was in shambles. Grosso felt that books and movies like *Serpico* (book published and movie made in 1973) and *Prince of the City* (book published in 1978 and movie made in 1981) were a disservice to the profession. As far as Grosso is concerned, he had, and still has, no fondness for cops who turn on other cops. In his view, it is hard enough to be a cop when you are attacked on all sides by civilians who do not understand your job and now you are concerned about the cops you are working with. Even today, decades later, he feels offended. As a producer, he has made it his life's work to show the positive side of policing.[39] The movies *The French Connection* (1971) and *Dirty Harry* (1971), both of which were released within two and a half months of each other, depicted officers fighting for what they believed was right, even if the law got in the way.

AFTER *THE FRENCH CONNECTION*

Four weeks after the movie *The French Connection* was released on October 9, 1971, Egan filed for early retirement. He was later quoted in *The*

New York Times[40] as saying, "I knew as soon as the film came out that I better get out of this job because there would be this guy sitting up there at headquarters reading his rule book and this guy would say, 'Either the job is done this way or we go by the book. It can't be both. We'll have to rewrite the book or get rid of that guy.'" Of the character based on him, Popeye Doyle, he said, "A cop has to be the way he [Doyle] was depicted on the screen or we'd better go hide in the woods." And about all the paperwork required by regulations, "I don't do it. Popeye Doyle throws the book away and he fights crime." As the article pointed out, Egan did fail to distinguish a difference between himself and the movie character. He had been with the force a little over fifteen years; it was a little over a year to the day that Patrick Murphy had taken over as commissioner.

Unfortunately, a major problem for Egan was that the film was released at a time when New York City was under a well-known reformer, Commissioner Murphy. It was no longer business as usual. There was no place in his police department for abusive or corrupt officers. In the police subculture, from which both Egan and Grosso came, officers believed that a cop put his life (most often it was a "he") on the line every day, did his job, and was not questioned about how it was done. It was a subculture that espoused a closed social society, where no one but a cop understood the life (both Grosso's and Egan's lives were totally wrapped up in the police department): total loyalty to other cops; cynicism of all "civilians" (Egan believed everyone was "dirty"); the right to arrest or punish anyone not respectful of police authority (a major factor in the 1960s was clashes of police with college students); the use of force for anyone deemed "deserving of it" (Egan's and Grosso's raids on bars); and the right to "hot pursuit" to apprehend criminals trying to escape arrest.[41] Police reform questioned these values with its goals of objectivity, following the law at all cost (even when the law itself is biased); justice for all groups (even when justice for one group counters justice for another); fairness (this can be interpreted as everyone getting equal treatment for the same action, without taking into account circumstances); accountability (everything is aboveboard and transparent; no organization works this way); and truth (there are often several ways to interpret events). These two models were constantly in conflict, but the point for us, Grosso says, is that those criminals out there had to be contained or nobody's safe.[42]

Three days later, on November 17, 1971, *The New York Times* reported that, according to Robert Daley, the deputy commissioner for public affairs, Egan had been charged with failing to return to the property clerk's office evidence used in a trial, something all cops did until their trials were over, and with failing to show up in court when scheduled to appear. After this announcement, the Police Department issued a brief statement that Egan had been brought up on three separate sets of charges and that he had already come to trial on the first set of charges the previous Friday, November 12.

It went on to say that the second set of charges was set for trial that Friday, November 19, and noted that the case against Egan had to be completed before December 2, 1971, because he had applied for early retirement.[43] Two days later *The New York Times* reported that Egan had been reduced in rank to patrolman. Instead of December 3 being Egan's first day of retirement, he went to his station house of record, the 23rd Precinct on East 104th Street in Harlem, turned in his shield and weapons, and quit the job he loved. He had been dismissed from the force, with no pension rights, twelve hours before he was to take retirement.[44]

Egan did not deny the charges. Instead, he stated that the punishment they were giving him was excessive for what he did (and all cops did it), and anyway, those weren't the real reasons for his dismissal. He showed that he had exactly $89.71 cents in savings, which was all he had in the world except for a 1964 car and an eviction notice for not paying the rent on his Queens apartment. His argument against the charges was that he had broken the rules because he was out making arrests rather than filling up his time doing paper work. Egan said, "I don't do it. Popeye Doyle throws the book away and he fights crime," addressing himself as the movie character.[45] As far as Egan was concerned, high police officials were also mixing him up with a film character. Egan knew he was the prototype for Doyle, and sometimes the two got fused in his mind, but in this instance involving alleged misconduct, he was clear about the separation.

On March 1 *The New York Times* reported that Egan, for whom the New York Police Department was home, went to the state Supreme Court to counter the charges filed against him. His lawyer, Frank L. Miller, said that Egan had been the focus of a smear and harassment campaign and that his dismissal came at this time because he was the real protagonist of the movie, which depicted a "tough" cop, an image the department was trying to negate. Miller said that the department wanted the image of the New York cop to be one of compliance with civil rights, of one who did not resort to force.[46] The judge ordered Commissioner Murphy and other high police officials to show cause the following Monday why Egan's dismissal shouldn't be revoked.

On April 5, 1972, Justice George Starke quashed the dismissal. The ruling entitled Egan to an annual pension of $7,000 starting in 1976, which would be twenty years after he joined the force. It also entitled him to get his .38 caliber service revolver back. The judge noted that Egan's prior superior officers, and other detectives, all testified to both his efficiency as an officer, as well as to his integrity. Egan, in Hollywood when he heard the result, said he was "very tickled—now I'll get my gun back and I'll feel much more comfortable." His friends in the department agreed that the police action against Egan was taken because the "film had highlighted his informal mode of operations."[47]

Then, eight months later, on December 15, 1972, the front page of *The New York Times* read "$10-Million Heroin Stolen From a Police Office

Vault." Commissioner Murphy announced that fifty-seven pounds of heroin, originally seized in the 1962 French Connection case, had been stolen from the property clerk's office and that a white powder had been substituted. The following day, the headline read: "Police Say That They Lost 24 More Pounds of Heroin." That meant that eighty-one of the original ninety-seven pounds were missing. Egan, who was still in Hollywood where he was working as a technical advisor/story consultant on *The French Connection II*,[48] held an improvised news conference where he said that he attributed the loss to "slipshod" police practices. He said he had never seen any of the heroin after it had been seized in the Bronx and used at trial. When asked about the additional twenty-four pounds that had just been found missing, he said he didn't know anything about that either.[49] According to Grosso, 260 pounds of heroin and 137 pounds of cocaine were also discovered missing and had been replaced with a mixture of flour and cornstarch. The Property Clerk's office was in total disarray, which only exacerbated the problem of locating the missing heroin.[50]

Robin Moore then published an article in *Show* magazine that added additional fuel to the fire. Grosso remembers that late in 1967, during the writing of the book *The French Connection*, Moore had invited Egan and Grosso to his home in Jamaica where they were writing the book *The French Connection* when this explosive story broke.

Another detective named Joe Nunziata had his signature forged in several places on the Property Clerk's sign-out sheet for the heroin, but he was cleared of the charges of stealing the narcotics. However, he was then questioned by federal authorities for taking a $4,000 bribe from a federal agent pretending to be a narcotics dealer, a man named Dandolo. It had been the plan that Dandolo would get arrested by a street cop, so that he could attempt to bribe his way through the court system. Instead he was arrested by Detective Nunziata who thought Dandolo was a wealthy narcotics dealer. Dandolo decided Nunziata was corrupt and set out to prove it. He told Nunziata he needed his passport back, which Nunziata had confiscated, and offered the detective $4,000. After talking back and forth, Nunziata took the money, which he later said was to make a bribery charge against Dandolo. Later that night both he and his partner were arrested and brought to the U.S. Attorney's office in lower Manhattan.[51]

After hours of interrogation, Nunziata was given one last chance to persuade authorities of his innocence. He had to pass a test. One of Nunziata's old cases, one he had worked on with Grosso, would be pulled. Nunziata would call Grosso and tell him that he (Nunziata) had a problem and that everyone was in trouble. If Sonny were an honest cop, according to the federal agents, he would ask what was wrong. However, if Grosso were to say that he, Egan, and Nunziata had to meet, that would prove Grosso was dirty and they would get him. Nunziata refused. According to Grosso, Nunziata told them, "Grosso and Egan never did anything dishonest."[51]

Nunziata was found dead, on March 27, 1972, sitting in the passenger seat of his squad car, shot through the heart. His friends said he was too vain to shoot himself in the face, but there were some details that did not add up. Nunziata was left-handed. The shot entered at a steep downward angle. It is very hard, if not impossible, for a left-handed person to shoot himself in the heart that way. His death was ruled a suicide.[52]

Grosso's book, *Point Blank*, coauthored with Philip Rosenberg, tells the story of Joe Nunziata, under the pseudonym Joe Longo. The narrative takes place during the Knapp Commission. According to Grosso, the Knapp Commission investigation did almost nothing except try to make police corruption highly visible and antagonize the public.[53]

Some of the names in the book have been changed for what the publishers said were "obvious reasons." The character "Gil Lacey" is the pseudonym for Robert Leuci, the corrupt cop who was turned by federal agents into an informer and who decided to wear a wire to help uncover corruption. Grosso says that it's difficult to know where an individual will draw the line between what he/she considers permissible and what is not. However, entrapment was something else. "Lacey's" normal mode of behavior was to approach his fellow cops with illegal schemes to see if they would bite. If they didn't, he would come back to them again and again. The rumor was that "Lacey" was part of the scheme to trap "Longo," and no one ever forgave him for that.[54] Both this book and *Prince of the City*, which tells Robert Leuci's side of the story, were published in 1978.

Grosso also expounds on his view of Internal Affairs (IA):

> It's a sad fact that Internal Affairs scares the average cop shitless. And with good reason. In the New York City Police Department, the federal government, and the police departments of other major cities in the United States, the Internal Affairs Division, or whatever its local variants may be called, is a set-apart force of investigators whose secret police-like powers far exceed the power of any other branch of our criminal justice system. They can bring a cop up on departmental charges, get him dismissed from the Force and stripped of his pension for all sorts of things that may not stand up in a court of law. In effect, they have the power to take away a man's job and his life savings without having to prove in a court of law that he did anything wrong, as they would with any other citizen.[55]

What Grosso's book, and work in general, illustrate is the humanity of the cop against the self-serving interests and political manifestations of the police administration. However, in the late 1960s to early 1970s it was a time for reform introspection and academic interest in police corruption and abuse of power. As Grosso puts it:

> In the spring and summer of 1972, police corruption was a headline issue, and the so-called anticorruption agencies were being hailed as the saviors of New

York. This story would tear that myth apart. Because it showed how a good man could be callously destroyed. Because it showed the amoral viciousness of his persecutors. Because it showed that the men who were supposedly cleaning up law enforcement were sometimes more lawless than the cops they were trying to put behind bars. Maybe it has to be that way, but that doesn't make it right.[56]

Grosso's first book, *The Murder at the Harlem Mosque*, also follows the path of decent cops vs. politicized administrators. It details this through one of his cases, the murder of patrolman Phil Cardillo in a Harlem mosque. Grosso was getting burnt out in the job, while seeing wider horizons, as he was now also consulting on several movies shooting in New York.[57]

Grosso was assigned to the Major Case Squad in the 28th Precinct. It was the early 1970s, and he was investigating the ambushes and shooting deaths of several police officers in the city. Some of these officers had been killed by bogus 10–13 calls ("cop in trouble"). The detective was wary, because he was staking out an important member of the Black Liberation Army (BLA), who was known to have been involved in the death of at least three officers.

The Murder at the Harlem Mosque details what happened when the police of the 28th Precinct responded to a 10–13 call at the Black Muslim Mosque, officially Muhammad Temple No. 7. It was a bogus call that turned into a near-riot, as officers entered the mosque with guns and were met with a wall of Black Muslims who would not let them pass. The mosque, located in a very populated area of Harlem, drew many people; then the sound of gunshots erupted. The two cops who had initially entered the mosque looking for an officer in trouble, responding to the call that had come over the police department radio, were beaten; one officer, Patrolman Phil Cardillo, was shot. He died six days later in the hospital. Meanwhile bedlam broke out outside, with cars overturned and set on fire and bottles and other implements thrown from the tops of buildings.

The incident was followed by an investigation, headed by Grosso, that was stymied at every turn. The book shows, though maybe not intentionally, how people have different values, and thus different reactions to the same situation. In a sense, Grosso acted more as a reformer, as he sought to find the truth about the murder, while Commissioner Murphy and the other upper-echelon of the NYPD were more concerned with the politics of the situation, to keep the city from exploding racially. His solution was to try and cover up the killing. Grosso quotes from *Report to the Commissioner*, "Cops get killed all the time. The killing of a cop can be handled."[58] Murphy has described this incident as "a low point" in his administration.[59] This incident was instrumental in solidifying how cops felt about the NYPD administration. They felt personally affronted that neither the police commissioner nor the mayor came to the funeral.[60]

Murphy has said that the reason he could not stand up for the police department was because a detailed agreement had been signed ten years earlier between Muslim ministers and the police commanders who had mosques in their precincts. The agreement stipulated that mosques were to be given special status as "sensitive locations" and that police officers would not rush into any mosque with guns. Because officers had done exactly that (with no knowledge of the agreement), he, Murphy, was put in a very uncomfortable position in his talks with the head of Mohammed Temple No. Seven, minister Louis Farrakhan, whom Murphy described as "anything but a rabble-rouser."[61] History has proven Farrakhan to be just that. Murphy explained that he could not in good conscience uphold the actions of the original officers, Phil Cardillo and Vito Navarra, and Victor Padilla and his partner Ivan Negron, because their actions had violated the standing order of which they had never heard. He then went on to explain that this was the result of poor police administration and that had the department been better managed and the officers reminded of the special circumstances of all black mosques, the incident would not have occurred. Grosso said: "What a crock of shit."[62]

Grosso had a different understanding of what had happened. The chief of detectives, Al Seedman, resigned over the incident, saying that what they had learned from their investigations of the shootings of four cops, the BLA was trying to enrage cops so that they would attack blacks and riots would break out between blacks and the police. This came very close to happening. Some observers said that the Black Muslims were law-abiding, but that was not the issue, as Grosso saw it. Rather it was whether the BLA was infiltrating the Black Muslims. He was convinced the 10–13 was initiated by the BLA. And he was equally convinced that the administrative officers, from Murphy down, did not trust their officers, nor did they believe that beat cops and detectives could understand complex situation as well as they, the administrators, did. For Grosso, the only way to survive in Harlem was to show no fear, and unfortunately, that was often construed by administrators as having no understanding. A cop's courage was mistaken for stupidity and bigotry.[63]

In April 1973, Grosso was put in charge of the Cardillo murder investigation,[64] He was also contacted by Abby Mann, the producer of *Kojak*, who wanted him to work on the series, which was to be filmed in Hollywood, as a technical consultant. Near the end of May, Grosso got more pressure from Hollywood, when Phil D'Antoni, the producer of *The French Connection* called and told Grosso he had to decide now what he wanted to do. Grosso had twenty years on the job, his legs were killing him, and the police surgeon was very concerned about his knee, which he had originally injured while in the Army. He then reinjured it during his first contact with the BLA. That occurred when Grosso chased the leader of the BLA, Twymon Myers, into an abandoned building on 113th Street in Harlem. Myers ran up the building's squared staircase, whose design created a shaft down to the basement. Grosso followed, tackling him on the fifth floor. The two men fought on the banister, which caused it to break. However, when it broke, the banister fell in toward the shaft and became entangled with the banister on the lower floor. This was lucky because the broken banister covered the shaft so that the two men only fell one story, to the fourth floor. However, Myers fell on top of Grosso, breaking Grosso's leg. When the other detectives heard what had happened they said, "God must have been on your side," to which Grosso replied "It must have been only a disciple, because if it had been God, he would have let me land on Myers." Now, two years later, Grosso was in rehabilitation therapy for part of every day. He decided it was time to retire.[65]

From New York, Grosso went to Studio City, California, where *Kojak* was filmed at Universal Studios. Jurgensen took over the lead in the investigation, but maintained his ties with Grosso, who came to New York often on business. The Cardillo investigation went on for three more years and ended with a hung jury first and then a dismissal. Grosso is still angry about it: "What a bullshit farce."[66]

Egan and Grosso went on to have careers in film and television (see Filmographies below). In the early 1990s, Egan was diagnosed with colon cancer. He always believed, up to the very end, that he would beat it. As his sister put it, he always had his own way and could not fathom why he wouldn't this time. He was sixty-five years old and living in Fort Lauderdale, Florida, where he had been since 1988.[67]

Grosso went on to found Grosso-Jacobson Productions with Larry Jacobson. They are still in business making television shows, made-for-television movies, mini-series, and films. Grosso's focus is on bettering the image of the police. Grosso-Jacobson Productions films mostly in Canada.

FILMOGRAPHY FOR EDDIE EGAN[68]

Actor:		
	1.	*True Blue* (1989) (TV) Detective
	2.	*Cold Steel* (1987) Lt. Hill
	3.	"Houston Knights" (1 episode, 1987)
		Mirrors (pilot) (1987) TV Episode
	4.	*Houston Knights* (1987) (TV)
	5.	*Out of the Darkness* (1985) (TV) Tom Duncan
	6.	*Mike Hammer* (1984) TV Series
		Hennessey (unknown episodes, 1984–1985)
		aka Mickey Spillane's Mike Hammer (USA: complete title)
		aka The New Mike Hammer (USA: new title)

(Continued)

7. *Murder Me, Murder You* (1983) (TV)   Hennessey
   aka Mickey Spillane's Mike Hammer: Murder Me, Murder You
8. "T. J. Hooker"   Max Silver (1 episode, 1983)
   "Requiem for a Cop" (1983) TV Episode   Max Silver
9. *Crazy Times* (1981) (TV)   Bartender
10. *Eischied*   Chief Inspector Ed Parks (9 episodes, 1979–1980)
    aka *Chief of Detectives* (UK)
    "Buddy System" (1980) TV Episode   Chief Inspector Ed Parks
    "Powder Burn" (1980) TV Episode   Chief Inspector Ed Parks
    "Fire for Hire" (1979) TV Episode   Chief Inspector Ed Parks
    "The Dancer" (1979) TV Episode   Chief Inspector Ed Parks
    "The Accused" (1979) TV Episode   Chief Inspector Ed Parks
    (4 more)
11. *Police Story: Confessions of a Lady Cop* (1980) (TV)
    Captain Harrison
    aka *The Other Side of Fear*
12. *To Kill a Cop* (1978) (TV) (uncredited)   Chief Ed Palmer
13. *Police Woman*   Brock (3 episodes, 1975–1977)
    Ambition (1977) TV Episode   Captain
    The Hit (1975) TV Episode   Jack Ballard
    The Bloody Nose (1975) TV Episode   Brock
14. *Police Story*   Captain Mead (6 episodes, 1975–1977)
    "Stigma" (1977) TV Episode
    "Nightmare on a Sunday Morning" (1977) TV
       Episode   Lieutenant   Holtzman
    "Trial Board" (1977) TV Episode   Captain Mead
    "Oxford Gray" (1976) TV Episode   Sean McLiam
    "Payment Deferred" (1976) TV Episode   Sergeant Harry
       Volmer
    (1 more)
15. "Baretta"   Thompson (1 episode, 1977)
    "Don't Kill the Sparrow" (1977) TV Episode   Thompson
16. *Joe Forrester* (1975) TV Series   Sgt. Bernie Vincent (unknown
       episodes, 1975–1976)
17. *Cop on the Beat* (1975) (TV)   Sgt. Malone
    aka The Return of Joe Forrester
18. *Badge 373* (1973)   Lt. Scanlon
19. "McCloud"   Al Barber (1 episode, 1973)
    "Showdown at the End of the World" (1973) TV Episode
       Al Barber
20. Night of Terror (1972) (TV)   Lt. Costin

	21. "Mannix" Lt. Paul Haber (1 episode, 1972)
	"The Open Web" (1972) TV Episode Lt. Paul Haber
	22. *Prime Cut* (1972) Jake
	23. *The French Connection* (1971) Walt Simonson
Miscellaneous Crew:	
	1. *Popeye Doyle* (1986) (TV) (technical advisor)
	2. *The French Connection* (1971) (technical consultant)
Writer:	
	1. *Badge 373* (1973) (inspiration)
Thanks:	
	1. *Making the Connection: Untold Stories of "The French Connection"* (2001) (TV) (dedicatee)
	aka "The French Connection 30th Anniversary Special" (USA)
Self:	
	1. "V.I.P.-Schaukel" Himself (1 episode, 1975)
	Episode #5.2 (1975) TV Episode Himself
	2. "The Tonight Show Starring Johnny Carson" Himself (1 episode, 1972)
	aka The Best of Carson (USA: rerun title)
	Episode dated 30 August 1972 (1972) TV Episode Himself
Archive Footage:	
	1. *Making the Connection: Untold Stories of "The French Connection"* (2001) (TV)
	Himself Retired NYPD Detective

FILMOGRAPHY FOR SONNY GROSSO[69]

Producer:	
	1. *Kings of South Beach* (2007) (TV) (executive producer)
	2. *N.Y.-70* (2005) (TV) (executive producer)
	3. *Judgment Day: Should the Guilty Go Free* (2003) (TV) (executive producer)
	4. *All Around the Town* (2002) (TV) (executive producer)
	aka Nous n'irons plus au bois (Canada: French title) (France)
	aka Mary Higgins Clark's "All Around the Town" (USA: complete title)

(Continued)

5. *Haven't We Met Before?* (2002) (TV) (executive producer)

   aka Mary Higgins Clark's "Haven't We Met Before?" (Canada: English title)

   aka Mary Higgins Clark's *Haven't We Met Before?* (Australia: DVD title)

   aka Mary Higgins Clark: *Vous souvenez-vous?* (Canada: French title)

6. *Lucky Day* (2002) (TV) (executive producer)

   aka Mary Higgins Clark's 'Lucky Day' (USA: complete title)

7. *Pretend You Don't See Her* (2002) (TV) (executive producer)

   aka Mary Higgins Clark's *Pretend You Don't See Her* (Canada: English title)

   aka Mary Higgins Clark's *Pretend You Don't See Her* (UK: complete title)

   aka Mary Higgins Clark: *Ni vue ni connue* (Canada: French title)

8. *The Red Phone: Manhunt* (2001) (TV) (executive producer)

   aka *AT13: Anti-Terror-Warfare* (Europe: English title)

   aka *Red Phone 2* (USA)

9. *Loves Music, Loves to Dance* (2001) (TV) (executive producer)

   aka Mary Higgins Clark's *Loves Music, Loves to Dance* (USA: complete title)

10. *Making the Connection: Untold Stories of "The French Connection"* (2001) (TV) (executive producer)

    aka The French Connection 30th Anniversary Special (USA)

11. *You Belong to Me* (2001) (TV) (executive producer)

    aka Mary Higgins Clark's *You Belong to Me* (USA: complete title)

    aka Mary Higgins Clark: *Tu m'appartiens* (Canada: French title)

12. *All-American Girl: The Mary Kay Letourneau Story* (2000) (TV) (executive producer)

    aka Mary Kay Letourneau: *All American Girl* (USA: new title)

13. *Moonlight Becomes You* (1998) (TV) (executive producer)

14. *Let Me Call You Sweetheart* (1997) (TV) (executive producer)

    aka *Let Me Call You Sweetheart* (Canada: English title)

    aka Mary Higgins Clark's *Let Me Call You Sweetheart* (USA: complete title)

15. *While My Pretty One Sleeps* (1997) (TV) (executive producer)

    aka Mary Higgins Clark's *While My Pretty One Sleeps* (USA: complete title)

16. *The Big Easy* (1996) TV Series (executive producer) (unknown episodes)

17. *Remember Me* (1995) (TV) (executive producer)
    aka Mary Higgins Clark's *Remember Me* (Canada: English title: complete title)
    aka *Souviens-toi* (Canada: French title)
18. *Secret Service* (1992) TV Series (executive producer) (unknown episodes)
19. *Counterstrike* (1991) TV Series (executive producer) (unknown episodes)
    aka *Force de frappe* (France)
20. *A Family for Joe* (1990) TV Series (producer)
21. *Top Cops* (1990) TV Series (producer) (unknown episodes)
22. *A Family for Joe* (1990) (TV) (executive producer)
23. *True Blue* (1989) (TV) (executive producer)
24. *Juvenile Justice* (1988) (TV) (producer)
25. *The Gunfighters* (1987) (TV) (executive producer)
26. *Diamonds* (1987) TV Series (executive producer) (unknown episodes)
27. *Night Heat* (executive producer) (10 episodes, 1985–1986) (producer) (1 episode, 1985)
    —"Children of the Night" (1986) TV Episode (executive producer)
    —"The Hit" (1986) TV Episode (executive producer)
    —"Friends" (1986) TV Episode (executive producer)
    —"The Fighter" (1986) TV Episode (executive producer)
    —"The Legendary Eddie Shore" (1986) TV Episode (executive producer)
    (6 more)
28. *Hot Shots* (1986) TV Series (executive producer) (unknown episodes)
29. *Pee-wee's Playhouse* (1986) TV Series (producer) (unknown episodes)
30. *Out of the Darkness* (1985) (TV) (producer)
31. *Trackdown: Finding the Goodbar Killer* (1983) (TV) (producer)
    aka *Trackdown* (USA: short title)
32. *A Question of Honor* (1982) (TV) (producer)
33. *Baker's Dozen* (1982) TV Series (producer)
34. *CBS Afternoon Playhouse* (producer) (1 episode, 1981)
    —"Portrait of a Teenage Shoplifter" (1981) TV Episode (producer)
35. *The Dain Curse* (1978) (mini) TV Series (associate producer)
    aka Dashiell Hammett's *The Dain Curse*
36. *Strike Force* (1975) (TV) (associate producer)

(Continued)

aka *Crack*
aka *Crackdown*

Actor - TV:

1. *Murder in Music City* (1979) (TV)
   aka *The Country Western Murders* (USA: new title)
2. *To Kill a Cop* (1978) (TV)   Mafitano
3. *The Godfather Saga* (1977) (mini) TV Series (uncredited)   Cop
   aka *The Godfather 1902–1959: The Complete Epic* (USA: video title)
   aka *The Godfather: The Complete Novel for Television* (USA)
4. *Contract on Cherry Street* (1977) (TV)   Rhodes, OCU
   aka *Stakeout on Cherry Street*
5. *Mr. Inside/Mr. Outside* (1973) (TV)   Detective
   aka *Hot Ice*

Actor:

1. *Cruising* (1980)   Det. Blasio
   aka William Friedkin's *Cruising* (USA: closing credits title)
2. *Report to the Commissioner* (1975)   Detective
   aka *Operation Undercover* (UK)
3. *The Seven-Ups* (1973) (uncredited)   Counterfeit Money Courier
4. *The Godfather* (1972) (uncredited)   Cop with Capt. McCluskey outside hospital
   aka Mario Puzo's *The Godfather* (USA: complete title)
5. *The French Connection* (1971)   Bill Klein

Actor - video:

1. *The Godfather Trilogy: 1901–1980* (1992) (V) (uncredited)   Cop

Miscellaneous Crew:

1. *Making the Connection: Untold Stories of "The French Connection"* (2001)
   (TV)
   aka *The French Connection 30th Anniversary Special* (USA)
2. *Cruising* (1980) (technical advisor)
   aka William Friedkin's *Cruising* (USA: closing credits title)
3. *To Kill a Cop* (1978) (TV) (technical advisor)
4. *Contract on Cherry Street* (1977) (TV) (technical advisor)
   aka *Stakeout on Cherry Street*
5. *Report to the Commissioner* (1975) (technical advisor)
   aka *Operation Undercover* (UK)
6. *The Seven-Ups* (1973) (technical advisor)

Eddie Egan and Sonny Grosso

    7. *Kojak* (technical advisor) (1 episode, 1973)
       —"Siege of Terror" (1973) TV Episode (technical advisor)
    8. *The Godfather* (1972) (technical advisor) (uncredited)
       aka Mario Puzo's *The Godfather* (USA: complete title)
    9. *The French Connection* (1971) (technical consultant)

Writer:
    1. "Night Heat" (1 episode, 1985)
       —"Obie's Law" (1985) TV Episode (story)
    2. *A Question of Honor* (1982) (TV) (book *Point Blank*)
    3. *Strike Force* (1975) (TV) (story)
       aka *Crack*
       aka *Crackdown*
    4. *The Seven-Ups* (1973) (story)

Self-TV:
    1. "Inside TV Land: Cops on Camera" (2002) (TV)   Himself
    2. *Making the Connection: Untold Stories of "The French Connection"* (2001) (TV)   Himself—Retired NYPD Detective/Producer
       aka *The French Connection 30th Anniversary Special* (USA)
    3. The Poughkeepsie Shuffle: Tracing "The French Connection" (2000) (TV)   Himself—NYPD Narcotics Agent

Self-video:
    1. "The Joe Spinell Story" (2001) (TV)   Himself

AUTHOR NOTE

Grosso graciously agreed to be interviewed for this chapter, and reviewed it, which gave the chapter greater depth and allowed the writing to reflect his personality and insights. The quotes at the beginning of the chapter are two of Grosso's favorites.

NOTES

  1. Carlo Rotella, *Good with Their Hands: Boxers, Bluesmen, and Other Characters from the Rust Belt* (Berkeley: University of California Press, 2002), 134–35.
  2. Robin Moore, *The French Connection: A True Account of Cops, Narcotics, and International Conspiracy*, 1969 (Guilford, CT: The Lyons Press, 2003), 15; Rotella, *Good with Their Hands*, 137; David M. Herszenhorn, "Edward R. Egan, Police Officer Who Inspired Movie, Dies at 65," *The New York Times*, June 11, 1995.
  3. Moore, 14.
  4. That decided him on a police career. As told to Moore, Egan put himself in a category with Mickey Mantle. He believed that if Mantle hadn't come along when

he did, he (Egan) would have had a chance at a major league career with the Yankees. Moore, *The French Connection*, 13–15; Rotella, *Good with Their Hands*, 137. As Rotella explains it, this was Egan's account of himself, which permeates all the movies in which he was involved. This includes both *French Connection* movies, and *Badge 373*, described as "inspired by Eddie Egan" Rotella, *Good with Their Hands*, 164–65. There is a scene in *The French Connection II*, when Popeye is in a French cell, trying to go cold turkey off the heroin that was pumped into his system by drug dealers. In a semi-coherent, drugged state, he goes on about how great a baseball player he was, only to lose out to Mickey Mantle, and yells out "Mickey Mantle sucks." That line caused many headaches for the film makers, as their legal department advised them to get permission from Mantle to keep that line in the movie. In order to do that, the producer, Robert L. Rosen, had to find Mantle, and when he did, wound up flying out to Mantle's home in Dallas with a copy of the film. It was screened for both Mantle and Mantle's lawyer. When Gene Hackman screamed the line, Mantle roared with laughter and after watching the rest of the movie, signed the waiver and the line remained (http://www.imdb.com/title/tt0073018/trivia).

5. Moore, 14–15.

6. Moore, 15–16; Robert M. Fogelson, *Big-City Police* (Cambridge, MA: Harvard University Press, 1977).

7. Moore, 16–17.

8. Moore, 11–12, amended by Sonny Grosso.

9. Sonny Grosso and John Devaney, *Murder at the Harlem Mosque* (New York: Crown Publishers, 1977), 16–17.

10. Moore, 12; Grosso and Devaney, 17.

11. Moore, 12–13.

12. Grosso and Devaney, 17; Moore, 305.

13. In my conversation with Grosso, he stated that he retired in 1976 after twenty-two years on the force.

14. Rotella, 138.

15. Rotella, 136.

16. Rotella, 139, amended by Sonny Grosso.

17. Rotella, 136–37, amended by Sonny Grosso.

18. Rotella, 136–37, amended by Sonny Grosso.

19. Rotella, 144, amended by Sonny Grosso.

20. Rotella, 140.

21. Rotella, 139–40, amended by Sonny Grosso.

22. Moore, 3.

23. Rotella, 137–38, amended by Sonny Grosso.

24. Moore, 3.

25. Rotella, 138–39.; *New York Times,* November 6, 1995.

26. Rotella, 138.

27. Rotella, 140.

28. Sonny Grosso, "Afterword: Sonny Speaks…." in *The French Connection,* by Robin Moore (Guilford, CT: The Lyons Press, 2003).

29. Rotella, 141.

30. Sonny Grosso, "Afterword: Sonny Speaks…." in *The French Connection,* by Robin Moore. An example of this is Robert Lipsyte's article on Egan and Grosso,

written in 1962, where Egan is described as dressed in a Santa suit, almost a decade before the Santa scene in the movie. Robert M. Lipsyte, "Cops in the World of 'Junk,'" *The New York Times,* October 14, 1962.

31. *The New York Times,* Nov. 9, 1971.
32. Rotella, 111–12, enhanced by Sonny Grosso.
33. Rotella, 114.
34. Rotella, 114, amended by Sonny Grosso.
35. Sonny Grosso, "Afterword: Sonny Speaks...." in *The French Connection,* by Robin Moore, 2003, enhanced by Sonny Grosso.
36. This was a term coined by Daniel Patrick Moynihan, in the book he wrote with Nathan Glazer, *Beyond the Melting Pot: The Negroes, Puerto Ricans, Jews, Italians, and Irish of New York City.* 1963. Reprint. (Cambridge: MIT Press, 1970), as opposed to the concept of the "melting pot."
37. New York (NY), *The Knapp Commission Report on Police Corruption* (New York: G. Braziller, 1973). Also see *The New York Times,* beginning June 19, 1970 through April 6, 1972; Peter Maas and Frank Serpico, *Serpico,* originally published 1973, in *Serpico,* Edition (New York: HarperPaperback, 1997).
38. Martin Arnold, "Murphy's Drive on Graft Is Deeply Affecting Police," *The New York Times,* September 20, 1971. The article uses the word "caught," which Grosso changed to "charged with." Gregory Wallance alludes to Murphy's two idols, the god of Efficient Administration, which could wipe out police corruption, and the Cop, who walked a beat and handed out chewing gum to the kids on the block. Gregory Wallance, *Papa's Game* (New York: Rawson, Wade Publishers,1981), 22, amended by Sonny Grosso.
39. Rotella, 109–10, enhanced by Sonny Grosso.
40. Joseph Lelyveld, "Detective Lays His Ouster to Movie Role," *The New York Times,* December 4, 1971.
41. Joycelyn M Pollock, *Ethical Dilemmas and Decisions in Criminal Justice,* 5th ed. (Belmont, CA: Thompson/Wadsworth, 2007), 200–201.
42. Personal conversation with Sonny Grosso. For an analysis of how these two police cultures function, see Elizabeth Reuss-Ianni, *Two Cultures of Policing: Street Cops and Management Cops* (New Brunswick: Transaction Publishers, 1983).
43. It was department policy that all of its business was required to be completed within a 30-day period after retirement papers are submitted. David Burnham of the *New York Times* wrote this article. He was the newspaper man Frank Serpico worked with to uncover police corruption during this period.
44. Lelyveld.
45. Lelyveld.
46. Interestingly enough, while the public supported police reform, they cheered the cops in both *The French Connection* and *Dirty Harry.* Jurgensen reacted very negatively to the scene when "Popeye" Doyle shoots the Frenchman, Frog Two, who is unarmed, in the back. (This is the poster picture.) He felt that Friedkin had done a great disservice to the police department. The scene was kept in. When the movie was previewed, the audience cheered. Rotella, *Good with Their Hands,* 147–48.
47. Eric Pace, "'French Connection' Patrolman Wins a Suit to Regain Pension," *New York Times,* April 6, 1972, enhanced by Sonny Grosso.

48. While Egan's filmography does not list his technical help on this movie, Rotella writes that in both the *Connection* movies and in *Badge 373*, Egan was given leeway to give his own fantasy account of himself. Pete Hamill, who wrote the screenplay for *Badge 373* says basically the same thing as the crew of *The French Connection*. He hung around with him and got the cadence of his speech. Eddie, according to Hamill, "was his own fictional creation." Rotella, *Good with Their Hands*, 164–65.

49. Alfred E. Clark, "Egan Links 'Slipshod' Practices in Police Office to Heroin Theft," *New York Times*, December, 16, 1972.

50. See also Wallance, *Papa's Game*, 27–28. For the full story of the disappearance of the narcotics, see Wallance, *Papa's Game*.

51. David Burnham, "Detective Pleads Guilty to Taking $4,000 Bribe," *New York Times*, May 22, 1973. Wallance, *Papa's Game*, 110–14, amended by Sonny Grosso.

52. David Burnham, "Detective Pleads Guilty to Taking $4,000 Bribe,"*New York Times*. Wallance, *Papa's Game*, 114–15, amended by Sonny Grosso.

53. Philip Rosenberg and Sonny Grosso, *Point Blank* (New York: Grosset & Dunlop, 1978), 21–22.

54. Rosenberg and Grosso.

55. Rosenberg and Grosso, 279, amended by Sonny Grosso.

56. Rosenberg and Grosso, 283. In the book "ultimately" is used, not "sometimes." For clarity here, the sentence that begins "Joe's story" in the book has been changed to "This story." These changes were suggested by Sonny Grosso.

57. Grosso and Devaney, 36–38.

58. Grosso and Devaney, 222.

59. Patrick V. Murphy and Thomas Gordon Plate, *Commissioner: A View from the Top of American Law Enforcement* (New York: Simon & Schuster, 1977), 173.

60. Grosso and Devaney, 87–88.

61. Murphy and Plate, 176.

62. Murphy and Plate, 173–78, responded in person by Sonny Grosso.

63. Grosso and Devaney, 96–97.

64. Grosso and Devaney, 119–20.

65. Grosso and Devaney, 18–23; 127–28; personal conversation with Sonny Grosso.

66. Grosso and Devaney, 145–224.

67. Rotella, 138. Egan's obituary, David Herszenhorn, *The New York Times*, November 6, 1995, and *South Coast Today*, November 6, 1995.

68. IMDb, "Eddie Egan," http://www.imdb.com/name/nm0250670/.

69. IMDb, "Filmography by type for Sonny Grosso," http://www.imdb.com/name/nm0343780/filmotype/.

FURTHER READING

Fogelson, Robert M. 1977. *Big-city Police*. Cambridge, MA: Harvard University Press.

Grosso, Sonny, and John Devaney. 1977. *Murder at the Harlem Mosque*. New York: Crown Publishers.

Herszenhorn, David M. Edward R. Egan, Police Officer Who Inspired Movie, Dies at 65. *The New York Times*. June 11, 1995.

Knapp Commission. 1973. *The Knapp Commission Report on Police Corruption.* New York: G. Braziller.

Maas, Peter, and Frank Serpico. 1997 [originally published 1973]. *Serpico.* In *Serpico*, Edition. New York: HarperPaperback.

Moore, Robin. 2003 [1969]. *The French Connection: A True Account of Cops, Narcotics, and International Conspiracy,* 309. Guilford, CT: The Lyons Press.

Murphy, Patrick V, and Thomas Gordon Plate. 1977. *Commissioner: A View from the Top of American Law Enforcement.* New York: Simon & Schuster.

Pollock, Joycelyn M. 2007. *Ethical Dilemmas and Decisions in Criminal Justice.* 5th ed. Belmont, CA: Thompson/Wadsworth.

Reuss-Ianni, Elizabeth. 1983. *Two Cultures of Policing: Street Cops and Management Cops.* New Brunswick, NJ: Transaction Publishers.

Rosenberg, Philip, and Sonny Grosso. 1978. *Point Blank.* New York: Grosset & Dunlop.

Rotella, Carlo. 2002. *Good with Their Hands: Boxers, Bluesmen, and other Characters from the Rust Belt.* Berkeley: University of California Press.

Wallance, Gregory. 1981. *Papa's Game.* New York: Rawson, Wade Publishers.

This annotated list cited is only a partial representation of the literature and resources available on the topics of urban police during the 1960s and 1970s, urban drug enforcement, and the French Connection case. However, they form a solid base from which to grow.

1. The French Connection and its Aftermath

Books

Moore, Robin. 1969. *The French Connection: A True Account of Cops, Narcotics, and International Conspiracy.* Boston: Little, Brown and Company. Reprinted with an additional preface by Robin Moore, and a new afterword by Sonny Grosso, Guilford, CT: The Lyons Press, 2003. The best factual step-by-step account of the police investigation.

Moore, Robin, with Milt Machlin. 1975. *The Set Up: The Shocking Aftermath to The French Connection.* Pyramid Books. Reprinted with a preface by Robin Moore. Guilford, CT: Lyons Press, 2004. A highly fictionalized account of what happened to the seized heroin from the French Connection case.

Wallance, Gregory. 1981. *Papa's Game.* New York: Rawson, Wade Publishers. The true account of what happened to the seized heroin from the French Connection case.

Film

The French Connection: Collector's Edition. DVD. 20th Century Fox, 2006. The 1971 film that won five Academy Awards, including Best Picture, Best Director (William Friedkin), and Best Actor (Gene Hackman). Based loosely on the actual case, Friedkin focused more on the way Egan and Grosso (Doyle and Russo) conducted themselves and NYC cops.

2. NYC Police

Conlon, Edward. 2004. *Blue Blood.* New York: Riverhead Books.

Daley, Robert. 1971. *Prince of the City: The True Story of a Cop Who knew Too Much.* Boston: Houghton, Mifflin Company. Many of the books by Robert Daley focus on the NYC police department during the 1960s and 1970s. Some, like *Target Blue* and *Prince of the City*, are factual. Daley was the Deputy Commissioner of Public Information of the NYPD under Commissioner Patrick Murphy.

Daley, Robert. 1971. *Target Blue: An Insider's View of the N.Y.P.D.* New York: Dell Publishers.

Knapp Commission. 1973. *Knapp Commission Report of Police Corruption.* New York: George Braziller Publishers. This commission investigated police corruption in New York and discerned between corrupted police who were grass-eaters as opposed to meat-eaters.

Leuci, Robert. 2004. *All the Centurions: A New York City Cop Remembers His Years on the Street, 1961–1981.* New York: HarperCollins. Leuci was the protagonist in Robert Daley's *Prince of the City*. In this book, he recollects his years as a NYC police officer. He has become a best-selling author himself.

Murphy, Patrick V., and Plate, Thomas Gordon. 1977. *Commissioner: A View from the Top of American Law Enforcement.* New York: Simon & Schuster. Written by Patrick V. Murphy about his life as a police officer, it focuses on his tenure and philosophy as commissioner of the NYC police force from 1970 to 1973. He also discusses his philosophy as a police reformer, and his feelings about the FBI. Murphy was one of the major police reformers of his time. Murphy reduced Eddie Egan in rank and then had him dismissed from the force. The charges were later invalidated by the New York state supreme court.

3. Urban Police

Domanick, Joe. 1995. *To Protect and Serve: The LAPD's Century of War in the City of Dreams.* New York: Pocket Books. A sweeping, detailed history of the LAPD, with all its abuse of power and racism.

Fogelson, Robert. 1977. *Big-City Police.* Cambridge, MA: Harvard University Press. One of the best histories of urban police. Its focus is on politics and reform.

Lane, Roger. 1967. *Policing the City: Boston 1822–1885.* Cambridge, MA: Harvard University Press. Although this book deals with the Boston police, much of what Lane discusses, with regard to the structure of the police, also applies to New York. This book gives the reader an understanding of where the police came from, and the differentiation between beat cops and detectives.

Rubinstein, Jonathan. 1973. *City Police.* New York: Ballantine Books. A classic. Insight into urban police, focused on Philadelphia, that details the way police really think and operate.

Walker, Samuel. 1977. *A Critical History of Police Reform: The Emergence of Professionalism.* Lexington, MA: Lexington Books. Also focuses on police reform.

4. Histories of Drugs in the United States

Courtwright, David T. 1982. *Dark Paradise: Opiate Addiction in America before 1940.* Cambridge, MA: Harvard University Press. This book focuses on opiate addiction from before the Civil War, and explains how the majority of addicts before the 1990s were white, southern, upper-middle-class women.

Musto, David F., M.D. 1987. *The American Disease: Origins of Narcotic Control.* Expanded edition. New York: Oxford University Press. Musto's book gives detailed facts about the use and abuse of drugs in the United States. He explains the social and political forces behind drug laws and how we, as a country, have not learned from our past.

5. Noble Cause Corruption

Film

Dirty Harry. 1971, DVD release 1997, starring Clint Eastwood, directed by Don Siegel.

The Seven-Ups: They Take Justice One Step Further. 1973, DVD release 2006, starring Roy Scheider, directed by Philip D'Antoni, story by Sonny Grosso.

Books

Crank, John P., and Michael A. Caldero. 2000. *Police Ethics: The Corruption of Noble Cause.* Cincinnati: Anderson.

Kappeler, Victor E., ed. 2006. *The Police and Society: Touchstone Readings.* Long Grove, IL: Waveland Press.

Klockars, Carl. 1991. Blue lies and police placebos: The moralities of police lying. In *Thinking About Police: Contemporary Readings,* ed. Carl B. Klockars and Stephen D. Mastrofski. 2nd ed. 424–32. New York: McGraw Hill.

Klockars, Carl. 1991. The Dirty Harry problem. In *Thinking About Police: Contemporary Readings,* edited by Carl B. Klockars and Stephen D. Mastrofski. 2nd ed. 413–23. New York: McGraw Hill.

Manning, Peter K., and Lawrence John Redlinger. 1991. Invitational edges. In *Thinking About Police: Contemporary Readings,* ed. Carl B. Klockars and Stephen D. Mastrofski. 2nd ed., 396–414. New York: McGraw Hill.

Skolnick, Jerome H., and James J. Fyfe. 1993. *Above the Law: Police and the Excessive Use of Force.* New York: The Free Press. While this book is about abuse of power, there are several chapters (e.g. the first, the fifth, and the seventh) that deal with noble-cause issues.

Sutton, Paul L. 1991. Getting around the Fourth Amendment. In *Thinking About Police: Contemporary Readings,* ed. Carl B. Klockars and Stephen D. Mastrofski. 2nd ed. 433–46. New York: McGraw Hill.

Courtesy AP Images

Bob Woodward and Carl Bernstein: Presidential Crime Fighters and Shapers of American Public Opinion

Christopher Larimer

To political pundits, journalists, political scientists, and indeed many others, the phrase "post-Watergate era" is a familiar and often-used phrase when discussing presidential politics. A casual observer of presidential approval ratings will often hear of such ratings couched in Watergate terms; i.e., "the approval ratings of the president are the lowest (highest) in the post-Watergate era." For political candidates with presidential aspirations, the effects of Watergate have also been substantial. Media events for presidential candidates have become no-holds-barred contests in which candidates relentlessly defend themselves against statements made five, ten, and twenty years earlier. But what is Watergate? Why did it have such a profound effect on American politics? Why is it often considered the worst scandal in modern political history? And, most importantly, who were the crucial figures in bringing this case to the public and creating such a powerful legacy?

"Watergate" refers to the scene of the crime that ultimately led to the first resignation of an American president. During the early hours of June 17, 1972, a break-in was reported at the Watergate Hotel in Washington, D.C., the national headquarters of the Democratic Party. On June 19, 1972, two days after the burglary, two reporters for *The Washington Post* were the first to report a link between the White House and the suspects involved in the crime. Over the next two years, the two reporters would collaborate in a series of articles for *The Washington Post* that would serve as the basis for one of the most serious and far-reaching scandals in American political history. Although first described by the White House as a "third-rate burglary," the subsequent investigation into the break-in would later result in the indictment of seven aides to President Nixon and ultimately force the president himself to resign to avoid indictment. Because of this, the journalists who broke the case, Bob Woodward and Carl Bernstein of *The Washington Post*, are icons of political crime fighting and political accountability. As Alicia Shepard writes, Bernstein and Woodward are "two of the most celebrated journalists in the world. Their names could be *Jeopardy* clues." (Shepard 2007). As testimony to their iconic status, Woodward and Bernstein's hand-scribbled notes from the Watergate years were recently purchased by the Harry Ransom Center at the University of Texas for $5 million.

Soon after their story broke connecting the White House to the Watergate break-in in October of 1972, Woodward and Bernstein were simply known as "Woodstein" by their peers. In 1973, *The Washington Post* received a Pulitzer Prize for "Woodstein's" investigative reporting of the scandal. The immediate and long-term effects of Watergate on presidential as well as congressional politics have been significant, both in terms of the relationship between the media and government and between the public and government. Most notably, in addition to instigating the investigation that led to first resignation of a sitting American president, as well as institutionalizing a new form of political reporting, Woodward and Bernstein's investigation has shaped the public's view of presidential administrations.

This chapter will focus on the enduring legacy of Bob Woodward and Carl Bernstein, and their investigation into the Watergate scandal, on presidential politics and political accountability. The chapter will proceed as follows. First, there will be a brief biographical sketch of these two figures. This will be followed by a more in-depth discussion of the Watergate case itself, including a discussion of Woodward and Bernstein's reporting from 1972 to 1974. The following section will then be split into two parts: the first examining the immediate effects of "Woodstein's" reporting and the second focusing on more long-term effects. The emphasis here will be on the inverse relationship between political accountability and trust in government caused by the Watergate story. This will be followed by a discussion of Woodward's ongoing assault on presidential accountability. Finally, the chapter will conclude with a broader discussion of Woodward and Bernstein's roles in modern presidential politics as well the implications of their work on the relationship between the media and political figures and public attitudes toward government.

WHO ARE BOB WOODWARD AND CARL BERNSTEIN?

The two figures that broke the Watergate story could not have been more different in personality and professional conduct. Prior to the Watergate scandal, the two rarely spoke to each other, let alone worked together. In fact, the duo's first account of the Watergate investigation, *All the President's Men* first published in 1974, presents a contrasting and initially distrustful relationship between the two men. Yet, despite these initial differences, the two were able to work quite well together in helping to bring down the most powerful man in American government. Moreover, despite their tenuous beginning, Woodward and Bernstein are credited with redefining the scope of political journalism.

Prior to covering the break-in at the Watergate Hotel, an event that ultimately would bring down the president, Bob Woodward had served only nine months at *The Washington Post* and had been a reporter for only two years. In fact, before Watergate, Woodward readily admits to having covered relatively mundane stories for *The Washington Post*. The portrait of Woodward is that of a prim reporter, ambitious yet obedient. A Yale graduate and former communications officer in the navy, Woodward's own description of himself in *All the President's Men* presents a portrait of someone who tended to be acquiescent to authority. In terms of talent, at the time of the break-in Woodward was certainly the lesser of the two reporters. Some scholars have speculated that Woodward's education at Yale, including his involvement in one of Yale's secret societies, afforded Woodward access to government documents not normally available to the public. Such comments have not been substantiated by Woodward himself.

Carl Bernstein, by contrast, was a college dropout, often challenged authority, and was incautiously ambitious. As Alicia Shepard writes, "If Woodward was strait-laced, clean-shaven, and determined to please his editors, Carl Bernstein was the opposite." (Shepard 2007, 17). Bernstein began his journalistic career as a copy boy at *The Washington Evening Star*. In 1965, he joined *The Washington Post* as a full-time reporter. In their account of the Watergate investigation, Woodward and Bernstein admit that Bernstein was the better writer, and in fact, was probably the better reporter at the time of the burglary. Colleagues tended to describe Bernstein as reckless and aggressive, but very talented. In her research on the two contrasting personalities, Shepard provides Woodward's own assessment of Bernstein following Watergate story. According to Woodward, "there is a kind of arrogance to him [Bernstein]. It's as if he's convinced that six hours of his work is worth twenty hours of someone else's. And he's probably right." Bernstein's style, because it was in direct contrast with Woodward's, initially created a level of antagonism between the two. As recounted by the two reporters in *All the President's Men*, during the initial coverage of the scandal Bernstein was incessantly harassing the editor about Woodward's work and would often rewrite Woodward's stories. Thus, it is safe to say that Bernstein was probably the more tenacious of the two reporters at the time of the scandal.

What was remarkable about both Woodward and Bernstein in 1972 was their persistence in tracking down sources, facts, and statements, and relating them to the Watergate break-in. Given the scant attention paid by most reporters and news organizations to the initial story, the ability of Woodward and Bernstein to keep pushing is testament to their political and crime-fighting instincts. As will be discussed in the chapter, the ambition and careful attention to detail by both reporters transformed a story described by the White House as "third-rate burglary" into an event that forced the resignation of an American president for the first time in the history of the United States.

WHAT IS WATERGATE?

The most extensive and politically in-depth discussion of the Watergate scandal comes from Woodward and Bernstein's own account in *All the President's Men*. As the authors discuss, the story began on June 17, 1972, in what was perceived as a relatively innocuous break-in at the Watergate Hotel in Washington, D.C., the national headquarters for the Democratic Party. That Woodward and Bernstein would cover the initial break-in was purely happenstance. Bernstein had been on probation and was assigned to weekend duty at *The Washington Post*. Woodward, who was awakened that Saturday morning and asked to cover the break-in, reluctantly made his way down to the courthouse for the initial hearing. The spark for

Woodward came when James McCord, one of the five burglars at the Watergate Hotel, admitted in the courtroom to having been a former employee of the Central Intelligence Agency (CIA). As Woodward and Bernstein began searching for more information on McCord, the two uncovered evidence linking the bank accounts of the burglars to the Committee for the Reelection of President, or CRP as it was commonly referred to, for President Richard Nixon. On June 19, 1972, *The Washington Post* ran a story by Woodward and Bernstein reporting a link between the burglars and the CRP. Woodward and Bernstein would later learn that the burglars were also connected to Howard Hunt, a political consultant in the White House. In August and September of 1972, Woodward and Bernstein reported that the burglars were in fact paid by a "secret fund" within the CRP that had been implemented to finance operations discrediting political opposition to President Nixon. It was at this point that the two reporters began to realize the magnitude of the case. A significant turning point in the scandal came the following month. Just four months after their initial story about the break-in, on October 10, 1972, *The Washington Post* published a story linking the Watergate burglary to efforts on behalf of members of President Nixon's reelection campaign to discredit any and all political opposition. The headline read, "FBI Finds Nixon Aides Sabotaged Democrats." The most famous political investigation of the twentieth century had now begun.

Just one month after the October 10th story in *The Washington Post*, President Nixon was reelected to a second term by one of the largest margins in presidential history. However, by January of 1973, indictments were already being handed out to the five burglars (including James McCord, Jr., former Nixon administration aide) and, more damaging to the White House, to Howard Hunt, counsel to the CRP, and G. Gordon Liddy, a former assistant to a top White House aide. What is remarkable is that despite the president's enormous popularity, Woodward and Bernstein continued to question details surrounding the Watergate burglary. The press in American politics has long been considered a linkage mechanism between citizens and government. However, in the years following the Watergate investigation that responsibility shifted to a more "watchdog" role. Following the general election in 1972, members of the media were singing the praises of the Nixon administration. Woodward and Bernstein could have easily slipped into this role, assuming that a widely popular president would never engage in illegal activity. They remained vigilant, however, in their investigation.

In the early months of 1973, pressure increasingly mounted to hold someone accountable for the Watergate break-in. The indictments of the five burglars as well as former Nixon aides were followed by resignations of H. R. Haldeman (White House Chief of Staff) and John Ehrlichman (a top assistant to President Nixon), as well as Attorney General Richard Kleindienst on April 30. That same day, John Dean, White House counsel, was also fired. The following month, the Senate Watergate Committee began holding public testimony regarding White House, and more specifically, President Nixon's involvement in the scandal. That same month *The Washington Post* received a Pulitzer Prize for their reporting of the scandal, in large part because of the investigatory reporting of Bob Woodward and Carl Bernstein. Testimony in June and July of 1973 revealed that not only did Richard Nixon have knowledge of and perhaps even ordered the burglary, but also that the president maintained a secret taping system in the Oval Office. It was believed that the tapes provided the "smoking gun" regarding the president's involvement in the scandal. Throughout the rest of the year President Nixon battled with Congress and special prosecutors over possession of the tapes, while several more aides resigned or were fired, many of whom were indicted by Congress.

In April 1974, the White House released transcripts of White House tapes to the House Judiciary Committee. The editing of the tapes, in particular an 18½-minute gap in one of the tapes, raised suspicion among committee members, and they demanded that the actual tapes be turned over to the committee. The White House initially resisted the committee's request, but was ultimately forced by the U.S. Supreme Court to turn over the tapes on July 24, 1974. Three days later the House Judiciary Committee passed an article of impeachment against President Nixon, charging the president with obstruction of justice. To make matters worse for the president, Woodward and Bernstein's *All the President's Men* was released in June of 1974. Moreover, in the month prior, *The Washington Post* ran a story by Woodward and Bernstein that indicated that President Nixon had requested "blackmail" payments for the burglars at the Watergate Hotel. Finally, on August 9, 1974, after a two-year public investigation led by Woodward and Bernstein, congressional hearings, and U.S. Supreme Court rulings, President Richard Nixon became the first U.S. president to resign from office. Two years later, the movie *All the President's Men,* starring Robert Redford as Bob Woodward and Dustin Hoffman as Carl Bernstein, was released, providing an in-depth look into the difficulties faced by Woodward and Bernstein during their investigation. That same year, *Final Days*, by Woodward and Bernstein, was published. The book is a more focused examination of President Nixon's last few days as president and provides a closer glimpse of his fixation on squelching any and all political opposition.

From the initial break-in on June 17, 1972, until the resignation of President Nixon almost two years later, Woodward and Bernstein were unrelenting in tracking down sources, details, leads, or any information suggesting a link between the burglary and the White House. They were the first reporters to suggest White House involvement in 1972, and in 1973 and 1974 were able to reveal President Nixon's direct involvement in the scandal. Woodward and Bernstein's unwillingness to let the story die is their ultimate contribution. Although nobody in the summer of 1972 believed the break-in to be linked in any way to the inner workings of the executive branch, by the summer of 1974, Woodward and Bernstein had convinced almost the entire nation that Watergate was part of a larger ploy by the Nixon White House to discredit political opponents.

LEGACY OF WATERGATE

The legacy of Watergate is profound. As evidenced by the discussion thus far, Woodward and Bernstein's investigation into the break-in at the Watergate hotel led to a significant shake-up in the executive branch of American government. But did the Watergate investigation lead to more practical reforms? Iconic figures are those who have had a lasting impact on one or more facets of society. Did the Watergate investigation affect the legislative branch, i.e., the U.S. Congress? If so, what sort of legislation was enacted as a result of the investigation? How did Watergate shape public opinion regarding the power of the executive branch? Is Watergate still relevant today? The following sections will examine the short- and long-term effects of Watergate on the American political system.

Short-term Effects

The immediate impact of the Watergate investigation was a significant shift in the role of the media. As noted earlier, the work of Woodward and Bernstein redefined the nature of the relationship between the executive branch and the media. No longer would the media sit idly by, passively accepting White House statements. Rather, the media became increasingly skeptical of presidential administrations and government generally.

Watergate's immediate impact can in part be traced through legislative action on the part of the U.S. Congress. Following Watergate, a series of bills was passed to prevent any further abuses of power. As would be expected, the bills sought to significantly reduce presidential prerogative and presidential power. Two prominent pieces of legislation include the War Powers Act of 1973, which requires the president to obtain congressional approval prior to waging war, and the Foreign Intelligence Surveillance Act of 1978, which requires the president to obtain a court order prior to conducting clandestine intelligence-gathering activities on U.S. citizens. In December 2005, it was revealed that President Bush bypassed the language of this legislation by gathering information on U.S. citizens without court approval. Ironically, such overreach of power invoked comparisons to the actions of President Nixon in the Watergate scandal and significantly reduced the approval ratings of President Bush.

Other pieces of legislation passed in the aftermath of Watergate were aimed more generally at presidential conduct and public accountability. The Ethics in Government Act of 1978 requires annual disclosure of all financial records by presidents and vice presidents, the Presidential Records Act of 1978 transferred ownership of presidential records to the federal government upon the president's leaving office, and the Government Sunshine Act of 1976 further increased government openness by placing tight restrictions on the ability of a federal agency to hold meetings that are not open to the public. The Ethics in Government Act also created the position of special prosecutor who could be appointed by the Congress or the attorney general to investigate high ranking officials, i.e., the president. (Archibald Cox was appointed in May 1973 by the attorney general to serve as special prosecutor for the Watergate case. On October 20, 1973, President Nixon fired Cox in what became known as the "Saturday Night Massacre" and eliminated the office of special prosecutor.) Like the two acts described in the previous paragraph, these three pieces of legislation were all a direct result of the Watergate scandal and were all aimed at restoring faith in the federal government and creating a sense of accountability among federal officials, particularly the president.

Reducing presidential power also extended to the budgetary process. The Budget Control and Impoundment Act of 1974 sought to reduce the president's ability to withhold federal money or reprogram federal money after it had been allocated. Like the other congressional acts mentioned above, the intent was to increase congressional involvement in the legislative process while at the same time reducing the president's. Two of a president's most formidable powers are those relating to foreign policy and those relating to the budget. Legislation following the Watergate scandal sought to reduce the president's authority in both areas. As Michael Genovese, a leading scholar on Watergate and the Nixon presidency, notes, all of these pieces of legislation share a common link to public attitudes surrounding the Watergate scandal—the president wielded too much power, and that power was corruptible.

Watergate also contributed to a growing distrust in government. Figure 1 presented on page 299 illustrates Americans' trust in government immediately after the Watergate investigation.

Although prior to Woodward and Bernstein's story of October 10, 1972, trust in government had been declining, the ongoing reporting of the scandal contributed to a sharp decline in trust in government. As Figure 1 shows, in 1972, 53 percent of the public trusted the federal government in the combined categories "just about always" or "most of the time." By 1974, that percentage had dropped seventeen percentage points to 36 percent. Woodward and Bernstein's two-year assault on White House involvement in the burglary at the Watergate Hotel significantly shaped public opinion about the federal government. No longer did a majority of the American public trust the federal government "to do what is right." Rather, in large part due to Woodward and Bernstein's investigation, only about a third of Americans trusted the federal government in 1974. In fact, the

Figure 1. Trust in the federal government, 1964–1978.

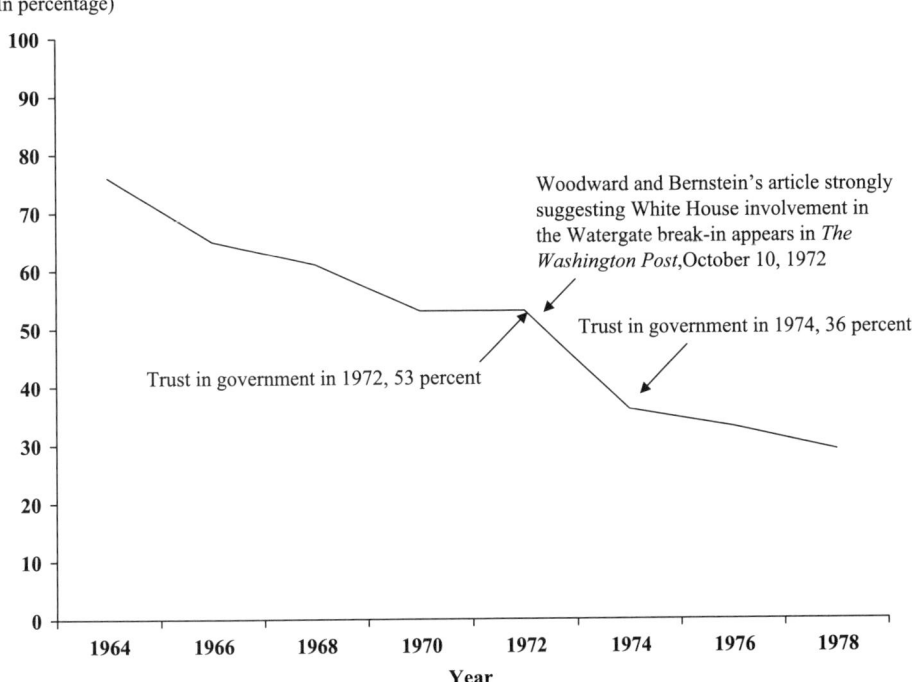

Source: National Election Studies (NES) for "Trust in Government."
Note: "Trust in Government" combines the answers "just about always" and "most of the time" from the following question:
"How much of the time do you think you can trust the government in Washington to do what is right– just about always, most of the time or only some of the time?"

seventeen percentage point shift is the largest two-year change through 2004 since the American National Election Studies began asking the question in 1958. (Data were unavailable from the National Election Studies for "Trust in Government" for the years between 1958 and 1964.)

The Watergate investigation, as expected, also had an immediate impact on the public's view of the presidency. Figure 2 displays the percentage of Americans who expressed a "great deal" of confidence in the presidency.

Although the decline is not as immediate as that displayed in Figure 1, the graph in Figure 2 shows a sharp decrease in the number of Americans who were confident in the presidency following the resignation of President Nixon. What is remarkable about this question is the lack of specificity. Scholars tend to find that approval of political institutions increases when questions are framed in terms of the "institution" rather than a particular individual or current makeup of government. Despite asking about the institution of the presidency, rather than a single individual, approval of the institution decreased sharply after 1974. In 1974, 28 percent of Americans expressed a great deal of confidence in the presidency, and by 1976,

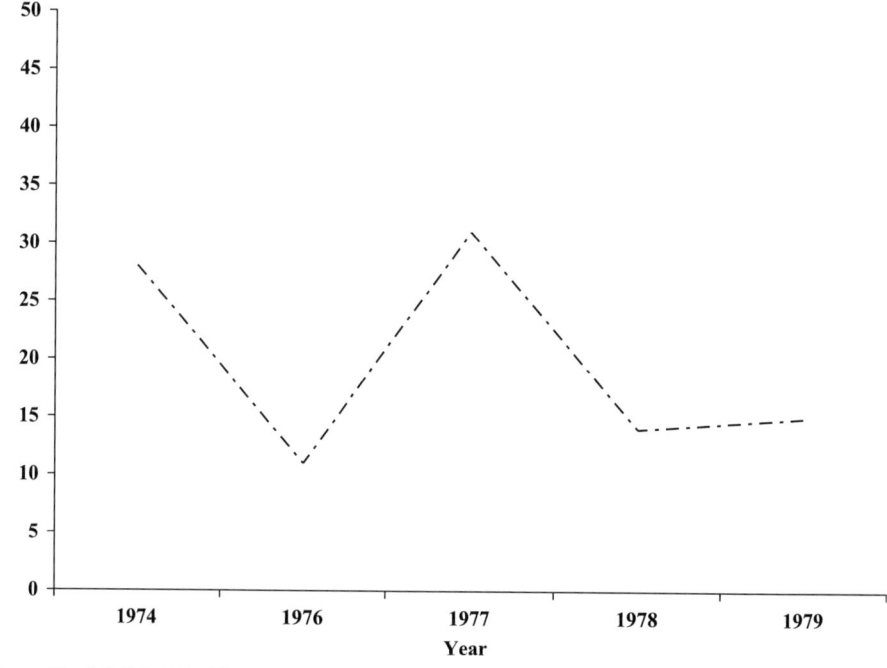

Figure 2. Confidence in the presidency, 1974–1979.
(In percentage)

Source: Harris Poll for "Confidence in Presidency."
Note: Data were unavailable for the year 1975. Confidence in the presidency is the percentage of respondents expressing "a great deal of confidence" in the White House from the following question:
"As far as people in charge of running the White House are concerned, would you say you have a great deal of confidence, only some confidence, or hardly any confidence at all in them?"

confidence had dropped by seventeen percentage points to 11 percent. It was not until after the 1976 presidential election that confidence in the presidency slowly began to increase. The resignation of President Nixon, an event that was set in motion by the investigation of Woodward and Bernstein in 1972, significantly reduced public confidence in the top elected office in the United States.

As evidenced by Figures 1 and 2, Woodward and Bernstein's investigation tended to affect perceptions of all government officials. Figure 3 shows the percentage of Americans who believed that government officials are "crooked."

The number of people who perceived "quite a few" government officials to be crooked increased dramatically between 1972 and 1974, going from 36 percent to 45 percent in just two years. In fact, the 45 percent mark is the highest mark for the entire decade of the 1970s. People tended to generalize from Woodward and Bernstein's investigation that politicians, not just the president, were self-interested decision makers unlikely to pursue the public good. The phrasing of Woodward and Bernstein's articles is worth

Figure 3. Perceived number of crooked government officials, 1968–1978.

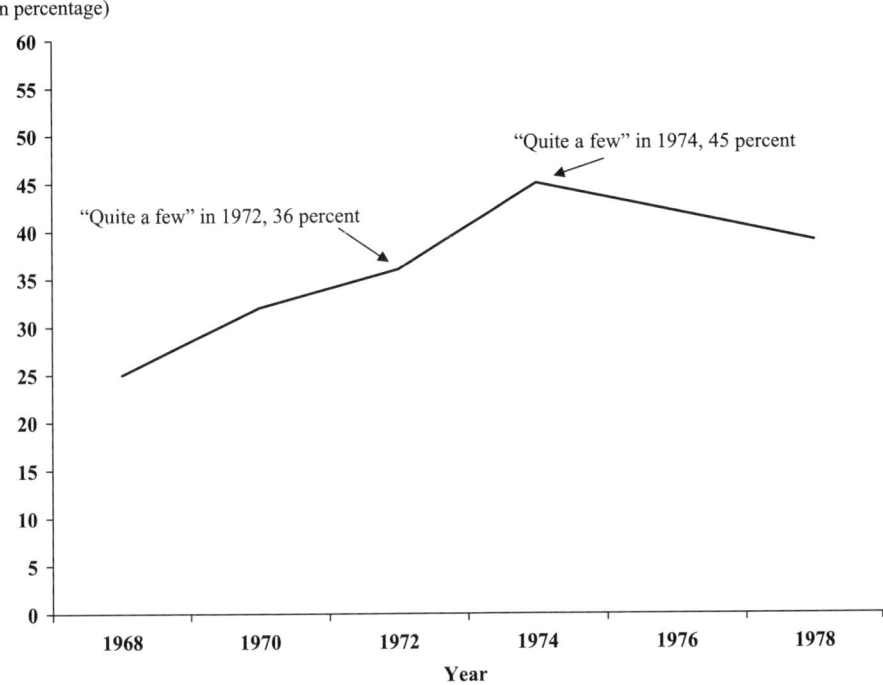

Source: National Election Studies (NES) for "Are Government Officials Crooked?"
Note: "Are Government Officials Crooked" uses the answer "quite a few" from the following question: "Do you think that quite a few of the people running the government are crooked, not very many are, or do you think hardly any of them are crooked at all?"

noting. By writing that the White House had "sabotaged" Democrats and that Nixon had "blackmailed" the burglars, Woodward and Bernstein were able to tap into the primary reservation the public has about politicians—that they will use their power to further their own interests at the expense of the public. Thus, from Figures 1–3, it is evident that the work of Woodward and Bernstein had a profound impact on public opinion and popular support for government officials and political institutions.

Finally, as expected, Watergate had a significant impact on the midterm elections of 1974 as well as the first presidential election following the scandal in 1976. In 1972, Republicans were already in the minority in both chambers of Congress. However, the results of 1974 midterm elections significantly worsened the situation for Republicans. Following the 1972 elections, Democrats held a fifty-seat advantage, 242 to 192, in the U.S. House of Representatives. After the 1974 elections, that advantage had increased to 147 seats, 291 to 144, with the president's party losing forty-eight seats. In the U.S. Senate, the story was just as bleak. In 1972, Democrats held a fifty-six-seat majority. After the 1974 elections, that number had increased to sixty, a politically significant number because sixty concurring votes are required to end a filibuster as well as act on budget resolutions and reconciliation bills. It is also suggestive of the impact of Woodward and Bernstein's claim that Democrats had been "sabotaged" by the White House.

The immediate effect of Watergate on presidential politics came first from the short presidential tenure of Gerald Ford from 1974 to 1976, as well as the 1976 presidential campaign. On September 8, 1974, President Ford, just one month into his presidency, made perhaps the most defining decision of his presidency—the decision to pardon Richard Nixon for his involvement in the Watergate scandal. Scholars have argued that President Ford's pardon of Richard Nixon just one month after Nixon's resignation, crippled his administration. Indeed, this is reflected in Figures 2 and 3, which show that although confidence in the presidency continued to decline after 1974 (Figure 2), fewer Americans perceive "quite a few" government officials to be "crooked" after 1974 (Figure 3). The pardon seemed to further indicate a collusion and abuse of power at the highest level of government. Moreover, the pardon connected President Ford to President Nixon. Ford's tenure as president seemed to be a continuation of the Watergate scandal, a scandal the public had reacted negatively and vociferously to. Two years later, in 1976, the American public would have a chance to elect their first president since the scandal.

Prior to the Iowa Caucus in 1976, Jimmy Carter was a relatively unknown former governor of Georgia. However, his message was simple and appealing—"I'll never lie to you. I'll never mislead you." (Woodward 1999). Coming on the heels of the Watergate investigation and President Nixon's subsequent resignation, Carter's message struck a chord with the American people. In their coverage of the scandal, Woodward and Bernstein repeatedly emphasized the covert and clandestine nature of the scandal—one particular headline read "Still Secret—Who Hired Spies and Why" (Woodward 1999, 41). The Watergate scandal had ripped a gaping hole through any preexisting perceptions that presidents are model public servants. Carter's pledge seemed to be exactly what the American public wanted to hear more than anything else from a candidate with presidential aspirations. Thus, it seems reasonable to suggest that the work of Woodward and Bernstein not only affected public perceptions of American political figures and political institutions, but also had a significant impact on political behavior.

LONG-TERM EFFECTS

One reason why Woodward and Bernstein's investigation resonated so strongly with the American public is that it taps basic human predispositions. Public opinion polls and political behavior experiments consistently reveal a strong predisposition against leaders perceived as power hungry.

Figure 4. Trust in the federal government and crooked government officials, 1974-2004.
(In percentage)

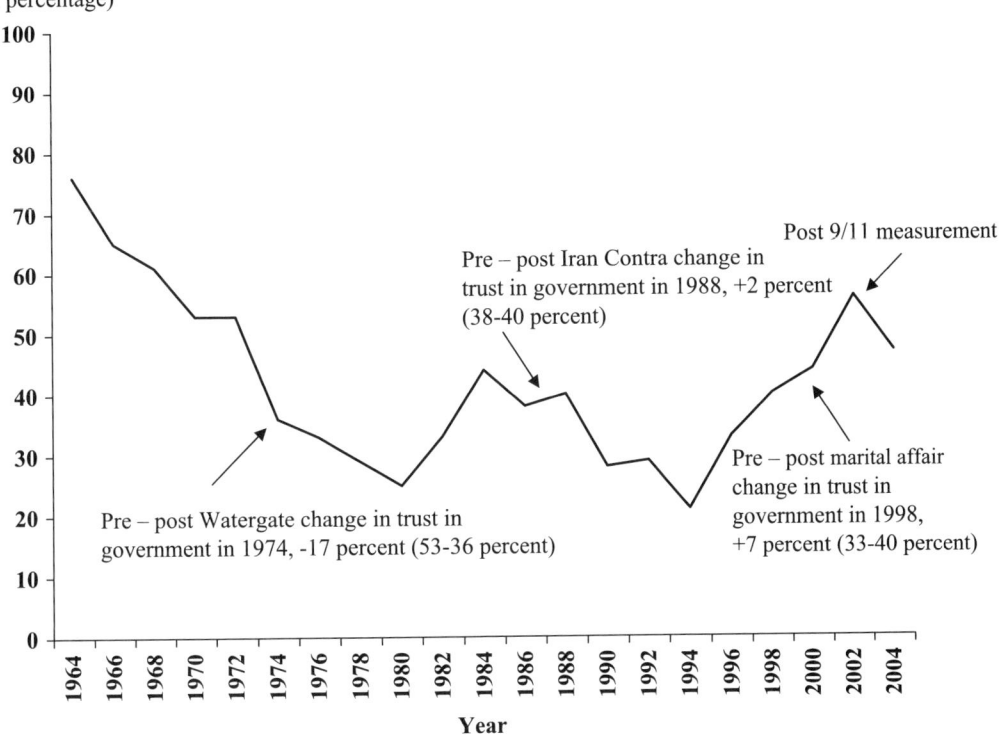

Source: National Election Studies (NES) for "Trust in Government."
Note: "Trust in Government" combines the answers "just about always" and "most of the time" from the following question: "How much of the time do you think you can trust the government in Washington to do what is right– just about always, most of the time or only some of the time?"

People tend to prefer leaders who are reluctant for power as opposed to leaders who are perceived as craving power. Watergate revealed that the public will respond very negatively and forcefully to leaders who overextend their power. The legislation cited earlier in the chapter that was enacted in the years following the Watergate scandal are testament to people's strong aversion to leaders who overextend their rule. Although such attitudes were dormant for much of American political history, Woodward and Bernstein's investigation ignited such suspicions, and they have yet to recede.

To demonstrate the public's sensitivity to abuses of power, Figure 4 presents the "trust in government" measure from the years immediately prior to the Watergate scandal through 2004, thirty years later. As Figure 4 shows, once such suspicions were aroused, faith in government was difficult to restore.

Figure 4 demonstrates that the Watergate scandal marked the beginning of a significant decline in trust in government. By 1980, only 25 percent of the population could trust the government in Washington to do what is right "just about always" or "most of the time." Although that number increased in the mid-1980s, the number bottomed out in 1994 at 21 percent. That year marked the GOP's "Contract with America" and the Republican takeover in the U.S. House of Representatives.

What is interesting, however, about Figure 4, is the relatively stability of the trust-in-government measure despite other presidential scandals. In late 1986 and early 1987 the Reagan administration was embroiled over a scandal involving illegal arms sales to Iran as a means of funneling money to Contras in Nicaragua. What is remarkable here is the fact that President Reagan went on television in November of 1986 initially to deny any wrongdoing. As the controversy continued to mount, Reagan went to the airways a week later to retract his earlier statement and in fact admitted that arms sales did take place, but that they were not in exchange for hostages. Similar to the Watergate scandal, the president of the United States initially denied any wrongdoing and then had to withdraw his statement. The integrity and honesty of the president were being questioned openly and publicly. However, the "trust" in government measurement in 1988, the first following what became known as the "Iran-Contra affair," was at 40 percent. That is, 40 percent of the American public still expressed trust in government to do the right thing "most of the time" or "just about always." That is four percentage points higher than the trust measurement after Watergate. Moreover, in the two-year period during the Watergate scandal the trust measurement decreased by seventeen percentage points. Before and after the Iran-Contra affair, the change in trust in government was a net *increase* by two percentage points. The Watergate scandal seemed to have a more dramatic effect on American public opinion, again highlighting the significance of Woodward and Bernstein's coverage of the scandal.

The other notable presidential scandal in the post-Watergate era involves the marital affair of President Clinton. In the summer and fall of 1997 reports surfaced that President Clinton engaged in sexual relations with a White House intern named Monica Lewinsky. Throughout the early months of 1998 President Clinton publicly and vehemently denied having any inappropriate contact with Ms. Lewinsky. Throughout the summer of 1998, an investigation by Independent Counsel Kenneth Starr revealed strong evidence that an affair did in fact take place. By August of that year, President Clinton became the first sitting president to testify about his own behavior before a grand jury. During that same month President Clinton went before the American public to withdraw and apologize for his earlier statements regarding the affair. The president admitted that he did in fact engage in an affair with Ms. Lewinsky. Like Watergate and the Iran-Contra affair, one of the primary issues here is presidential honesty. President Clinton blatantly and knowingly lied to the American public about his behavior while in office. However, as shown in Figure 4, the trust-in-government was measured at 40 percent in 1998 and 44 percent in 2000, four and eight percentage points, respectively, higher than the first trust measure after the Watergate scandal. Moreover, the net change from 1996 to 1998 in trust in government is a positive seven percentage points. Similar to the Iran-Contra affair, there is actually a net gain in trust in government following an executive scandal involving presidential integrity and honesty. This suggests one of two things: (1) that the reporting of Woodward and Bernstein numbed the American public to presidential transgressions or (2) that Watergate was a significant and unique event in presidential history. Most likely, the answer is both.

What is more revealing about the scandal involving President Clinton is that in December 1998 the House Judiciary Committee passed four articles of impeachment, including obstruction of justice. In July 1974, less than one month before he resigned, President Nixon was given the same indictment. Moreover, unlike President Nixon, President Clinton was actually impeached. On December 19, 1998, the U.S. House of Representatives passed two articles of impeachment against President Clinton, including obstruction of justice, making Clinton just the second president in the history of the United States to be impeached. Although the U.S. Senate voted in February 1999 not to impeach Clinton, the vote in the U.S. House and subsequent party line vote in the Senate spoke to the seriousness of Clinton's misconduct.

Because the impeachment proceedings formally began in late December 1998 and extended through the early months of 1999, it is useful to look at the trust-in-government measure for 2000, the first assessment after the Lewinsky affair. As Figure 4 shows, trust in government actually increased between 1998 and 2000, going from 40 percent to 44 percent of the American public expressing trust in the federal government. Again, what is revealing is the lack of any substantive change in American attitudes toward the government in Washington. Unlike Watergate, which precipitated a major change in beliefs about the trustworthiness of government, the Clinton affair had little effect. This suggests that Woodward and Bernstein's investigation was unique not only to American politics, but also to presidential scandals.

The lasting effect of Woodward and Bernstein's investigation on the presidency is also shown in Figure 5. Confidence in the presidency declined significantly following the Watergate scandal (Figure 2). Figure 5 extends the poll to 30 years after the Watergate scandal.

As Figure 5 shows, not only did confidence in the presidency decline significantly following the Watergate scandal, but the scandal was a particularly low point for Americans' perceptions of the institution of the presidency. Woodward and Bernstein's investigation uniquely affected public attitudes toward occupants of the White House. That only 11 percent of Americans expressed a great deal of confidence in the presidency in 1976 is worth noting. Following the Iran-Contra affair, confidence ranged from 17 percent to 23 percent. During the aftermath of President Clinton's affair and subsequent impeachment, confidence did not dip below 20 percent. Only in 1994–1995, immediately prior to the government shutdown in December 1995, did public attitudes toward the presidency approach

Figure 5. Confidence in the presidency, 1974–2004.

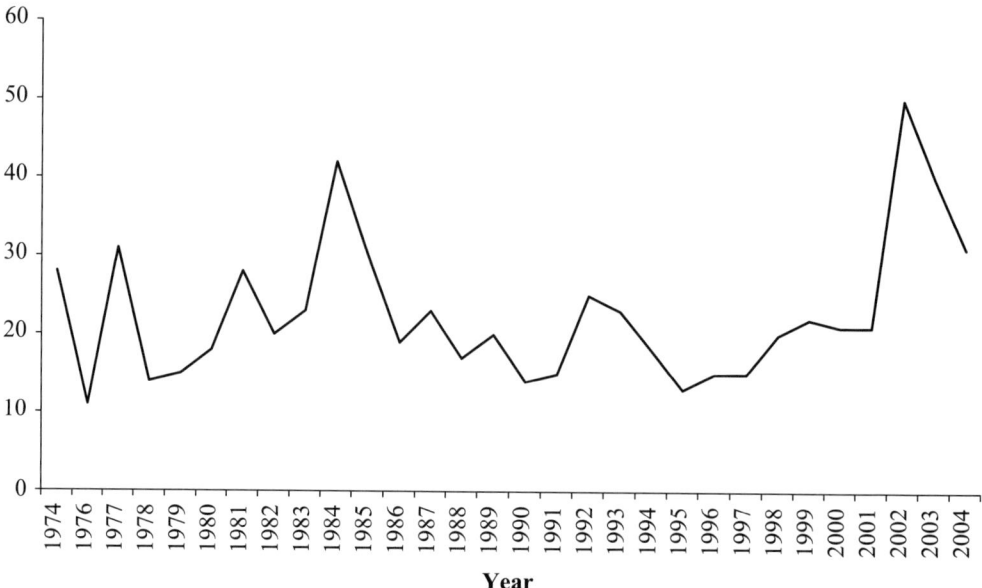

Source: Harris Poll for "Confidence in Presidency."
Note: Data were unavailable for the year 1975. Confidence in the presidency is the percentage of respondents expressing "a great deal of confidence" in the White House from the following question:
"As far as people in charge of running the White House are concerned, would you say you have a great deal of confidence, only some confidence, or hardly any confidence at all in them?"

Watergate levels, bottoming out at 13 percent. Woodward and Bernstein's coverage of the scandal in 1972 through 1974 was a direct challenge to presidential authority and revealed the problems of centralizing presidential power. And, as Figure 5 shows, their work had a profound effect on attitudes toward the institution of the presidency.

Ultimately, what Figures 4 and 5 demonstrate is that Woodward and Bernstein's investigation into the Watergate scandal was a watershed moment in American politics, particularly how the public viewed government and the president. Other presidential scandals have come and gone with relatively little change in public opinion about the federal government. This was not the case with Watergate. Woodward and Bernstein's investigation exposed fraud, dishonesty, and abuses of power at the highest level of government, and the American public reacted strongly and negatively to such abuses—more so than they would for other presidential transgressions. Even the terrorist attacks of September 11, 2001, failed to produce a more significant change in trust in government than the Watergate scandal. Between 2000 and 2002, the percentage of people expressing trust in government "just about always" or "most of the time" increased by twelve percentage points; after Watergate that same percentage decreased by seventeen percentage points.

Figures 4 and 5 suggest that Watergate shaped long-term beliefs and attitudes about government, but is it possible to establish a direct connection between Watergate and American attitudes toward government ten or twenty years after the scandal? What evidence is there that people believe Watergate to be a serious and defining moment in American politics? In 1997, "All Politics" conducted a survey of American attitudes about the scandal as part of a twenty-fifth anniversary forum on Watergate. Participants in the survey were asked whether Watergate was "a serious matter or just politics." A majority of the respondents, 52 percent, responded that Watergate was a serious matter, compared to 44 percent who said it was "just politics." Although 52 percent is not an overwhelming majority, it does suggest that even after twenty-five years Watergate still resonated with the American public. Perhaps even more telling is the fact that 78 percent of the respondents agreed that Watergate was a "turning point for trust in government." This provides more empirical backing to the notion that Watergate shaped American attitudes about government for a generation (Figure 4) and thus speaks to the importance of Woodward and Bernstein's investigation. Woodward and Bernstein's coverage of the scandal is viewed as a turning point in American politics: the relationship between the executive branch and the public was significantly altered by their reporting.

To be sure, Figures 4 and 5 show that people are extraordinarily sensitive to any abuses of power. People tend to be highly sensitive to fairness norms, particularly related to those making decisions on our behalf. What Figure 4 demonstrates is that once the American public became aware of an elected official, in this case, the top elected official, engaging in an abuse of power, trust in government was lost. Louis Liebovich writes that "a palpable public mood alteration took place in the immediate post-Watergate years. Presidents were liars. Government was bad." (Liebovich 2003, 119). Figure 4 demonstrates that this mood has yet to reverse course. Other scholars have also taken note of the significance of Watergate in American political history. Robert Spitzer writes that "Watergate was a transformative moment for the institution of the presidency...it altered the nature of the imperial presidency." (Spitzer 1999, 541). Figures 1–5 and the "All Politics" survey indicate that Watergate did in fact usher in an era of reduced credibility for presidents and politicians generally. After Watergate, the public was strongly anti-politics and anti-government. Figure 4 indicates this trend had long-lasting effects; in the thirty years after Watergate, the public remained convinced that politicians, and by nature, government are untrustworthy. Again, this can be attributed to Woodward and Bernstein's coverage of the scandal—that abuses of power permeated the executive branch of government.

In the book *Shadow*, Bob Woodward discusses the lasting effects of Watergate on presidents and presidential administrations. As discussed earlier in the chapter, the Watergate scandal had an indirect, but profound impact on the first president after Watergate. President Gerald Ford's decision to pardon President Nixon is often considered by presidential scholars to not only be the defining characteristic of his presidency, but also the main reason for his failure to be reelected. The presidential election of 1976 was thus significantly affected by the legacy of Watergate, from Ford's pardon to the campaign slogans of Jimmy Carter. As Woodward writes, President Carter's election in 1976 was a "direct response to Watergate" and the election was entirely about "trustfulness and honesty" (Woodward 1999, 84). Although presidential elections tend to be part policy and part personality, Watergate shifted the focus to personality. Moreover, the 1976 election was not just about personality generally, but specifically about the traits of honesty and integrity. But did this trend affect future presidents? Did the effects of Watergate diminish over time? Were there any long-term effects on presidents?

Consider the two most prominent presidential scandals in the two decades after Watergate: the Iran-Contra Affair in 1985–1986 and President Clinton's marital affair in 1997–1998. It is not uncommon to see both instances placed in the context of Watergate by scholars and reporters other than Woodward and Bernstein. For example, Robert J. Spitzer, when discussing the differences between the scandals of President Nixon and those of President Clinton, writes of "Watergate vs. Monicagate" (Spitzer 1999, 541). A database search of political science journals reveals that the phrase "Irangate" appears in thirty different academic works between 1987 and 1999 in reference to the Iran-Contra affair. This suggests that the work of Woodward and Bernstein defined the nature of investigative political reporting. Presidential transgressions following the Watergate scandal tended to be couched in Watergate nomenclature. Thus, beyond shaping public attitudes toward government, Woodward and Bernstein were, in a sense, able to create a standard language for discussing presidential scandals.

Finally, a more general result of "Woodstein's" investigation was the effect their reporting had on presidential power. As Aaron Wildavsky notes, the Watergate scandal raised serious questions concerning the legitimacy of the institution of the presidency. Concerns over legitimacy, Wildavsky argued, are significant, because they cut across policy domains and governing institutions. The president significantly affects both domestic and foreign politics and policy. Thus, because Watergate affected fundamental attitudes regarding the scope and legitimacy of presidential power, the reverberations were felt throughout the entire political system. The after-effects of the scandal, as a result, were aimed at limiting presidential power.

Genovese notes that Watergate affected both the policy activities of the president as well as presidential–congressional relations. According to Genovese, "the aftermath of Watergate led to a decline in the presidency and a rebirth of congressional power." (Genovese 2003, 168). As discussed earlier in the chapter, Congress passed several pieces of legislation after Watergate aimed at curbing presidential power, particularly budgetary and war powers. What is significant is that even thirty years after the scandal, executive branch officials contend that the power of the president has been severely diminished in light of the Watergate scandal. Indeed, scholars and pundits often noted the frustration of the Bush-Cheney administration in 2001 and 2002 in terms of increasing presidential power. As Kenneth Jost writes, "Bush entered the White House in 2001 convinced that the presidency had been weakened since Nixon was forced to resign in August 1974." (Jost 2006, 173). Although President Bush, and particularly Vice President Cheney, the former chief to President Gerald Ford, favored increasing the power of the president, they were met with resistance from both the public and the Congress. Presidential scholars often talk of both a strong- and weak-presidency models. The former is one in which the president commands authority and respect and is relatively unchecked in pursuit of his agenda. The latter is just the opposite: the president is unable to wield discretionary control over his policy or political agenda. Genovese writes that, "Watergate turned out to be the final nail in the coffin of the unambiguous acceptance of the strong-presidency model." (Genovese 2003, 168). In short, the investigation by Woodward and Bernstein shaped the discussion surrounding scope of presidential power.

Richard Neustadt, a leading authority on presidential power, notes that the ability of presidents to influence the legislative process is not dependent so much on their formal powers, but on their informal powers, particularly their "power to persuade" (Neustadt 1991). Lawrence Jacobs also discusses the obsession presidents have in pushing their agenda and attempting to frame the public debate. The work of Woodward and Bernstein significantly affected the public and the Congress's view of presidential power. Suddenly, as a result of their investigation, presidential authority was not only closely monitored, it was also questioned and often severely limited. Woodward and Bernstein single-handedly crippled the ability of presidents to persuade and push their agenda on the public and the media. Genovese notes that Watergate was significant because it represented a "systematic subversion of the political rights of American citizens" (Genovese 1990, 231). What Woodward and Bernstein were working on in the early 1970s represented more than just front-page news. Their investigation was critical to the functioning of a legitimate democracy. Specifically, their work was in defense of the basic rights of citizens to an open and free government.

The Media and Deep Throat

Without question, Watergate has had a lasting impact on American politics. Any public library will contain volume upon volume of material about Watergate and its effect on all aspects of the American political system. Woodward himself devoted an entire book to the effect of Watergate on the five presidential administrations immediately following Nixon's resignation. However, one of the enduring legacies of Watergate is its effect on the media.

Prior to Woodward and Bernstein's investigation, the press maintained a relatively cordial relationship with presidents and members of presidential administrations. Like most presidents, Richard Nixon enjoyed a bit of a honeymoon period with the press following his overwhelming reelection in 1972. However, as allegations emerged linking the White House to the break-in at the Democratic headquarters, the honeymoon period quickly faded, only to be replaced by feelings of anger and contempt. As Michael Nelson writes, after Watergate, "White House reporters felt that a breach of trust occurred." (Nelson 2006, 8). No longer did the press corps trust the words of presidents. The Watergate scandal created a hostile relationship between the press and presidential administrations. Nelson writes that this adversarial relationship even affected daily press briefings by presidential press secretaries. Such tension between presidents and the press can be disadvantageous to democratic debate. Jacobs documents the ability of presidents to dominate the press by "pounding" away at core issues. What Jacobs finds is that the more presidents and staff pound away at the press, the more likely the press are to report on the "gamesmanship" and strategizing of the White House rather than the details of the policy in question. And, as Jacobs notes, this tends to increase public skepticism about the executive branch and the presidency.

So, how does this relate to the work of Woodward and Bernstein? Woodward and Bernstein, unlike members of the other news organizations and the Washington press corps, were able to look past presidential statements. They were unwilling to accept White House statements that didn't confirm their own research. Woodward and Bernstein displayed an extraordinarily high level of confidence in their abilities. Although during the 1980s, 1990s, and into the twenty-first century it seemed relatively common for reporters to question, and almost interrogate, presidential press secretaries and even presidents themselves, that was not the case in the early 1970s. Woodward and Bernstein broke the mold of deference to presidential authority, and as a result, shifted the norm for presidential reporting. As Genovese writes, after Watergate, presidents were perceived as "vulnerable" (Genovese, 1999, 113). Although most scholars agree that the role of the media is to serve as a "watchdog" over government, this was not necessarily the case prior to Watergate. Woodward and Bernstein fundamentally shifted the role, as well as perceptions of the role of the media in American politics.

Quoting the executive editor of *The Washington Post* during Watergate, E. J. Dionne, Jr., writes "The press won in Watergate." (Dionne 2004, 84). Continuing in his own words, Dionne states that "Watergate encouraged an increasingly adversarial journalism, which helped undermine government's credibility." As discussed earlier in the chapter, such animosity tended to diminish public trust. Figures 1–5 show there was a significant decline in government's credibility as defined by the public's willingness to trust the federal government to do what is right. As the media became more cynical toward the president, so too did the public. This resulted in a shift in public mood. No longer was the government innocent until proven guilty. Instead, most people believed the opposite—that the federal government was corrupt and untrustworthy until proven otherwise.

One final lasting effect of Woodward and Bernstein on political reporting is their ability to highlight the importance of confidential sources. Woodward and Bernstein's investigation introduced the American public to the source simply known as "Deep Throat." As revealed in Woodward and Bernstein's book *All the President's Men*, Deep Throat was critical to the Watergate investigation in terms of linking the White House to the initial break-in, as well as larger attempts by the Nixon White House to quell political opposition. The importance of Deep Throat is evident by the fanfare over Deep Throat's unveiling in 2005, thirty-three years after their initial meeting. Woodward and Bernstein's efforts to keep their source secret for such an extended period of time resulted in what Shepard declares "the most famous confidential source in American journalism" (Shepard 2007, 249).

In June of 2005, the American public learned that Deep Throat was W. Mark Felt, second in command at the FBI during the Watergate scandal. What is remarkable about Felt's notoriety is the public's enduring interest in his identity. Because of Woodward and Bernstein's insistence that Deep Throat remain anonymous until his death, the public was exposed to the value of confidential sources in journalism. Deep Throat also symbolized the importance of nonexploitive investigative reporting. Woodward and Bernstein, following the worldwide fame they received in 1974, could just as easily have exposed their source. However, they vigilantly protected Felt's identity despite enormous public pressure. As a result, one of the legacies of Woodward and Bernstein is their ability to maintain journalistic integrity through perhaps the most significant and turbulent period of political reporting in the history of the United States.

Ultimately, Woodward and Bernstein changed the nature of political reporting. No longer did the media passively accept executive statements. Watergate ushered in what Genovese describes as "special prosecutor" mentality. The public and the press were now eager to seek out and investigate any suspicious wrongdoing by presidents or personnel in presidential administrations. Of course, the media are not the only ones to capitalize on the Watergate scandal. Members of Congress are also quick to exploit presidential transgressions. The public tends to be highly skeptical of "power-hungry" leaders. As such, attempts by members of Congress to reign in presidential power tend to play well with constituents.

After Watergate, people felt it was their duty to expose any suspicious activity by presidential administrations. All of this shifted public attitudes toward the president: people were now distrustful of presidents and apprehensive regarding their public actions. Such wariness no doubt contributed to the sharp decline in trustworthiness toward the federal government as shown in Figures 1 and 4. Presidents now must deal with a new, aggressive style of reporting and questioning by the media. As Woodward writes, the reaction among presidents was an incessant "fear" of leaks, resulting in an ever-growing distrust between the media and presidential administrations. It is now a basic requirement for presidents to have a "war" room full of staff whose sole responsibility is to control White House leaks. Every member of the Washington press corps is fearful of being scooped on the next major presidential scandal, resulting in a media feeding frenzy every time the president steps to the microphone to deliver a speech. As Genovese writes, "the media began like a lamb but ended like a lion." (Genovese 1999, 121). The lions leading the charge were two reporters from *The Washington Post*.

Woodward's Lasting Legacy

In 1976, Carl Bernstein left *The Washington Post* and went on to work for various publications, including *Rolling Stone*, *Time*, and *The New Republic*. During the 1980s and early 1990s he worked for ABC news as a bureau chief and correspondent, before teaching at New York University. Although he went on to write more books about public officials, his role in the Watergate scandal tends to be viewed as the highlight of his journalistic career. For Bob Woodward, however, the story is a bit different. Since the Watergate days, Woodward has written extensively about many facets of the American political system. In addition to writing about the effects of Watergate on future presidents, Woodward has written books on the U.S. Federal Reserve, the U.S. Supreme Court, the CIA, the Clinton administration, and the Pentagon. During the administration of President George W. Bush, however, Woodward returned to the theme of presidential accountability, writing three books detailing President Bush's wartime strategy.

Following the terrorist attacks of September 11, 2001, there was enormous pressure to hold someone or some group accountable for the damage and carnage inflicted on the United States. In the fall of 2001, the United States engaged militarily with Afghanistan with the intent of removing the Taliban from power. Following the attacks of 9/11 and subsequent war in Afghanistan, questions arose as to how the United States would govern in a new "post-9/11 world." In 2003, Woodward released *Bush at War*, describing how President George W. Bush and his cabinet dealt with the terrorist attacks and set a course of action for engaging militarily with Afghanistan. The book was widely heralded as presenting a behind-the-scenes look into crisis decision making at the highest level of government.

Following military engagement in Afghanistan in the fall of 2001, the United States, in the spring of 2003, engaged in a war with the nation of Iraq, which

Presidential Scandals

The Watergate scandal, uncovered by Bob Woodward and Carl Bernstein, has changed the American political lexicon. Indeed, today nearly every political scandal on the national level invariably becomes labeled with the suffix "-gate." The fact that modern scandals tend to carry a moniker from the Nixon-era scandal is a testament to just how serious Watergate was.

Watergate, however, was not the only serious scandal to affect and damage an American president. Indeed, there have been several scandals before and since President Nixon was forced to resign in disgrace. Below are just a few of the serious scandals to have an impact on presidents and their administrations.

The Whiskey Ring Scandal (1875): More than eighty high-level government officials, including President Ulysses S. Grant's private secretary (Orville E. Babcock), were prosecuted for conspiring with liquor distillers to evade federal sales tax on whiskey. This scandal, along with the impeachment of Grant's secretary of war, William Belknap, for bribery, cast a cloud over Grant's presidency despite his never being accused of a crime.

The Teapot Dome Scandal (1922): This scandal is widely thought by historians to be one of the most serious scandals in American history. In 1921, President Warren G. Harding transferred control of naval oil reserve lands to the U.S. Department of Interior and by extension, to the Secretary of Interior, Albert B. Fall. In 1922, Secretary Fall granted exclusive rights to the reserves to the Mammoth Oil Company and the Pan American Petroleum Company in exchange for cash. Secretary Fall was eventually arrested, prosecuted, and found guilty of bribery. He was sentenced to a year in prison and assessed a $100,000 fine.

The Iran-Contra Scandal (1986): This scandal tarnished the otherwise popular Ronald Reagan presidency. In an effort to curb the spread of communism in Latin America, high-ranking government officials illegally sold U.S. weaponry to Iran and then diverted the proceeds of those sales to fund the pro-American Contra rebels in Nicaragua. Although the Contras set themselves against the communist Sandinista government, the Contras were notorious human rights violators themselves. Congress had banned providing support to the Contras through the Boland Amendment in 1983. President Reagan's National Security Advisor Robert McFarlane pleaded guilty to withholding information from Congress concerning the Iran-Contra operation. McFarlane's successor, Admiral John Poindexter, along with National Security Counsel staff member Lt. Colonel Oliver North, were convicted of multiple charges related to the scandal. However, their convictions were thrown out on appeal because they had been granted immunity by Congress during the investigation of the Iran-Contra affair.

(continued)

> **Whitewater and Monica Lewinsky Scandals:** From the beginning of Bill Clinton's presidency in 1993, a number of accusations of impropriety plagued the administration. One of the major scandals focused on Bill and Hillary Clinton's connection to the failed and fraud-ridden Whitewater land scheme in Arkansas. Ultimately, the Clintons were never prosecuted for anything relating to Whitewater, but several business partners were. During an independent counsel investigation of Whitewater, other problems surfaced for President Clinton. In particular, President Clinton was found to have lied under oath about his sexual relationship with Whitehouse intern Monica Lewinsky (by saying he had never had a sexual relationship with Lewinsky) during depositions taken as a part of a sexual harassment suit against President Clinton by former Arkansas state employee Paula Jones. On December 19, 1998, President Clinton was impeached by the U.S. House of Representatives for perjury and obstruction of justice. The impeachment trial took place in the U.S. Senate in January and February of 1999. He was acquitted on both counts.

the United States suspected of harboring weapons of mass destruction. The following year, Woodward wrote his second book on President Bush's "war on terror." *Plan of Attack* was focused on explaining the Bush administration's reasoning and plan for the war in Iraq. In this text and *Bush at War*, Woodward was able to provide with incredible detail the conversations between high-ranking officials concerning war-time decisions. Both books, however, were aimed more at discussing, rather than criticizing the president's war strategy.

Although President Bush was quick to claim success for the war in Iraq, controversy surrounding the decision soon mounted as the conflict extended into 2004. In 2006, Woodward completed his third book on the Bush administration's war policy, titled *State of Denial*. As the title suggests, it is in this third text where Woodward begins to return to his Watergate days in terms of questioning the reasoning of those in the executive branch, including the president. Throughout *State of Denial*, Woodward details the internal power struggles between the trio of President Bush, Vice President Cheney, Defense Secretary Donald Rumsfeld, and the rest of the cabinet. As Woodward discusses in the book, President Bush and Vice President Cheney courted former Secretary of State Henry Kissinger as another ally against what Woodward perceives to be the more rational and logical members of the Bush administration. Ultimately, in *State of Denial*, Bob Woodward resurrects his Watergate style by seriously and adamantly questioning the decisions and actions of the Bush administration in conducting war with Iraq. Like many of his other books since the publication of *All the President's Men* and *Final Days*, Woodward's analysis of President Bush as a war-time president places a strong emphasis on public accountability. Moreover, his focus on mistakes and fallacies in presidential decision making furthers his status as an icon of journalistic and political crime fighting.

Conclusion

Iconic figures leave a lasting legacy in their respective fields. Bob Woodward and Carl Bernstein have left a legacy in *two* fields: presidential politics and journalism. Their legacy can most aptly be summed up by one word: accountability. Michael Genovese writes that "Watergate was the most serious scandal in the history of the U.S. presidency." (Genovese 2003, 165). However, this would not have been the case had it not been for the foresight and determination of Woodward and Bernstein. After Watergate, the public demanded accountability from their elected officials. And that demand tended to increase the higher up one moves in the federal government. People clamored for accountability and openness from their public officials. The public derided any government official even remotely suspected of criminal activity. More generally, however, the Watergate scandal and subsequent investigation layered the American political system with a heightened sense of skepticism.

While accountability may be Woodward and Bernstein's lasting legacy, they also ushered in an era of increasing distrust with government. It is one of the interesting paradoxes of any society, as well as a basic psychological reaction, that as trust decreases, the desire for accountability increases. Woodward and Bernstein's investigation into the Watergate break-in removed whatever veneer had been in place over the White House, and exposed the office as one that is subject to corruptibility. As Woodward would later write, after Watergate, the presidency became a "resignable office." (Woodward 1999, 12).

During and immediately following their investigation, trust and confidence in government significantly declined. Statements by politicians were viewed with intense skepticism, and their motivations were constantly questioned, and, more significantly, such skepticism did not decline with the passage of time. Rather, the work of Woodward and Bernstein ushered in a new era of political reporting, and, as a byproduct, a new era of public attitudes toward government. Trust in government has rarely achieved pre-Watergate levels, and if it has, it has been only for a brief period of time. The public tends to view politicians as more likely to act in their own self-interest rather than the public interest. Such skepticism, however, is not inherently bad. To be clear, Woodward and Bernstein did not cause the public to lose faith in their government; the actions of a few elected and appointed officials did that. Rather, what Woodward and Bernstein did was expose the transgressions of those operating at the highest level of government. They revealed to the American public that even the president is not immune to illegal activity, and nor should the public expect him or her to be.

As this chapter has pointed out, there were both short- and long-term effects to Woodward and Bernstein's coverage of the break-in at the Watergate Hotel on June 17, 1972. It is important to note that these long- and short-term effects are a direct result of Woodward and Bernstein's reporting of the scandal, not the scandal itself. Without their diligence in tracking down sources and persuading editors to continue to let them cover the story, there never would have been a "Watergate." To be sure, it would be easy to get wrapped up in the details of the scandal or the personality of President Nixon. But it is critical to remember why the Nixon presidency is viewed as such a watershed moment in American politics. Woodward and Bernstein brought the abuse of power and corrupt nature of the Nixon presidency to the American people. Unlike many members of the media at the time, these two reporters were quite willing to challenge the status quo of presidential reporting.

One measure of iconic status is an ability to affect the manner in which people approach a particular field of study. Woodward and Bernstein have had a profound impact on the study of media and politics. In 2007, a keyword search on "The Syllabi Finder" for college courses developed by George Mason and linked through the American Political Science Association's Web site, the leading organization for political scientists, reveals the significance of the work of Woodward and Bernstein. Searching for "All the President's Men" and "American government" resulted in more than ten thousand hits. This suggests that even thirty-five years after the incident, Woodward and Bernstein's coverage of the scandal is still viewed by many scholars as fundamental to the study of American government. This is quite remarkable considering that the two reporters had never worked together prior to the Watergate investigation.

Perhaps one of the more telling legacies of Woodward and Bernstein's investigation is the interest it sparked in presidential personalities and the workings of American government. Woodward and Bernstein were able to shape public attitudes toward government, legislation crafted by Congress, the role of the media in American politics, and more generally, how people view the relationships between the president, the press, and the public. In 2007, Web sites remained devoted to the Watergate scandal. (For example, see "The Nixon Era Times," Mountain State University: Nixon Era Center. http://www.watergate.com.) A simple *Google* search of "Bob Woodward" in 2007 returned 1.6 million hits, whereas the same search for "Carl Bernstein" returned 1.27 million hits. Perhaps even more telling is the fact that the same search for "Woodstein" and "Watergate" returned more than thirteen thousand hits. Thirty-five years after the Watergate scandal, not only do Bob Woodward and Carl Bernstein remain highly celebrated journalists, but their collective nickname is also renowned not just in journalistic and political circles, but also among the general public.

FURTHER READING

Baker, Peter, and Charles Babington. "Bush Addresses Uproar over Spying." *The Washington Post*. December 20, 2005. http://www.washingtonpost.com/wp-dyn/content/article/2005/12/19/AR2005121900211.html (accessed May 15, 2007).

Bernstein, Carl, and Bob Woodward. "Bug Suspect Got Campaign Funds." *The Washington Post*. August 1, 1972. http://www.washingtonpost.com/wp-dyn/content/article/2002/06/03/AR2005111001229.html (accessed April 1, 2007).

Bernstein, Carl, and Bob Woodward. "Mitchell Controlled Secret GOP Fund." *The Washington Post*. September 29, 1972. http://www.washingtonpost.com/wp-dyn/content/article/2002/06/03/AR2005111001231.html (accessed April 1, 2007).

Bernstein, Carl, and Bob Woodward. "FBI Finds Nixon Aides Sabotaged Democrats." *The Washington Post*. October 10, 1972. http://www.washingtonpost.com/wp-dyn/content/article/2002/06/03/AR2005111001232.html (accessed April 1, 2007).

Bernstein, Carl, and Bob Woodward. "Still Secret—Who Hired Spies and Why." *The Washington Post*. January 31, 1973. http://www.washingtonpost.com/wp-dyn/content/article/2002/05/31/AR2005112200788.html (accessed April 1, 2007).

Bernstein, Carl, and Bob Woodward. *All the President's Men*. New York: Simon & Schuster, 1974.

Dionne, E. J., Jr. 2004. *Why Americans Hate Politics*. New York: Simon & Schuster.

Genovese, Michael A. 1990. *The Nixon Presidency: Power and Politics in Turbulent Times*. Westport, CT: Greenwood, Press.

Genovese, Michael A. 1999. *The Watergate Crisis*. Westport, CT: Greenwood Press.

Genovese, Michael A. 2003. *The Power of the American Presidency, 1789–2000*. New York: Oxford University Press.

Harry Ransom Center. "The Woodward and Bernstein Watergate Papers." University of Texas. http://www.hrc.utexas.edu/exhibitions/online/woodstein/ (accessed April 15, 2007).

Havill, Adrian. 1993. *Deep Truth: The Unauthorized Biography of Bob Woodward and Carl Bernstein*. New York: Carol Publishing Group.

Hibbing, John R., and John R. Alford. Accepting authoritative decisions: Humans as wary cooperators. *American Journal of Political Science* 48 (January 2004): 62–76.

Hibbing, John R., and Elizabeth Theiss-Morse. 1995. *Congress as Public Enemy: Public Attitudes toward American Political Institutions*. Cambridge, MA: Cambridge University Press.

"Investigating the President: The Trial." CNN.com/Inside Politics. http://www.cnn.com/ALLPOLITICS/resources/1998/lewinsky/ (accessed May 1, 2007).

Jacobs, Lawrence R. 2006. The Presidency and the press: The paradox of the White House communications war. In *The Presidency and the Political System*, ed. Michael Nelson. Washington, D.C.: CQ Press.

Jost, Kenneth. Presidential power: Is Bush overstepping his executive authority? *The CQ Researcher* 16 (February 24, 2006): 169–92.

Kinder, Donald R., Mark D. Peters, Robert P. Abelson, and Susan T. Fiske. Presidential prototypes. *Political Behavior* 2 (1980): 315–37.

Liebovich, Louis W. 2003. *Richard Nixon, Watergate, and the Press*. Westport, CT: Praeger.

Nelson, Michael. 2006. Evaluating the presidency. In *The Presidency and the Political System*, ed. Michael Nelson. Washington, D.C.: CQ Press.

Neustadt, Richard E. 1991. *Presidential Power and the Modern Presidents: The Politics of Leadership from Roosevelt to Reagan*. New York: Free Press.

"Serious or 'Just Politics'?" All Politics: CNN Time. Public Perceptions of Watergate, June 17, 1997. http://www.cnn.com/ALLPOLITICS/1997/gen/resources/watergate/poll/ (accessed April 15, 2007).

Shepard, Alicia C. 2007. *Woodward and Bernstein: Life in the Shadow of Watergate*. New York: John Wiley & Sons.

Smith, Kevin B., Christopher W. Larimer, Levente Littvay, and John R. Hibbing. 2007. Evolutionary theory and political leadership: Why certain people do not trust decision-makers. *Journal of Politics* 69 (May 2007): 285–99.

Spitzer, Robert J. Clinton's impeachment will have few consequences for the presidency. *PS: Political Science and Politics* 32 (September 1999): 541–45.

"The ANES Guide to Public Opinion and Electoral Behavior." Ann Arbor, MI: The National Election Studies, Center for Political Studies [producer and distributor], University of Michigan. http://www.umich.edu/~nes/nesguide/nesguide.htm (accessed April 30, 2007).

"The Nixon Era Times." Mountain State University: Nixon Era Center. http://www.watergate.com (accessed May 15, 2007).

"Watergate Chronology." *The Washington Post*. http://www.washingtonpost.com/wp-srv/onpolitics/watergate/chronology.htm (accessed April 15, 2007).

Wildavsky, Aaron. 2001. *The Beleaguered Presidency*. New Brunswick, NJ: Transaction Publishers.

Woodward, Bob. 1999. *Shadow: Five Presidents and the Legacy of Watergate*. New York: Touchstone.

Woodward, Bob. 2003. *Bush at War*. New York: Simon & Schuster.

Woodward, Bob. 2004. *Plan of Attack*. New York: Simon & Schuster.

Woodward, Bob. 2005. *The Secret Man: The Story of Watergate's Deep Throat*. New York: Simon & Schuster.

Woodward, Bob. 2006. *State of Denial: Bush at War, Part III*. New York: Simon & Schuster.

Woodward, Bob, and Carl Bernstein. "GOP Security Aide among Five Arrested in Bugging Affair." *The Washington Post*. June 19, 1972. http://www.washingtonpost.com/wp-dyn/content/article/2002/05/31/AR2005111001228.html (accessed April 1, 2007).

Woodward, Bob, and Carl Bernstein. "Break-in Memo Sent to Ehrlichman." *The Washington Post*. June 13, 1973. http://www.washingtonpost.com/wp-dyn/content/article/2002/05/31/AR2005112200793.html (accessed April 1, 2007).

Woodward, Bob, and Carl Bernstein. "Nixon Debated Paying Blackmail, Clemency." *The Washington Post*. May 1, 1974. http://www.washingtonpost.com/wp-dyn/content/article/2002/05/31/AR2005112200804.html (accessed April 1, 2007).

Woodward, Bob, and Carl Bernstein. 1976. *The Final Days*. New York: Simon & Schuster.